Best Wishes & Kindest Regards,

...AND THE HORSE YOU RODE IN ON, SAUNDERS!

Barry Saunders

A collection of columns by
Barry Saunders

News & Observer Newspaper
Raleigh, NC

ISBN #9780692355855

Cover photo by Rick Crank
Rickcrankphotography@gmail.com

Cover Art, Graphics and Layout by
Karmen Piland | YEMDesigns.com

Printing by
Progressive Business Solutions
508 S. New Hope Road
Raleigh, NC 27610
www.progform.com

Foreword

Dear Reader,

This book is a compilation of my columns that appeared in the News & Observer from 1999-2005. They are not intended to represent the best of that period – each reader's idea of what constitutes the best will differ – or the worst.

Rather, I hope it represents a range of subjects that I hope you will find entertaining and thought-provoking.

I have not re-edited any of them for content, so errors I made in the original – like, say, that Streets of Southpoint Mall will never take off – are reprinted as they appeared in the newspaper.

Over the months preceding publication of this book, I asked scores of readers to suggest their favorite columns and to submit possible titles for the book. Submissions ranged, unsurprisingly, from the sublime to the ridiculous – which, now that you mention it, was one of the suggested titles.

The title settled upon, "... And The Horse You Rode In On, Saunders", was not suggested by a reader, but it definitely came from one.

A couple of years ago, in response to some now-forgotten column, an elderly female reader called on the telephone to excoriate me over something I'd written with which she disagreed. After several minutes of raging and, seemingly on the verge of apoplexy, words failed her.

She finally managed to sputter "You... you... you know what, Saunders? #@$% you and the horse you rode in on."

Just like that, a book title was born.

Enjoy,
Barry Saunders

A BAD CASE OF OVERDUE DILIGENCE

The message was unmistakable, like a dead fish wrapped in a bulletproof vest or a finger-slash across the throat: Give us the money or else.

Only this wasn't a Mafia movie where we learn that some unlucky dolt is sleeping with the fishes or is about to get his throat cut.

Uh-uh. This ominous message was delivered by Duke University Health System to the Durham County commissioners. "Give us $3 million or these poor blokes over here get it." Or, to be more precise, they won't get it - as in won't get medical treatment.

Of course, William "The Don" Donelan, the health system's executive vice president, and the other highly compensated suits at Duke are too smooth to try such blatant extortion outright. The intent of their prepared statement, however, was clear.

Duke claims that the value of Durham Regional Hospital was overstated, leading Duke to pay more to lease the hospital than it was worth. Because of that - and because profits from their acquisition aren't rolling in as quickly as they'd anticipated - they want to renegotiate the deal they signed with the county in 1998.

The commissioners' response to Duke's po'mouthing was a thoughtful, well-articulated "Fuhgeddaboutit." In its own statement, the county said, "There are no provisions ... for a renegotiation of the lease terms."

I empathize with Duke if it feels that it was hornswoggled and that the hospital's financial prognosis was not nearly as bright as presented. That happens to me, and probably to you, every time we buy a used car that has only been driven to church by a little old lady. When we get it home, though, we discover that the car was a Demolition Derby stalwart and is held together with duct tape and spit.

Despite our fervent pleas and moans, the seller is under no legal or moral imperative to refund any of our moola.

Duke must realize that neither is the county under any such imperative. Of course, when we get stuck with a lemon, we don't have the option - as Duke does - of holding thousands of residents' health care hostage.

Me, I find it hard to imagine that Duke would purchase a pig in a poke - that is, buy a hospital without going over the books assiduously, kicking the tires, asking all the right questions.

When Duke implies that it might cut service to poor, uninsured residents or ax programs that target drug abusers, the county would be well advised to take the threats - oops, the warnings - seriously.

After all, this is the same outfit that recently axed the 22-year-old Host Homes program that provided free housing for patients' families. For less than $25,000 a year - salary and benefits for a part-time program coordinator - Duke helped provide more than 118,000 free nights' lodging with volunteers for people who otherwise would've had to go into hock for a hotel room, sleep in their cars or simply not visit their sick loved ones.

1

Given Duke's obvious willingness to play hardball when money is involved, I certainly don't envy our county commissioners. Why, they're liable to wake up and find a horse's head - or at least a soiled bedpan - under the covers with them.

6/27/2000

A BURR GETS THE YANK

If at first you don't succeed - just wait a few years and the dude'll mess up. For real this time.

That appears to be the philosophy over at UNC-Chapel Hill, where they finally got rid of burr-in-the-saddle campus cop Edwin Swain.

Swain was fired -- most recently -- in May 2004. His dismissal was upheld last week by an administrative law judge.

Among the reasons cited for his dismissal after 17 years' service were that his officers sometimes took longer breaks than allowed and that on the night of March 28, 2004, he didn't enforce the rule requiring -- get this -- neckties with their long-sleeved uniform shirts.

If you believe that's all there is to it, then I'd like to sell you some cheap courtside tickets to the next Duke-UNC basketball game.

Swain was fired the first time in 1997, about a month after he issued a citation for underage drinking at a Tar Heels football game to the daughter of university trustee Billy Armfield.

Considering the problems caused by alcohol at college football games -- ask administrators over at N.C. State University if they wish somebody had written some citations on a fateful afternoon last year -- Swain should have been given an award for enforcing the rules.

He wasn't, but he was given his job back when it couldn't be proven that he lied on his time sheet.

This time, he was fired for the far harder to disprove charges of "grossly inefficient job performance and inappropriate conduct."

A university spokesman declined to comment but referred me to a statement released by Campus Police Chief Derek Poarch on Sept. 8, three months after the firing. "Swain was terminated from his position ... after an internal investigation. The investigation showed that Swain's job performance was inadequate and that he failed to follow department policies and properly supervise officers under his command."

It would be easy to argue, as Swain and his attorney plan to do when they appeal the latest ruling, that Swain has had a bull's-eye on his back since 1997.

I mean, in order to make this case, Chief Poarch and Maj. Jeff McCracken rented a car so they wouldn't be recognized and, armed with a video camera, taped officers as they entered the Paul J. Rizzo Center to shoot pool and watch television -- neither of which is forbidden.

The tape had no time bar, making it impossible to tell how long the surveillance lasted -- although you'd occasionally hear somebody intone, "It is now 2:37 a.m.," or something.

What you can tell from the tape is that minutes after Swain arrived, the officers left. Or tried to. Their exit was blocked when Poarch and McCracken swooped down upon them.

Poarch, in a transcript I read, told the officers, "This is one of the saddest days in all my 27 years in law enforcement because I hired every one of you guys."

Yeah, but he didn't fire every one of them. Just Swain and a new cop who was on probation. Even that cop has since landed another cop gig; Swain's name, unfortunately, appears to be mud in local cop shops. He's still unemployed.

The message other officers will take from Swain's persecution is, "Do your job, but be careful who you do it to."

8/30/2005

A DONOR, A KIDNEY, A HEART

Of all the things for which Miverna Fields and her daughter, Barbara Hibbert, gave thanks Thursday, none was as important as a single overheard conversation.

One Sunday after a service at White Rock Baptist Church in Durham, friends were asking Hibbert about her health, her search for a matching kidney. Patty Baskette overheard them. "She walked up," Fields recalled this week, "and said, 'I have two good ones. I'll give you one.'"

Hibbert said, "I couldn't believe it. She gave me her phone number, but I didn't call for a couple of days. I had to absorb what was happening." After she absorbed her good fortune, a series of tests determined their compatibility. Hibbert received the kidney Nov. 16 at UNC Hospitals in Chapel Hill.

"My new kidney is working well. I am feeling on top of the world," she said Wednesday. "My doctor says I'm on track."

Had the two women been relatives or lifelong friends, Baskette's sacrifice would be a heartwarming holiday tale. That they were, in Hibbert's words, "casual acquaintances" makes their story close to miraculous. Both women attended N.C. Central University during the 1960s, and both moved to New York after graduation. "Because of work, we only saw each other at monthly alumni meetings. We were alumni buddies," Hibbert said.

Baskette retired from the cardiology department at Westchester County Medical Center in New York in 1995 and returned to Raleigh. About the same time, Hibbert headed south, too. She retired from IBM and became a consultant for Blue Cross Blue Shield in South Carolina. Both attended White Rock Baptist Church.

"I am oh-so-thankful," Hibbert said. "It's like having a second chance ... a new lease on life knowing that I don't have to go to dialysis three times a week. She overheard friends saying I need a kidney and stepped right in and never wavered throughout the entire process. She's my angel."

Baskette doesn't feel like an angel. She sees her contribution as practical, not celestial. "I'm a donor. This is really to make African-Americans aware of donating," she said. "We're the ones most in need, but we do the least donating."

Statistics from the United Network for Organ Sharing confirm that 36 percent of the 55,000 people on waiting lists for organs are blacks, while blacks make up roughly 13 percent of the general population.

Skepticism of the medical profession is one reason that about one in 10 blacks register as organ donors. History and urban legend abound with tales of us being used as guinea pigs. Remember Tuskegee Experiment 626, in which black men were deliberately infected with syphilis in Alabama?

As smart as I am, even I resisted for a long time becoming an organ donor lest I enter the hospital with, say, a hangnail and come out minus a kidney or eyeball. That fear became indefensible, though, after I realized how often we need transplants but how infrequently we give them. Besides, if I really end up where everyone tells me to go, I'll neither need nor want eyes.

Barbara Hibbert said, "You never know where your blessings are going to come from."

Nor, she might have added, do we know when we might be in a position to be a blessing.

————————————————————————————————⊣ 11/26/2004

A DREAM OF BANNING THE SPEECH ⊢————————

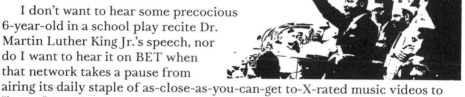

I have a dream that I can make it through this whole day without hearing "I Have a Dream."

I don't want to hear some precocious 6-year-old in a school play recite Dr. Martin Luther King Jr.'s speech, nor do I want to hear it on BET when that network takes a pause from airing its daily staple of as-close-as-you-can-get to-X-rated music videos to "honor" Dr. King.

Chill, Homes. I haven't been kidnapped by some cult and had my brain replaced by Jesse Helms'.

I am just sick and tired of having that speech trotted out yearly, as though it is the only thing King ever said. The speech, the greatest oration ever, now packs about the same emotional wallop as "We Shall Overcome," the anachronistic theme song of the civil rights era: none.

Both, through a combination of overuse, misuse and misappropriation, have been rendered meaningless, almost powerless, because they allow some people to think that merely listening to either and nodding solemnly in the appropriate places makes them a Rosa Parks-like freedom fighter.

That's crap. While criticizing Dr. King's speech will strike some as blasphemous - it would've struck me the same way a few years ago - and invites vituperation upon my head, I mean the big guy no disrespect. The Roman Catholic Church recently named him a candidate for martyrdom, and I'd be the first to say King deserves that and any other honor that can be bestowed upon him.

Criticizing anything about the dude is not something I do lightly, and I wouldn't be doing it now if someone else hadn't done it first.

That someone was the Rev. Michael Eric Dyson. Surely y'all remember Dyson. He is the former University of North Carolina faculty member, now at DePaul University, who had tassels spinning after bravely and justifiably criticizing Michael Jordan at a UNC graduation ceremony.

Dyson is now taking aim, albeit lovingly, I'd say, at the brightest star in black America's firmament. Among other things, he is calling for a 10-year moratorium on "The Speech."

Dyson, who is touring the country promoting his new book on King - "I May Not Get There With You" - feels that the King we purport to honor today bears little resemblance to the one who gave his life for his beliefs.

Dyson and I missed connections all weekend, but in an interview with another reporter, he railed against the "namby-pamby, We-are-the-world-Michael Jackson - and I could add Quincy Jones" revisionist image of King as a "safe Negro" who merely traveled around making eloquent speeches. "Dr. King wasn't killed because he had a dream," Dyson reminds us.

Nowhere in these almost-cartoonish images, Dyson declares, is the King who vehemently opposed the Vietnam War, urged civil disobedience and even favored reparations for descendants of slaves. Dyson bravely writes about the adulterous and plagiarizing King, as well as the one that FBI Director J. Edgar Hoover called "the most dangerous man in America."

Far from diminishing King, Dyson's discomfittingly honest, three-dimensional portrayal is infinitely better than the deification - Disneyfication? - of King to which we are usually subjected on this day. Happy Birthday, Doc.

1/17/2000

A GOOD NIGHT'S REST: $579

Thank goodness someone besides me recognizes the need for a little class around here.

That's what the Triangle is getting now that the Goodnights of Cary are building that $35 million luxury hotel near their SAS Institute.

If you're anything like me, you're tired of having no answer when visiting friends and family members ask, "Say, hoss, you know where I can blow a week's salary on one night of lodging?"

Now, you can direct them to The Umstead, Ann and Jim Goodnight's contribution to high-class hotels.

Groundbreaking on The Taj Ma-Goodnight won't begin until August, but we already know this is not going to be like the old Rock 'em, Sock 'em Motel in Rockingham, where rooms could be had for $35 a night, less if Linda Kay was working and her boss wasn't around.

Ann Goodnight said she convinced her husband, Jim, that there was a need for a luxury hotel.

"We get a lot of executives coming into our area -- certainly SAS does -- and it would be wonderful to have a quality hotel for these visitors."

A room at the Four Seasons Hotel in San Francisco -- the one whose design inspired Ann Goodnight, she said -- starts for about $300 a night. Suites start at $579.

I called up Akbar "I've got your wake-up call right here, pal" Throckmorton, manager of the notorious No-Tell Motel -- whose motto is "Where every couple is named Mr. & Mrs. Smith" -- and asked what guests at his motel could get for $579.

"The whole place," he said. "I've been looking to dump this sucker since I won it in a poker game last year."

Throckmorton just laughed when I asked if the No-Tell had, as The Umstead will have, a first-class restaurant.

"No, but there's a Waffle House next door where the waitresses wear orthopedic hose and call you 'Sweetie' if you tip 'em right."

Lest the Goodnights alienate us natives by focusing entirely on well-heeled visiting execs, a few of The Umstead's 17 proposed suites should be named for personages of cultural significance to North Carolinians, like Richard Petty.

I don't know about you, but I'm already saving my scratch so I can be the first to sleep in the Barney Fife Suite, which should, for historical accuracy, be a corner room overlooking the YMCA.

Married Southern Baptists will certainly want to stay in the Jesse Helms Suite -- because of the strategically placed camera over the bed. It'll be there to make sure no one is having too much fun. If you do, a Republican will rush in and threaten to cut off your funding.

Want to make a bet on how long it'll take to hear a guest from Rockingham, up with the family for the State Fair, say, " 'Continental breakfast' my butt; that's a honey bun and glass of orange juice, Martha, and we ain't payin' $18 for it."

Or this conversation between some John Deere salesman from Monroe and The Umstead's front desk clerk:

CLERK: Beg pardon, sir, but we explained to you that the room was $579.

JEB: I know, but you didn't say for one night.

2/20/2004

A HAND HELD OUT IS DENIED

For once, I offered to the one-legged dude in the wheelchair a hand that didn't contain money. He slapped that sucker away.

"I don't have any money today," I told him after parking my car and darting through traffic to reach him on the traffic-divider island, "but I'd like to write a story about your situation."

Because Triangle residents are so generous to neighbors who need help, I knew that a story about a man with one leg -- the left one is gone clean up to the kneecap -- who spent each day humming and bumming in the heat would easily raise money.

Larry -- the name on the city-issued badge that gives him a license to beg -- said he needed to raise less than $400 to pay for a kidney transplant, and I assured him that would be a piece of cake to raise once people knew of his plight.

Alas, he didn't want people to know.

"I don't want any publicity," he said politely but firmly. Five minutes of persuasive arguments, scores of oblivious drivers and a merciless noonday sun failed to weaken his resolve. He thanked me for previous contributions, but he still wouldn't talk.

Our five-minute conversation was interrupted three times by people pulling up to give him a buck or two. He thanked each with a sincere "God bless you."

The law requiring panhandlers to get licensed went into effect in January and has cut down on the number of people soliciting on city streets. Theoretically, it also cut down on the number of people trying to scam softhearted residents. Thus, anyone with the badge probably has a legitimate cause for which they're seeking donations.

Larry has spent the past three months in the median of Club Boulevard at Duke Street, holding up and out a hand-lettered sign seeking donations for his kidney transplant.

Larry often has a bottle of something cold -- juice, a bottle of water -- although it couldn't stay cold for long on the unshaded median. When I stopped to talk to him Monday, all he had was a giant, opened bag of potato chips that was attracting the attention of a line of ants.

I don't know about the motives of other motorists who pull up and hand him a dollar or two or five, but mine were always purely selfish: If I hadn't given him something, I'd have felt bad all day.

Not anymore I won't. The switch that turns on sympathy flipped off after my efforts to get him out of the sun were rebuked. Illogically, irrationally, I wanted to tell him what he could do with that sign.

Why, I asked him and later me, would someone choose to sit out in a broiling sun when there was an easier way to achieve his goal?

His answer was a most dissatisfying one: He didn't want to publicize himself.

I was immediately reminded of a man who slept under the bridge near my house a few years ago. I took him for breakfast -- again, spurred purely by self-interest -- and asked whether he'd like a job.

"Man," he said, "if I got a job, the first thing I'd do when I got paid would be to go buy some more crack."

I thanked him for his honesty and left him in the restaurant munching on an Egg McMuffin.

The same way I left Larry with his potato chips.

7/20/2004

A LANDLORD DURHAM CAN'T AFFORD

Betty Perry is one of those people who, it could be said, fell through the cracks of life.

It's a wonder she didn't fall through the cracks of her front porch. Or drown because of the leaking cracks in her roof.

These days, she barely gets by. Perry subsists on a small government disability check -- I didn't have the nerve to ask how small -- since suffering serious injuries in a car crash several years ago.

On top of that, the former nurse's assistant until recently had the misfortune to have as her landlord one of Durham's most notorious slumlords, Chester "Shaft" Jenkins.

When I christened Jenkins "Shaft" in 1994, it wasn't because he reminded me of that cool private eye who was a sex machine with all the chicks; it was because that -- the shaft -- is what he gave to tenants of his various properties.

That Jenkins pulls down $72,862 from the city of Durham as human relations director -- $16,000 more than he made when he was hired six years ago -- while owning buildings that are a blight on the city is unconscionable to many people. But to Perry -- known to people in her neighborhood as Miss Betty -- it was convenient.

"I could pay my rent when I went to City Hall to pay my water bill," she said.

Hooboy. The image of Jenkins chillin' in his office -- did I mention it was inside City Hall? -- collecting money from people too uninformed, too disconnected or merely too tired to complain is an image the city cannot afford.

While it's convenient for tenants and housing inspectors who serve citations, having a slumlord right inside City Hall is unacceptable.

City Manager Lamont Ewell told me Monday that he would make a decision on Jenkins' future with the city later this week. If he needs help making the right decision, he should talk to Miss Betty. When I told her that workers were busy fixing up her former home at 603 Linwood, the one that was cited for 47 housing code violations, she plaintively asked, "I wonder why he didn't work on it when we were there?"

The reason, of course, is that no one forced him to. Jenkins has gotten away with providing the minimum required by law -- and in some cases less than that -- to people like Miss Betty.

On Monday, though, housing activist Steve Hopkins cited Jenkins by name as the king of slumlords when he announced his candidacy for mayor.

Jenkins weathered the criticism directed at him after he was first hired to the city post in 1994 and it was learned that many of his properties were not just dilapidated but also havens for illegal drug activity.

When told about that, Jenkins replied, "I am not responsible for crime that goes on in Durham. That's a police problem."

Yikes. Such civic insensitivity would be reprehensible coming from anyone, but it is especially galling coming from a former Durham mayor, the city's first black one.

Ewell, who is leaving at the end of the month, can give the city a great going-away gift: Shaft's pink slip. Durham can't afford officials or landlords like Shaft Jenkins.

12/5/2000

A LAPSE LOOKS COSTLY

I'll tell you one thing. If the sight of Donnie Harrison traipsing through the woods with bloodhounds wasn't enough to get Wake County's black voters to the polls, nothing will ever be enough.

Harrison, in his TV ads and in an interview with me, noted that he favors bloodhounds to search for lost Alzheimer's patients, children and criminal suspects, but his use of them nonetheless sent chills down my spine because of their historical symbolism.

Judging by voter turnout, Harrison's use of dogs that were at one time used specifically to track down black slaves resonated with hardly anyone else.

Thus, it appears that Harrison has edged out John Baker for the office of Wake County sheriff. Overall voter turnout in the county was 55 percent, but in the predominantly black precincts where Baker was strongest, the figure didn't reach 40 percent.

For instance, Baker got 98 percent of the votes cast at sites in Chavis Heights and Walnut Terrace, but turnout there was a disgraceful 25 percent and 19 percent, respectively.

We shall overcome, indeed.

Show me a bloodhound -- except for ol' Duke on "The Beverly Hillbillies" -- and I think of slavery. It's hard to read anything about that "peculiar institution" and not see references to the hellhounds.

Since reading Richard Wright's short story "Big Boy Leaves Home" when I was 12 years old, I'd rather rassle an agitated alligator than pet a sleeping hound.

Frederick Douglass, speaking to an anti-slavery audience in Scotland in 1846, stated, "There is no spot ... where the slave is secure. He is still exposed to the bloodhounds that may be let loose against him."

Yet the man who could be Wake County's new sheriff featured them prominently in his ad campaign against a qualified black incumbent. And apparently won.

Harrison said, "When you've found people like I have, black and white, you don't think of slavery. ... I like bloodhounds because they're one of the best 'trailers' you can get. That's what's bred into them."

I believe Harrison, and if he's guilty of anything, it's of being insensitive to how the ads could affect some people.

If Baker's only qualification were his color, I'd be indifferent to Harrison's victory.

Baker, though, has been an outstanding public servant and role model. The first time I met with him, he had summoned me to his office to talk about a program he wanted to implement that would allow inmates in the county jail to get their GEDs. That, he said, would lessen their likelihood of returning.

As good a sheriff as he was, though, he made one politically fatal mistake: He thought his record would speak for him.

Alas, he obviously put too much faith in Wake County's electorate.

If you haven't seen Donnie's dogs, trust me, you will: They'll be sniffing around your children's school lockers and anywhere -- or anyone -- else arousing suspicion.

9

To the county's black voters who lolled around and didn't vote -- for either Baker or Harrison -- I say, with all due disrespect, "You ought to be ashamed."

To Big John -- and with apologies to Willie Tee -- I just want to say, "Thank you, John."

11/8/2002

PLEASE, CALL OFF THE DOGS

After hearing from several hundred people who were angry at me for calling Sheriff-elect Donnie Harrison a racist for using bloodhounds in police work, I had to consider the possibility that I was guilty of muddled thinking, that I didn't clearly state my views.

"That many people surely couldn't be wrong, could they?" I asked myself.

You're darned right they could. And they were.

I never called Harrison a racist who was going to sic dogs on blacks. Not even close. But that didn't stop me from being labeled a "dog-hatin' racist" living in the past.

All I said was that seeing Harrison roaming the woods with bloodhounds in his TV campaign ads evoked for me the images I think of anytime I see a bloodhound -- of slavery, when some bloodhounds were trained expressly to track down runaway slaves.

I also wondered in the column why the dog ads didn't propel more blacks -- the real target of my column -- off their sofas and into the voting booths.

Race, let's face it, is still the hottest hot-button topic in America, and people are understandably hypersensitive to having their candidate -- and, by extension, themselves -- accused of being racist.

I'd have felt the same way if I thought my candidate -- if I had one -- was being unfairly labeled and attacked.

I'm not backing off of anything I said -- in the words of Willie Nelson, "If you see me backing up, it's just to get a running start" -- but I understand how some people either misinterpreted the column or read it wrong.

Others who took my name in vain were probably just absent from school the day they taught cognitive thinking skills.

I don't want to get off on the wrong foot with a cat who leads armed men and women, so if Big D thinks the column called him a racist, I apologize. To him. When I talked with Harrison, he said he uses the dogs to search for Alzheimer's patients and missing children. Who could oppose that?

Nothing he said or did makes me think he's a racist. He aggressively went after Sheriff John Baker during the campaign, but they're both big boys who know that, in the immortal words of the late Chicago Mayor Harold Washington, "Politics ain't beanbag."

I wasn't even angry at the rabid, right-wing radio host who got on the air and misrepresented what I wrote. The dude, I knew, was merely trying to make his show interesting. It would've been a lot more interesting if I could've gotten ahold of him on the air.

Alas, the most vociferous responses came not from people who thought I disparaged their candidate. They came from dog lovers who objected to me mentioning ol' Duke from "The Beverly Hillbillies" -- "If you think that is typical of bloodhounds, you are an idiot" -- or saying that I'd rather rassle an agitated alligator than pet a sleeping hound.

That was fine with the hound-loving and -raising woman from Oklahoma who wrote, "You are off the wall, and I don't think I'd want you to pet my children."

Did you know that there are organizations out there committed to protecting the image of bloodhounds?

I didn't either, but I do now.

11/19/2002

A MATTER OF DADS' SUPPORT

Michael Gross of Raleigh should write a book. He could call it "New York on less than $6 a week."

The downside is that if you took the advice, you'd have to sleep in a garbage truck.

That's what Gross did, even though he was no bum badgering strangers for change; he was a New York City garbageman making $450 to $550 a week.

Not enough, even during the 1980s, to put you in the lap of luxury, but certainly enough to keep you out of the cab of a garbage truck, right? Wrong, especially after factoring in what Gross paid in child and spousal support after his divorce.

Of the dozen or so men I talked with about this issue in the past month, nary a one -- no, not one -- was a "deadbeat dad" or lamented having to support his children.

None wanted -- OK, none expected -- sympathy. They all wanted some understanding of what they considered the injustices inflicted upon them by a court system that they think gives not a hoot for fathers.

Several men showed me their pay stubs, post-deductions, but those offered by Gross were the ones that made every man, including me, clutch head, chest, then wallet.

In one particular week, Gross grossed $583.49. After taxes and child support, he had $40.32 left to live on. Other take-home paychecks were for $17, $11 and the nadir, $5.39.

"When I told the judge, 'I can't afford to do this,' he said, 'Then you need to get another job,'" Gross said.

Gross, whose children are now grown, resembles singer Billy Davis Jr. and smiles almost as much. During our 90-minute conversation, the smile left his face once: when I asked why he wanted to talk about child support now, years after his last court-ordered payment.

He said, "I have a couple of friends who are younger who are going through the same thing. It's really messing with their minds. ... They're talking about killing these women, making them disappear.

"I've been trying to chill them out and let them know that if I can survive what the system put me through, they can survive."

Gross has reason to be concerned. So do many pregnant women in America:

Barry Saunders

A University of Maryland study showed that the leading cause of death for mamas-to-be is -- get this -- daddies-to-be.

A yearlong examination by The Washington Post of death-record data in states across the country last year documents the killings of 1,367 pregnant women and new mothers since 1990. This is incomplete, because no reliable system is in place to track such cases.

Even without such a system, we've all become aware in recent years of women who were murdered while pregnant and whose boyfriends or husbands were responsible. Contrary to the endless news coverage their cases received, Scott Peterson in California and Rae Carruth, the professional football player in North Carolina, are not the first men to kill the expectant mothers of their children.

Gross, who proclaims triumphantly that "I've endured," is doing his small part to ensure they'll be among the last.

Men feeling that they can't endure can log onto the American Coalition for Fathers and Children Web site -- www.acfc.org -- for support.

Or else look up Michael Gross and learn to live off $6 a week.

5/13/2005

A NEW STAMP CANCELS SOME OLD WRONGS

Every now and then we -- Americans, that is -- get one right. We did earlier this week, when the U.S. Postal Service came out with a stamp honoring Paul Robeson.

That this country is bestowing such an honor upon a person who was at one time treated as an enemy of the state -- and, worse, a nonperson -- shows a great capacity for change.

Paul Robeson is mistakenly called one of history's greatest black Americans. Wrong! Robeson was one of the greatest Americans of any hue we've ever produced. Educator Mary McLeod Bethune, who was no slouch in the "greatness" sweepstakes, once referred to him as "the tallest tree in our forest." She was referring specifically to black America, but she could just as easily have meant all of America, since no objective measurement of greatness could exclude Robeson.

He excelled academically -- a Phi Beta Kappa graduate of Rutgers and senior class valedictorian -- and athletically, twice named to the All-America football team.

Alas, don't go looking for him in some of the sports history books: his name was stricken from the record books because of his outspoken criticisms of America's racial and Cold War policies and because he refused to deny that he was a member of the American Communist Party.

Robeson, an admitted socialist sympathizer, was never a member of the party but he chose as a matter of principle not to answer the question while being grilled by the ironically named House UnAmerican Activities Committee during the McCarthy red hunt period.

He also was a great social activist and singer, whose voice actually stopped a war: during the Spanish Civil War, both sides supposedly ceased hostilities while

12

Robeson sang, among other tunes, his signature "Ol' Man River." That song, from the musical "Showboat," was written specifically for him by Jerome Kern.

After World War II, Robeson was hounded and persecuted by the State Department, which took away his passport and forbade him to travel outside the country. As a result of that action, which the U.S Supreme Court eventually overturned, his income reportedly dropped from $104,000 in 1947 to $2,000 in 1950.

For those of us who love the guy, though, one of the greatest indignities visited upon Robeson was the selection of James Earl Jones to portray him in a one-man play during the 1970s. It was a travesty that Jones, an at-times buffoonish and admittedly apolitical actor, should portray Robeson, the personification of the activist artist. Robeson left no doubt about his feelings on that matter. "The artist," he wrote in 1937, "must elect to fight for freedom or for slavery. I have made my choice."

What say you, James Earl?

The same play was resurrected during the 1980s with the acclaimed Avery Brooks in the title role. Not one word was changed, but the play succeeded because of Brooks.

More than anything, the posthumous recognition given Paul Robeson is proof that, if you're right, the world will sometimes come around to your view. At the least it will admit, if begrudgingly, that you had the courage of your convictions and were a worthy adversary.

It's regrettable that Robeson has been dead so long — he died Jan. 23, 1976, a largely forgotten, broken man. If there is a Heaven we can take some solace in knowing that he knows his good fight was not in vain. America, we got one right this time.

⊢ 1/24/2004

A NIAGARA OF VIAGRA ON YOUR TAB ⊢────────────

What a truly remarkable, inspiring sight that was earlier this week - thousands of state employees marching between the Capitol and the Legislative Building demanding a larger pay raise.

I know, I know. There is nothing inherently remarkable about workers picketing for more money. Happens every day, right?

The amazing part is that state workers would have the energy to walk and carry signs at the same time, considering the amount of moolah the state is spending on Viagra prescriptions for them.

The state - that's you and me, pal - is expected to spend more than $2 million this year for the erectile dysfunction drug, leading one to conclude that state government is peopled not by pencil-pushing bureaucrats as previously thought, but by insatiable, lusty lotharios who get turned on at the sight of a copy machine.

Another fear is that some state workers are selling the danged pills on the black market.

"We've never seen anyone who needed 400 pills a year," said Heather Van Ness, a spokeswoman for Pfizer, the company that makes Viagra. That probably came as a surprise to the state worker who bought 473 last year.

To most people, that's an open-and-shut case of abuse and fraud, and it would be hard for even Johnnie Cochran at his most dramatic to get him off.

Cochran: Your Honor, my client, Vinnie Viagarino, is an honest man who did not abuse the system. If you've ever seen Mrs. Viagarino, you'd realize that he sometimes had to double up on the number of pills he took. In closing, I'd just like to say, "If you didn't see him sell the pill, the state must foot the bill."

Indeed, instead of cynically assuming fraud and forcing the prodigious pill popper to reimburse the state, why not give "Vinnie" the benefit of the doubt? Since it would be medically disastrous for him to take that many pills in a year, it's possible he was a beneficent sexual Johnny Appleseed who, instead of planting apple trees across the countryside, is spreading little blue pills among the lovelorn and encouraging them to be fruitful and multiply - or to at least have a heckuva good time trying.

But some might consider that too generous. Despite my sympathy for state employees suffering what Bob Dole so famously calls "E.D.," the amount of our tax money being spent to put these cowboys back in the saddle is too high.

Worse yet, state employees are also using the state health plan to lose weight and grow hair. That's ironic, since one side effect of the hair-growth drug Propecia is impotence. I don't want to deprive state employees of access to these "happy" drugs, but when I'm paying for it, they should have to choose to either look good or love good.

Don't accuse me of player-hating. I want state employees to be happy - maybe then they'll treat us better when we renew our driver licenses - but I don't want to have to pay for them to have more fun than I do.

My suggestion for easing the burden on taxpayers' pocketbooks is for the state, instead of spending $10 per pill for Viagra, to buy a bottle of Ripple and a Barry White greatest hits CD for employees and tell 'em they're on their own.

And for those who're bald and fat? Buy 'em a big hat and a six-pack of Slim-Fast.

———————————————————————————————— 5/19/2000

A ONE IN A MILLION MARRIAGE

Pam Gattis knew that her chance of finding true love in a newspaper ad was one in a million. She found it anyway.

The way she lost it was also one in a million. Literally.

Gattis' husband, William Harrison -- whom she met through a newspaper personal ad -- died in August of Creutzfeldt-Jakob disease. The disease strikes one in 1 million people worldwide.

I introduced you to Gattis several years ago in a column with the headline "Cupid answers the ad." It described how the Wake County educator met the man who was to become her soulmate and husband through a News & Observer personal ad.

"I had given up on finding 'Mr. Wonderful,' " she said at the time, "so I figured I might find 'Mr. Somebody-to-do-something-fun-with.' He was looking for an ACC sports fan, so I called him up and told him, 'If you find a bigger one than me, you'd better grab her.' "

Harrison was indeed Gattis' "Mr. Somebody-to-do-something fun-with" -- at the time of his first seizure this past summer, they were packed and ready to leave on a trip to South America. He also turned out to be the man with whom she intended to spend the rest of her life.

14

They were married in January 1995, months after she responded to the ad.

I described Gattis at the time as a perky liberal in her 40s and her husband as a conservative Republican who cherished his autographed picture of Jesse Helms. Not even that could derail their love train.

Gattis is no longer in her 40s, but she is still perky. "I was married to a wonderfully ordinary man," she said, which, to her, made his affliction with such a rare ailment even harder to bear. "I nearly blessed that poor lady out when she told me" he had CJD, Gattis recalled.

"That poor lady" was Dr. Laura Jozewicz, a Raleigh neurologist. Jozewicz said CJD "is very, very rare." Most cases are sporadic, she said, occurring for no known reason, although one specific form of it is caused by exposure to cattle that have mad cow disease.

CJD is a degenerative brain disorder, which, Jozewicz said, is usually fatal within three months. It is characterized by blindness, deafness, the loss of memory and personality changes.

Gattis sees irony in her husband dying of an illness that incapacitates victims mentally and physically.

"Bill was such an intellectual, and from that standpoint, he would have been fascinated with CJD and how it affected his mind and body," she said.

Alas, the disease held no such fascination for her. "Watching somebody you love more than yourself being eaten alive and falling apart is tough," she said.

"I'm pretty good at premonitions, so I said, 'If this is our last trip together, we're going to go for it,'" she said.

The two-week South America trip would have been arduous for all but the fittest person. For Harrison, Gattis said, it was "extremely difficult. I don't know how in the world he ever pulled that off. ... I think he knew he was going to die, and he wanted that to be his legacy.

"We climbed volcanoes, hiked the Andes and the Galapagos Islands. We climbed 500 steps up a volcano with someone holding him up on each side," she marveled.

When Harrison died, nearly 30 family members were also at his side, holding him up.

11/19/2004

A ROOF IS JUST A START

Langston Hughes' transcendent poem "Mother to Son" contains these lines:

"Well, son, I'll tell you.

"Life for me ain't been no crystal stair.

"It's had tacks in it, and splinters,

"And boards torn up,

"And places with no carpet on the floor -- Bare."

Well, count your blessings, sister, because at least you had a stair, splinters notwithstanding.

When Helen Thomas of Chapel Hill sits on a tattered sofa and talks to her son, who turns 12 Saturday, it is with the knowledge that, not too long ago, they were sleeping outside.

So for Thomas, 36, and her three children, just having a roof is as good as it's been in a long, long time.

The two-bedroom duplex apartment in which the four of them now live is paid for by the Orange-Person-Chatham area mental health agency.

The family is scheduled to move into a three-bedroom Section 8 home in Hillsborough next week. It's a modest place, but their excitement rivals that of someone fixing to move into the Biltmore House.

I met Thomas through Hillsborough dentist Joseph Gatewood, who owns the house, and his staff. They met her through the Orange County Department of Social Services.

"It was beyond rough," she said. "We've slept on the street, outside behind buildings. We'd wash up at McDonald's and spend time, a lot of time, at the library when it got cold."

The weather outside the rickety screen door was sunny and over 70 degrees when I met with Thomas, but I felt a chill when I thought of her girls, ages 13 and 17 and blossoming into womanhood, being exposed to the streets' hazards, natural and man-made.

When I asked Thomas what she needs for her new home, it was a rhetorical question. The truth is they need everything.

"I don't want to wish for too much, 'cause I don't have nothin'," she said.

There's a dresser she got from a local church and a gray stuffed rabbit. That's it.

Everything else -- the 13-inch television, the mismatched sofa and lumpy chair -- belongs to the mental health agency and stays for the next distressed family.

Her children, she said, "are good kids, to be under the kind of pressure they're under, the circumstances they're under. So far, they seem to be OK. They know that I suffer from depression, and the voices, and they take it good."

Thomas has been diagnosed as bipolar and clinically depressed, conditions that make it hard for her to work, she said.

She tried to kill herself recently after losing her last fast-food job, she said.

I asked, again rhetorically, why.

She began a litany of misfortune -- domestic abuse, a sick daughter, a boyfriend who split -- which she said occurred "back to back to back."

A streak of bad luck like that would make the luckiest person with the strongest constitution ask, "To be or not to be?" For Thomas, whose life had never been a crystal stair, it was too much.

Despite mental illness, bad luck and bad decisions, Thomas said she feels she now has a reason to live. "Just having a roof and being together, that's my main thing," she said.

Of course, a washer, dryer and some beds would help, too.

3/25/2005

A SIMPLE MATTER OF TRUST

We Are, in the Lingo of the Hip-Hoppers on the Street, "Fixin' to Get Paid, Dawg." Ta-Dow.

Turns out that a couple of African guardian angels -- one in Nigeria and the other in Sierra Leone -- were looking out for The Kid and are offering to cut me a slice of a multimillion-dollar piece of cheddar.

All they need is my checking account number.

Check this out. I was cruising the Internet late one recent eve, answering adoring letters from fans -- and trying to ignore unsolicited sales pitches from sleazy companies offering to make me bigger or smaller for a fee -- when an offer from a doctor yanked at my heartstrings.

"I have a widow in my clinic who is on political asylum" in an African refugee camp, wrote Dr. Aliu D. Francis. The widow is destitute now, Dr. Francis said, but -- wouldn't you know it? -- her late husband was a top military officer who left her $28 million in cash. In a trunk.

The widow, whose name I didn't get, "has a limited knowledge in the business world and cannot manage this [sic] funds herself," my new best friend, Dr. Francis, wrote.

He picked me, he said, because he'd heard that I was "credible and trustworthy."

Funny, those are the very words I use -- but no one else does -- to describe me.

All I have to do to get a piece of this pie is give them my checking account number, wait for word from Dr. Francis and then scoot over to some as-yet-undisclosed country in Europe and get my moolah. I merely have to promise to be fair with the widow when she gets to America.

That's the least I can do.

While pondering which color Bentley I'd purchase to drive my young'un to school in, I received a letter from a concern in Nigeria called the National Petroleum Corp. It was seeking my help in smuggling $35 million out of the country.

It's a complicated story how they came upon said funds, but suffice it to say that they simply must have a trustworthy -- there's that word again -- U.S. agent into whose account they can wire the money.

Once they get the money into my account, Mr. Ugo Nwosu wrote me, I get to keep 25 percent of it. I'm no math whiz, but I figured out that 25 percent of $35 million is ... hmm ... Let's just say you won't ever again see me waiting anxiously for that blue light special at Kmart.

All my buddy Ugo needs from me to begin and complete this enriching transaction is, you guessed it, a checking account number into which they will place the money.

And here I was thinking there were no such things as angels.

Just one thing separates me from unimagined riches, though: no checking account. My bank, Walk Over Ya' National, canceled my account because it said I was no- account. Something about 47 overdrawn checks.

That's where you come in. The bank said I must deposit $2,000 before it'll give me a new account. All I need from you is a little good-faith cash with which to open an account, and I'll cut you a piece of cheddar, too.

You know I'm trustworthy: I've got two letters that say so.

9/20/2002

A SIN, A STAIN, A STRUT

As that noted civil rights activist Trent Lott has said many times -- at least in the past week -- segregation was a sin and a stain on our nation.

But for a sin and a stain, it wasn't all bad.

Contrary to common misperceptions, black life in the segregated South was not one of unrelenting misery, with us shuffling around going, "Oh, lawdy, we's bein' segregated."

No sirree. We lived, Jack, even as our leaders battled to end segregation.

While some current so-called leaders would have us believe that nothing has changed -- so they can keep a job and remain relevant -- the truth is that conditions and opportunities for most blacks in the South have improved beyond anything we could've dreamed.

I'm not trivializing or romanticizing what was a dreadful period in our history, so keep those accusatory letters.

Just between us, though, many black institutions thrived during segregation, and many black students thrived despite inferior school resources. Kids have new books now, but as Jesse Jackson asked -- back when he was relevant -- "What does it matter if you have old or new books if you open neither?"

I'm of the last generation of blacks who remember being forced by law to sit in the balcony at the movies or having to fry up a couple of yardbirds for long road trips because you might not find a restaurant that would serve you.

Psst, lean closer: We liked sitting in the balcony -- but not being forced to -- and nothing in any restaurant has ever tasted as good as my grandmother's fried chicken on a piece of light bread.

"Drumline," a new movie about competition between bands at historically black colleges, reminded me of the fun to be had in a small Southern town during the mid- to late 1960s, when legal segregation wheezed its last, labored breath.

Sure, Leak Street School, which went from first grade through 12th, received less money per student from the state than all-white schools, and the hand-me-down textbooks were often obsolete by the time we received them.

But we made do. When the Christmas parade rolled around, however, we did more than make do: We made up -- for all we'd been denied. Each year, Leak Street's Marching Tigers, led by band director Lewis Broadnax, high-stepped through downtown Rockingham and just tore the place up. I mean.

The Morrison Training School Drill Team, all black except for one or two white kids whose parents obviously didn't have the juice to keep them out of the joint, owned the parade with its precision marching drills. But Leak Street's band was a strong No. 2.

The school was blessed with two great drum majors, both of whom -- by cosmic coincidence -- were named Larry Diggs. When the first one graduated, the band never missed a step.

Now, I consider myself to be a dancing fool when I want to be, but both of those dudes had more rhythm in their big toe than I have in my whole body.

Junior Walker, in his song "Way Back Home," wrote, There are good and bad things about the South/And some leave a bitter taste in my mouth.

Mine, too, Junior. But some bring a smile to my face.

12/17/2002

A SOUL WITHOUT A NAME

No doubt about it, murder is the worst thing you can do to a person.

But being killed and then lying unclaimed at the morgue for several days is an added indignity that should be visited upon no one.

Not that John Doe, the young man found dead on a sidewalk in front of a stranger's East Durham home early Saturday morning is aware of this indignity; at least I hope not for his sake. It's more comforting to think that the victim's earthly concerns are over and his soul is departed and has already gone on about its business.

No, the affront is to us the living. Think about it. We are constantly told of the sanctity of human life, that every life matters, yet this life passes in a violent, well-publicized manner and nobody comes forth to claim it. Where's the sanctity in that?

How would you feel -- if you could feel anything -- after being slain or dying accidentally and no one knew or cared that you'd passed from this Earth and the only notice taken was in the form of impersonal news reports?

If you're anything like me, you want to think that family and friends would move heaven and earth to find out where you were if you were 15 minutes late getting home from the office. Or that their anguished wailing would alert the angels in heaven to the fact that something was amiss here on Earth.

The thought that a fellow human being's body could lie in a drawer at the medical examiner's office for days unclaimed, unspoken for, is discomfiting -- mainly because it makes us wonder if we, too, are living an unremarkable life that, when it ends, will be unremarked upon.

Police, proceeding under the assumption that the victim is Hispanic, canvassed Hispanic neighborhoods and contacted the Mexican Consulate. They think they are close to identifying the dead man, who wore three rings, one of which appears to be a wedding band.

But if a positive ID is made, the big break cited by police won't be a distraught young wife desperately seeking a husband who didn't come home or anxious parents looking for their missing son.

If John Doe is identified through the latest lead, Durham Police Cpl. R.C. Spivey said, it'll be for the most mundane of reasons: "Someone didn't show up for work Monday" and a person at the job called to check the identity of the dead man, he said.

Spivey said police have been working since Saturday to find out who the dead man is, who killed him and why. Except for the rings, he said, there was nothing distinctive about the 5-foot-8, slightly built man with brown hair and brown eyes.

"Detectives have been working hard" to determine the victim's identity, Spivey said. "He's just your average guy. It's an 'Any Man' situation. ... If we identify him, at least for friends and family, they'll know who it is and what happened to him."

And then maybe "Any Man's" soul can rest. And ours, too.

————————————————————————————————— 5/8/2001

THEY KNOW PABLO; NOW WE DO, TOO ————————————

Remember that "soul without a name" I told you about earlier this week?

Jackie Thomas and the rest of the staff and students at Neal Middle School want you to know that the soul did, indeed, have a name. When they learned that the man who had laid unidentified in the morgue for three days after being slain last week was "Pablo," a beloved janitor at their school, they opened their hearts.

Now, led by Thomas, a secretary at the school, they are also opening their pockets to see whether they can send his body back to his hometown, Tenango del Valle, Mexico, for burial.

Some students, said Don Bryson, a technology teacher at the Durham school, "just automatically turned their pockets inside out" and gave all the money they had upon learning that the dead man called Pablo was German Gomez Benites, the soft-spoken, hardworking janitor with the big smile and the bike he rode 12 miles to work each day.

I introduced you to Gomez, 24, earlier this week, when I wrote about the double tragedy of a man who was shot to death in an apparent robbery and then was left, unspoken for, in the medical examiner's office. I didn't tell you his name because I didn't know it. No one did. His sister only came forward to identify the body the day I wrote about him.

The story's headline referred to the body as a "soul without a name." That prompted students and staff at Neal to fire off more than a dozen letters to emphatically let you - and especially me - know that Gomez, who looked so young that he was sometimes mistaken for a student, was loved and will be missed.

Some of the letters were angry, some pained. All mentioned Gomez's ever-present smile. And all were heart-wrenching.

Typical was one from Shana Gillen, who teaches English as a Second Language at Neal. "Soon after beginning work at Neal," she wrote, "he began to approach me for help in learning English. ... I would sometimes work with him while he was cleaning. The broom never stopped, the mop never stopped. He was trying really hard to better his life."

Thomas, the secretary, simply said, "He was such a sweet, gentle man." In addition to trying to raise enough money to send Gomez's body back to Mexico, Thomas would like to raise enough to allow his sister, who lives in Durham and speaks no English, to accompany him. As of now, she said, the sister won't be able to attend her younger brother's funeral - if, that is, enough money is raised to send Pablo home.

So far, the school has collected just over $300, and another $800 has been contributed to the funeral home handling arrangements by "different people in the community," said Martha Sandlin, a spokeswoman for Professional Mortuary Services. "When people hear about it, they just come in and give" whatever they can.

The cost of sending Gomez back for burial is $3,346. If you are interested in helping, you can contact Thomas at 596-7308.

While it is comforting to realize that Gomez is no longer a soul without a name. It is disturbing to know that the person responsible for his death, a name without a soul, is still out there.

5/11/2001

A TELEVISION SHOW OUR DEMOCRACY SHOULD IDOLIZE

Hey, get over it already. Your man lost and there's nothing to be done about it.

The virulence of those voters upset that their candidate lost is frightening. You'd think people would be over that "Al Gore-really won-the-presidency" mind-set by now, wouldn't you?

They are. The stolen -- oops, lost -- presidential election is yesterday's news. The real anger now is over whether Raleigh's Clay Aiken got cheated out of being the true "American Idol."

In "Citizen Kane," publisher/gubernatorial candidate Charles Foster Kane had two front pages of his newspaper printed on election night: "Kane Elected" in case the election came out in his favor, and "Charles Foster Kane Defeated, Fraud at Polls!" if he lost.

Likewise, it's a certainty that both camps, Aiken's and winner Ruben Studdard's, were similarly armed with the immortal cry of losers the world over -- "We wuz robbed" -- in case the results weren't to their liking.

One local woman vented that she was unable to cast her vote for Aiken because the telephone lines were busy for hours. She's demanding a recount.

"What's so different about recounting this and recounting the general election in Florida?" she and other conspiracy theorists asked. And asked, reporters assured me, with disconcerting earnestness.

The fact that so many people are livid and crying "fraud" -- with seemingly far more virulence than they contested the presidential election results in 2000 -- confirms for many cultural doomsayers that Americans are mindless lemmings and that the country is in trouble.

Me, I see it as exactly the opposite.

That people can accept a justifiably contested presidential election -- heck, even a war -- with far more equanimity than they can the ultimate made-for-TV event is evidence that, hey, the kids are alright.

At first blush, it could be a bit -- OK, tremendously -- disturbing that 24 million votes were cast for two singers, neither likely to become a household name once his 15 minutes of media-induced fame are over.

(In what was meant as a putdown of Barry Manilow, one critic hoped that Aiken wouldn't become the "next" Manilow. The dude with the funny 'do can only wish that he develops Barry's pleasing persona and songwriting skills. For instance, if he ever writes and sings anything half as pretty as "Mandy," I'll become the next American Idol.)

Far from ridiculing the rabidity of "American Idol" fans and fretting about what it portends, politics should take a tip from the show.

Here's an idea: Leaving aside the difficulty of getting through to an open "American Idol" phone line, why not make it as easy to vote for city council representatives, governors, even presidents, as it was to cast a ballot for Clay or Ruben?

A democracy should seek ways to encourage participation, something the creators of the TV show succeeded in doing. After all, some people said they dialed in for hours trying to cast a vote. Such tenacity would redound greatly to the glory of a local pol.

The potential for fraud with phoned-in elections might increase, but in a country where dead folks cast votes, and where many say, only half-whimsically, "Vote early, vote often," what's a little fraud among friends?

Besides, more than a few politicians seem to "phone in" their terms and commitment, so why not let voters phone in their votes?

———————————————————————————— 5/24/2003

A WORLD WITHOUT KINDNESS ⊢————————————————

Instead of some weapon of mass destruction bringing about the world's end, it'll most likely be a weapon of mass indifference, where good people just say, "T' hell with it."

The first apocalyptic sign appeared a few months ago, and it made me weep for our world.

Mike Hickman, a guy I'd met only briefly, knocked on my door at home and told a tale that proves no good deed goes unpunished.

At least, his wouldn't have gone unpunished if he hadn't driven really fast.

Hickman told how he was driving down the Durham Freeway when he spotted a pickup truck with metal flying off the back. "I pulled up beside the driver and tried to tell him and his friends they were losing stuff," he recalled.

After doing what he thought was his duty as a decent human being, Hickman veered off at his exit. He noticed the truck, with three cursing, scowling men wielding baseball bats and a hammer, following him.

They chased him, but he lost them in traffic. He was shaken by the experience.

"I'm never going to try to help anybody again," he resolved on my front porch.

That would be a shame, because when I first met Hickman a few months earlier, he was trying to help somebody.

A well-known neighborhood creeper had stolen Hickman's daughter's bicycle off their front porch and refused to return it.

Hickman, driving down the street, recognized me at a traffic light, flagged me down and -- aware of my well-documented delinquent and misspent youth -- asked me to speak to the kid to try to set him straight. "I don't want to call the police and get him in trouble," is how he put it. Wow.

I agreed to speak to the thief, who of course never showed up for our scheduled meeting. I was impressed that Hickman cared enough for a kid to try to help him before calling the cops.

Days before Hickman told his woeful tale of trying to be a good Samaritan, I'd experienced a similar one in which my rare effort at being a good-deed-doer was rebuffed.

A young woman in the parking lot of Marshalls department store on Glenwood Avenue in Raleigh was struggling to back her mammoth car out of a parking space, so I tried to show her how much room she had. When she'd finally backed out and put her car in gear, she turned and angrily snapped, "Next time, would you please let me drive my own car? THANK YOU."

She dismissively held up the palm of her hand to squash any explanation from me and screeched out of the parking lot, leaving me feeling, and no doubt looking, stupid.

Hickman, for his good deed, could have gotten his head bashed in; I merely had my feelings bashed in. Like him, though, I vowed to never try to help anybody again. T' hell with it, I say.

I plan to be true to my vow. And you can thank that ugly woman with an ugly car -- and an uglier attitude. (Boy, I hope she reads this.)

It's possible that these are isolated incidents, involving socially maladjusted cretins, that have no larger meaning.

But what if they're not? What if we're becoming a world in which people not only can no longer appreciate random acts of kindness but also in which people stop doing them?

2/1/2005

AN ANGEL APPEARS OUT OF THE DARK

And here I was thinking I had a lot to be thankful for just because my aunt made her Sweet Potato Surprise for Thanksgiving dinner.

That was before I talked to Linda Shields, a Fuquay-Varina woman who, just a couple of months ago, was ready to write off all mankind as greedy thieves.

Of course, that was just after someone stole all of her credit cards for the second time this year but before an angel appeared out of the dark and saved her choking daughter's life.

Shields, 40, still gets emotional when talking about the night of Oct. 29. She was driving along Holly Springs Road in Cary with her 3-year-old daughter, Claire. They were going to get ice cream for the little girl's Halloween party when Shields heard a gurgling sound coming from the back seat.

"It was dark, and I couldn't see anything, so I pulled to the side of the road, got

out and unfastened her car seat," Shields recalled, choking up at the memory. "The minute I saw her face I knew something was wrong."

Shields reached into her daughter's mouth and felt a piece of candy lodged in her throat. Unable to push it in or pull it out, she panicked, grabbing her daughter by the ankles and shaking her.

"I had her upside down, I was screaming as loud as I could, 'Somebody help me!' I was hysterical," she admits now, laughing and crying at the same time.

Like an apparition, a car suddenly emerged from the darkness, sending gravel flying before screeching to a stop inches from her own car.

"This girl jumped out and grabbed my daughter," Shields recalled. "It was like she was a professional. One push on her ribs and this little ball of candy flew out. It was truly like a miracle."

Michele DeMarco, a 20-year-old pharmacy student at the University of North Carolina, is no professional, but she has taken emergency response classes.

"It's kind of weird, because we don't usually go that way," DeMarco said of the night her life fatefully intersected with that of Linda and Claire Shields. "We just decided to take another way to avoid a red light ... I see this woman standing there holding her little girl and screaming at the top of her lungs, so we swerve over."

The girl was not breathing, she said, so "I did the Heimlich maneuver, and it popped right out."

Shields, tearful and incredulous, wanted to express her gratitude somehow, but DeMarco's friend, Jamie Bradshaw, who'd held and comforted Shields during the ordeal, replied, "We're just glad we were here."

DeMarco told Shields she owed her nothing. "Just let me baby-sit for her sometime," Shields recalled her saying. "She's so cute."

Shields plans to register for cardiopulmonary resuscitation (CPR) classes at WakeMed and has become fanatical about what she lets her tot eat.

"I hate to make her paranoid, but I don't even let her eat suckers now," she said.

11/28/2000

AN ATTACK ABETTED BY THE LAWYER

I used to think that being raped by some masked thug was the worst thing that could happen to a woman. Now, I think being raped by the law is.

Rape is already the most under-reported major crime - only about 18 percent are reported - and if an apparent new defense strategy continues, even fewer victims may be willing to step forward.

A man accused of rape copped a plea to a misdemeanor in Hillsborough this week and emerged from court relatively free - three years of supervised probation and counseling. The deal was OK'd by the victim, in part because of a furor over the defendant's request to have her counseling records scrutinized by a judge and possibly a defense attorney.

Amos Tyndall, the Chapel Hill lawyer representing the defendant, had subpoenaed the records of the woman's counseling sessions at the Orange County Rape Crisis Center. He said he was looking for specific information; Robert Epting, who represented the rape crisis center in its efforts to protect its records, said Tyndall was conducting a vague "fishing expedition" designed either to impeach the woman's story or to discourage her from pursuing the case.

Epting views the subpoena as an unscrupulous arrow in a defense attorney's quiver. "Subpoenas have become a tool of the trade as defense counsel understand the stress they create is directly related to the victim's willingness to continue" with the case, Epting wrote in a brief to the court and repeated to me Thursday.

"Some defense lawyers have followed victims from therapist to therapist, counseling center to counseling center, looking for something to impeach her," he said.

"The first question every woman asks when they call a rape crisis center is, 'Is this information I'm about to give going to remain confidential?' If you can't say yes, they hang up."

Wouldn't you? Can you imagine pouring your heart out to a counselor immediately after a traumatic rape and then sitting in court months later and having those same words used to bludgeon you?

Tyndall, of course, sees it differently. "When someone comes into court, their credibility is an issue," he said. "We wanted to see if she told the center the same thing" she'd told police, he said.

Whether or not Tyndall's goal was to intimidate the victim - something he adamantly denied - you've got admit that things turned out swimmingly for his client, not so swimmingly for the victim.

Going after a counseling center's records not only compromises the victim's right to confidentiality, as Epting said, but also slows her healing process. "The whole premise of the rape crisis center is that it's a respite for women who've been raped, a place where they can unload the secrets of their lives and begin to heal," he said.

You really can't expect a lawyer not to use every weapon at his disposal - even one Epting calls "pallid" and "unconscionable" - to get his client off.

That's why we should all hope Epting's successful when he beseeches, as he said he plans to, the state legislature to institute a law protecting victims' counseling records from subpoenas.

9/22/2000

ANGERED CHRISTIANS REVEAL UN-CHRISTIAN LIKE SIDE

Bless y'all's hearts. Because so many people took such a special interest in my spiritual welfare last week, I made sure that the first thing the deacon saw when he came to open up church Sunday was me.

What was it Shakespeare said? "Hell hath no fury like a woman scorned"?

Forget that, pal. He should've said "Hell hath no fury like a Christian dissed."

Not that the Triangle's Christian population had been dismissed or disrespected. At least not by me. I merely said that I saw church parking lots full of cars last week and suggested that people who spent all of their time in church singing "Wade In the Water" would've done far more good had they actually waded in the water Down East, helping families toss out water-logged furniture and pull up soaked carpet that had been ruined by Hurricane Floyd-related flooding.

Oooweee, what did I want to say that for? Judging by the angry calls and letters I've been receiving since then, you'd have thought I'd bad-mouthed Billy Graham. (I did that, too, a couple of years ago, and there are people who still haven't forgiven me for it.)

Some letter writers and callers compared me to Jesse "The Body" Ventura, not because we have similar physiques - I'm much more buff than he - but because the Minnesota governor in this month's "Playboy" magazine called organized religion a crutch for the "weak-minded."

I, as someone who was raised in the Baptist church, don't believe that, and I never said a word disparaging anyone's beliefs.

But that didn't prevent me from receiving some very un-Christianlike suggestions from people professing to be Christians. Being told to go to - aw, you know where - is not unusual for me, but being told to go there by people quoting scripture is. Or was.

One creative Christian caller said "I'll go 'wade in the water' when you go jump in a lake." Another said, "Why were you riding through parking lots instead of being Down East yourself?" (Psst. Just between us, I was just returning from there.)

In criticizing Sunday morning saints, I wasn't making a universal indictment of Christians. I was talking specifically and unapologetically about people whose faith is, as we cowboys say, "all hat and no horse."

I had a college roommate, a minister, who never involved himself in any aspect of campus life or anything outside the church.

"I don't bother nobody," he said, as though that were something to recommend him.

"Well, pardner, of what use are you to God?" I asked, although not in those exact words.

Believe it or not, something good came of our confrontation. Naw, he didn't suddenly become outspoken, but he did move out, leaving me with a room to myself for the rest of the semester.

There is a saying down in my hometown, Rockingham, that "a hit dog will sure bark." Thus, my only conclusion is that the people who yelped loudest at my quite temperate criticism last week are the ones who indeed think that singing, praying and looking solemn will get them into heaven.

10/11/1999

APOLOGIES WOULD HELP EASE PAIN

Being a doctor must mean never having to say you're sorry, even when you wrongly give an order that could let an old man die.

Doctors at the VA Medical Center in Durham and at Wake Medical Center in Raleigh wrote out DNRs - "do not resuscitate" orders - on Sam Hicks Jr. within weeks of each other despite not discussing it with Hicks' family. Both decisions not to revive Hicks in the event of a medical crisis were rescinded as soon as the family found out about them, but not one mea culpa - not one "Goshdarnit, we're sorry, y'all" - was uttered.

Brenda Alston knows her granddaddy is sick. He is 79 and has been diagnosed with chronic renal failure, among other things. But she wants to give him a chance to fight, just as he fought for his country in the U.S. Army during World War II.

"They say he's incompetent and can't decide for himself, but we can," Alston said while recounting her family's medical nightmare.

Dr. Mark Rothman, the doctor at Wake Med who issued the DNR on Nov. 4, wrote on Hicks' discharge chart that a discussion with the family ruled out "aggressive care." But Alston strongly disputes Rothman's contention that he had difficulty pinning down the family for any type of discussion.

"It took 10 days just to get them to come in and discuss" Hicks' treatment, Rothman told me.

Alston says the family came as soon as they got a call requesting a meeting.

"'DNR' doesn't change [patients'] treatment," Rothman said. "It just means we don't resuscitate them if they have an arrest ... [DNR] was only on the chart for 15 minutes. It was never instituted or signed off on."

On his discharge summary, Rothman wrote, "When the granddaughter was informed [of the DNR], she became quite agitated and angry with us and I said that we would just rescind it from the chart and that it was really just put on and that she was being informed and requested to respond."

Say what?

The incident at Wake Med must have seemed like deja vu to Hicks' family, because less than a month earlier a doctor at the VA also had written off Hicks - you guessed it - without family input.

In that case, Dr. Eugene Kovalik, chief of nephrology at the VA Medical Center, responded to Alston's concern by letter.

"It seems to me that unfortunately there was a miscommunication between Dr. Oliverio and your family," he wrote. "In general, I am sorry that you had this miscommunication. ... But in reviewing the records, it seems to me that the major issues that you are worried about concerning the 'DNR' order were taken care of [within] a very brief time."

Call me naive, but can't somebody just say "sorry"? As medical advances enable us to survive formerly fatal illnesses, decisions will sometimes have to be made on when and whether to curtail the use of those advances. Such decisions, when possible, should be made by family, not doctors.

My favorite general, Douglas MacArthur, once said, "Old soldiers never die, they just fade away."

If he'd been treated the way veteran Sam Hicks Jr. has been, he might have amended that to, "Old soldiers never die, they just don't get resuscitated."

─────────────────────────────────────── 3/14/2000

AT 9 OR 95, WORLD CAN BE AN AWFUL PLACE ────

I'm no quitter, but after what's happened around here lately, I'm about ready to take a powder. Feel free to join me.

First, a 9-year-old boy is killed - and the confessed killer was someone he trusted and loved. Then, a 95-year-old man who left church early and stopped for a cup of coffee at his favorite hangout has his life taken from him for, apparently, a couple of dollars.

Clarence "CJ" Wilkerson III of Wake Forest was found stuffed inside a suitcase in some woods almost before his life got under way. Alton "Bob" Carson of Durham was found laid out - again, in some woods - behind a furniture store last week as he neared the inevitable end of a long, giving and, by all appearances, happy life. Makeshift, heartwarmingly impromptu shrines materialized in the woods where both died because everyone knows they didn't deserve to die like that. Nobody deserves to die like that. Except, perhaps, those who committed these two atrocities.

I don't know about you, but I'm thinking, "If a 9-year-old young'un and a 95-year-old man aren't immune to violence, who is? What hope can there possibly be for the rest of us?"

The answer, obviously, is "not much."

What caught my attention about Carson's death, aside from the horrific thought of someone as old as he meeting a violent end, was his obituary. Reading it, I learned that he was a church deacon and played baseball for the Durham Bulls before the team became a professional franchise and that he still loved the game.

Not only will one monumentally senseless act of violence prevent an old man from watching games with his grandsons, I keep thinking, but it will prevent his grandsons from watching those games with him, from hearing him invariably compare the way they play it now with the way it was played "in the good ol' days."

The year in which Carson was born, 1905, the Wright brothers were still trying to work out some kinks in their flying contraption, the first electric freight locomotives were introduced, and a New York restaurateur served the first slice of pizza in America.

It just doesn't seem right for a dude who lived through those times and all those that have transpired since to die in the woods at the hands of a vicious predator.

If Carson's killer merely wanted his car or the little chump change he reportedly carried with him, it seems that it would have been a simple matter to take it without facing too much resistance.

Alas, the person who committed this vicious act had more than a car or money on his mind: He had evil, pure and simple.

I've since changed my mind, but I used to think that if you lived long enough, eventually you'd get out of the "danger zone" where you were a threat to others and others were a threat to you. I'm still trying to imagine what was going through

Carson's mind when he realized that he, at 95, hadn't yet reached that point.

On second thought, you don't have to stop the world for me to jump off; just slow it down a little.

── 6/2/2000

AT THE FUNERAL, THE LAUGHTER WAS MISSING ├──────

You aren't supposed to be mad when you leave a funeral, are you? I didn't think so, but I was. And I wasn't the only one. My cousin, sitting next to me during the service last week, leaned over and whispered "If I go before you do, and some jackleg starts preaching like this about me...."

He wasn't kidding, either.

We were attending the funeral of a childhood buddy, a 44-year-old man whose accomplishments in life could probably be written on the head of a pin. The only thing he was ever good at was being a great friend and making us laugh until we hurt.

He was one of the wittiest, brightest people you could ever meet, but somewhere along the way the schools decided he belonged in special education -- the educational equivalent of banishment to Siberia in those (and often in these) days. Without an advocate to speak up for him, he languished in special ed until he got old enough to quit going to school altogether.

In deference to his family, I won't mention his name, but most people in Rockingham of a certain age will know my friend.

My cousin and I spent the entire 90-minute drive to Rockingham for the funeral -- and nearly the entire trip back -- talking about our friend, reminiscing about the childhood mischief we all got into, the fun we had. And we still didn't make a dent in our fond memories.

Even though we'd both known him since we were 9 or 10 years old, neither of us could ever recall seeing him angry about anything or at anyone. "I don't think he had the 'mean' gene," my cousin noted.

Yet, and this is what had us ready to jump on the preacher, the good reverend could think of nothing good to say about our buddy except that -- in the final few days of his life -- "he found Jesus."

That's great, Rev., but aren't funeral services supposed to be a celebration of a dear, unique friend, not a "wake up" call that we, too, had better get saved lest we spend eternity in hell?

"I've preached enough funerals to know that I'm supposed to say something about the departed," the preacher began, "but..." He then proceeded to say hardly anything about the departed.

It's true that my buddy wasn't a member of that church, and so the preacher's personal knowledge was limited -- but there were two other ministers and a church full of people who knew him well. And loved him.

As the service neared its end, I sat there hoping -- nay, praying -- they'd invite mourners to say a few words. They didn't, and it's probably a good thing, I realize in retrospect. Because I already had in my mind what I wanted to start out with.

"Hold on a minute there, Mr. Preacherman. That was a terrific sermon you just preached, but that's not the way to send off a beautiful person like our friend.

"It's true that our pal's life was unremarkable by conventional standards, but that life deserves better than to be presented merely as some cautionary tale of 'this could happen to you if you don't get your soul right.'"

Our friend had a hard, unremarkable life -- except for the joy and laughter he brought to so many -- and as another friend said, "Never has somebody who deserved so much gotten so little."

I'll never read another cold, sterile obituary without wondering if the person was happy, sad -- and if he or she brought a lot of joy or sadness to others. Those things help make a life.

I'm nobody's preacher and my knowledge of the Bible is spotty. If you recall, earlier this year I had Moses piloting the ark. But I'd still like to give the preachers a bit of advice.

Don't use the life of anyone as a cautionary tale. Most lives have something good in them, and my buddy's had a whole lot. Too bad that preacher didn't realize it.

─── 10/19/2002

AT WORK ON THE DENTS OF LIFE ────────────────

Thursday was dreary and overcast, with the smell of impending rain heavy in the air.

There are a lot of things such weather is good for, but getting a car wash is not one of them. Thus, there was no work going on inside the Men at Work Car Care Center near downtown Raleigh shortly after noon.

But the place was still full of life. Luther Vandross blared out of the radio, and a couple of dudes shot hoops inside the garage. Others stood or sat around, just chillin'.

Even though no work was being done and thus no moolah was being made, there was a palpable sense of joy inside the garage.

"This is the happiest place in town," owner Mike Phillips said.

And why shouldn't it be?

The auto detailing and repair center is not just a place for cleaning up and repairing cars. It is, equally importantly, a place for cleaning up and repairing lives.

You know how when you've just been released from the joint and you have to fib on your r"sum" to be considered for a job because the boss won't hire an ex-con?

OK, maybe you don't. But take my word for it: it happens. Not here, though. At Men at Work, having a record is essential because the bald, loud and loquacious Phillips has made fixing and cleaning up lives as important a facet of his business as cars.

"Somebody's got to help them," Phillips said when I asked him about his hiring philosophy: Everybody who works for him has done time. "Most people don't want to give a brother a chance when he comes out of jail. He's already been 'exed' out.

"If I give up on them -- whew! -- we're in trouble. By them seeing me change, it helps them see that they can change."

With no arrogance, he added, "I'm a beacon for other dudes."

Phillips, ironically, has never been in jail, but he admits to having had a wild side when he was younger. He is now happily married with four children.

He also admits, sadly, that there have been a few dudes who just wouldn't do right despite the second chance he offered. "But you don't let that stop you," he said. "I have few 'no-nos' as a boss. They are 'no stealing, no stealing and no stealing.' That's important because people are trusting you with their cars.

"We have quite a few success stories, and in 12 years, nothing has been missing" from any customer's car, he said.

He said he hopes to persuade Wake County judges to sentence some young men to the Men at Work program, and he plans to enlist the aid of retired plumbers and carpenters, among others, to help train them. "There are a lot of old dudes who'd love to help young brothers," he said.

Because he figures it's "easier to get a job if you already have one," he wants Men at Work to serve as a way station for men trying to move up.

In its classic 1970s-era song "Car Wash," Rose Royce sang, "You might not ever get rich, but let me tell ya' it's better than digging a ditch."

Phillips loves the song and the movie of the same name -- he wants to make "Car Wash II" -- but he thinks you can become rich, if not in money, at least in restoring fractured lives.

11/10/2000

BACK TO THE DISCO

What the #@$*&!

Did I stumble into "Soul Train" or the 25-year class reunion for NCCU, Shaw or St. Augustine's College?

That, no doubt, is what people asked themselves if they happened upon Kool & the Gang playing at the Sheraton Imperial Hotel several days ago.

But it wasn't "Soul Train" or a black college reunion that had hundreds of people on the dance floor. What it was was part of a -- get this -- sales and marketing training event for SAS.

Yes, that SAS. I asked John Dornan, a SAS spokesman, why Kool & the Gang -- a band known for its soul and funky rhythms -- was performing for SAS, a company not known for its soul and funky rhythms.

More important, I asked the dude why I wasn't invited.

To someone who is unapologetically still living in the '70s -- and I've got my albums, stacked-heel shoes and lime-green jumpsuit like the one Jim Brown wore to such great effect in "Slaughter's Big Rip-off" to prove it -- that party sounded like the place to be.

Since SAS founder Jim "Get Down Tonight" Goodnight is obviously a shrewd businessman, I figured bringing Kool & the Gang -- and earlier in the day, motivational speaker Les Brown -- to entertain and motivate the troops was somehow related to the company's desire to boost productivity or change its image before eventually going public.

Wrong, said Dornan. The public offering of SAS stock, which is now on the

31

back burner, had nothing to do with the entertainment. "We do this every year," he said of the event that brings in 1,200 SAS employees from across the country. The training sessions, he said, are "a lot of work. We do a lot of stuff that isn't fun, so on the last night we ... try to make it as much fun as possible.

"I realize we might not have the most exciting image in the world," he said, since talk about software and sales projections "doesn't exactly bring thoughts of dancing the night away into your head. But we're just regular folks like everyone else. When 5 o'clock rolls around, we like to have a good time, too."

You just know that some of those SAS executives making millions today as stolid, pinstriped conservatives were, 25 years ago, polyester-wearing disco fools like me. And if they're anything like me now, they've retained a fondness for the music they liked then.

Just because they now think Kenny G is cutting edge doesn't mean they've forgotten the words to "Celebration."

Jim Goodnight can afford anybody he wants to perform at his private shindigs -- last year it was Hootie & the Blowfish -- and because of some of the things I've written about him, I don't expect an invitation to any of them.

But I'd pay to see SAS' founder sing along to "Can't Get Enough of That Funky Stuff."

Dornan didn't know who they'll pick to perform at future SAS sales and marketing soirees, but if the eventual offering of company stock is successful, they should pick James Brown.

That way, everyone who owns SAS stock could join in with the Godfather of Soul and the Godfather of Software in a rousing rendition of "Say It Loud (I'm Rich and I'm Proud)."

2/5/2001

BALM OF SLEEP HAS PRICE

Getting a good night's sleep for some of us is difficult under the best conditions.

Going to bed with wires stuck to your head, legs and chest -- plus having what feels like a Chihuahua gnawing on your index finger all night -- is not the best condition.

It is, however, the condition under which I found myself twice in recent weeks at the Second Breath sleep clinic in Durham.

As if those wires weren't enough of an impediment to sleep, there were also the video cameras recording every move. Have you ever tried to doze while thinking, "Oh Lord, please don't let me do anything embarrassing in my sleep"?

I've never been able to sleep -- four hours is a good night -- but in recent months I haven't been able to get up, either. Not only would I wake up angry and more tired than when I lay down, but I'd have one of those hangovers you usually have on New Year's Day after drinking too much Cold Duck or other cheap champagne. Only problem is, I hadn't drunk a thing.

I asked my doctor, Ron Fleming, for a drug to help me sleep -- and whether he had anything to help knock off this last 10 -- OK, 20 -- pounds.

Sewing up my mouth was his suggestion for the weight. For sleep, he suggested that I might be suffering from sleep apnea, a condition that causes you to stop breathing during sleep. He had me make an appointment at Second Breath.

"New Age mumbo jumbo," I figured, but since Dr. Fleming is usually right, I played along.

The clinic receptionist gave me instructions that ended with, "Oh, and don't take a nap."

So, of course, I took a nap. You learn, as a lifelong insomniac, that when that sleep train pulls into the station, you'd better jump on it. With eyelids drooping, I turned the dudemobile into the parking lot of Crabtree Valley Mall about 4 p.m. and slept for nearly an hour a mere five hours before I was scheduled for my sleep test.

Like Evelina, the witch in the Broadway play "The Wiz," I "wake up already negative," but waking up at the sleep clinic the next morning found me more negative -- and angrier -- than usual. It's "lights out" at 11 p.m., but I tossed and turned for hours before dozing off.

I felt like saying something bad when the nurse shook me awake at 5:30 a.m., my usual bedtime. I felt like saying something worse when she called a week later and said I needed to come back because -- get this -- "You didn't sleep long enough" the first time.

"I would have if y'all hadn't woke me up at 5:30," I snapped, without regard for grammar.

The second time at Second Breath, they applied all of the same electrodes to my head, chest and legs -- and attached the Chihuahua to my finger again. This time, though, they placed over my nose a mask that blew air into my nostrils throughout the night.

I begged the nurse not to wake me at 5:30 this time, and, bless her heart, she didn't: She let me sleep until 5:45.

Again, I woke up angry, but something miraculous occurred moments after taking off the mask: I felt great. And rested.

If the mask continues to work, I'll be faced with a tough choice: going to bed sexy or waking up rested -- but looking like the Elephant Man.

4/15/2005

BEG YOUR PARDON, GOVERNOR

A few years ago, I dialed up a local radio station to request a song. The DJ answered with, "Sorry, you're caller number 5," and hung up.

Turns out I'd almost won a contest -- $5,000 to the seventh caller -- that I didn't even know I'd entered.

Do you ever feel that Mike Easley won a contest he didn't know he'd entered and that's how he ended up as governor?

I swear, sometimes it seems as if da' gubna doesn't want the job and goes out of his way to show it by blowing off innocuous public relations events or refusing to address important topics.

Terry Sanford was known as the "education governor," Jim Hunt as the "children's governor." Will Easley, especially when compared with Hunt -- who never met a back he didn't want to slap -- be remembered as the "accidental governor"?

Most of you probably don't give a rat's toenail that Easley eschews news conferences or that he'd remain hermetically sealed inside the governor's mansion if the recent discovery of mold hadn't forced him to seek new digs.

Considering the harm politicians often do, you're justified in feeling that he who governs least governs best.

Despite his apparent inaction, Easley campaigned hard for the honor of serving us. Only problem is, he isn't.

If Easley were doing his duty, the state would be trying to help Leo D. Waters get on the good foot after wrongly taking 20 years of his life. Waters was released from prison in 2003 after DNA evidence cleared him of raping a Jacksonville wife and mother. DNA has identified another man, already imprisoned, as the attacker.

In his request for a pardon of innocence, Waters' attorney, Mark Raynor, wrote, "Despite the fact that he was wrongfully incarcerated, he made every effort to serve his sentence with peace and dignity. ... During that time his wife divorced him, he was estranged from his children, lost his father, lost his home."

Nothing and no one can return to Waters the years, his wife, his kids, his father. A pardon would, however, make him eligible to receive $20,000 for each year he was imprisoned. That would at least provide some traction in getting his life back on track.

Easley received the pardon request in January, yet he still hasn't signed it.

Waters' mother, Pauline, is baffled and angry at the lack of response. "We don't know what the holdup is. It's going on three years. We'd sure 'preciate anything you can do."

What could be more important than ensuring that a poor bloke who had a huge hunk of his life unfairly taken away by the state at least gets a hand in reclaiming what's left of it?

The governor's office has been as unresponsive to my telephone calls as it has been to Waters' request for a pardon.

In another case similar to this one, in which a man went to prison on very shaky evidence and questionable cop conduct, Easley granted a pardon. So we know he has a heart.

Life for Pauline Waters' son hasn't been a crystal stair since his release from prison. It may never be, but a pardon would sure smooth what remains of his journey.

With the mere flourish of a pen, Easley can give Leo Waters some justice. And money.

Sign the pardon, governor.

8/12/2005

BEST HAS A PRICE TO PAY

It was, if I remember my history, the late philosopher Sir John Taylor -- that's Johnnie Taylor to you -- who first said "It's cheaper to keep her."

John Best, the Durham City Council member in jeopardy of going to jail for not paying child support and alimony, can testify that Sir John was right.

So can scores of divorced men I've heard from over the years, men who learned that the grass on the other side might be greener, but when they get over there they have no time to enjoy it because they're working two jobs -- or, in Best's case, three -- to support their new family and the one they left behind.

Best repeated in a telephone conversation Monday what he'd said in an N&O interview last week: that "there is no way in Helsinki" he can come up with $11,000 by December -- plus nearly $2,000 a month -- required to keep him out of the pokey.

Best is not the first man who didn't fulfill his financial obligations to the court's satisfaction and got hauled before a judge as a result. It is his misfortune, though, to be a public official who made his name attacking the financial ineptitude of other officials. Few of them, he acknowledges, feel sympathy for him.

"I'm sure that people who don't agree with me politically will go after me," he said. "They're enjoying this."

He's probably right. Wanna bet that, somewhere, former City Manager Marcia Conner is kicked back with a box of Bon Bons and a 40-ounce, gloating over the public problems of the man who criticized her management skills and led the protracted but ultimately successful effort to oust her?

Oh, so I'm the only one who celebrates with Bon Bons and a 40 when a nemesis gets in trouble? I didn't think so.

Best said he doubts that his private issues will hurt him politically. "I've been telling my constituents that I'm simply going through what other Average Joes go through," he said. "I'm sure there are mothers who wish the judges would go after the fathers of their children the way they're going after me.

"There may be a personal or political motivation behind what is happening. Most people don't care about my private life unless it affects them. When I fail to balance my checkbook, it only affects me," he said. "When you forge documents and don't balance the city's checkbook, as some have done, then you're dealing with the public's money."

No sound in the world is worse than that made by the growling belly of a hungry child. Men who fail to take care of their children must be made to do so, but locking them up only puts taxpayers on the hook -- for feeding their children and providing them with three hots and a cot.

Here, as a public service to men who think the grass is greener on the other side, are more words from Sir Johnnie:

"When that little girl makes you mad

"And you get an attitude and pack your bag.

"Them five little children that you're leaving behind?

35

"Son, you're gonna pay some alimony or do some time ....

"When that judge gives you that dirty look --

"you may as well put your money in Mama's pocketbook

"That's why it's cheaper to keep 'er."

———————————————————————————————— ⊣ 11/9/2004

BET SHOULD BE BOUNCED ⊢————————————————

I love lap dances. I also love the Lord. But lap dances and the Lord together?

Nah, homes. Not feeling that.

Yet that's what you get with Destiny's Child, the trio of singing sistuhs who'll be performing in Raleigh on Sunday.

Michelle Williams, the group's newest member, has sold lots of gospel records and will probably release more after the group's latest farewell tour ends.

I wonder whether, after performing "Bootylicious" -- which goes, "Is my body too bootylicious for ya, babe?" -- Williams will break into a heart-stirring rendition of "Come Unto Me, Ye Weary"?

Nothing wrong with that. But hold on a second. Didn't I just see Williams and her comely co-horts giving lap dances on BET's televised awards show?

They weren't the lap dances you'd get at the late, deeply lamented Brothers III gentledudes' club in Durham, but they were too much for prime time.

Alas, we're talking BET here. That network, which started out promising so much 25 years ago, has done more to degrade black people -- especially our women -- than anything since slavery.

At first, BET stood for Black Entertainment Television. Now, though, it deserves to be called, as it derisively is by many, "Booties Every Time."

BET founder Bob Johnson should be tried for treason. As if he hasn't insulted us enough, he stunned everybody when, on the awards show intended to honor the best black entertainment has to offer, he implied that he'd like to bounce Beyonce on his lap.

What a hoot, Bob.

Since our arrival here, Africans in America have been battling the stereotype that we were sexual animals with no self-control. Just ask Thomas Jefferson and Strom Thurmond. Of course, if you dehumanize a race, that makes holding it in bondage easier to justify.

Years ago, when the Rev. Jesse Jackson still had a claim to moral authority, he attacked the Rolling Stones for one line in a song called "Some Girls" about the presumed hyper-sexuality of black women.

Now, it appears, we seem intent upon living down to the racist stereotypes that were used to rob us of our humanity.

A local musician who produced tracks for Destiny's Child said in an N&O story, presumably without laughing, that he was impressed by the group's "relationship with God."

Me, too. Every time I see lead singer Beyonce slither across the ground -- as she does in many videos -- in her Daisy Duke shorts, I go, "Oh, God."

Before taking the stage to titillate on BET, Destiny's Child no doubt gathered in the dressing room and prayed thusly:

Oh Lord, thank you for bestowing upon us these bodaciously bootylicious bodies. Let the wiggling of our jiggly parts be acceptable in thy sight and be used to deliver unto thee the souls of those who are lost.

Also, may it be used to help us buy matching Mercedes CLKs. Forever and ever, amen.

Don't get me wrong, now. Bootyliciousness is a good thing, but there is a time and a place for everything.

Verily I say unto you: That place is not on prime time TV.

7/22/2005

BIG BROTHER HELPS PINCH PENNIES

There are two things guaranteed to make you feel like a chump. One is seeing Sweet Thang locked in an intimate embrace with the same dude she swore the night before was her cousin.

The other is going to the grocery store and forgetting to carry your $@%*#% store discount card.

Oooowee, talk about panic. The cards - just about every major grocery store in the Triangle has one - save you just enough dough to make you feel like an irresponsible schmo when you forget them.

The stores I called contend the cards are a hit with customers and that gripes about them are minimal. If that's true, it's only because most people probably figure that - just as you can't fight city hall - you can't fight the mega-grocery store food-card cartel, either. Thus, for the sake of saving a few coins, people uncomplainingly allow Big Brother to peer right into their shopping cart and see precisely what they're eating.

What? You didn't know that the cards allow the stores to catalog your purchases? Why else do you think they demand a picture ID before giving you a card? I discovered that little requirement when the clerk at my neighborhood Harris Teeter refused to believe I was "John Shaft" without proof.

As much as I want to save 50 cents per pound on white seedless grapes or a dollar on a 48-ounce jar of apple butter, I refuse to concede this last vestige of privacy without a fight. Don't tell anyone, but I switched cards with a friend of mine - a move sure to have Big Brother scratching his head if he tries to decipher my shopping habits.

Someone at Master Control perusing the purchases on my card will surely think, "Gee, that guy must be some kind of gourmet," or, "Hmmm, he sure buys a lot of feminine products for a single man." They're probably equally miffed that a single woman buys so much "guy" food, which reminds me of one of my favorite grocery store jokes:

A dude comes up to the counter ready to check out. The female cashier looks at him and his purchases - orange juice, milk, Cap'n Crunch, Ramen noodles - and purrs "You must be single."

The guy looks at his stuff again, scratches his head and goes, "Uh, what makes you think I'm single?"

"Because you're ugly." Ba-dump.

To ensure that you have the chump-change-saving card with you at all times, you may be tempted to fasten it onto your car keys. Don't do it, Hoss.

Saving money is fine, but the moment you stick one of those food cards onto your key chain, you have given up any pretense of coolness, any hope that Tyra Banks or Cindy Crawford will someday saunter up to you on the beach and coo, "Will you rub some of this goose grease on my back, Governor?" or "Can I have a bite of that apple-butter sandwich?"

It doesn't matter if you drive a Porsche, BMW or Jaguar and have Led Zeppelin pumping on your stereo at 80 decibels, there is just no way to be cool when you're cruising around with a brightly colored discount food card banging against the dashboard.

Face it, Horace: Put one of those things on your key chain, and you might as well trade in that 'Vette for a minivan with twin baby seats.

———————————————————————————————— 1/10/2000

BIG WIND FROM TEXAS USHERS IN HURRICANE SEASON

Seventy years ago, George Schuyler, a black conservative writer and publisher, skewered racism -- both the black and white kinds -- in his novel "Black No More."

In the book, everyone in America became the same race. Far from creating a racism-free oasis of harmony, this development caused much consternation and an increase in unemployment -- as people who made their livings off of racial hostilities between blacks and whites were thrown out of work.

The book dealt with what would happen if whites didn't have blacks to kick around anymore, and what race pimps -- a term Schuyler (1895-1977) didn't use but could have -- would do once there were no racial flames to fan.

Thanks to U.S. Rep. Sheila Jackson-Lee of Texas, we know what they would do: make up something stupid to rail against.

Racism has by no means disappeared from America, and anyone who says otherwise has probably been listening to too much Rush Limbaugh or Clarence Thomas. Yet, judging by the latest crusade on which Jackson-Lee is engaged, you'd think racism had disappeared, along with every other serious problem our nation has yet to adequately confront.

Jackson-Lee, whose fiery speeches from the House floor are often the most entertaining things on C-Span, has been complaining this summer that there are no hurricanes with black names.

Go back and read that paragraph again: I'll wait. Now check your calendar so you'll see that this is not April Fool's Day.

My efforts to reach the Democratic representative were unsuccessful, but I wanted to ask her if there weren't, perhaps, a couple of issues of slightly more importance than ethnic names for hurricanes.

Apparently not. She has said in published reports that the "lily white" names of hurricanes should be made more inclusive by adding names like "Keisha, Jamal and DeShawn."

I hate to admit it, but I was initially ready to lampoon Jackson-Lee by concluding that she had braided her hair -- a style she wears well, I might add -- a bit too tight.

Alas, after further review, I now see the genius of what she was attempting. With just a little imagination, it is easy to see how giving future hurricanes black-sounding names could help us conquer the myriad problems faced by blacks in America.

Take the problem of education, in which black students often lag behind their white and Asian counterparts in standardized test scores. Jackson-Lee has apparently and brilliantly concluded that if little Tyquan or Laqueisha had hurricanes to which they could relate, they'd be more motivated to study hard.

Think about it: the next time some young black kid was teased by his peers for studying, he could respond proudly "I want one of those hurricanes named after me." He could then turn to The Weather Channel and burrow deeper into his textbook while listening to Ludacris sing "You're Nobody 'til Somebody Names a Hurricane After You."

What about the devastation being wrought by AIDS among young blacks? That, too, would be a thing of the past if we only had some hurricanes to which our kids could relate.

Don't look at me like that. Promiscuity, or at least unprotected sex, would decline dramatically if kids knew that at the end of a long, productive life, they might be honored with a hurricane-- or at least a tropical storm -- in their name.

Of course, if meteorologists acceded to Jackson-Lee's wishes and gave hurricanes ethnically identifiable names, she and others would have nothing to complain about, right?

Wrong. Even if the next hurricane was named Shaniqua Shante, LaTanya or Donnell, Jackson-Lee could then complain "Hey, how come all of the -- pick one: "weakest," "strongest," "most destructive" -- hurricanes have to be named after us?"

8/16/2003

BLADDER CONTROL OF GRADES

Parents buying school supplies for their kids next year may also want to pick up some scuba gear, swimming lessons or Depends.

That's because the ability to keep your head above water in class could take on an entirely new meaning as a result of the bathroom pass policy at West Lake Middle School in southern Wake County: Students in some classes are given extra credit if they don't go to the bathroom during class.

The idea behind the "don't ask, don't go" policy is that teachers think that cutting down on the number of students parading to the toilet also will cut down on classroom disruptions.

John Ringo, assistant superintendent for Wake County schools, said, "We're not trying to promote bladder infections ... but teachers are trying to promote responsibility by encouraging them to go to the restroom before class.

"They're trying to keep them in the classroom so they can teach" without being constantly interrupted by raised hands, Ringo said.

Hmm, let's see. What's more disruptive -- a couple of kids slipping discreetly out of class to answer nature's call or a roomful of squirming kids turning blue?

Robin Boettcher, whose daughter attends West Lake, thinks that rewarding students for their bladder control is ludicrous, and she said so in a letter to Superintendent Bill McNeal.

"The policy makes a mockery of the higher academic standards" that county schools claim to aspire to and may even be a violation of students' civil rights, she wrote.

Ringo, though, said no student is penalized for going, while those who don't go receive one grade point at the end of the semester.

Because gaining admission to top-flight universities is so competitive, I'm guessing that many students vying for top schools will do anything to add points to their average. Folks, this could get ugly and rupture friendships.

Susie: "I just hate that Mary Ellen Throckmorton. She thinks she's all that. Hmmph, the only reason she got into Harvard and I'm going to Tyrone's School of Toenail Art is because she has better bladder control than me."

Tenisha: "That's right, girl. I know for a fact that she goes just before school starts and then refuses to even walk past the water fountain until school's out."

One good thing about the policy, though, is that it could allow kids with otherwise undistinguished academic records to receive recognition.

Superintendent McNeal: "I'm proud to present this lifetime achievement award to Roscoe "Joe Camel" Meriwether, the student who caused the fewest classroom disruptions by ignoring nature's call for 12 years.

"Unfortunately, Roscoe couldn't be here today. He's in intensive care at WakeMed having his bladder removed."

Now, Dr. Connell Covington, a Raleigh pediatrician, said delaying a visit to the toilet for the duration of one class shouldn't adversely affect a child "unless there's some underlying problem or incontinence."

Dr. Covington may be right, but that doesn't mean the policy won't result in injuries: Think of how many kids will be trampled rushing to the bathroom after class.

⊢ 5/1/2001

BOOTLEG T~SHIRTS A THREAT? ⊢

If you're anything like me, every time you've been arrested for a crime short of murder, you probably asked the arresting officer, "Why aren't you out arresting real criminals?"

I wasn't even collared by the cops Saturday night, but that's still a good question to ask now.

Seven people were arrested for selling bootleg Rolling Stones T-shirts and other paraphernalia at the aging rock group's concert at Duke University's Wallace Wade Stadium.

All together now: "Why, darnit?"

If some bloke with a silk- screen printing machine is enterprising enough to fleece chumps willing to pay $20 for a $3 Fruit of the Loom T-shirt with Mick Jagger's lips stamped on it, why should cops care?

None of the arrested dudes was local, and efforts to reach them in cities ranging from the Bronx, N.Y., to Bedford, Ohio, failed. Judging by their far-flung addresses, though, many apparently came here solely to hawk T-shirts to Stones fans.

If each T-shirt sold by a bootlegger was taking money out of the mouths of the babes of Keith, Ron, Charlie and Mick, perhaps you could work up sympathy for the devils. After all, rock stars have to eat, too.

This, though, is a case of greed, not need. The London Telegraph newspaper estimated that the Stones' tour this year will earn more than the group's 2003 tour, which grossed more than $300 million.

Expenses are being underwritten by loan company Ameriquest, which recently paid $325 million to settle lawsuits over its business practices. And even after expenses, each Stone will earn several million dollars. (The Telegraph also reported that the group practices in Canada for its bi-annual U.S. tours to avoid our taxes.)

If people want to pay $350 to see a 61 year-old Don Knotts-look-alike prancing across the stage, more power to them.

But those of us who pay the salaries of Durham's cops should be asking, "Don't we have enough real crime that impacts our quality of life without cops wasting time making sure megarich rock stars' T-shirts aren't ripped off?"

While the Rolling Stone 7 were waiting to be arraigned over the weekend, guess who paid for their lodging at the city jail and their food?

It wasn't Mick Jagger -- it was you and I.

There are neighborhoods throughout the city where the presence of those cops would have been more appreciated and needed than at Duke on a Saturday night.

No one from the police department returned any of several messages left seeking justification, but it's hard to imagine how putting officers on the Stones' T-shirt detail represented anything other than a misappropriation of manpower.

Bruce Springsteen once said that rockers who claim they got into the business for any reason other than to meet girls is lying.

Likewise, rockers over 60 who claim they're still rocking for any reason other than money are lying, too.

We shouldn't begrudge the Stones getting paid for what they do. We should begrudge them for begrudging others from getting paid for what they do, though.

10/11/2005

BURNING CROSSES BACKFIRED

Don't you just hate it when you burn a cross -- three of 'em, to be precise -- and nobody runs, shrieking, for cover?

It's unlikely that whoever burned the three crosses in Durham one night late last month imagined that it would unite the community and provoke positive discussion and soul-searching.

Far more likely, the retromingent slugs thought resorting to a symbol of domestic terrorism would set Durham residents -- black, white, brown and everything in between -- at each other's throats in an orgy of acrimony and hate.

If you've ever seen a Durham school board meeting, you know that some Bull City residents are always at each other's throats. The city thrives despite such behavior. So there.

Even as the ashes smoldered, the odds-on favorite fire-starting suspects in the minds of many were those perennial pyromaniacs, the Ku Klux Klan. These wouldn't be the first three crosses they've burned, and a city such as Durham -- esteemed by many for its inter-racial cooperation and decried by others for its interracial conflict -- must grate on such a group's last nerve.

Alas, not all fingers point to the Klan. For instance, the burning of three crosses in separate parts of town required coordination and synchronization -- two words the KKK is not traditionally noted for, nor could many of its members be expected to spell if you spotted them the first 10 letters in each.

If the Klan really did burn the crosses, though, somebody is in trouble with the Grand Kleagle.

Grand Kleagle: "Say, did you krazy kats drop the leaflets at the site like I told you?"

Rookie KKK dude: "Sure, your lowness. But the wind was blowing, and they must have gotten scattered."

Grand Kleagle: "Well, that's a fine howdy-do. It says in the paper that they don't know who burned them crosses. What's the use of striking fear if you don't get credit for it? Why, I'll probably be the laughingstock of the next Klan konklave."

Indeed, other groups are trying to steal the fire of whoever set them. Some people who apparently possess an ability to read ashes the way cops read arcane clues on those crime scene investigative shows have ascribed other intentions, even a noble one. I've heard from community leaders and readers who think the burning crosses were meant to illuminate Durham's gang problem.

Say what?

Then, the host of a cable TV show that allows residents to speak out on problems within the city said he thinks the crosses were meant to intimidate him for being so outspoken and providing such a forum.

Regardless of the intention of the cross burnings, they succeeded only in galvanizing Durham residents to common causes: survival and prosperity.

Rallies, forums and discussions were held in the weeks following the cross burnings, and anyone who cares about the city must be encouraged by the overall response.

But before Durham residents injure their shoulders patting themselves on the backs, they need to acknowledge that rallies or linking arms and singing "We Shall Overcome" won't amount to much without follow up.

Still, whether or not the cops find them, we should all say "Thank you" to the cross-dressers -- uh, cross-burners -- for bringing the community closer.

6/7/2005

BUSINESS ISN'T SO HOT, NOW

Revenge, history teaches us, is a dish best served with a tall glass of cold milk.

Say what?

Oops, that's "doughnuts" that're best served with a tall glass of cold milk. Revenge, too, goes down well with milk, especially when it's served with doughnuts. Krispy Kreme doughnuts.

We in the Triangle who've watched aghast as North Carolina's own burgeoning Krispy Kreme doughnut conglomerate ignored us feel a tinge of satisfaction at the news that the company isn't as sweet as it used to be.

C'mon, it's OK to admit that you take some pleasure in Krispy Kreme's loss of its chief operating officer, its plummeting sales and the SEC probe into some of its practices.

Oh, so I'm the only one gloating because the company was getting above its raisin' and forgetting where it came from?

Ever since it went public in 2000 and expanded globally -- London, Australia, California -- the Winston-Salem company has been beloved by Wall Street. Its lard-based fare became the gustatory equivalent of slumming, a low-class snack that high-class people craved.

Gosh, who would have ever thought that the same doughy treat we used to sell to finance our elementary school road trips would one day be sold amid the pomp and flash of Harrod's in London?

Amy Hughes, a company spokeswoman, told me that the Krispy Kreme phenomenon is still hot, despite the cooled- off sales. Hughes admitted that carb-watching has lowered doughnut consumption, but she described the company's acceptance as "phenomenal ... It's still unbelievable the way the brand is being received ... People are still lining up around the block to get them hot whenever a new store opens. In Australia, a woman showed up at the opening dressed from head to toe" in Krispy Kreme colors, she said. "She'd even painted her Doc Martens boots."

Hughes, who has the boots in her office, said the globalization is continuing, with a deal struck to open 25 stores in South Korea over five years. As I do each time we speak, I asked Hughes whether KK has another Triangle store in the oven. She, as she does each time, refused to say: "I'm not going to comment on specific growth plans, but we look forward to continued growth, especially in North Carolina, our home state."

Whew, at least they still recognize that.

Despite the woman who donated her boots and Hughes' rosy assessment of KK's future, it seems that the glaze is off the doughnut -- sorry, that won't happen again -- for the 67-year-old company. At least, for some people it is.

The company was sued by people who bought its securities and say they weren't told the low-carb craze was eating into KK's profits. Its chief operating officer resigned last week.

The problem here, though, isn't low carbs but low location: There's only one store in the Triangle, and sometimes driving all the way to Raleigh isn't appealing -- especially when you can hop a couple of jets to Australia and say, "Tie me kangaroo down, sport. And hand me a box of those glazed, mate."

⊢ 8/24/2004

CAN YOU EAT WATERMELON IN PUBLIC ⊢

Hmmm, I wonder: Was the perfessor talking about a melon or the last woman I almost married?

The watermelon described by N.C. State University scientist Jonathan Schultheis in a recent N&O story was afflicted with a "hollow heart," making it, his assistant said, good for nothing but "throw[ing] it in the hog pen."

Funny, that's what I said about her.

Some people lie awake pondering deep philosophical questions, like "Who actually spends good money on Kenny G CDs?"

Not me. The questions that keep me awake nights are along the lines of "Has anyone ever OD'd on watermelon?"

Grits and watermelons are the only two foods worthy of rhapsody and they also happen to be, respectively, the perfect cold- and hot-weather foods. Nothing warms you up on a cold morning like a plate of hot grits, and nothing chills you out on a blisteringly hot day like a huge hunk of sweet-to-the-rind melon.

While it is safe for me to sing grits' praises, rhapsodizing about watermelons is quite dangerous. It is, as Lord Alfred Bruce Douglas said about something else, a love that dare not speak its name.

Sure, they look harmless, but walking through a watermelon field, even journalistically, is akin to walking through a minefield of racial politics.

Remember the assault upon my sterling character by some hypersensitive black people two months ago when I deigned to mention that I actually eat pork skins and listen to the blues? Oy vey!

Even as a boy in Rockingham, I knew people in my neighborhood who placed watermelons in the same category as chitlins and dipping snuff: Oh, they ate and dipped, but not publicly, because they considered such indulgences "low-class." With proper investments, I could've become rich from all the moolah I earned running up to King's Grocery and buying a certain high-class lady a can of Tube Rose snuff, with strict instructions not to tell anyone whom it was for.

I am not belittling the sensitivity that causes some of you to give up pleasurable diversions because they are associated with negative stereotypes. I, too, grimace each time I walk into a flea market and see salt-and-pepper shakers featuring little black pickaninnies with big ol' half-moon-shaped slices of watermelon - slices rivaled in size only by the idiotically rapturous grins on their glistening faces.

That image causes many people to dissociate themselves from watermelons even when - as it has been the past two weeks - it's too hot to sanely eat anything else.

Comedian Dick Gregory told of a woman he knew who had her watermelons gift-wrapped so no one in her neighborhood would know of the delectable treat she carried, and Stokely Carmichael wrote of how he and other student radicals at Howard University in Washington induced apoplexy in school administrators by eating watermelons on the campus's front lawn.

What, they sputtered, would passing motorists think of seeing students at such an august institution publicly eating watermelons?

Beats me, but here's what I'd be thinking: "Man, I sure wish I had me a hunk of that."

8/2/1999

CHANGING FOR THE CHILDREN

Linda Bonner is a quitter. Why, when she was a 12th-grade science teacher in Columbia, Md., and encountered a student who could barely read his name, she quit -- teaching seniors, that is.

"I taught one year of high school, went back and got a reading degree and began teaching first grade. That's where I thought I could make a difference."

Years later, when she noticed many of her public school students, primarily black boys, lagging, she quit again -- to start her own school.

That's where I caught up with her, in the three-room, double-wide trailer on Raleigh's Hunter Street that serves as Bonner Academy.

On the day I visited, Bonner was teaching a class of 10 students, eight boys and two girls ranging in age from 13 to 17. Although the topic was how to figure interest rates, she also seamlessly -- and in the children's own lingo -- included math, science, physiology and life in the lessons.

For instance, when she pointed to a skeleton in the classroom and asked students to identify the bone that a friend of hers had broken, thus ending his professional sports career before he learned to save any money -- and consigning him to a lifetime of relatively menial labor -- Kevin Kirby raised his hand and said "fibula."

After the class, Kirby, 16, said he never would have had the confidence to answer the question a year ago while at Garner Senior High School.

"I was having trouble there and came here to get more one-on-one attention," he said. "It's easier here because there's not as much moving around" between classes.

The school is not a job but a mission for Bonner, who works nights to support it. "I put my whole salary into this place to prove that these kids can learn," she said.

"But it's not about me. It's more about the people who help me. I have so many people who've been laid off who say, 'I come here to help just to keep from going crazy,'" she said.

Talking to Bonner and one of those volunteers, Carolyn Cameron, I was reminded of a story I read as a kid of Mary McLeod Bethune, who started her own college despite being so poor that she had to mash up blackberries to make ink.

Bonner hasn't had to make her own ink, but she has made sacrifices. Before getting the trailer, Cameron said, Bonner turned her house over to the school. "She used every inch of it for the school," Cameron said.

Not quite every inch, Bonner corrected: "I pulled two chairs together to sleep in because we didn't have room for a bed."

Bonner Academy was a charter school for one year, but Bonner, a 1972 N.C. State University graduate, felt constrained by the rules, regulations and paperwork required of a school receiving public money, of a school expected to do things just so. "So they told me, 'It's my way or the highway,' and I chose the highway," she said.

Now it's a private school with 40 students. Some pay tuition, some don't. Money often is tight. "Every year we run into a bind around April," Bonner said.

Bonner Academy, in all honesty, is not much to look at. But, boy, is it something to see. If you're interested in seeing what Bonner and her volunteers are doing, or if you want to help, call the academy at 571-4617.

5/7/2002

CHARLOTTE IS CASTING STONES?

Silly me. Here I was, thinking I lived in a pretty decent place, a city with more culture, diversity and attitude than any other in North Carolina.

I didn't know I was actually residing in the armpit -- actually, more like an unprintable body orifice -- of the state.

That, anyway, was the implicit pronouncement of the Charlotte Observer in a recent front-page story on Durham.

As much as it hurts, I'm inclined to take their word for Durham's shortcomings, because if anyone knows a second-rate city, it would be the good people of Charlotte.

Unlike a lot of Tar Heels who despise Charlotte on principle because of its perceived -- perceived, my eye, its undeniable -- arrogance, my antipathy toward the Queen City developed over a period of years. Growing up in Rockingham in the early 1970s, we considered Charlotte to be New York, Paris and Los Angeles wrapped up in one. At the time, a big night for my buddies and me was driving the 60 or so miles to Charlotte, where you could find a business that stayed open -- get this -- 24 hours. In a row! So what if it was only a Krispy Kreme.

Alas, something happened to Charlotte over the years, and it went from being a welcoming, big little city proud to be the crown jewel of the state to a would-be kingdom unto itself.

Were the city a person, it could be accused of "puttin' on airs," like that cousin of yours who went to New York for a week but came back speaking with an accent so proper you'd have thought he'd been raised having tea and crumpets with Queen Elizabeth.

I'm guessing the change came about when all those banks started relocating their headquarters to the Queen City and it had the good fortune (ha ha) to snare professional football and basketball teams. What a blessing, eh?

Charlotte is beset by many of the problems the paper attributed to Durham, and its crime rate is consistently higher. Yet, a boosterish newspaper article noted several years ago that Charlotte's problem is not crime, but -- dig this -- a conscientious police department. "Charlotte is so good about investigating and reporting crime, it may just seem more dangerous." Who wrote that? The Chamber of Commerce?

The "volatility" the paper ascribed to Durham is a good thing. Durham is a city that takes pride in its raw politics, and a lot of people would have been happy to say so.

I mean, the people interviewed for the story were a state representative, a City Council member and a former City Council member who said, "General public morale is low." That former council member was Floyd McKissick, who did not exactly bathe the city in glory during his tenure in public office.

Had the newspaper talked to my neighbors, people in Charlotte would have learned that the volatility means only that the city embraces, nay, revels in dissent.

It also acts as a repellent to people from Charlotte who might be seeking to relocate.

The story noted that Durham might consider changing its moniker to "The City That Can't Catch a Break." Splendid idea, because there's another North Carolina city more deserving of being called "the Bull City."

12/6/2002

FELON GIVES FRIGHT IN THE NIGHT

If it was up to me, I might've let him go - the man who broke into my house after midnight several months ago while I lay upstairs trying to sleep.

True, I should've first bloodied him up a little - all right, a lot - but deep down I wouldn't have wanted him tried as a habitual felon and possibly sent away for 25 years.

But I now realize that would be the best thing that could happen to him. And to society. Otherwise, this hoodlum might break into another house - mine was the sixth for which he has been caught, I was told - and kill someone. Or get killed.

So, in a way, I may be saving his life. Or someone else's, because the person whose home he burglarizes next may not be as lucky as I - an insomniac who got up, unaware of a prowler, and stumbled downstairs for a snack. Instead of assaulting a bowl of Cap'n Crunch with Crunchberries, though, I found myself strangling a burglar.

Confirming my theory that most criminals are spineless weasels, this one was as meek as a newborn kitten when I fastened my hands around his throat.

And then, when I asked him - although not in these exact words - "Pray tell, whatever are you doing in my house?" his response was almost comical. "But I knocked three times, " he said. Honest.

I fear that if the inhabitant had been some sweet, vulnerable young thang, her house would have been roped off by police the next day with that yellow crime-scene tape that connotes a major crime, and neighbors would be fearfully double- and triple-checking their locks before going to bed.

Durham County District Attorney Jim Hardin is facing accusations from some defense lawyers that he only lowers the boom - the habitual-felon charge - against black defendants.

Maybe he does, and it should be easy enough to prove if true. But the defense lawyers have not proved it. So put up or shut up. Otherwise, let the man do his job.

Besides, my burglar does have a choice when we go to court next month: He can plea bargain and get 10 years without parole, or he can fight and get 25 if he loses.

All I know is, the guy who broke into my house - he's black, but certainly no "brother" - is a habitual felon and deserves to be sent away for a long time.

And he's lucky to be alive. For someone dumb enough to break into a house with two autos parked in the driveway, he was smart enough not to fight when the homicidally angry homeowner - me - grabbed him.

After checking to make sure my son, past whose bedroom he'd crept, was safe, I opened the front door and slung him off the porch - hoping he'd fall and break a leg or something. Of course, if he had, he'd have sued and my house would now be his and I'd be a nomad going from friend to friend asking, "Yo, homey, can I crash on your couch?"

Durham Police spokesman Dwight Pettiford talks often about protecting the community's "quality of life." As distressed as I am about sending some dude to the big house, there is no doubt that getting him off Durham's streets will improve the city's quality of life by giving us one fewer predator to worry about.

━━━┥ 5/17/1999

CIVIC DUTY SOMETIMES HURTS ┝━━━━━━━━━━━━━━━━

Sending a dude to prison is like making love to a porcupine: Even if you do it right, it's still going to hurt.

A couple of months ago, I sat at a table in Courtroom 2 of the Durham County courthouse and heard a judge sentence the man who'd broken into my house - while my young 'un and I were there in bed - to at least 10 years in prison.

As the cops led him away, I waited for the feeling of elation that should come from knowing I'd done my civic duty and made the streets safer.

It never came. Instead of elation, all I felt was sadness and a tear that I couldn't keep from falling. "Uh, it's just something in my eye," I nearly blurted out when the assistant district attorney turned to me, but all she said was, "Good job."

Being an insomniac is a curse that usually means I am assaulted all night by repeats of Rush's right-wing radio rants or bad music. But 'round midnight Sept. 2, 1998, I stumbled downstairs to assault a bowl of Cap'n Crunch with Crunchberries. Instead, I found myself assaulting a burglar.

"I say, old bean. What're you doing in my house?" I asked, although not in those exact words.

When I confronted the perp - that's cop lingo for "perpetrator" - in court, he didn't look nearly as terrifying as he had that night. Fact is, I was so much bigger than him that I feared the jurors would find me a wholly unsympathetic victim.

From the witness stand, I glared at him and tried to work up a good head of hate. Couldn't do it. All I felt was pity for his plight and anger at his stupidity for putting himself - and me - in this position.

The person for whom I did feel hatred, at least until the assistant district attorney reminded me that he was merely doing his job, was the defense attorney. The burglar's silk-stockinged mouthpiece kept twisting my words, trying to trip me up. I'd stood all I could stand by the time he told the jury that "perhaps Mr. Saunders took poetic license" with the truth when I told how I tossed his client off my porch.

"I'm going to take 'poetic license' with your #@$#%," I whispered through gritted teeth when he sauntered back to his seat a few feet from mine.

I still lie awake nights wondering whether I did the right thing, whether perhaps I should have just administered a good whomping and sent the thief on his way.

But then I think of what would have happened after I'd extracted my foot from his anatomy and after the scars I'd inflicted on him had healed: I'd either have to look over my shoulder for the rest of my life - fearful that he would seek vengeance - or he'd continue breaking into people's homes as they slept. Only next time, he might encounter some small, terrified woman instead of a big, angry me.

Remember the story I wrote last week about a murdered mother and her 9-year-old daughter who were stabbed a couple hundred times? Had I let this joker slide, I'd never be able to write or read another such story without wondering, "Was that the same cat I let go?"

As painful as it was, I now know I did the right thing because it's much better lying awake nights regretting sending someone to prison than lying awake nights wishing I had.

11/15/1999

CLAY'S PRICE TAG UNFAIR

We all remember that beloved children's bedtime story about the hooker who approached the old man on the street and said, "Hey, pops, I'll do anything you want for $100."

The man, whose interest in what the woman was really selling had long since died, thought it over. "OK," he said, "paint my house."

I felt like that old man upon hearing that the N.C. State Fair is paying Clay Aiken an obscene amount to perform this year: Long after our interest in what Clay is selling has, if not died, at least passed its peak, he's making $100,000 to perform at Dorton Arena.

Tiffany Budd, the fair's promotions specialist, said, "It's worth it to us" even though the fair will lose money on the booking.

Can't you just hear Meg Scott Phipps in her cell saying, "And they arrested me for my State Fair shenanigans? Oy vey!"

I rode the short bus to school -- I really did, so don't look at me like that -- so someone must explain to me how paying Clay $100,000 is good business when Dorton Arena seats only 6,000 and tickets are $15. Even if you sell out the joint, which you will, you're still $10,000 in the hole -- and you haven't even paid his opening act.

That's indefensible, especially when you see Aiken constantly on TV or when there's a grand opening of a Fred's Beds in, say, Rat Spit, Wyoming.

Budd seems unaware that, for many of the people venturing forth annually from their tiny hometowns to gape at the state's award-winning livestock or produce, any attraction is worth the trip. She could stick a microphone in front of three bleating sheep, two kumquats and a giant squash -- and nobody would notice.

The fair's own survey from 2002, Budd said, showed that few people actually go to the State Fair for the concerts.

What makes the fee paid for Aiken's performance even more distressing is how prices at the State Fair have ballooned.

Budd assured me that prices on fair staples -- cotton candy, fried Snickers bars, turkey legs -- won't increase to offset the Clay-induced shortfall. An evening at the fair for a family of four can easily cost $200 -- more, if you eat. Fairgoers suffering sticker shock called me complaining last year about the higher price of everything.

Turkey legs, for me the fair's main attraction, were $7 last year, which helps explain why you might have seen that family of four I mentioned earlier taking turns nibbling on one. I didn't resort to that, but I did take the bone home to make soup the next day.

Aiken's solo tour begins July 8 in Grand Forks, N.D. Chris Semrau, director of events at Grand Forks' Engelstad Arena, declined to say what our boy is taking them for, but he said admiringly, "The boy's getting paid. He's doing all right."

When I told Semrau that we're paying him $100,000, he was not surprised. "Clay is not entertaining offers for much less than that," he said.

Come on, folks, let's face it. Clay Aiken seems like a nice enough chap, and no one should begrudge his milking this cow dry. Still, it's hard to think of anything he can do that's worth that much money.

Unless it's come over and paint all of our houses.

———————————————————————————— 5/14/2004

COACHING THE GAME OF LIFE ————————————————

By some accounts, it took Leo Tolstoy 10 years to write "War and Peace," one of the most famous -- and certainly one of the thickest -- books in history. It's now considered by some to be one of the greatest literary works ever.

What, then, would you call a book that took four decades to write? A masterpiece?

Harvey Heartley doesn't care what you call it, as long as it helps make your life better. Heartley, the retired basketball coach of the St. Augustine's College Falcons, timed the release of "A Book for All Families: Life Lessons from a Coach, a Teacher and a Parent" to coincide with this week's CIAA Tournament, a tournament he played or coached in for nearly 30 years.

"It took me 40 years to write it," he said of the self-published tome. "It's all of the things I've learned in life and the things I've seen help people succeed."

Heartley, who is known by some people as "the father of Falcon athletics" and by others -- OK, just me -- as Harvey Heartless because he cut them from the college's basketball team and ruined their shot at pro sports stardom, calls his book "a personal behavioral map for self-fulfillment." Talk to Heartley about his years as a basketball coach, and he doesn't dwell on the on-court success of his teams or players. He dwells on their lives after they remove their uniforms for the last time, when the crowd stops cheering and the dudes have to go into a store and buy their own athletic socks and jockstraps, many of them for the first time in their lives. That's when Heartley's pride beams through.

"They usually measure you by how many games you win or how many players you send to the pros," he said when I talked with him Monday about the book, which is available at local bookstores and from vendors at the CIAA Tournament at the Raleigh ESA. "I like to look at how my guys turned out after they left St. Aug."

In a conversation about five years ago, I asked Heartley of which team he was proudest. I expected him to say the 1984 team, which made it to the NCAA Division II championship, or the team that sent power forward Ken Bannister to the New York Knicks for a cup of coffee. Some of his other players have played, and are still playing, professionally in European leagues.

He never mentioned them. Instead, he singled out the 1975 team -- the one I failed to make -- but the recognition had nothing to do with the team's on-court success. "I think all of those guys turned out great," he said at that time and repeated Monday. He cited the paths they've followed since leaving St. Aug's -- a counselor, an aircraft company executive, a New York police detective, a postman -- and it was obvious he considers them all candidates for the hall of fame of life, if not hoops.

"I taught life, not just basketball," he said.

Consider this: If your high school son was a hotshot hoopster with a great jump shot or terrific crossover dribble, St. Aug's under Heartley wouldn't have been your first choice. But when you see the abysmal graduation rates -- and life success rates -- of many big time college hoops programs, you couldn't do better than a coach who sought to teach his players to execute the crossover from the court as well as on it.

2/26/2002

COLD WATER ON THE WARM GLOW OF U.S. UNITY

Oh well, it was a nice dream while it lasted.

Ever so briefly, it appeared that the ghastly terrorist attacks in New York and Washington would bring us closer together as a nation, united in comforting the families of victims of last week's attacks and warding off future ones.

The sale of U.S. flags skyrocketed, along with patriotic fervor. So did our national resolve to find and punish the perpetrators of the attacks - and there was talk of America becoming the kind of culturally harmonious country many of us have long hoped it would become.

Fat chance. Even before the bodies have been removed from the

smoldering ruins that were the World Trade Center and the Pentagon, the forces of divisiveness began plying their trade. The cracks in our week-long display of unity are beginning to show.

It started fewer than 48 hours after the attacks, when the Rev. Jerry Falwell pointed his stubby, self-righteous finger at all of the groups he abhors - which is just about everyone. In Falwell's myopic view, God allowed the attacks on America's symbols because we dare countenance the presence of the ACLU, liberals, pro-choice advocates and - egads! - homosexuals.

"I point the finger in their face and say 'You helped this happen,'" Falwell stated while on the "700 Club" television show, which is hosted by his kindred spirit, the equally batty Pat Robertson. Robertson "totally" concurred with Falwell's hatemongering.

Falwell later apologized - if you can call what he said an apology - by acknowledging that his comments were "insensitive and inappropriate at this time."

By that, one can only assume that he would consider them appropriate at another time - say, after all of the victims have been removed.

Theories even more bizarre - if that's possible - abound on the Internet, given credence solely by the fact that they can be disseminated around the world in a matter of minutes. Fortunately for us all, most of these are so ludicrous they defy belief.

For instance, one of the most popular, or at least most prolific, e-mails making the rounds claims that President Bush orchestrated the attacks - for which nonsensical reason escapes me - and made sure he was out of town when the attacks went down.

Even more recently, Curtis Gatewood, president of the Durham chapter of the NAACP, garnered attention when he issued a press release urging blacks in America not to participate in the imminent war because of past and present instances of racism by both the government and the companies that were destroyed at the World Trade Center.

Gatewood's comments were quickly disavowed by Kweisi Mfume, national president of the group, but too late to prevent yet another crack in the bell of our national unity.

There will indeed be a time for the country to address some of the issues Gatewood so indelicately and ill-timedly raised. As for Falwell? There is never a good time to promote the particularly rancid brand of intolerance he preaches.

Oh well, it was a good dream while it lasted.

9/22/2001

COMIC ROUTINE BOMBS

When Dave Chappelle did it, he got laughs and a $30 million TV deal.

When Durham resident Kenyart Ali Williams did the same thing, he got thrown in jail.

Durham cops apparently don't share Williams' and Chappelle's sense of humor, because when Williams called with what he thought was a guaranteed way to get a rapid cop response -- using Chappelle's comedy skit about a report of a white woman in distress -- the cops weren't amused.

About 10:45 Saturday morning, Williams called police for assistance in moving some belongings out of the house he had shared with his girlfriend.

"That's common when people are getting divorced or separating and they don't want any trouble or retaliation," police spokesman Cpl. David Addison said.

Indeed, if you've ever been asked by an angry woman to pack your albums, barbells and your beloved velvet portrait of Teddy Pendergrass and leave -- and who among us hasn't? -- you know that inviting the cops to stand by was a smart decision by Williams.

Alas, it was probably the last smart decision he made that day.

The officers, Addison said, apparently didn't arrive fast enough for Williams, so he dialed 911 and employed a trick he admitted getting off of Chappelle's Comedy Central TV show.

"A white woman is being raped and killed," he frantically told the 911 operator. "My wife is about to die."

When police arrived at 114 Davidson St., Addison said, they discovered a woman lying in bed -- in no distress -- and children playing a video game in the front room.

Williams told officers he'd made the call. He also told them where he got the idea.

The officers, Addison said, "weren't pleased at all. When they confirmed that everything was all right, they placed him under arrest."

Williams, 30, was charged with filing a false police report, a misdemeanor.

He was remorseful when I talked to him Thursday and acknowledged that he had "made a foolish mistake. I lost my head ... . I talked nicely the first time, and I'll bet I sat there for 35 or 40 minutes.

"When I called back and told them a woman was being raped, -- whew! -- they were there in two minutes, as though they were right around the corner."

Williams' treatment by Durham cops was very different from that given by Gary, Ind., police to an unthinking man who used a similar trick to get a response several years ago.

While covering a double murder there, I watched as police cruisers zoomed in and parked everywhere, including in the parking lot of a nearby bar. One frantic bar patron whose car was blocked rushed up to an officer and claimed that a man inside the bar was having a heart attack. He needed to rush the man to the hospital, he said breathlessly.

The officer obligingly moved his car and watched the man get in and drive away. Or try to.

Turns out no one needed medical attention -- at least not until the irate cop got through with the driver.

Williams said he is fixing to seek treatment to control his anger. "I've been listening to too many comedians," he said. "I'm going to leave Dave Chappelle alone."

10/15/2004

COSBY'S TRUTH HURTS

Homeslice must have OD'd on some Jell-O Pudding Pops.

That's as good an explanation as any for why Bill Cosby recently committed an unforgivable boo-boo: He told a truth about race.

Not the whole truth, you understand, and not the only truth. But a huge one.

Commenting at a commemoration of the 50th anniversary of the Supreme Court's Brown v. Board of Education ruling at Constitution Hall in Washington last week, Cosby criticized some poor blacks for "not holding up their end in this deal."

You know what deal. The one, unspoken but written in blood, in which black people in the 1950s and 1960s would march in the streets, get bitten by dogs, slammed into buildings by high-pressure fire hoses, get fired and killed -- and those of us who came later would take full advantage of the opportunities their sacrifices created.

It hasn't happened, at least not to the extent that it should have. "These people marched in the street and were hit in the face with rocks to get an education," Cosby said, "and now we've got these knuckleheads standing around."

He could have also criticized middle-class blacks, the primary beneficiaries of those civil rights pioneers and warriors.

For instance, when less than 30 percent of blacks vote in many elections, that's a failure to uphold their end of the deal.

One of the problems was exemplified moments after Cosby's speech -- before he could sit down. Ted Shaw, head of the NAACP Legal Defense Fund, rushed to the podium to reassure the audience that many problems confronting blacks are not self-inflicted.

No, but dammit, many of them are. And until we acknowledge that, our race won't reach the hoped-for Promised Land.

Only a fool -- or Clarence Thomas -- thinks racism no longer exists.

But racism is not as bad as it was 40 years ago and can't be solely to blame for the 50 percent dropout rate among black students nationwide.

Cosby, who has contributed millions of dollars to black colleges, lambasted many parents for "not parenting" or placing enough emphasis on education. They buy "$500 sneakers" for their kids but won't spend $200 for Hooked on Phonics to teach them to speak proper English, he said.

One black columnist, in attempting to discredit Cosby's criticism, pounced on the fact that there are no $500 sneakers.

Maybe not now, but when there invariably are, wanna bet who'll be lining up to buy them?

Comedian Chris Rock didn't take nearly the heat that Cosby did when he cracked on the anti-intellectualism among many younger blacks. That attitude is typified, he said, by a subculture that respects time spent in prison -- that's called "keepin' it real" -- more than time spent in school.

In subsequent interviews and in response to the criticism he's receiving, Cosby said he was tired and frustrated. No doubt he and a whole generation of blacks are tired, frustrated, saddened and sickened by what has become of our once-righteous struggle.

Do these kids think we have reached "the promised land" that Dr. King spoke of the night before he was murdered?

Do they even know who King was?

5/28/2004

CRUSADE DESERVES AN 'AMEN'

If you went to Patrick Wooden's church Sunday expecting an apology, you were at the wrong place.

Among the first words from Wooden, the Raleigh pastor who sparked a firestorm last week when he urged shoppers to avoid stores that don't include "Merry Christmas" in their holiday advertisements, were, "This is warfare."

He and his Upper Room Church of God in Christ congregation and band then jumped into the most soulful, most defiant version of "We Wish You a Merry Christmas" I've ever heard.

Who am I kidding? It was the only soulful, defiant version of "We Wish You a Merry Christmas" I've ever heard.

Wooden, a big ol' Otis Redding-looking and -singing dude who grew up in Rockingham when I did, was unfairly compared to Adolf Hitler because of The News & Observer ad.

In it, he decried the absence of Christmas songs and challenged "all Christians to spend their ... dollars with merchants who include the greeting 'Merry Christmas' in their holiday advertising."

The comparison to Hitler, who forced Jewish store owners to place a yellow star on their businesses in the years leading up to the Holocaust, "is too ignorant to respond to," Wooden said.

He eagerly responded to the criticism that his ad excluded people of other faiths.

"If you look at the ad, you see that we say shop with 'merchants who include the greeting.' That doesn't mean exclude anybody," he said. "Our hope," he said, "is for those who profess to be Christians to say, 'Hey, come to think of it, you don't see 'Merry Christmas' anywhere or hear Christmas carols anymore.' "

The ad, under the heading "Attention Christians," asks "Have you noticed you don't hear 'Silent Night' " and other traditional Christmas carols?

I've noticed, but thought it was because radio stations simply preferred playing "Grandma Got Run Over by a Reindeer" 500 times a day.

Wooden said during Sunday's sermon and in an interview Monday that he feels the absence of Christmas carols is part of a "clandestine effort to de-Christianize Christmas."

Response to the ad, he said, has been "overwhelmingly positive." Opposition has come from "multiculturalists with a desire to do away with Christmas... They want to re-name it 'the winter festivals.' "

Wooden is charismatic and courageous, with the chutzpah to accomplish whatever he wants to. If you doubt that, just go check out that impressive school he's built next to his church. I only hope that when he finishes putting the "merry" back in Christmas, he'll confront issues that too many other preachers shy away from, like the disdain for educational achievement too many black youngsters and their parents seem to have embraced or the proclivity of so many black boys to kill one another.

I didn't find the ad bigoted or exclusionary. Of course, not much offends us Baptists.

Wooden's crusade is well-intended and should cause people to think about why we celebrate Christmas. Alas, most people will be motivated more by ads that save them a buck or two on Baby-Wets-a-Lot or whatever is this year's hot new toy than by ones wishing them "Merry Christmas."

11/30/2004

DEATH CAN'T BE UNCERTAIN

No one, the Bible states, knows the day or hour that death will come. Right on.

If, however, we could choose where to give up the ghost, I suspect many of us would choose Franklin County.

After what happened there this week, being pronounced dead in Franklin County is merely a suggestion, not a fact.

Monday night's gaffe, which led to Larry D. Green's being erroneously zipped into a body bag after he was hit by a car, might have been a once-in-a-lifetime mistake. But when you're dealing with life or death, once is too many times.

As a result of an error that has focused national attention on the area, people will be tormented for eternity by the thought that maybe, just maybe, Uncle Louie or Papa Daddy wasn't really dead when zippered.

No one will ever know, though, because if they're zipped up alive, they're not likely to be unzipped that way. Bill Brummond, a spokesman for a company that makes body bags, said in an e-mail Thursday that the tiny needle holes through which the zippers are sewn into the bags are the only possible places for air to enter.

"It's amazing he survived," Brummond said.

Not only was his survival amazing, but it also makes you wonder how many people died in a body bag, gasping for air, after being prematurely pronounced dead.

Residents of Franklin County and people injured or ill there deserve to know that their lives won't hang by a thread or, more accurately, a threaded hole, if there is doubt.

The four paramedics involved in the case have been suspended with pay. Someone deserves punishment for such obvious dereliction of duty. Far more important than punishment, though, is the need for systemic changes to reduce the likelihood of this happening again.

"That," Franklin County Manager Chris Coudriet said, "is the major focus of our investigation. What could we have done differently, and what should we have done differently on the scene to prevent what happened to Mr. Green?"

Coudriet also promised a "subsequent rewrite of our protocol" to determine who can declare a person dead.

"Someone clearly made the decision on the scene," he said. "I'm not certain there is anything in the law that spells out who can make that decision. This case opens up a clear opportunity" for the county to do that.

In the movie "The Wizard of Oz," the coroner of Munchkin Land arrived to check on the condition of the Wicked Witch of the East after she was crushed by a house. He sang:

"As Coroner, I must aver

I thoroughly examined her

And she's not only merely dead

She's really most sincerely dead."

Alas, in Franklin County, where no one is admitting to declaring Larry Green dead, a similar figure of authority is needed who can pronounce an inert person most sincerely dead -- to spare other families the emotional trauma inflicted upon Green's loved ones.

The difference between "inert" and "inept" is but a single letter of the alphabet. The difference between, say, Larry and Lazarus, two guys who apparently came back from the dead, is even smaller.

───────────────────────────────── 1/28/2005

DEMOCRATS' DECISION TO MOVE ├─────

LOS ANGELES -- Whew, that was close. For a minute there, it appeared that I was going to have to go to a party with a bunch of nekkid women.

Democratic Congresswoman Loretta Sanchez spared me that indignity by canceling her political fund-raiser at the ultimate den of iniquity, the Playboy mansion.

It's unlikely that the Playmates would have actually been topless during a political fund-raiser - especially with Bill Clinton not even a candidate - but just being surrounded by a bevy of airbrushed Playmates who have been topless at some point in their lives might have been a distraction in my quest to get the big story at the Democratic National Convention.

So thanks a lot, Loretta.

Sanchez, considered a rising star of the Democratic Party until she decided to throw a party, bowed to political pressure - and political correctness - after being besieged by the party's puritanical and hypocritical elements.

"Have that party at the Playboy mansion," they wagged their finger at her, "and your political career will be as dead as Ambrose Merriwether's."

Who?

Precisely.

To show that they meant business, party officials banished Sanchez from a speaking role at the convention here this week. She was reinstated after succumbing to their pressure.

The fund-raiser now will be held at Universal Studios, the family-friendly mega-corporation that brings us movies of stomach-churning violence and mayhem, the kind of Hollywood movies that Democratic vice presidential candidate Joseph Lieberman has criticized repeatedly.

But hey, violence ain't S-E-X, and the Democrats are extremely skittish about anything having to do with S-E-X after eight years of Clinton and his peccadilloes. Since nothing has more to do with S-E-X than the Playboy mansion, the Democrats were afraid the Republicans would turn pipe-smoking, pajama-wearing, Viagra-popping Playboy founder Hugh Hefner into a personification of the party's moral laxity. Remember when George W. Bush's daddy made convicted rapist Willie Horton a symbol of the Democrats' softness on crime in 1988?

Bush: We're the party of family values - the only reason we didn't have our convention at a Baptist church was because Philadelphia didn't have one big enough - and they're out at the Playboy mansion in Los Angeles. Nyah nyah nyah nyah nyah.

Isn't it sad to think that someone running for president might stoop to such a childish tactic? Isn't it even sadder that it would have probably worked?

Now that the party has been canceled at the mansion, I will have to find something to do with these silk jammies I bought - you know, the ones like Hef wears.

I won't miss going to the mansion - I drove past it three times today while trying to think of a reason to go ring the bell - but I am sorely disappointed that I won't be able to ask the in-depth political queries I spent the flight out here poring over. I imagined the Pulitzer-Prize-winning interview starting something like this:

Me: Miss December, what do you think of Al Gore's environmental record?

Her: Oooh, I loved it, but I prefer it on CD.

8/14/2000

DIRTY HANDS FINGERED

Who knew you could earn a living hanging out in public restrooms?

Get your mind out of the toilet, pal. I visited a few men's rooms throughout the Triangle over the past few days just to see if men in this area are more hygienic than those in other parts of the country.

Sadly, such was not the case. Our hands are as dirty as everyone else's.

Research by spies for the American Society of Microbiology that shows that a lot of men don't wash their hands sent me to the restrooms to see where we rate.

It is my civic duty, and great shame, to let you know that when it comes to hands, many of us would be better off standing on our hands and eating with our feet.

Over three days in restaurant and mall restrooms, only 18 of 30 men I saw washed their hands. Most of the filthy-fingered philistines checked themselves out in the mirror, and some even turned on the water but didn't touch it, before going out to eat or shake your hand.

I pretended to talk on a cell phone or wash my hands for several minutes in case cops from the vice squad wandered in and wondered why I was hanging out in restrooms.

Fortunately for me, no cops questioned me, but you'd be surprised at the dirty looks you get standing around in public toilets for longer than the prescribed time.

My initial plan -- to ask the nonwashers why they didn't wash -- was scrapped after only two attempts. "Say, homes, didn't you forget something?" I asked, nodding toward the unused sink. I intentionally picked two of the smallest men, dudes I could take if either responded violently.

Neither did, but both, in the words of Woody Allen, told me to be fruitful and multiply -- alone. Although not in those words.

Laugh if you want, but you'll thank me one day. The health risk associated with dirty hands is severe and might even deserve a national hand-washing czar.

How serious is the risk? So serious that a guy who served in Iraq said soldiers were prohibited from entering the mess tents until they'd washed up in sinks set up outside.

If men who worry every minute about roadside attacks and suicide bombers are paying that much attention to their hygiene, shouldn't we all?

Several people said they seldom eat out any more precisely because of people's lax attitude toward hand-washing.

I know that's the reason Sweet Thang and I don't dine at high-class restaurants like Golden Corral as much as we used to.

Nothing makes their exquisite nanner pudding less appetizing than seeing some bloke pull into the parking lot, climb down out of a septic tank trunk and sidle right up to the chow line without washing his hands.

The one good thing about people not washing, though, is that it could help in our battle against obesity.

If Jenny Craig and Sweatin' to the Oldies doesn't help you lose those last 20 pounds, go hang out in public restrooms. Watching people walk out without washing up should decrease your appetite by 30 percent.

If it doesn't, then maybe you'd better look in the mirror -- and wash your hands.

9/27/2005

DON'T BAN GUNS

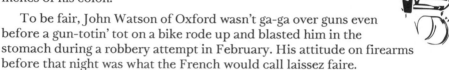

If it's true that a liberal is just a conservative who hasn't been mugged yet, then it must also be true that a gun nut is just a gun-control advocate who hasn't yet been shot in the belly and lost 18 inches of his colon.

To be fair, John Watson of Oxford wasn't ga-ga over guns even before a gun-totin' tot on a bike rode up and blasted him in the stomach during a robbery attempt in February. His attitude on firearms before that night was what the French would call laissez faire.

"If someone wanted to be licensed to carry and they were responsible, I didn't have a quibble with that," he told me.

But the colon that doctors took from Watson's belly has since been replaced by fire, and he is now passionate about holding gun manufacturers liable for the mayhem attributed to their products.

The change wasn't just the result of his nightmarish experience in the parking lot of the Durham Clinic on Roxboro Road.

Oh no. Sounding like a lawyer, which he is, Watson lamented society's vulnerability "to those who don't even have the capacity to be responsible."

He cited not only his own youthful-appearing assailant - he estimates the kid was between 13 and 16 - but the 11-year-old twins in Kittrell who earlier this month allegedly blew away Dad and seriously wounded Sis and Mom.

Then there was the Colorado massacre by another pair of youthful gunslingers. (OK, chill, all of you NRA members: They slung bombs, too. Feel better?)

Watson spoke to a state House committee considering a bill called, too innocuously, the "Right to Keep and Bear Arms Protection Act." The bill seeks to protect gun manufacturers from municipalities wanting to make them accountable for the human and financial toll of their products.

Watson said that medical care for his shooting cost nearly $50,000. Although he was insured, many shooting victims aren't, and the cost of their treatment is borne by municipalities and taxpayers.

The House passed the bill Tuesday despite Watson's pleas, and a companion bill is moving through the Senate. (Psst. I'll bet you they'll wait for this Colorado stuff to cool down so they can genuflect to gun makers when no one's looking.)

Some people, such as the General Assembly, are downright shameless in their efforts to absolve gun makers of any liability. First, they point out - and point out often - that the deadly Beavis and Butt-head duo in Colorado also used bombs, not just semi-automatic weapons.

Then, two nights ago Neal Boortz, an Atlanta talk show host - a fraternity that, we all know, epitomizes mental stability, right? - ridiculed efforts at gun control. He giddily noted that a London television show host was gunned down on the street last week. I swear, the dude sounded so disgustingly gleeful to inform his listeners that this occurred in a country with "absolute" gun control that I disgustedly cut off my radio before he had a chance to tell them that - ahem - more people are killed by handguns in the United States in a week than in all of Western Europe in a year.

Y'all don't reckon he forgot to mention that, do you?

— 4/29/1999

DON'T LET 'SMART CARDS' FOOL YOU

Just in time for Christmas, we hear that those benevolent credit card companies are unleashing a "smart card" on the public.

This technology is supposed to make our lives better and everyday tasks easier. Don't believe it. Matter of fact, as they say in the movies, be afraid. Be very afraid.

I hate to look a gift card in the mouth, but the idea of consumers expecting credit card companies to do something good for them -- with no expectation of recompense at a usurious interest rate -- is like chickens expecting Col. Sanders to do something good for them out of the goodness of his heart.

You, dear consumer -- like the chicken -- stand an excellent chance of getting plucked in that transaction.

I'd be a lot less skeptical of the motives of Visa and MasterCard, among others, if they weren't always bombarding me with solicitations to take on yet another card.

How, for instance, can one trust the motives of an industry that congratulates me for being such a good customer when my benign "9 percent introductory interest rate" leapt, unbeknownst to me, to 26 percent after I innocently forgot to make two payments on time?

Of course, upon further reflection, maybe that's precisely why they think I'm such a good customer.

The much-touted smart cards would enable us to make certain telephones operate like ATM machines, check out books at the library and even make calls at pay phones.

Wow. I don't know about you, but I am thrilled at the prospect of potentially paying $800 -- once you add interest and late-payment penalties -- for an overdue library book or a 35-cent phone call.

What's so smart about that? Nothing, unless you own a credit card company, because a smart card for credit card companies would serve a different purpose from a smart card for consumers.

For credit card companies, it would be one that, through a microchip imbedded in it, transmits subliminal messages to consumers.

"Go ahead, buy that suede sport coat. You'll look just like Denzel Washington," it'll tell your brain. Or, "Sure, you can afford those $500 open-toed shoes. You'll come up with the money somehow. That gorgeous, nominally employed babe on 'Sex and the City' always does, and just look at the way men go gaga over her. Besides, you'll probably hit that lottery by the time the first payment is due."

Hmm, come to think of it, my credit card already tells me that one, and it's not even a smart card.

A true smart card for consumers, on the other hand, would be one that warns us away from those impulse purchases that get us in so much trouble, especially at this time of year.

"Nah, Homey," it would whisper insistently, "that $2,700 lynx jacket isn't going to make Li'l Mama forgive or forget the fact that you stayed out all night 'with the boys' and came home smelling like Chanel No. 5."

And it would certainly warn you that putting those seven visits to the Magic Fingers Massage Parlor on your credit card is not such a good idea.

—————————————————————————————————————→ 12/19/2000

DON'T TELL ME HOW TO VOTE ——————————

The bearded man didn't like it at all when I called him a stupid, insensitive lout who was an insult to his ancestors.

He couldn't do a thing about it, though -- not because I was bigger or meaner than he (we're the same size and tempera-ment), but because, you see, he is me.

Yep, I was flagellating myself Tuesday evening for one of the worst offenses a grown black man can commit: I thought about not voting.

It was after 6 p.m. Tuesday, I was stuck in traffic across town and I knew the candidates I was supporting would win easily.

Why bother? I asked myself.

Then I thought about Medgar Evers, Viola Liuzzo, Chaney, Goodman, Schwerner and hundreds of others who gave their lives so that I could vote.

With that heroic roll call in my head, I braved the traffic and did my duty.

Still, unless I'm forgetting something, those martyrs died so that I could vote, not so that I could be told how to vote.

To enter my polling station, you have to walk a gantlet of people offering tickets with candidates already marked. In my usual pleasant way, I told them all -- the Durham Committee on the Affairs of Black People, the People's Alliance, the Ya Ya Sisterhood -- to get lost.

I'm a big fan of the Durham Committee, and not just because it's the only organization that would have me as a member. (You just have to be black and live in Durham).

Voting, though, is too precious a right to let anyone, even some tradition-bound organization, tell you how to do it. If you don't know where the candidates stand on an issue, grow a brain and find out.

For proof that not everyone has a brain, you need look no further than the case of Thomas Stith, the only incumbent seeking re-election to the City Council. Despite what he and others described as a "positive" freshman term, Stith apparently won by fewer than 200 votes.

True, he has never met a developer he didn't like, but his main liability is that he's a black Republican. That makes him unacceptable to many black voters on general principle. The Durham Committee only grudgingly supported him.

Why? "People got caught up in partisan rhetoric," Stith said. "What party you were in became more important than what kind of service you provided."

Stith isn't the only black Republican on the council, nor is he the only one who has had to battle uphill because of it. Howard Clement, the coolest Republican I know, has served seven terms on the council, but he told me, "The Durham Committee has endorsed me only twice, and I suspect they'll be going after me in two years.

"I just wish the partisanship would end ... . There's no Republican way or Democratic way to pick up garbage, put out fires or make the streets safe."

When you realize that the Republican Party is the party of the terrifying triumvirate of John Ashcroft, George Bush and Clarence Thomas, you can see why some blacks find supporting it as odd as a chicken supporting Col. Sanders.

Alas, it's possible, but highly unlikely, that I'm wrong and that the Democratic Party alone is indeed the light and the way for blacks.

If not, though, some of us ought to be willing to try the darkness of the Republican Party.

⊢ 11/7/2003

DOOMSDAY SHOPPING MADE EASY

Time was, all a bloke needed for a good time was "a jug of wine, a loaf of bread and thou."

At least those are the timeless ingredients that "The Rubaiyat of Omar Khayyam" recommended for romance.

That prescription for love might seem woefully outdated now, however, because with all of the contemporary threats faced by modern man, some might need a little more than that to set the mood.

Like what, you ask?

How about a gas mask, some antibiotics, a vial of stuff to grow hair on your head and some Viagra to go along with your special thou?

That's what I concluded earlier this week after visiting a Web site that bills itself as "the Internet's online pharmaceutical source." For a price -- deliberately vague -- you can "Get what you need here NOW." In case the seriousness of the threats we face escapes you, those words are emblazoned against an apocalyptic background of red clouds or smoke.

What you will need, apparently, are gas masks "certified by the Israeli Defense Authorities," along with Cipro, "the only anthrax antibiotic available."

For those unsure whether they need the drug and gas mask, the site lists a supposed news story from CNN. "Agents made from anthrax first produce fever and stomach pains. A horrible death can occur within ... hours."

Many experts doubt the effectiveness of the gas masks, because many biological and chemical weapons have no warning odor. Also, although Cipro has been approved for biological attacks, this use of the drug has never been directly tested on humans. Doctors should not prescribe it until they know you've been infected.

With the threat of annihilation hanging palpably in the air, you'll want to stop smoking, so the online pharmacy is offering Zyban. And, because one's amorous interests -- and, most likely, abilities -- will wane in such a dire situation, the company, seeking to capitalize on man's two most basic instincts, survival and having a good time, is also offering Viagra. "Order while supplies last," it urges.

In the event you survive a biological attack and live to love again, you'll want to look good. So they're offering, apparently as part of their doomsday survival package, Xenical, to help you lose weight, and Propecia, to give you a thick head of hair.

Makes sense to me. Think about it. What's the use of surviving a biological holocaust if you're going to be fat and baldheaded? (Never mind that I'm already fat and baldheaded.)

I predict I'll hear from some of you yapping about "There is nothing funny about the threat of biological Armaggedon, which is what we'll have if anthrax gets into the wrong hands."

You're right, but shut up anyway. I know there's nothing funny about the threats we face, but, to quote that great seafaring philosopher Jimmy Buffett, "If we couldn't laugh, we'd all go insane."

Besides, tell me there is nothing funny about the thought of some dude popping antibiotics, Propecia and Viagra like jelly beans. While wearing a gas mask.

—— 10/12/2001

DUMB THING TO DO AT A COLLEGE

When I used to rob people, I was not the smartest criminal you'd ever hope to meet.

For instance, it took me a while to realize that the reason I was netting so little moolah from my victims was that they had already been robbed by the bootleggers whose houses they were staggering from when I'd accost them.

(I hope the statute of limitations has run out on strong-arm robbery.)

But I no longer hold the title of dumbest criminal, not since I learned that there are some chumps out there who are robbing - get this - college students.

Next to robbing drunks, rolling college students strikes me as the least profitable criminal endeavor imaginable. Yet we've got reports of robbers who are intentionally targeting them.

Isn't that a hoot? At least when I was vying for the title of world's dumbest criminal I was never armed, so the person most likely to get hurt was me.

But these idiots who are terrorizing students at or near N.C. Central University are loaded for bear, armed with a pistol-grip shotgun, NCCU campus police said.

About 25 years have passed since I was running around thinking I was a teenage John Dillinger, and two decades have passed since I was in college. My one indelible memory of college life, though, is of being broke and hungry. As were most of my pals.

Anyone who bothered to rob us would have been extremely, perhaps homicidally, disappointed, because we didn't even have money to pay street insurance. That's the cash you carry in case you encounter a robber so he won't feel he's wasted his time. A robber who feels that way is more likely to plug you for the heck of it.

Since no one with good sense goes to a college campus seeking a big score, we're obviously dealing with people who are - hmm, let's see, what's the word I'm looking for? - STUPID. Which makes him (or them - the number of assailants varies) even more dangerous, especially with a pistol-grip shotgun.

But stupidity can't be the sole reason. I'm guessing, based on what I learned in Psych 101, it is also jealousy. The main guy who has NCCU students looking over their shoulders - they've named him "Bolo" - knows he won't net much loot rolling college kids, but he does know he can terrify them and give himself a fleeting, albeit false, sense of superiority.

Since the bed-wetting bandit feels inadequate in an academic setting armed with books, pencil and paper, the gun represents his ... aw, nevermind.

I went to the NCCU campus yesterday and asked several students, "How much money do you have in your pocket?" After I assured them I wasn't some bold daylight robber, they told me.

None of the students I surveyed, not surprisingly, was flush with dough. Typical was Demetris Long, a High Point freshman who answered: "I've got zero in my pockets. If I have cash, it's for a short period, like when I'm on my way to do laundry."

Hardly enough to justify getting out of bed, is it?

Willie Sutton's famous comment, when asked why he robbed banks, was "That's where the money's at."

I wonder what Bolo and his idiot pals would say if someone asked them why they're terrorizing kids with a pistol-grip shotgun?

4/19/1999

EGGNOG GIVES NOD TO SEASON

With eager merchants putting up store decorations in October -- while touting their "unbelievable" sales as a way of enticing us to buy, buy, buy -- and cities staging their parades just after Labor Day, it's becoming hard for some people to tell just when the Christmas season begins.

But not for me. The holiday season begins the exact day the Piggly Wiggly and other grocery stores break out the eggnog. This year, that was about the first of November, and I was delighted to be in my neighborhood grocery store when the dude delivered the first batch.

"Kind of early to be putting that stuff out," I said, trying to ingratiate myself to the shelf stocker lest he tell me it was all reserved for others. The look he shot me told me he was not in a festive mood. It also told me where he thought I could stick one of those quarts.

Despite his inhospitableness, I purchased two quarts -- one of which, sad to say, never made it out of the parking lot alive.

A great philosopher -- OK, it was just me -- once noted that eggnog, like only a couple of other things in life, is a lot like liquor: Even when it's bad, it's good.

But like a lot of other things -- say, for instance, moonshine and homemade cookies -- the first batch is rarely the best. Perhaps it was my anticipation, or the fact that I gulped most of it without actually tasting it, but the first sip of the season was a disappointment.

Could it be that they milked the eggnog cow too soon? Or plucked the tree before it was ripe?

Even though I consider myself an eggnog connoisseur, lots of people I asked thought the stuff should be poured down the sewer.

No holiday staples get as much bad press, ridicule and disdain as eggnog -- someone once said it was made from elf snot -- and fruitcake, which make up the two essential food groups.

Every time I hear people joking about fruitcakes -- according to lore, there's only one fruitcake in the world, and everybody keeps sending it to somebody else -- I want to stand up and defend my nutty buddy.

I know there's more than one fruitcake extant, because I polished one off yesterday and hope to find another just as good. (I even discovered what that green thing is in fruitcake: a dyed cherry. Like you, I'm sure, I'd hoped it was something more exotic -- like green eye of newt.)

That fruitcake discovery was a bit of a letdown, but what I learned about eggnog was fascinating. The name, according to some history I read (I told you I was serious about the stuff), comes from an Old World concoction of egg-based milk and rum, the latter also being known as grog.

According to legend, the Old World dudes got tired of saying "Arghhhh, gimme a pint of that egg and grog, matey," so they shortened it to the name we now know and love.

Years ago, I learned that George Washington loved eggnog, especially after he added rye, whisky, rum and sherry to it. After drinking that, I'll bet he was the father of more than just our country. Nor is it any wonder that he had wooden teeth.

11/29/2002

E~MAIL DELIVERS A BIG LIE

There are three ways to know you're fixing to get hit with a big lie: when a DJ says, "Hey, here's a great song by Michael Bolton," when Sweet Thang tells you, "Those pants don't make you look fat" or when you receive e-mail that begins, "This is for real, yo."

People know not to try those first two lines on me, but I received just such an e-mail recently alerting me to the grave national threat posed by throngs of terrorists posing as -- get this -- UPS deliverers.

In a letter addressed to the police chief of Washington, D.C., someone supposedly from the U.S. Department of Homeland Security warned him -- and us -- to "BE ALERT!!!" There has been "a huge purchase, $32,000 worth, of United Parcel Service uniforms on eBay over the last 30 days."

Being somewhat dense, I couldn't fathom what danger -- other than uglying up the sartorial landscape -- thousands of people walking around in hideous brown suits and matching knee socks could pose.

Hmm. Perhaps the uniforms were props in a joke played by French fashionistas to flood runways with models sporting the "ironic chic" look -- outfits so unhip that they became hip.

They'd then sit back, sip espresso from tiny little cups and laugh at "the silly Americans who'll fall for anything."

Scoff if you will, but if Tommy Hilfiger can persuade millions to pay $90 for a pair of khaki britches that even Richie Cunningham would've found too plain, imagine what clever marketing could fetch for a matching brown-pants-and-shirt ensemble?

My other theory is that thousands of faux UPS drivers could wreak maximum havoc by double-parking and causing panic on city streets.

Alas, the e-mail warned that the mass purchases "could represent a serious threat as bogus drivers can drop off anything to anyone with deadly consequences! ... Make people aware so that we can prepare and/or avoid terrorist attacks ... TAKE THIS SERIOUSLY!"

Here's another tip: Disregard any e-mail that USES ALL UPPERCASE LETTERS TO GRAB YOUR ATTENTION!

I called UPS headquarters in Atlanta to inform them of the possible misuse of their signature attire and to ask whether they were going to make changes -- like adding a colorful sash -- to distinguish them from fakes. I expected UPS would be so grateful that it would deliver my next package for free.

Instead, they laughed. "That's an old hoax," Rob Haskins of UPS' security department told me between chuckles. "It's crazy. This is at least the third time this [rumor] has reared its head."

Boy, did I feel dumb -- but relieved. This may get me in trouble with John Ashcroft and his truth squads, who are the ones who really should don brown shirts, but terrorists could find an easier way to deliver mass destruction. They could dress up as, say, Hooters waitresses or Catholic schoolgirls in those plaid skirts and knee socks. I guarantee you that either of those outfits would get them in any door they knocked on.

Thanks to the hoax, I've discovered an even greater threat to national security than hordes of fake UPS workers: the one posed by asinine e-mail warnings from people with too much time on their hands.

8/22/2003

E~MAILING IT LIKE IT WASN'T: AN ACTOR'S UNDELIVERED LINES

It's not often you actually get to see an urban legend born. Who, for instance, knows where the one began about the giant alligator emerging from the toilet?

But I was there at the creation of the most recent urban legend, saw it as it emerged from the womb -- and then from the fevered mind of someone who desperately wants a celebrity to feel as he does.

If you've fired up your computer in the past week you've probably seen an e-mail lauding Denzel Washington for putting Katie Couric, Meryl Streep and all like-minded liberals in their place.

One sure way to tell a whopper is forthcoming in an e-mail is when it starts with "Did you see...?" If the answer is "No," the sender can proceed to tell his version of events, even if it's make-believe.

The dozen or so versions of this one begin "Did you see Denzel being interviewed by Katie Couric? Not many people are talking about it. They are wishing it would go away and are trying to sweep it under the rug...The women became enraged. Meryll Streep turned blood-red and she sat with her legs crossed and one leg shaking up and down, fuming."

Gee, I've never seen a fuming leg before.

Denzel Washington, according to the story, gave Couric and fellow guest Streep the what-for, for, among other things, expecting him to be a liberal simply because he's black. Had he seen Michael Moore's "Fahrenheit 9/11?" Couric asked.

No, Washington replied, "and I don't plan to." He also pounced on her for referring to him as "you people."

Denzel -- whom I've been told I resemble when the lights are just right (real low) -- then told Couric that the film was nothing but lies and propaganda to support a cynical film director's views.

Man, it was riveting television except for one thing. It never happened.

Couric never asked if Washington had seen the movie. Instead he volunteered "You know, I haven't seen 'Fahrenheit 9/11' because I live in America... I'm an ex-slave. I'm a product of what this country can do. So it's nothing new to me. I'm not surprised at all.

"What I want to talk about is what we're doing right now for these young kids that are coming home."

Somehow, those thoughtful -- REAL! -- comments didn't make it into the jingoistic account.

Expecting Couric to attack a guest for not toeing the liberal line is balderdash, anyway, especially to anyone who saw her interview last week with Michael Moore. She was her usual chirpy self throughout, but did backstands to distance herself from the left-wing moviemaker, lest anyone think she was sympathetic toward him.

For instance, when Moore asked Couric to tell her viewers that he was, deep down, "not a jerk," Couric responded -- with a bit more harshness than necessary given the tone of the interview -- "I don't know you well enough to make that assumption."

When he asked her to hang out with him and find out, she responded that she'd "rather re-arrange my sock drawer."

And this is the woman who attacked Denzel Washington for not spouting the liberal party line?

One person who forwarded me an account of the alleged confrontation even said of Denzel, "Now there's a celebrity that deserves to wear the uniform in movies and I don't mind at all. Everyone else is a hypocrite."

Well, darn, if that's all it takes, perhaps my correspondent will agree to let me wear the uniform, too. After all, I wasn't in the war, but I've watched every episode of "Combat" twice.

ENJOY LEISURE, BIG GUY

Don't do it, Big Guy. That's what I said when word on the street reached me that former Wake County Sheriff John Baker is planning to run again for that office. I hoped that this was just an unfounded rumor.

Alas, when I reached Baker on Monday, he confirmed that he is indeed considering a run for the office he lost in a close race to Donnie Harrison last year.

"It's on my mind, sure," Baker told me. "I've been moving around, making speeches, and people are saying to me, 'You ought to consider running again.' I gave 24 years of my life to Wake County, and I felt I made a contribution. I still feel I have something to offer.

"If the time is not right when I have to make a decision, then I won't run. ... It looks like it's going to be right."

If Baker can predict the future like that, I wish he'd tell me so I can go play the lottery in Georgia and Virginia. Far more likely, Baker, like most politicians, is being swayed by the sweet nothings being whispered by people saying what he wants to hear: Run again.

Don't do it, dude. These people pledging their support -- ask 'em where the heck they were last year, when voter turnout was criminally low and you lost by a narrow margin?

Anyone who has known the adoration of the masses -- Baker has had it as a professional athlete and as a politician -- will have a hard time letting it go or, as Mike Tyson said after a defeat in the boxing ring, "fading off to Bolivia." Rejection by one person can devastate, so imagine how painful rejection by an entire county can be.

As someone who has been rejected by the people -- I received 14 votes when I ran for City Council in Rockingham -- and by hundreds of women individually, I can attest that it hurts, and your first instinct in both instances is to come back and say, "Baby, I'll do better next time."

Baker will be 70 in 2006, and although he swore he's "in the best shape of my life," there must be better ways to spend one's twilight years than trading barbs with Harrison or being attacked by rabid right-wing radio talk show hosts.

I want to see the dude enjoying his retirement without having it marred by what will surely be a nasty campaign. Just as the first one was.

If Sheriff Harrison is doing a bad job, surely there is someone else who can challenge him and drive him and his hunting dogs back to the farm.

If he's doing a good job, then his incumbency is going to make him hard to beat -- especially when turnout among blacks who are urging him to run was abysmal.

Baker said "the margin of the loss" makes him believe "the citizens weren't dissatisfied with me. ... If I'd lost by 10,000 votes, then they're saying to me, 'It's time to go somewhere and sit your [rear end] down.' That didn't happen."

As an experienced pol and athlete, Baker knows that being close counts only in horseshoes, hand grenades and slow dancing.

The Big Guy served Raleigh and the Triangle admirably for two and a half decades; it would be sad to see his memory tarnished with an ill-considered bid to serve it again.

10/14/2003

FALSE NOTE ON THE NET

Relax, Sweet Thang. You know you can't believe everything you read. Or see, either: They doctor those photos to make them show things that aren't true.

Oops, sorry. Y'all caught me in the middle of practicing my defense presentation to Sweet Thang in case she opens up the National Enquirer or some other tabloid and sees the story a reader sent me this week.

Turns out that someone with more time than sense has started a rumor on the Internet (imagine that) alleging that Clay Aiken and Big Papa -- that's what some people (OK, just me) call me -- are lovers.

"Huns, all the details aren't in yet, but it looks as though Clay and Raleigh editor Barry Saunders are a hot couple. Barry is the man who has repeatedly attacked Ruben and his fans in his biased column. An official announcement is coming. Clay is tired of hiding it."

The posting was removed by America Online -- it was deemed libelous -- before the official announcement was made. Darn. I was so looking forward to hearing the sordid details.

This is just further proof that no good deed goes unpunished.

Public service is something I've always aspired to, and it was as a public service to Studdard that I wrote a sensitive column suggesting that the dude lose some weight before he dies of a heart attack at a tragically early age. As too many brothers do.

Then, I wrote months later that the Internet push to help Ruben's debut album outsell Clay's -- with its unseemly element of "We'll show them who's tops" -- was stupid, since the same company owned both artists and would be the main beneficiary of this misplaced racial pride.

Alas, many of you didn't take either suggestion in the altruistic spirit in which both were offered.

"To hell with you, I'm getting my CD" was a common response.

Most were along the lines of "What are you doing ... besides talking out of the side of your neck, you old fool?"

Hey, I'm not that old.

Or, "As an African-American man, you should be ashamed" for saying Ruben needs to lose weight. "You wouldn't want anybody talking about that pit bull you sleep with."

Hold on a minute, now, Dawg. That's a low blow. Talk about me if you

70

want, but leave Sweet Thang out of this.

Both sides are guilty of introducing race into the issue from the beginning, with Clay's supporters claiming Ruben won only because he is black -- yeah, we brothers get breaks for that all the time -- and Ruben's faction claiming that Clay still gets more publicity even though he finished second.

How, I innocently asked, is buying Ruben's CD en masse going to benefit anyone but Ruben and his record company?

I dismissed the woman who first wrote linking Clay and me as a disgruntled mountain climber who didn't like the view from the top of Mount Barrymore.

Just between us, it isn't true. But if Clay and I were, as one chump put it, "an item," I'd tell him to try a new hairstyle.

And eat something.

————————————————————————————————— 1/23/2004

FATHERHOOD MORE THAN JUST A PAYCHECK ├————————

In the end, it's not going to ease the pain in the dude's heart one bit, nor stem the flow of tears he sheds for the dead little boy found stuffed inside a suitcase in the woods.

Naw, finding out that Clarence Wilkerson III is not really his son - make that not really his biological son - won't lessen Clarence Wilkerson Jr.'s emotional devastation or allow him to sleep any more peacefully.

Whatever anger and sense of betrayal Wilkerson feels toward Tracey Gill, who is the young boy's mother and his former lover - or even toward Derrick Glover, the troubled soul suspected of killing CJ - will have to wait. Right now, he's got some grieving to do for his son.

And that, unquestionably, is what the young boy had become. You know the intense debate between pro-lifers and pro-choicers over when human life begins - how some say it's at the moment of conception and others say it's much later, say, after the eyes and fingers and toes have developed?

That's all bull. While people with nothing better to do argue over such philosophical fine points as that, most men know precisely when a boy becomes a son. The moment varies from man to man, but they know in their hearts. Judging by men to whom I've talked over the years, it might be the first time you hold the squirming infant and see a part of yourself reflected in his face and eyes. It could be the first time you change his diaper and don't gag. Or it might even be the first time he makes solid contact with a pitch and the pride in his eyes is exceeded only by that in your heart.

Wilkerson held CJ, changed his diapers and played ball with him just like a father, so don't expect his paternal concern or heartache to dissipate simply because his former girlfriend admitted quite late and only under duress that he wasn't the biological father of the boy to whom he unquestioningly gave his name.

Gill admitted the paternity deception after being confronted by police with the confounding evidence that blood found in her car matched Glover's - but not Wilkerson's offspring.

Doesn't matter, Wilkerson told the cops. That's his young'un, he said, and he vowed that as long as CJ III was missing, CJ Jr. would keep looking. "I'm not trying to be a hero," he told an N&O reporter. "I want CJ. ... That's all I want."

That may not be a hero, but it most definitely is a father, regardless of what blood tests or DNA results say. There is an important distinction between being a father and being a daddy: A daddy is a male who can make a baby - just about any adolescent boy can do that - while a father is someone who can raise a child and supply it with love and discipline.

A buddy of mine told me years ago how, when he was in paternity court disputing that he was a baby's daddy, he'd said, "Judge, that baby don't even look like me."

The judge, unmoved and unconvinced, replied, "He'll look like you if you feed him long enough."

Likewise, if a dude loves a young'un long enough and raises him, then he is his father - regardless of who's the daddy.

———————————————————————————————— 5/12/2000

FEELING TAPPED OUT? IT'S THE 8 GLASSES A DAY ├────

Wow, I could have had a V-8. Or a soda. Or even a beer. Or some collard greens.

Like many people, I was a believer in the maxim that human beings need a minimum of eight glasses of water a day to keep hydrated and healthy, and to keep the skin aglow.

Now, though, like so much of what we were led to believe -- that, for instance, consuming fat makes you fat, or that David Hasselhoff was really a good actor -- we're seeing the water balloon burst too.

A report from the National Academy of Sciences has confirmed what we should have known all along: when it comes to water, we should drink until we're simply no longer thirsty. Forget the "eight glasses."

Not only that, the study said water consumed secondarily -- such as when you eat collard greens or other foods with water in them -- is also helpful. National food surveys cited by the academy say that 20 percent of our necessary fluids come from the foods we eat.

Previous studies have shown the same thing, albeit to a lesser extent. Unlike those, the new study says that all beverages -- including tea, coffee, even alcohol -- contribute toward our daily required intake.

Who hasn't been besieged by guilt because we didn't -- or were unable to -- guzzle our eight glasses of water daily? Who hasn't felt that each teen-aged zit was punishment for drinking too many grape NeHis and not enough H20?

Despite drinking enough water to float the Titanic, the zits that were my constant companion during adolescence usually stayed put, and my teen-aged face usually bore a close resemblance to a pepperoni pizza.

Dr. Jeffrey Scales, a Durham dermatologist, says "Staying hydrated is important, but there is nothing magical about eight glasses of water. Your body knows how much water it needs and how little. When you need water it conserves what you already have, and when you have too much it discards it."

Speaking of discarding, this country's sluggish economy would likely be flush it weren't for the lost productivity caused by workers whose slavish and misguided adherence to drinking eight glasses a day sends them constantly scurrying to the bathroom during working hours.

Just between you and me, it's hard imagining anyone drinking eight glasses of water -- without some Kool-Aid, tea or Jack Daniels added for flavor.

Some folks, though, are so swept away by water as an elixir that, for awhile, drinking it even became a symbol of status or style. During the "designer decade," people walked around conspicuously carrying huge jugs of so-called designer water, as if to snub their well-hydrated noses at the faucet-sipping masses.

Their naive efforts at living a healthy lifestyle were commendable, but I wonder how they feel upon learning that they could have derived the same health benefits from drinking tap water -- or sucking on a collard.

2/14/2004

FIERY WORDS START FIRE

Just from its name, Blacknificent Books doesn't sound like the kind of store where you expect to find books touted by Oprah's book club or the ladies at the North Raleigh tea club.

Neither, though, was I expecting to see a book titled "Nuts Are No Good For You."

This was disappointing not just because it goes against the conventional wisdom of diet and nutrition, but also because I thought I was being health-conscious by munching a fistful of pistachios when I entered the store.

That the first book you see upon entering Blacknificent defies conventional -- some say logical -- thinking isn't surprising. The man who owns the store does, too.

Kamau Kambon, the dreadlocked former teacher at N.C. State University and St. Augustine's College, became a pinup boy for right-wing radio gabbers last week when comments he made earlier hit the Internet.

On the few occasions that I've spoken with Kambon, he was polite, soft-spoken, even serene. Serenity left the building when he spoke Oct. 14 at the Howard University conference on coverage of Hurricane Katrina.

Broadcast on C-SPAN, Kambon said, "We have to exterminate white people off the face of the planet to solve this problem. ... So we just have to just set up our own system and stop playing and get very serious and not be diverted from coming up with a solution to the problem, and the problem on the planet is white people."

Say what? Was this some type of urban legend in response to the furor over equally incendiary comments made by former Education Secretary William Bennett? Bennett, the nation's self-anointed moral mack daddy with a taste for the slot machines, angered some blacks -- while others of us didn't give a rat's toenail about what he said -- when he opined that aborting all black babies would lower the crime rate.

He argued, as those with foot-in-mouth disease always do, that his comments were taken out of context.

I wondered if Kambon would trot out the same defense, although it's hard to imagine a context where either his or Bennett's comment would be acceptable.

I called Kambon before entering the store and asked, "You reckon I could have a few minutes to talk with you, to give your side of the tempest your comments made?"

"No," he said.

"You're kind of the man of the hour" because of the comments, I said. "You wanna explain, clarify or repudiate anything you said?"

"No."

No explanation would've placated the people who called Chris Whirl, a switchboard operator at C-SPAN. "We got a lot of calls Friday and Saturday" after the comments were broadcast, she said.

What, I asked, was the consensus? "They weren't very happy," she said.

Two punks, both of whom were afraid to leave their names, called profanely demanding that I publicly repudiate Kambon's comments. One said I wouldn't because I feared losing my standing and popularity in the black community.

I didn't have a chance to tell the fool that I have no standing or popularity in any community.

After Kambon's comments, it's hard to imagine that he does, either.

10/25/2005

FINALLY, A WORD WITH JESSE

You can say what you want about Jesse Helms, and if it's uncomplimentary, chances are I've already beat you to the punch.

For instance, every time he said something bad about Martin Luther King Jr. -- which was every time he said something about King -- I seethed and wished he was 40 years younger so I could challenge him to a showdown.

But nothing Helms ever did or said angered me as much as what he said Monday: Hello.

Yep, I was ready to rip into the legendary "Senator No" yet again for his parting shot at King -- he said in a recent interview that King caused more harm than any good he ever did, a laughable assertion. I called him up at home to ask what was his main beef with the slain civil rights leader.

Now, I've called Helms' office in Washington probably 100 times over the years and never even got close to talking to him, so I was all ready to write, "The senator couldn't be reached for comment" this time, too.

But he could be reached for comment this time, and comment he did -- graciously and politely.

As for his main stated objection to King, he said, "He had another woman with him when he traveled, and he had a nice lady at home."

He also pointed out that during the civil rights movement, "Many black city officials invited him not to come to their cities because violence followed him everywhere."

The conversation was going so surprisingly smoothly that I didn't have the heart to tell the senator that there weren't "many black city officials" before the civil rights

74

movement. I do know, though, that some blacks didn't welcome King with open arms: either because they were sniveling cowards or because they had a vested, selfish interest in maintaining the status quo, regardless of how unfair it was to most blacks.

After suggesting that we sit down "eye-to-eye and nose-to-nose" and chat someday, Helms delivered yet another low blow, one that I'll have a hard time forgiving him for: He put his wife on the telephone, further disarmingly, and she was as gracious as you can imagine.

I expressed great admiration for her character and patience, since anyone who stays with Jesse for more than 60 years must have an abundance of both.

No matter how much you deplore Jesse's politics, you have to respect him for standing up for his beliefs, for refusing to be swayed by public sentiment. Could you ever imagine Jesse going on BET-- as Trent Lott did after expressing his pre-civil rights-era, nay pre-Civil War-era, sentiments -- and pretty much renouncing everything he once solidly stood for?

Never.

The News & Observer's Rob Christensen wrote an excellent column Sunday in which he noted the similarities between Helms and Furnifold Simmons.

Who?

Precisely. Simmons, once a powerful U.S. senator, was on the wrong side of the racial issue in North Carolina and the country, and he is now a mere historical footnote.

Jesse, despite our pleasant conversation Monday, is destined to end up the same. For the same reason.

1/7/2003

FORGET DURHAM DISSER

Perhaps the dude got a hold of a bad taco. Or maybe Mrs. Dude had a headache that night and sent him off to work ornery.

Those are two possible reasons Michael Skube wrote a poison-computer column in the News & Record of Greensboro disparaging Durham.

Another reason for Skube's gratuitous swipe could be that he wants to draw his News & Observer counterparts -- and former colleagues -- into a bare-knuckle civic brawl.

Sorry, Mikey. I refuse to throw mud in response because, for one thing, I'm saved. Okay, not really, but that's what I told Sweet Thang's mama.

For another, my respect for Greensboro is too great for me to act as though it alone has problems. Which is what Skube -- rhymes with booby -- did to Durham.

If those four A&T students hadn't sat down at that downtown Greensboro lunch counter in 1960, I might still be having my fatback sammitch handed out a window around back of the local Biscuitville.

The worst I'll say about Greensboro is that it was home to my first ex-fiancee and its newspaper is home to a columnist who uses his forum to impute to others his prejudices against Durham.

For instance, who are these people Skube cites, in a story titled "The City

We'd Like to Forget," who are "embarrassed to call Durham one of their own"? He also called Durham the state's "family outcast."

Say, chump. I've got your 'family outcast.' Right here.

Durham has its share of problems and often addresses those problems with veins a'poppin'. That's what makes it fun.

Nobody has been more critical of Durham than I. Who proposed selling tickets to its chaotic school board meetings? Or having a WWF steel-caged Texas Death match between warring council members?

Who offered to buy a one-way bus ticket to anywhere for an incompetent, shady city manager? And who, finally, would do the same thing if Skube agrees to leave? Yep, Skube voluntarily lives in a city he called "dysfunctional and dangerous" and which has, according to him, "cornered the market on crooks as candidates for public office."

Chill, homes. Just about anybody can run for office in America: Besides, none of the tainted candidates you referred to won.

Calls to his home and office were not returned, so I couldn't ask how much it'd cost to send him packing.

I don't know what kind of doobies Skube's smoking to inspire his indefensible blather, but wouldn't you like to have some for your next party?

He attributes his most incendiary blast to some unnamed friend with, he said, "an appreciation for Joseph Conrad" who called the city "Heart of Darkness Durham."

I'm guessing that it is the darkness of Durham's citizenry -- half of which is black and Hispanic -- and not of its heart that causes Skube heartburn. Otherwise, why isn't he attacking other cities in the area whose problems are just as bad and as numerous as Durham's?

You don't have to live in the Bull City to be full of bull, but as Skube showed, neither does living here make you immune to the condition.

Besides, everyone knows that the city North Carolinians are most ashamed of is Charlotte.

11/15/2005

FRANKLIN GRAHAM GOES BACK TO THE WELL

You'd have to flip a coin to tell which is worse -- a daddy who never spoke out against anything or a son who speaks out in ignorance.

I'm talking, of course, about the Rev. Billy Graham and his young 'un, evangelist Franklin Graham.

Once again, young Franklin is in the news for comments about Islam and Muslims. You'll recall that soon after the Sept. 11 terrorist attacks, Graham called Islam a "very evil and wicked religion." He seemed, in subsequent statements, to backtrack a bit, but now he's at it again.

Muslims, he said on a Charlotte radio station earlier this week, have not sufficiently apologized for the attacks, and should help compensate victims' families.

"I'm certainly not preaching against Muslim people," Graham said, as he seemingly preached against Muslim people.

Call me cynical, but I'm guessing that much of Graham's renewed criticism is driven by his desire to sell copies of his book, "The Name." He is -- surprise, surprise -- just finishing up a tour promoting the book; he must know that incendiary comments would garner attention for it.

I'm no theologian, but I'd bet that every religion has its share of wicked and evil people. That, however, doesn't make the religion itself wicked and evil.

It's funny, but I don't remember Franklin or his daddy demanding that, for example, all Christians apologize for the terrorism other Christians inflicted upon blacks during this country's darkest days. Yet that seems precisely what he is asking now of Muslims around the world following the attacks of Sept. 11.

Oy vey.

Funnier still is Graham's indictment of Muslim clerics for not condemning the attacks as vociferously as he thinks they should.

"How come they haven't come to this country, how come they haven't apologized... (and) reassured the American people that this is not true Islam?

"The silence of the clerics around the world is frightening to me," he said.

Frankly, Frank, that's precisely what so many people said about your daddy, who remained mostly silent in the midst of the civil rights, antiwar and women's liberation movements.

When the younger Graham castigates Muslims for not coming to this country and apologizing, doesn't he realize the role he and other Islam-bashers may be playing in their reluctance to do so?

Demonizing their religion is certainly not going to make Muslims rush to these shores, roll up their sleeves and join in rebuilding America. Yet that -- demonizing Islam -- is what Ibraham Hooper, communications director for the Council on American-Islamic Relations, accuses people such as Graham of doing.

"Mainstream political leaders and religious figures must speak out against the growing demonization of Islam by extremist right-wing commentators and by representatives of the evangelical Christian community," Hooper said in a prepared statement.

Faiz Rehman, director of communications for the American Muslim Council in Washington, told me he thinks Graham suffers from "selective hearing. He hears only what he wants to hear. As a Muslim activist, I don't know one Muslim leader in this country who has not condemned the horrific attacks of Sept. 11."

During our telephone conversation, Rehman said of Graham "He's not paying attention. He should talk to some Muslim organizations before he, a responsible religious leader, makes such irresponsible statements. He's not serving his country well."

Probably not, but he's juicing up sales of his book.

8/17/2002

GO EASY IN JUDGING THE JUDGE

Ricky Mardell Sewell, the 19-year-old male -- you can't in good conscience call him a man -- who stood up in court this week and admitted that he had raped a 7-year-old girl, is not the most despised person in the Triangle.

That dubious honor, judging by the word on the street, probably goes to Superior Court Judge Orlando Hudson, who sentenced Sewell to five years' probation.

Or to prosecutor Tracey Cline, who allowed Sewell to plead to a lesser charge. Her answering machine, when I visited her office, was full of calls from people angered both by the plea and the sentence.

Outrageous, right? Another example of a judicial system that doesn't know its habeas from its corpus, huh?

Not so fast, Matlock. Turns out that the case is not as clear cut -- or as much of a judicial travesty -- as televised reports indicate.

Sure, Sewell pleaded guilty to taking indecent liberties with a child and must register as a sex offender. And yes, he stood right up in court and said that he had engaged in anal, oral and vaginal intercourse with the girl.

So why didn't Hudson drop the bomb on Sewell and hand-deliver him to those dudes in prison who love nothing better than getting their hands on pedophiles?

Because, Hudson said, Sewell didn't plead guilty to the more serious charges, and the prosecutor knew she would have had a hard time winning a conviction on them based on the skimpy evidence at hand.

The crime to which Sewell was allowed to plead -- indecent liberties -- is a class F felony, one that the prosecutor knew, Hudson said, had "a strong possibility of a probation-type sentence."

Cline, an aggressive, energetic and able prosecutor, said she argued for an active prison sentence. She contends the victim's family agreed to the plea bargain only to spare the little girl the horror of reliving last year's trauma, experienced when she was left in Sewell's care while her mama went shopping.

Any parent would want to spare her child such trauma, but Hudson isn't buying that as the main reason Cline and the girl's family agreed to the plea bargain.

"They allowed him to plead down because they know they didn't have much, except the allegations made by the girl," Hudson said. "That's why they let him plead down to not just a lesser offense, but to a seriously lesser offense."

Cline, reached in her office Thursday, disagreed. "I never predict what a jury will do," she said, "but I think the evidence was strong."

Sewell's graphic courtroom admission, Hudson said, "was just for the girl's family" and was read because Cline was prepared to nix the plea agreement.

"That's gamesmanship," the judge said. "It's unfair to load up on him with the admission that he raped her and then want me to sentence him for rape when that was not his plea."

Imposing a heavy sentence for a light plea, he said, is "deceptive sentencing. They can't have it both ways."

Whatever. You can waste your anger on the DA or the judge. Me? I know who the real villain is in this sad case. And I'm guessing he'll mess up again before his five years are up.

3/16/2001

GOOD BUSINESS, BAD NEWS

Ted Turner is guilty of sour grapes when he says Fox News helped push the United States into war with Iraq. Turner even called it "Murdoch's War," in honor of Fox owner Rupert Murdoch.

Turner, founder of CNN, used to be the big dog of cable news. Now the self-styled Capt. Outrageous has to sit back and watch Murdoch's network garner all the high ratings -- but not necessarily high accolades -- for its coverage of the war.

Turner, who called Murdoch a "warmonger," is undoubtedly jealous of Murdoch's war-brought success.

But he's also right. Murdoch and his media brethren who love war and the riches war brings to their networks pounded the drums and helped propel the country into war.

Cable news channels must fill their telecasts regardless of whether some washed-up jock is accused of killing his wife.

So, what did Murdoch and the other network owners say when President Bush set his sights on a villain more despised than O.J.?

Saddam, glad to see you.

War is the ultimate reality TV and the perfect antidote to sagging ratings -- featuring, as it does, death, mayhem, explosions and plenty of opportunities to wrap yourself in the flag in between commercials.

Many U.S. media outlets have been guilty of trading in their objectivity for patriotism, but none were as blatant as Fox.

Murdoch, who once acknowledged that he became a U.S. citizen for the tax advantages, is probably no more patriotic than anyone who opposed the war. Backing the war, it seems, was just good business.

Good business can be bad journalism, though. How bad was Fox during the war? This bad: I watched as Shepard Smith -- a supposed Fox news anchor -- interviewed former Republican congressman Newt "Neutron" Gingrich as the invasion began last month and thousands of American citizens showed their displeasure by marching in city streets throughout the country.

Smith, with no attempt to conceal his disdain for the marchers, asked Newt what he thought of people who would march against the war even as U.S. soldiers were putting themselves "in harm's way"?

It was left to Gingrich to give Smith -- who stopped just short of donning a cheerleader's uniform and grabbing some pompoms -- a civics lesson by telling him that, golly gee whiz, even though he disagreed with the marchers' position, it was their right as American citizens to protest if they wanted.

Now, when Newt Gingrich, who once blamed Democrats for the murder of two little boys by their mother, has to impart to you a lesson on the

79

Constitution, you're in trouble.

In 1897, legend has it, artist Frederick Remington cabled his boss, New York Journal publisher William Randolph Hearst, from Cuba and told him there was no war. Hearst is said to have cabled back: "You furnish the pictures. I'll furnish the war."

He set out to do just that by, among other things, claiming with no evidence that Spain had blown up the battleship USS Maine. Voila, we soon had the Spanish-American War.

The media are more sophisticated these days: It appears many of them furnished the pictures -- and the war -- this time around.

———————————————————————————————— 4/29/2003

GRIEF BURDENS SUNSHINE ——————————————————

It wasn't the singing or the bagpipes that did it, although beautiful both were.

Nor was it the lofty words about duty and sacrifice.

The thing that tugged at my heartstrings was the look on the faces of the fallen cops' family members when they emerged from the muted light of St. Michael the Archangel Catholic Church into the sunlight.

The mamas, daddies, wives and children, the brothers and sisters, cousins and nephews of the six officers saluted for making the ultimate personal sacrifice last year were not hard to spot if you looked closely.

They squinted reflexively, as everyone did, but then they -- one and all -- resumed the slow, unsteady walk of the bereaved.

Small children looked uncomfortable in suits on a day better suited for running and laughing. Elderly parents walked a bit more slowly, their backs more bent, than when they'd entered the church for the North Carolina Peace Officers Memorial Day commemoration.

One older lady, escorted by and holding onto the arm of a ramrod-straight state trooper, faltered briefly as she walked past the honor guard of troopers lined up directly outside the church doors. It was hard to tell whether her unsteadiness was caused by the 80-degree-plus heat or her own grief -- until you looked into her face.

Then you knew: It was the grief.

I wanted to ask her to give voice to their sorrow but didn't. Intruding upon her grief at such a moment would have been loutish.

Several months have passed since the honored officers died, long enough for time to ease the pain. If only slightly.

Monday's service trumped time, though, and reawakened anguish. It did mine, and I didn't even know the officers.

Neither did Gale Buck, whose mournfully wailing bagpipes had some inside the church dabbing at their eyes. Buck has played at eight such observances for fallen officers, he said, and the tune that touched so many was an original piece. It's called "Peace Officers' Prayer."

"I wrote it for one of these events," he said. "I do it simply as a tribute to the officers."

As Durham County Sheriff Worth Hill read the names of the fallen officers, an officer solemnly stuck a red rose commemorating each of them onto a large white wreath.

The officers honored Monday were Glenn Harold Hicks of the Avery County Sheriff's Office, Toney Clayton Summey of the Randolph County Sheriff's Office, Anthony Greg Cogdill of the state Highway Patrol, William Franklin James II and Phil Owens, both of the Wake County Sheriff's Office, and John Fitzgerald Strickland of the Harnett County Sheriff's Office.

Cops have a thankless job, and time was -- back when the cops in Rockingham had my telephone number on speed dial even before speed dial was invented -- that I'd have been the last one to thank them.

After considering the sacrifices made by those honored Monday -- and by their families -- let me now be the first.

5/11/2004

HARMONY ISN'T HARD TO FIND

It was a good question, although I'd never heard it put quite that way before.

"Who sucked all the red off your candy?" the woman caller asked earnestly last week. "You sure have been mean lately."

Mean? Me? "Sorry ma'am, you obviously don't know me," I said.

She responded by citing a list of what she called recent negative columns -- about our beloved senior senator, about his prospective replacement Liddy Dole, even about Kweisi Mfume.

Hmmm, maybe she does know me after all.

Anyway, after she hung up I decided to humor her: I went out looking for something positive to write about.

I didn't have to look long. Throughout this past weekend in Cary, Durham and Raleigh, it was hard not to be hit smack dab in the face by sterling examples of the kinds of racial harmony and interaction that we only think we have year-round.

It all started Friday night at the annual Bull Durham Blues Festival, when a racially mixed crowd of thousands gathered to listen to black and white blues performers. (I actually used to doubt that white people could sing the blues. After all, I'd wonder, what y'all got to be blue about? But that was before George W. Bush got elected.)

That was also before I heard Bonnie Raitt and Maria Muldaur. Those women can flat-out sing and bring the pain, honey.

It did my heart good to see people of all races enjoying the same thing, oblivious to anything as superficial as race.

Sure, I thought as I surveyed the frolicsome scene, but this is Durham. People in Durham are a little, hmmm, what's a good word for it -- STRANGE; we have to be, to listen to what others say about our city and still live here. Nothing as groovy as this could ever happen in Cary or Raleigh, I said rather self-righteously to a buddy of mine as we picked our way through the revelers.

But it did, the very next day. In Cary, an annual male rite of passage -- the Hot Hoops 3 on 3 tournament -- was going on, and boys of all ages, shapes and colors were trying to prove their mettle in one of the last proving grounds available to men: basketball.

The mood wasn't nearly as serene and peaceful as in Durham the previous night, but the voices raised in anger were raised about important stuff, such as whether the dude's foot was behind the three-point line when he shot or whether he got fouled when he drove to the basket.

And peace and love reigned in Raleigh on Sunday night when thousands of people gathered at The Alltel Pavilion at Walnut Creek to see a concert by Earth, Wind & Fire.

The group's music was as timeless and enjoyable as ever, but the most smile-inducing part of the evening was the way blacks and whites lounged unselfconsciously and unconcernedly on the grass, allowing themselves to be moved by the music.

It's possible that my thinking was affected by the aroma coming from the funny-smelling cigarettes the two dudes - one black, one white - were sharing a couple of lawn seats over, but late in the evening, under a blanket of stars, I couldn't help but think, "I'll bet even ol' Jesse and Kweisi could get along on a night like this."

Want to tell Barry what you think?

9/11/2001

FASHION FAUX PAS

When I make a fashion faux pas, as I am wont to do - just look at the picture below - the only thing that happens is that my son laughs and says, "Dad, I know you're not going to wear that out in public, are you?"

Benson police are investigating whether Curt Collier of Dunn paid a much higher price for his fashion misstep last week: Some black dudes allegedly beat the crap out of him when he drunkenly wandered into their neighborhood wearing a T-shirt emblazoned with a Confederate flag.

Benson Police Capt. Kenneth Edwards said police didn't know whether the suspects arrested Wednesday - Jimmy Wayne Banks, 23, Bob Junior McArthur, 26, and an unnamed juvenile - would be charged with a hate crime in addition to the assault charges they already face because of conflicting reports from neighbors that they shouted racial epithets at Collier as they beat him.

Banks, who is charged with assault with a deadly weapon - a chair - with intent to kill, is in the Johnston County jail with his bail set at $75,000. McArthur was released after posting $5,000 bail on charges of assault inflicting serious injury.

Edwards said police are seeking at least one other person connected to the attack.

Beating someone because of his color, sexual orientation or attire is despicable, and the cowardly attackers deserve the same punishment they meted out. I'd like to think that if I took a wrong turn and wandered into a trailer park wearing my red, black and green Afrocentric Speedos, that I'd be safely escorted back to my car with a pat on the head and a "Y'all don't come back now, y'hear?"

Even though I'd much rather have hate-crime laws that lower an extra boom on homophobes or racists of any color than not have them, when someone is whaling away on my behind, what they call me in the process is irrelevant; I probably couldn't hear them anyway above my screams.

It seems surreal that somebody could beat the black - or white - off you and that the severity of their punishment depended on whether they called you a bad name while doing it. Does anyone really think that Collier's injuries would hurt any less if the dudes had professed their undying love as they trounced him?

Attorney: Your honor, my clients are not guilty of a hate crime. As they pounded on the plaintiff, they continuously expressed unbridled admiration for his ability to take a punch.

Furthermore, I intend to prove beyond a shadow of a doubt that my clients attacked him because they're merely mean, rotten vermin who would've beat the crap out of anyone who came along.

Don't laugh. If you've spent any time in courtrooms, you've heard attorneys put forth even more outlandish suppositions than that.

It's not hard to imagine some creative attorney arguing that the defendants attacked Collier not because of racism or because he wore a shirt with a Confederate flag, but because they considered themselves the public housing fashion police and were making a citizen's arrest.

"Yup, they beat him," an attorney might say, "because they were offended that he was wearing white after Labor Day."

9/29/2000

HE HAS 'HEART TO DO RIGHT'

Alisa Smith thought she was just making small-talk with the vanload of privileged 9-year-olds, her daughter's classmates at Durham Academy, she was ferrying in her carpool one day.

To her question "What do your parents do?" she heard replies of surgeon, lawyer, teacher and various other professions.

When Antoine Hunt's turn came, his reply befuddled her. "My mama's dead, and my daddy's at the courthouse," he said bluntly.

"Oh, he's a judge?" Smith asked, not getting the picture.

No.

"A lawyer?"

No.

When she glanced in the mirror she saw her embarrassed daughter, Lizzie, frantically giving her the "CUT!" sign, pleading with her to change the line of questioning.

That's when she learned that Hunt 's dad, Charlie Lamont Jones Jr., was an involuntary guest at the courthouse, in jail.

Jones spent a lot of his life in jail -- "He wasn't a bad man; he just had a severe drug problem," Smith said -- and he died there: He hanged himself June 12, 2002, leaving his son to be raised by his grandmother, Gwen Hunt, in the sometimes unforgiving Few Gardens housing development.

"Antoine has had more death in his life than anyone I've ever known to be just 18 years old ... He called me one day, very upset, and asked me to come and get

him. A 15-year-old had shot a 16-year-old near where he lived. When I got there, the body was still there."

Coming from such a place, you could understand if Hunt had been content just to run out the clock in time-honored fashion -- blaming life's bum circumstances for his fate -- and adopt a popular but self-defeating "what the heck, I just can't win" attitude toward life.

Lots of people, facing fewer obstacles than Hunt -- whose mother died in a car crash when he was 1 -- have become bitter, destructive, self-destructive. But not Hunt.

He got into Durham Academy after Durham dentist Curtis Bowen recommended him for a scholarship. It was a struggle culturally, financially and academically -- "Nobody at Durham Academy knows what this kid was overcoming just to go to school," Smith said -- but last year he graduated from Christ School, a private institution in Arden.

He is enrolled in college -- pretty much on credit -- and Smith is trying to help raise money to keep him there. As she explained it to me, the president of Georgetown College in Georgetown, Ky., has assured her that, with various grants and scholarships, Hunt 's college education can be assured -- if he can keep up his grades and pay half of this first year's tuition. That's $14,000.

When I asked Smith what made her and her family seemingly adopt the boy, she recalled a comment by her own adopted brother. "'Antoine,' he said, 'has a heart to do right.' He's just eminently lovable."

That may be why so many people have become guardian angels to shepherd him .

He needs more help to clear this latest hurdle. If you want to contribute to the fund to help Hunt stay in school, and to become a role model for other kids stuck in similar seemingly hopeless situations, you can make a donation at any Central Carolina Bank.

———————————————————————————————— 8/26/2003

HELP OUT ONE LAST TIME ——————————————————————

If you were one of those Raleigh residents angered by Johnnie Miller's presence, incited to rancor by his very existence, please chill.

Miller was Raleigh's, perhaps North Carolina's, most talked-about bum since Otis Campbell wandered Mayberry's streets on a cow. But he died Wednesday at Rex Healthcare. He was 50.

In case you've forgotten, Miller was the homeless beggar whose daily pleas for money at the off-ramp near Crabtree Valley Mall in the mid-'90s had Raleigh radio listeners split between those who wanted to turn him into roadkill or deify him as his own man, one who lived by his own standards. If, that is, you can call humming and bumming spare change from strangers living.

Dudes begging for spare change at highway off-ramps are a dime a dozen and generally make no impression on the people who simultaneously see and yet don't see them. Miller's notoriety came when he became fodder for a local radio talk show host and his outraged callers.

For weeks, Miller provided a hot-button topic for conservative talk-show host

Tom Joyner and his listeners on radio station WPTF, even though Miller was incidental to the seldom-mentioned real issues -- poverty, welfare, laziness and whether we really are our brother's keeper.

Miller even became a figure of mythology, as some callers to the station and to me stated authoritatively that he earned $40,000 a year and lived a comfortable middle-class life -- a caller once said she knew someone who lived next to him in a nice North Raleigh neighborhood -- or that they'd seen him dash into a nearby service station wearing a suit and emerge moments later in his bumming attire.

Superbum, eh?

There was, alas, nothing super about Miller. Unless you count his ability to rile people.

"My brother was a good boy," his brother, Joe, told me Thursday, "but he sure could aggravate you to death."

After being the subject of often-rancorous debate on the radio station for weeks, Johnnie Miller apparently decided to aggravate the callers and the conservative host.

He called in to defend himself and his refusal to accept a job that wasn't just right for him. (Potential employers called in, making offers.)

He sidestepped the city's anti-panhandling laws -- by operating, meticulously, on property owned by the state instead of the city -- as adroitly as he sidestepped cars driven by angry motorists who tried to run him over. Then-City Council member Paul Coble, in whose district Miller had set up shop, complained that Miller was "flaunting" his ability to avoid panhandling ordinances.

Beggars don't have burial plans, and Bruce Lightner of Lightner Funeral Home is trying to raise enough money to bury him in a manner as dignified as the way he lived. No, make that more dignified than the way he lived.

If you want to make sure someone's burial is more dignified than his life, send contributions to the Community Burial Fund, P.O. Box 27462, Raleigh, 27611. Anything raised beyond what's needed for Miller's burial, Lightner said, will be used to help pay for services for other indigent people.

In addition to helping to bury him, it would be nice to remember Johnnie with a horn toot the next time you drive past his favorite off-ramp.

8/27/2004

HER SAD, FINAL MISSION FOR A GRANDSON

Dontravius Jones died Saturday lying in his grandmother's lap. He was 9.

Oh, the medical examiner's report will show that he was pronounced dead at WakeMed, and that is indeed where his heart stopped beating for the final time.

But if you ask Mary Jones, his grandmother, he really died in her lap about an hour before that.

"I had just given him his medication. He came and sat up in my lap, looked up at me and smiled, then he tilted over," Jones told me Thursday.

She thought Dontravius was merely tired. He had every right to be. I mean, the frail little kid had undergone hip surgery about 10 days before and was no doubt exhausted from dragging around the metal braces he had to wear on his legs after that.

Upon realizing her grandson wasn't breathing, she called paramedics. They arrived within minutes, got his heart beating again and transported him to

WakeMed. Dontravius, a fourth-grader at Creech Road Elementary School in Raleigh, never regained consciousness. The exact cause of death wasn't immediately available.

Grandmothers, some of us feel, are the best thing ever invented, and his grandmother's lap was Dontravius' favorite nesting place. It was the one place, it seems, where he was assured warmth and security in a life in which he was seemingly shortchanged of both. Thus, it's better for all who knew him to think of him taking his last breath there instead of in a cold, impersonal hospital emergency room.

Life was not easy for Dontravius, a frail boy afflicted with brain damage from birth. His mother, who, Mary Jones said, "didn't come around much," suffered from spinal meningitis during her pregnancy, and Jones thinks that condition contributed to Dontravius' infirmities.

Taking care of Dontravius with his myriad disabilities was tough for Jones. For instance, she ruefully recounted years-long -- and vain -- efforts to get oxygen tanks to alleviate his asthma.

That, alas, was impossible with limited resources and no insurance.

So she is burying him. A funeral for the boy who liked to be read to is scheduled for 2 p.m. Sunday at Mount Pleasant Worship and Outreach Center on Sawyer Road in Raleigh.

That's where they'll be if the family can find the money. Right now it's a struggle. Bruce Lightner of Lightner Funeral Home said the family needs $3,100 just for the cemetery plot, casket and embalming. "We're not profiting at all from this," Lightner said.

Still, $3,100 for someone of Mary Jones' limited means might as well be $31 million.

A couple of community groups, including the Martin Luther King Jr. Committee -- led by Lightner -- are trying to raise money for the funeral, but they could sure use your help.

People around here are famous for their generosity to neighbors in need. What need can be greater than helping a family say a dignified "farewell" to a 9-year-old whose life was hard?

If you want to help, make checks payable to the Dontravius Jones Burial Fund, c/o Passage Home, P.O. Box 28696, Raleigh, N.C. 27611. Happy holidays.

12/8/2000

HIGH TIMES IN CHATHAM COUNTY

The question Chatham County sheriff's deputies must be sick of hearing is not, "How do you lose 5,000 pounds of pot?"

No, the question I'm sure they're sick of hearing is, "Hey, dude, where's the party?"

Chatham County is no Sodom of the South, but once the story makes the rounds that 2 1/2 tons of pot went poof right under cops' noses, it could become the destination of choice for anyone looking for a high old time.

If you're not familiar with the baffling case, the pot disappeared -- or, more precisely, was discovered missing -- from law enforcement custody on Sept. 28. On Sept. 29, every pack of Doritos, Krispy Kreme doughnuts and Ding Dongs -- stuff you eat when you get the munchies -- disappeared from the county, too.

Sheriff Ike Gray resolutely maintains that none of his deputies is responsible for the missing marijuana, and I believe him. But if any of his deputies is helping to dispose of the wacky weed in an unapproved manner, that would make routine law enforcement matters quite interesting.

Deputy: Wha's hap'nin', baby? Say, Homey, do you know how fast you were goin'?

Driver: No, deputy.

Deputy: Me, neither. Ha, ha. Now, sir, I'm going to ask you an important question, and I want you to be honest with me: Are you gonna eat those Pringles there on the front seat? I've got a case of the munchies you wouldn't believe.

Or ...

Deputy: Sir, I noticed you weaving a bit back there. Would you step out of the car and blow into this Breathalyzer?

Driver: Sure, deputy. I was ... Hey, wait a minute. That's not a Breathalyzer. That's a ...

Deputy: Oops, wrong pipe. You can go.

If Sheriff Gray is serious about solving the case of the purloined pot, he might want to watch out for telltale signs of marijuana use. Here are a few subtle signs that deputies might be smoking more than Marlboros:

- If they begin engaging in prolonged, intense debates over the nutritional merits of powdered doughnuts vs. the pink ones with the little sprinkly things.

- If kids come home from school marveling that "Officer Friendly was a lot friendlier than usual."

- When officers start wearing their "Puff Daddy was framed" T-shirts over their uniforms.

Lots of people are criticizing the sheriff's department for keeping the pot in an unsecured truck, and then dropping it in an unsecured hole, instead of burning it as soon as it was logged in as evidence.

Not me. I'm glad they didn't burn it. We all know people who've gotten a buzz merely from being in the same room with friends who were toking up; can you imagine what effect 5,000 pounds of pot wafting through the air would have on the citizenry of a county that doesn't even have a liquor store?

Burn that much wildwood weed, Hoss, and Chatham County instantly replaces Mount Mitchell in Yancey County as the highest spot in the state.

After hearing about what went down in Chatham County, I don't feel so bad about spending 20 minutes each morning looking for my car keys. I figure it's easier to lose car keys than 5,000 pounds of pot and two suspected drug dealers.

3/20/2001

HONOR FOR A LIFE WELL-LIVED

Perhaps that adage is true: It's not how long you live, but how well.

Otherwise, why are people still gushing over a kid who barely made it out of high school before dying of cancer nearly 40 years ago?

"Gushing" is the only way to describe what happens when anyone who saw him play football for Ligon High School in Raleigh talks about Willie "Pat" White, the star athlete who took ill the night of his high school's graduation ceremony in 1964.

He was spirited to the hospital, where X-rays revealed that White, 19, was gravely ill. Doctors gave him three to five days to live.

Typically for him, said his sister, Adline Keith, he fought the virulent cancer and lasted three weeks. Newspaper accounts from the period note that more than 2,000 people braved the rain for his funeral.

"He never complained once" before the advanced cancer was diagnosed, Keith said, sitting in the living room of her Chavis Heights apartment. "The most he would say was, 'Sis, I have a stomachache. Do you have anything I can take?' "

White excelled at all things athletic, but it was because of football that his mom's apartment was bombarded with scholarship offers -- many from faraway universities.

He spurned the bigger schools and had accepted a scholarship to Morgan State University in Baltimore when he died.

For Carol Gartrell, a guidance counselor at Leesville Road High School and White's former high school sweetie pie, it's painful to talk about the tragic end of such a promising life.

"I marvel at how he could have been so sick and achieved what he did athletically," Gartrell said. "The only thing I ever heard him complain about was that he was getting out of shape. He was extremely conscientious, so he just got up earlier and ran harder."

Alas, he couldn't outrun the cancer that snuffed out his life.

Dr. W.F. Clark, quoted in The Carolinian newspaper a day after his patient's death, said, "White played with cancer all last season and perhaps longer. ... He was an amazing young man. He never complained once."

His refusal to complain, along with his humility, are common threads running through every conversation about Pat White. Thus, it's unlikely he would mind there being no memorial to his athletic prowess.

Some friends and family members mind, though, and are trying to rectify what they consider a historical oversight.

Bruce Lightner, a childhood friend and former teammate, is helping the family raise money for a memorial to replace White's nondescript headstone at Hillcrest Cemetery.

Any money beyond the amount needed for the memorial, Lightner said, would go to a burial fund for the indigent in Wake County. Ralph Campbell, the state's bulldog of an auditor -- and the team statistician when White starred -- will see to that, he said. Contributions may be made to the Pat White Memorial Fund, Mechanics & Farmers Bank, P.O. Box 28696, Raleigh, NC 27611.

I read that when Ernie Davis, the all-America football player from Syracuse University, died of leukemia at 23 -- before ever playing in a pro game -- someone asked his best friend, "What was it like watching a great young athlete die?" The friend replied, "I don't know. I was too busy watching him live."

Pat White's friends would say the same thing.

5/30/2003

HOW COULD A DADDY ALLOW IT

As Howard Hunichen settles into his new digs at Central Prison, preparing, presumably, to preach his peculiar brand of salvation to other guests of the state's penal system, I'd like to suggest a couple of cellmates for him.

Those would be the parents of Zachary Fortner, the little baby Hunichen abused and left mentally and physically disabled.

Lisa and Kevin Fortner indeed still face child-abuse charges, but they'll likely skate because they testified in court against "Brother Howie."

That's cool. No judge could sentence them to a worse prison than they've sentenced themselves to, a prison in which the door'll shut a little tighter each time they hear babies crying or see children running and laughing - all the things Zachary won't get to do.

Religion gets a bad enough name already, and many good ministers have to battle cynics and negative stereotypes to do what they see as God's will.

Testimony portraying Hunichen as a jackleg Svengali who had the Fortners under his spell won't make easier the task of legitimate men and women of God who counsel people in need.

Of course, any parents whose minister counsels them to stomp or whup their infants so they won't become "mama's boys" should either break his neck or their own getting away from him.

You might've seen, on the evening news one night last week, the baby's daddy testify how he gradually ceded his parental duty to Hunichen, and how last April he saw Hunichen emerge from a back room dangling his 7-month-old son by one leg, and how at various times he stood by as Hunichen stomped the infant during sadistic attempts to make him crawl, walk or hush.

"I felt helpless, I felt powerless ... like a shell of a man," he testified.

You got that right.

Help me out here: What kind of daddy sits back while some cut-rate Elmer Gantry fractures his baby's body and mind?

If I sound as though I lack sympathy for the Fortners, that's only because I do. My real sympathy is for Baby Zachary who - if doctors are correct - will never completely shake the cobwebs from his brain or run and jump and play like other kids, so devastating was the neurological damage inflicted by Hunichen. With his parents' acquiescence.

Me? I'd love to visit Brother Howie in the cell he'll call home for the next six years - 4 1/2 if he's good - and discuss his wacky child-rearing philosophy.

But even more than probing Hunichen's psyche - or his skull with a baseball bat - I'd love to know how Kevin Fortner sat idly by as some fool convinced him

his child - an infant, remember - was "lazy" and a "crybaby."

Isn't there an instinct, a primal instinct, that's supposed to kick in when your young'uns are in danger? Isn't that what makes eagles attack when you get too close to their nest? That instinct, sadly, was somehow short-circuited in the Fortners.

Maybe Kevin Fortner doesn't deserve jail time, but I hope every day, every hour of his life he hears a tiny voice saying, "Daddy, how could you let him do this to me?"

———————————————————————————————— 1/24/2000

I'M EDGY ABOUT JESUS AND VEGETARIANS ⊢————————————

Earlier this year, two books came out hinting or declaring that Abraham Lincoln was gay.

My response? Big deal. The claim, whether true or not, neither increases nor diminishes Lincoln's historical significance.

Human nature dictates that we all seek to identify with greatness, and it's not hard to understand why some gay people might seek to claim the 16th president as one of their own. The reasoning apparently goes that if a great man like Lincoln was gay, then perhaps rabid homophobes will ease up on their persecution of other gays and say "Y'all ain't so bad, after all. Let's go drank a cold one, hoss."

One group, though, has gone too far in trying to claim the ultimate historical ally - Jesus - to their struggle.

I recently received a tract asking the question "Was Jesus a vegetarian?" That question - and the hypotheses backing it up - are being floated by People for the Ethical Treatment of Animals. What, you were expecting Burger King or KFC?

In addition to the tract, PETA has a website - www.Jesusveg.com: now really, could I make that up? - with a picture of somebody who's supposed to be Jesus sporting a halo that doubles as a slice of an orange. On the website you can find supposed scriptural support for PETA's meatless thesis as well as mouth-watering veggie recipes.

The PETA people quote Isaiah 11, which states that, in the last days, "the lion and the lamb shall lie down together." (Yes, but according to Woody Allen only the lion will get up.)

I'm no biblical scholar, but I remember reading something about Jesus with some loaves and fishes. PETA, conveniently, doesn't mention that anywhere in its tract.

I used to wonder about the so-called great ancient philosophers who sat around pondering such profound issues as "How many angels can fit on the head of a pin?" Sheesh, you'd think that people living in a period with no indoor plumbing or cable TV could think weightier thoughts than that.

But at least they weren't trying to push an agenda, as PETA is. My problem with PETA is not that they have an agenda - which seems to include everybody eating tofu burgers and black bean burritos - nor is it that they are engaging in unprovable speculation.

No, my problem is that PETA is unwilling to consider anyone else's views. For all we know, the key to spiritual enlightenment could well be found in that third

Big Mac I had for lunch.

Just as reprehensibly as attempting to co-opt Jesus to their side, the folks at PETA are seeking to wrap themselves in the moral cloak of the anti-slavery movement and the anti-Nazi struggle in France during World War II. In what may be a lame attempt to justify extremism by the Animal Liberation Front, PETA said on the web, "The Underground Railroad and the French Resistance are both examples of people breaking the law to answer to a higher moral authority."

What bull. I respect PETA's efforts to end the gratuitous barbarism of the meat and fur industries and to call attention to the unnecessarily cruel testing on animals. I respect people who choose not to eat meat, whether they do it for philosophical or health reasons. But PETA's zealotry and self-righteousness is enough to make a dude want to rush out and eat a pork chop sandwich just for spite.

I recall a country music song, the refrain of which was sung by a group of winos who'd just scored a bottle of grape, went:

Will they have Mogen David in Heaven?

Dear Lord, we'd all like to know.

Will they have Mogen David in Heaven, sweet Jesus?

If they don't, who the hell wants to go?

Sorry PETA, but I feel the same way about bacon.

9/18/10

IN A CRISIS, PRIVATE ENTERPRISE OFFERS AMERICA TRUE GRITS

The Bush administration may at last be doing something to help small business.

Thanks to its ineptitude in rescuing and serving residents of the Gulf Coast following Hurricane Katrina, companies pledging to do what the government couldn't do -- or wouldn't -- seem to be thriving.

Bodies were still floating in the fetid waters of New Orleans and people were still waving "Help Me" signs made of sheets and awaiting government help when I received an automated telephone call from one such company.

Yet Steve Schenk, director of JMS -- the J. Michael Stevens Group -- insists that the company's current boom is not directly related to people's fears of Hurricane Katrina. "We've seen a huge spike in business in the past two weeks," he said when I called him Friday. "Not because of the storm, but because of government's response to the storm.

"People saw the fiasco created by the system, where instead of being a relief organization, the government became a police organization. That makes people see they are on their own and can't depend on support from

91

government. Food is the only way they can be sure."

Fears tend to become exaggerated late at night, so I had dialed the toll-free number left by the phone message, hoping to get the kid and me some of those grits, powdered eggs and meat substitutes that would survive a nuclear holocaust.

Schenk sent me printed material and a cassette tape stressing, among other things, the need for "liberty through self-reliance."

It was a concept I'd never considered: freedom through grits.

Remember after 9/11 and Y2K, when doomsayers were selling everything from gas masks to protect us from chemical attacks to parachutes to help us glide unharmed from bombed skyscrapers?

People who believe that government is incapable or unwilling to take care of it citizens in a disaster say such enterprises are just fulfilling a need.

Those who think the fears and governmental haplessness are overstated accuse them of exploiting our fears.

Such fears are not new. Thirty five years before JMS told me that "food is the ultimate medium of exchange" -- in other words, better than money -- our neighborhood grocer in Rockingham and Baptist church deacon, Mr. King, said the same thing.

Even though some days I can't even remember my computer password, I still remember him solemnly telling me that the day would come when grocery stores would be guarded like banks because we would run out of food and people would resort to any means to get it.

Being an ill-informed adolescent who'd never experienced a natural disaster, I took his warning of a coming food Armageddon to mean I should stock up: I think I purchased three packs of Now & Laters instead of two.

Schenk, of JMS, said lots of people still think that way despite the chaos along the Gulf Coast.

"The time right after a disaster is a total waste of time to even bring up the subject" of preparing for the next one, Schenk told me. "People have a tendency after they're hit to spend their time reacting to the disaster. They don't prepare."

But, "Most people who are politically and scripturally aware have already had an awakening that a lot of the stuff they feared and expected is coming to fruition. Those people prepare prior to" a disaster, he said.

I didn't order anything from JMS, but the next time I go to the grocery store, I plan to buy an extra bag of grits.

9/24/2005

...and the horse you rode in on, Saunders!

IN A DESPERATE NEW ORLEANS, THE INSTINCT TO SURVIVE

On the night of April 4, 1968, my next-door neighbor in Washington, D.C., Tyrone Taylor, was returning home from karate class. He got caught in the middle of the conflagration that erupted when Dr. Martin Luther King Jr. was assassinated.

The Taylors were one of the nicest, most honest families imaginable, so it was no surprise that they stayed at home when many in the city went out and, in an orgy of anger-abetted opportunity, burned and looted stores throughout the city.

Tyrone didn't burn anything, but as he explained to me later, he grabbed an iron through a broken store window and took it home.

I haven't seen Tyrone in more than 20 years, but wherever he is, I know he still regrets that decision.

His father, Big Percy, beat him so bad that a similar assault today would no doubt net the old man some jail time. Back then, though, it wasn't considered child abuse; it was called parenting.

As adolescent boys are wont to do, we joked afterwards that Big Percy was most angry that his son got only an iron; anyone who knew him, though, knew that his response was based on his belief that stealing is wrong.

Mr. Percy, the Taylors and civil disorder have been on my mind a lot lately while watching the deteriorating situation in New Orleans, where people have been grabbing things they need for survival and things they simply want. Even if they were so inclined, they'd be unable to pay for them, since there were no working clerks or cash registers to take their money.

Mr. Percy died a couple of decades ago, but I can't help wondering what he'd say about the people who grab food and clothing from waterlogged stores in New Orleans.

For instance, is it stealing when a man wades into a drug store and grabs insulin for his diabetes, as has reportedly happened? What about when a desperate man grabs some soggy hot dog buns and semi-edible meat from a grocery store to feed his starving family?

That is not the same as grabbing some superfluous item such as an iron, and I think Mr. Percy would be more concerned with the survival of those residents than with whether what they're doing can be considered looting.

Our president, on the other hand, is showing far more concern for property than for human beings. He echoes the Republican mantra about "law and order" and says insurance fraud won't be tolerated.

Insurance fraud?

Man, you've got people lying dead in American streets, a major American city obliterated, and you're talking about insurance fraud?

Oy.

Aside from complaints about looting, the most common one I've heard is that the residents of New Orleans are being impatient.

"Why are they chanting 'We want help. We want help'?" one caller asked me.

The president, he said, went on the air and assured them that help is on the way and the situation is under control.

I didn't have a chance to tell the caller that most of the people he labeled impatient didn't have access to a television set to hear their president. Even if they had heard his assurances, they might have compared them to similar ones he's made about the war in Iraq -- where the situation, despite two years of promises, most definitely is not under control.

That would have only made them angrier.

9/3/2005

IN THE EYE OF THE BEHOLDER

Man, I sure wouldn't want to be gay right about now.

Never mind that this would seem to be a good time to emerge from the closet and openly profess one's orientation, if that was it. Among other things, gay TV characters have become popular, and the Supreme Court recently ruled that gays are entitled to the same right to privacy as anyone else.

So what's the problem, yo? The pressure, that's what. Judging by such shows as "Boy Meets Boy," "Will & Grace" and "Queer Eye for the Straight Guy," gays are immaculately attired, fabulously hip and look as if they just stepped out of GQ magazine or a cognac ad.

In case you haven't seen "Queer Eye," it involves five trendy gay dudes with impeccable taste in fashion, furnishing and decorating who each week undertake a project -- a style-retarded heterosexual guy -- and remake him, at the urging of his despairing lady.

There is, at the end of each show, a noticeable improvement in the straight slug's appearance. So far, no one has been transformed into a Denzel or Brad Pitt, but after the makeover, no one thinks any longer that putting on a new John Deere cap and pressing his dungarees constitutes dressing up for the evening, either.

"Queer Eye" blatantly disparages straight men by implying that we all lack style. But it's equally unfair to gays by implying that they are imbued with a style gene. What if you're gay and lack style, class or fashion sense, as many straight men do?

Thanks to the unreal reality show, there is no room at the inn for such a person.

I don't know about you, but it'd drive me batty having to wonder, each time I left home, if the cuffs of my flat-front, Italian gabardine trousers break precisely one-quarter inch above the top of my shoes. Or if I ordered the appropriate wine with my stuffed duck.

Anything that contributes to the male aesthetic should be encouraged -- for instance, when I'm president, I'll forbid men to wear fanny packs -- but that is too heavy a burden to be borne by one group alone.

I'm guessing that gay slobs who want to lie around on their sofa watching football, eating pizza and drinking wine from a box feel pressure to project an urbane image more in keeping with the "Queer Eye" aesthetic.

Even Barney Frank, the gay congressman from Massachusetts, sees danger in "Eye." He said in Newsweek last week that "the notion that gay men have a superior fashion sense is not true, and it's damaging."

Ian Palmquist, a representative with the gay advocacy group Equality North Carolina, thinks ol' Barn should chill. "I think the show is all in good fun," he said. "There are different parts of our community. If some of the images represent stereotypes that people have, there are enough other images to counteract them."

But Keith Hayes, spokesman for NC Pride, would prefer to ditch the stereotypes altogether, even if those conveyed by the show are reasonably positive.

"Twenty years ago," he said, "the stereotype was a flamboyant, limp-wristed, promiscuous hairdresser. 'Queer Eye' is trading on a kinder stereotype, but one of the reasons I'm involved in Pride is to get across the notion that there's no typical gay male."

9/19/2003

INJUSTICE DESERVES JAIL, TOO

So, you still think the state ought to continue sentencing people to death, even after the disgraceful prosecution -- and tepid punishment of that disgraceful prosecution -- of Alan Gell?

Gell had one foot in the death chamber and the other on a banana peel, thanks to overzealous prosecution and possible misconduct by former prosecutors David Hoke and Debra Graves.

You can buy their argument -- as the State Bar did last week when it merely reprimanded them -- that their failure to play by the rules was an honest mistake. I don't.

How do you honestly overlook and fail to turn in evidence that proves the suspect was in jail when the murder occurred? Hoke admitted that he had evidence that might help Gell in his office for two years before the trial began. He never turned it over, as the law requires.

It's nothing to put on a resume, but I have been locked up four times. Believe it or not, I was innocent each time. Don't look at me like that: The statute of limitations has expired, and I can afford to tell the truth.

Three of those times, it's conceivable that the law actually thought I was guilty. On one occasion, though, I sat in court and listened as one of Atlanta's finest and a prosecutor lied.

Fortunately for me, mine was not a life-or-death case, but trust me: You have not known helplessness until you've been in that situation with your freedom on the line.

Some people will argue that Gell's exoneration, after nine years in prison, half of them on death row, is proof that the system works and that innocent people are not executed.

What a crock. Prosecutors, many of whom have designs on political office, know that no one around these here parts has ever lost an election because he executed too many people. Gell, it appears, was about to be a pelt in their belts.

If I ruled the world, there'd be a network that aired "Sanford & Son" 24 hours a day, grits would be the state food, and Hoke and Graves would be behind bars, slurping runny grits and fighting off the romantic overtures of

95

cellmates named Roughhouse and Big Bertha, respectively.

Attorney General Roy Cooper deserves punishment, too -- maybe not a shared cell, but something, for subjecting Gell to another trial and keeping him locked up an extra year and a half even after his innocence became clear.

Superior Court Judge Erwin Spainhour of Cabarrus County testified during the bar hearing that he was "appalled" that Hoke was subjected to a hearing. Funny, but he expressed no similar outrage for what Gell was subjected to.

Say, judge, I'm guessing that whatever the discredited duo experienced during their two-day lovefest of a hearing didn't come close to what Gell experienced during more than 3,000 days in prison.

I don't know about you, but my heart aches for Gell, Darryl Hunt and those still locked up for crimes they didn't commit -- especially when corner-cutting prosecutors view the law as a game to be won by any means necessary.

If you don't think innocent people go to prison or get executed, you'd better wake up and smell the daisies -- before even more innocent people are planted beneath them.

9/28/2004

INNOCENT OUTING TURNS TRAUMATIC

You'd think that going to the store with your mamma would, temporarily at least, stop the cops from considering you a "prime suspect."

Think again. Despite being with his mamma earlier this month, 14-year-old Shawn Robinson of Chapel Hill found himself handcuffed and kissing the cold pavement after some gun-waving dude - much later identified as a plainclothes cop - chased him out of the store where his mamma was paying for gas and he was trying to buy some of his beloved Hot Fries.

"I told him to go to the car to see if his sister wanted anything," Shawn's mother, Diane Edwards, recounted, "and the next thing I know he's running past me screaming 'Diane, Diane, a man's robbing the store.'"

"I liked to have had three heart attacks," Edwards recalled of the incident at the Texaco Zip Mart at Hope Valley and Garrett roads. "I saw a man with a big gun run past me. ... My son ran through the side door and shattered it."

The sight that greeted Edwards outside nearly made her keel over. The man and a uniformed police officer had her young 'un on the ground, handcuffed, with guns pressed to his head.

"That's just my 14-year-old son," she screamed frantically, prompting the man with the gun to pull back his shirt, reveal a badge and identify himself as a cop.

She recalls that the officers then indelicately snatched up her son and yanked him into the store.

"Ma'am, is this the man who was robbing you?" Edwards recalls the cop asking the clerk, who spoke halting English.

" 'No, no, no,' " Edwards says the clerk told police, he was a customer, not a robber.

So, what happened to turn a kid's outing with his mother - they'd come to

Durham to pick his 7-year-old sister up from church - into a terrifying episode of "The Twilight Zone"?

Apparently this: The clerk accidentally and unwittingly set off the robbery-in-progress alarm, which was heard by the Rambo-esque cop and some uniformed colleagues who were greasing at a nearby McDonald's restaurant.

After that harrowing experience, Edwards, who works five jobs a week - yeah, that's right - to raise her three children, recalled only a perfunctory apology. She questioned the sincerity of that apology when the cop added repeatedly, " 'I'd do it the same way if I had it to do all over again.' He just kept saying that."

That arrogance angered Edwards, who is now demanding a formal apology. Only problem is, there doesn't appear to be a police report of the incident.

Capt. Dwight Pettiford, a police spokesman, said there was no official report because Edwards hadn't filed a complaint, and Edwards said she was told she'd need a report to file one.

Pettiford called the incident as related to him "troubling," but he said he wanted to wait to hear the officer's version. The officer didn't return several messages left for him last week by a reporter.

After the incident, 14-year-old Shawn Robinson has understandably developed an aversion to Hot Fries. I only hope the recklessness of one cop doesn't cause him to develop a similar aversion to police officers.

3/25/1999

INNOCENT'S DEATH WAS UNDESERVED

Boy, talk about a tough crowd.

As soon as I heard the heart-breaking story of a beautiful 16-year-old high school honor student being shot in the head while riding in a car 11 days ago, I knew I'd be deluged with calls from people distraught and angered by the senseless violence, by the death of one so full of promise.

Fuhgeddaboutit. Oh, I got lots of calls about the incident in Selma in which some creeps with more ammo than brains pulled up behind the car carrying Seleana Nesbitt and three friends, and fired, killing Seleana and injuring her 15-year-old friend. But not one caller expressed the expected sympathy. Not one.

There was outrage up the wazoo, but it, incredibly, was directed at the victims. Or at their parents.

"What was she doing out at 4 in the morning?" was a typical query, as though anything that happens after a certain hour is your own fault. Or, "Why would her parents let her go out at that time of night with grown men?"

Stephen Potts, Seleana's stepfather, has heard those questions, too, and when I asked him about them, he was forthright and a lot nicer than I had any right to expect.

"She wasn't dating a 23-year-old," Potts told me. "She had been waiting for her ride at the club, and it didn't show up."

Indeed, it's been a while since I've dated, singly or doubly, but I don't recall the girls sitting in the back seat and the guys in the front, as was the case when

Seleana was killed and Brandy Smith was wounded in 23-year-old Gregory Lamont Brooks' car.

"We know Greg; he is cool with me," Potts said. "Everyone needs to step into reality. Everybody was young at one time .... Kids grow up, they have bumps and bruises, do things you tell them not to do, but you love them anyway.

"I have morals in my house, and Seleana set the example for the others. She didn't smoke or drink. She liked to listen to her music, and she did a lot of stuff around the house. She cooked and cleaned and took care of her sister. But you can't keep a teenager caged in."

While Potts maintains he had no problem with his stepdaughter catching a ride home with Brooks, Johnston County Sheriff Steve Bizzell isn't so sure: He told me he has not decided whether Brooks would be charged with anything relating to his squiring of two underage girls in the wee, small hours. "We're still investigating," Bizzell said.

I know I'm cynical, but what in the heck happened to make the rest of you think that people only get what they deserve? When the brutal death of an innocent young girl prompts more criticism of her mom and stepdad's parenting skills than of how some murderous dingbats got guns in the first place, we are in a bad place emotionally and intellectually.

A famous TV preacher once wrote a book called "When Bad Things Happen to Good People." If the people I heard from had written that book, I suspect they'd call it "When Bad Things Happen to Good People (They Probably Weren't So Good, Anyway)."

7/18/2000

IT MUST BE THE PICTURES

Let's hope Algie Toomer has those negatives stored in a safe place.

As long as he does, the former state employee with a penchant for turning state government into his own personal pension system may never have to work again.

The only explanation many can think of for the state's decision to roll over like a dyspeptic dachshund in a fight with a pit bull when Toomer comes calling is that the dude has pictures of his former bosses rasslin' in Jell-O with hookers or making nice with fluffy, domesticated farm animals.

Another possible explanation is that state officials don't relish the prospect of seeing Toomer testifying in court about the patronage system that allegedly -- ha-ha, that's a good one -- permeates state government.

Toomer in the 1990s was assigned to the Division of Motor Vehicles' emissions program, but DMV officials and Toomer have acknowledged that he actually performed the relatively cushy task of driving then-Commissioner Alexander Killens and various state legislators.

The Department of Transportation has agreed to pay Toomer $36,000, and the Department of Correction ponied up $12,000 more to make the Big Toom happy. The official explanation -- that they opted to pay to avert court costs and a possibly higher award -- would be easier to digest if Toomer hadn't already received $100,000 in a settlement seven years ago. Also without a court fight.

That payout was a settlement for Toomer's claim of job harassment after he was apparently caught in the middle of a feud between two bosses -- both of whom were political appointees.

To maintain DOT's integrity after his firing -- that is, to cover its butt -- state officials made Toomer's personnel file available to the skeptical news media.

That decision just bit the state in the very butt it tried so hard to cover -- and bit us taxpayers in our wallets -- when the state's litigation-leery lawyers advised settling out of court instead of fighting Toomer's claim that releasing his files violated his privacy.

Say, homes, for $48,000 you can violate my privacy -- once I've made sure the statute of limitations has run out on some youthful peccadilloes, that is.

Big bureaucracies, of which the state government is one, are not in the habit of paying out money without a fight -- unless they know they have a weak hand or unless they're trying to avoid the spotlight that a trial would shine on certain aspects of their operations.

Nobody should begrudge Toomer a cent that he receives, even though we're the ones paying the price for the state's reluctance to go to court. As for his depression-related disability payments, being made the scapegoat in a battle between warring superiors -- one who wants to keep you behind the wheel, the other who wants to kick your behind out the door -- would cause anybody to become depressed.

Repeated efforts to reach Toomer on Monday were unsuccessful, but if I could've reached him, the first question I'd have asked was: "Where does one hide the camera at a Jell-O rasslin' match?"

4/27/2004

IT WASN'T WORTH A LIFE

Here's a test to tell what kind of human being you are.

Do you say "toe-may-toe" or "toe-mah-toe"? Do you say "poe-tay-toe" or do you say "She should've blown the lowdown car thief to Kingdom Come"?

A whole lot of people, astonishingly, expressed the latter sentiment after an off-duty Raleigh cop last month shot and killed a man who apparently was stealing her car.

Officer Michelle Peele was placed on desk duty after the shooting death of Nyles Arrington, who was trying to drive off in Peele's 2005 Nissan Xterra from the parking lot of La Rosa Linda. Peele was working at the Mexican restaurant as a security guard in her cop uniform.

Many readers, apparently those lacking the human compassion gene, said "Nice shot."

If you're one of those who think the penalty for stealing a car should be a bullet to the chest, what should the moonlighting officer have done to somebody trying to rip off an enchilada from La Rosa?

Don't answer that.

Arrington was shot under his left arm, which means Peele was to the side as he got behind the wheel. She was in no danger, except of having to call her insurance company and explain that she'd left the auto running with the windows down.

No matter how much she loved her black Xterra, the law says that she could shoot only if someone was in danger.

The State Bureau of Investigation is still looking into the case.

Anger, even the homicidal kind, at being ripped off, is understandable. The burglar I caught inside my house at midnight some years ago has no idea how close he came to suffering Arrington's fate.

OK, if they get the newspaper at Central Prison and he reads this, he knows.

None of the items he'd stacked up by my front door was worth any man's life. What, then, made me go hunting for him minutes after throwing him off my front porch?

Perhaps it was the sense of violation I felt seeing him standing in my living room when I came downstairs to get some Cap'n Crunch. Or maybe it was the leisurely way he strolled into the darkness -- probably to find another, more accommodating house to break into.

I ran upstairs, got my gun and jumped into my truck. Fortunately, I saw a Durham cop before I saw the perp. The cop broadcast a description and sent me home. I never adequately thanked him for that.

The cops found the guy, he went to court and was found guilty. He's doing 11 to 15 years in prison.

That's precisely the way things should have played out then, and that's the way things should've played out last month in Raleigh.

I can't help but wonder what would have happened had the first cop I encountered been a quick-draw specialist as Peele appears to have been. Would he have sent me home, as the Durham cop did, or would he have asked, "You got a gun? Here, take mine. Let's go execute that dirty #$%#@&*."

Nobody, not even his family, is portraying Nyles Arrington as Bishop Tutu. Despite having a rich-dude, patrician-sounding name, Nyles had had his troubles and had caused some.

The fact remains, though, that whether you say "poe-tay-toe" or "poe-tah-toe," he wasn't supposed to die for trying to steal a car.

—— 9/20/2005

IT'S A MALL, NOT STROKE OF DOOM ⊢————————————————

Now that Southpoint mall is a *fait accompli*, I wonder if its opponents will shop there.

Yes, the people carrying signs and chanting "No mall" Tuesday night in the lobby of Durham's City Hall obviously felt strongly that the proposed mall will devastate the area. Some will be so upset at the intrusion of the huge, landscape-altering mall into their idyllic neighborhood that they will curse the earth movers clearing away the trees.

But their anger, regardless of how intense and principled, will melt like snow in April the first time some store they like puts up a bright red "Clearance" sign.

I could be wrong - which, as you know, is quite unlikely - but I predict that those screaming loudest at the mall developers' "desecration" of South Durham will be among the first to inquire of some minimum-wage-earning sales clerk, "Is this on sale?"

To people such as that clerk, Southpoint represents a way to earn a living. To others, it represents a way to go to the bathroom without relying on septic tanks and wells: The mall developers promised to hook up area residents to city water, something they've been unable to get from the county.

When a man is broke, his appreciation of the beauty of trees, streams and squirrels nibbling on nuts becomes secondary to the desire to provide for his family.

That's something many of the mall opponents - not all of whom are granola-munching environmentalists - fail to acknowledge. They should.

Nobody bemoans the unregulated, willy-nilly growth that threatens to turn the Triangle into Atlanta - which epitomizes a soulless, characterless metropolis - more than I do. It was I, remember, who warned y'all about that shopping debacle on U.S. 15-501, New Hope Commons.

As I predicted, the shopping center is a traffic and conceptual nightmare. That site was lusted after by high-tech companies from around the world promising high-paying jobs, yet a short-sighted City Council approved a #$*&% Wal-Mart.

But Southpoint won't be New Hope Commons, nor is it the death knell for Durham that opponents fear it will be - especially now that the mall developer has agreed to spend millions more to upgrade roads near the mall.

By initially proposing to pay for road improvements to handle projected traffic only a couple of years beyond 2001, the year mall construction is scheduled to be completed, the developer treated the City Council like a bunch of weed-bending Jethro Bodines and Minnie Pearls who, blinded by the glitter, would not realize that the real traffic problems begin after the mall is completed.

The council acquitted itself well. The owners of South Square mall didn't, though. They have no one to blame but themselves if the new mall decimates their mall. Had they made capital improvements - they belatedly pledged a $50 million upgrade - instead of making a lame plea for city loyalty, they could have staved off this predatory, deep-pocketed challenger. Instead, they now are like the dude who has neglected his woman but tries to get her back after someone else successfully woos her.

The council's vote told South Square, as scores of women have told me in similar circumstances, "It's too late for that, Homey."

1/21/1999

IT'S NO KINGLY HONOR

If you ever decide to bestow an honor upon me -- which is unlikely, seeing as how there are no awards for, say, knowing every line of dialogue from every episode of "Sanford and Son" -- here's a tip: Don't even think about naming a street after me.

Martin Luther King Jr. would probably say the same thing to the residents of Chapel Hill who've made the naming of Airport Road in his honor their cause of the moment.

Nobody in my lifetime is more deserving of honors than King, but there are far better ways to do that than by naming a stretch of asphalt after him.

For instance, I initially thought I'd honor him by becoming a preacher, too. Then, after a week at Bible college and discovering how much I liked women and liquor, I chose to honor him by not becoming a preacher.

You want to honor the great man? Vote. Raise your kids to be respectful of others and of themselves. Volunteer to help close that achievement gap that exists between black and white students in schools.

Those problems are not unique to Chapel Hill, but they exist there and would cause King far more consternation than not having that road changed to honor him.

Town Council member Cam Hill, a supporter of the measure, said that if how one votes on the issue is a test of one's racial feelings, "then a lot of people in Chapel Hill have failed."

"I think a lot of the arguments against the road are being used to cover true racial feelings," he said. Some of the arguments, he said, are "a load of crap. ... I'm very disappointed in our town" for not approving the change.

Does a "yes" vote on the renaming automatically mean a council member is -- to dust off a phrase from the '70s -- down with the cause?

Does voting "no" for any reason mean that the opposing council member is a closet klansman who wears a sheet in private and uses two-ply King toilet paper?

Of course not. Just as someone could vote for the name change with the cynical aim of keeping the natives quiet or in lieu of making real change, so, too, could someone oppose it for some rational -- to them, at least -- reason.

Hill is right that many of the arguments against naming the road for King are lame. The expense would be minimal, there is no need for more dialogue, and the resulting confusion that some opponents cite is a smoke screen.

Supporters claim that naming a major thoroughfare after King would set the town apart from other municipalities whose King streets, drives and boulevards are in poor, mostly black neighborhoods.

Indeed, comedian Chris Rock had one word of advice for anyone lost on a street named for the man revered as the prince of peace: run -- because there's some violence going down.

Would having it in a central artery really, as council member Sally Greene said and NAACP representatives seconded, somehow work King's nonviolent message into the community's consciousness?

If so, that means the chap I inadvertently cut off on Airport Road a few years ago would now extend to me his whole hand -- in brotherhood -- rather than one finger.

6/18/2004

'I'VE JUST CALLED MY OPPONENT...AN @&*%!'

They're as much a part of politics as chopped barbecue or sending hookers to your opponent's hotel room after posting a dozen photographers outside.

No, not pollsters. Concession speeches.

When one candidate wins, another loses -- requiring the loser to stand before the true-believers on election night and feign graciousness toward the person who, a day earlier, was Satan's hand puppet.

Once it's clear that the only way victory can be attained is for somebody to find a big box (or, in some cases, state) of heretofore uncounted votes -- a la LBJ in his first Senate race, resulting in the nickname "Landslide Lyndon" -- the losing candidate reads the tea leaves or goat entrails and concludes that he's as done as last Thanksgiving's turkey.

He clambers onto the stage, clears his throat and begins. "I just called my opponent and congratulated him..."

This opening statement is always -- ALWAYS -- interrupted by obligatory groans and cries of "no, no!" by campaign workers and diehard supporters who apparently believe that delaying the concession staves off the inevitable.

As someone who has felt the sting of voters' rejection -- I received 14 votes when I ran for the Rockingham City Council -- I feel a kinship with political losers. Mass rejection by the people you want to serve is something you have to experience in order to realize how much it hurts. Nothing hurts as bad, except perhaps the specific rejection you feel when Sweet Thang confesses that her aerobics instructor is actually her new main squeeze.

That hurt can be dealt with in private, with a bottle of 90-proof something and a stack of your favorite G-rated videos. You certainly don't have to stand before a battery of microphones and say nice things about the person who just broke your heart.

Most candidates, we'd like to believe, are good people who adopt incivility only as a cynical appeal to voters -- because polls show that saying nasty things about your opponent really does help. Thus, losing candidates may actually mean it when they call and offer the victor "best wishes."

Of course, losing candidates also know that coming off as a sorehead loser will derail any chances they have of ever winning another election. And the winner can afford to be gracious when he applauds his vanquished opponent for "a spirited campaign."

The closest thing to a heartfelt concession speech I've heard came from Richard Nixon, who petulantly declared after one loss that "You won't have Dick Nixon to kick around anymore."

Alas, we know how sincere that vow turned out to be.

The concession speech most of us would like to hear begins like this:

"I just called my cross-dressing opponent and told him to go kiss a snaggle-toothed llama what's been eating Oreo cookies for all I care.

"My opponent is still a man who couldn't spell 'truth' if you spotted him 'r-u-t-h.' He's a low-life, vote-stealing warthog who's going to have you ruing the day you rejected me.

"As for you, my dear voters, here's a dime. In the words of Don Rickles, 'take it, go outside and find a parking meter -- and violate yourself.'

"I just spent $75 million trying to show you that I am the way. How stupid do you have to be to buy that extra large bag o' whale vomit my opponent peddled? Well, you deserve each other.

"Me? I'm taking what's left of my millions and spending my time on my yacht off the south of France with my mistress, Bubblicious."

Turning to his stunned wife, he proceeds. "That's right. Now that this election is over, we don't have sit still for any more of those family photo ops. A lot of help they were.

"Oh yeah, just in case I do decide to run again -- God bless America."

11/13/2004

JACKSON TRIES ON A CONGRESSIONAL CLOAK

Talk about playing the race card. Imagine, Michael Jackson trying to act black.

Feeling the heat of prosecution after being charged with felony counts of child abuse, Jackson moonwalked to Washington last week to meet with black lawmakers and offer his help "in whatever way I can."

Fortunately for the Congressional Black Caucus, most of its members stayed as far away from Jackson as he had stayed from them during the years when he was actually an important entertainer.

It's entirely possible that most of the caucus members really did have important work to do -- their collectively issued excuse -- which precluded a meeting with the Besieged Gloved One. I'm guessing, though, that some had nothing better to do than, say, renew their subscriptions to Jet and remain outside camera shot. There is little or no political upside to being photographed with the King of Pop right now.

Whatever their reasons for shunning this human train wreck, they should be commended.

Unfortunately, some caucus members allowed themselves to be pimped by the not-quite-as-Beloved One in return, ostensibly for any publicity he could give their cause -- AIDS relief on the continent of Africa.

"The Congressional Black Caucus has held dozens of press conferences on this subject," Jesse Jackson Jr. reportedly said, explaining why he participated in what he acknowledged was a "sideshow" with Michael Jackson.

Jesse Jr., whose father is a master of media manipulation, mistakenly assumed that any buzz is good buzz, even when created by an eccentric -- if Michael Jackson goes broke, as rumored, he'll just be "crazy" -- 45-year-old man who openly admits he sees nothing wrong in being in the same bed with young boys.

Like far too many blacks -- O.J., Vanessa Williams, to name a couple -- Michael

Jackson obviously views his rejection by the larger society as a convenient time to go back home.

Home, they say, is the place where they have to take you back.

Not so fast there, partner. Jackson Jr., fellow Illinois congressman Bobby Rush and Texas Rep. Sheila Jackson-Lee may view Michael as a politically enhancing prodigal son and photo op, but most Black Caucus members wisely made themselves scarce when the Con of Pop strode in.

This is the fellow, remember, who when abuse charges surfaced a decade ago, showed up for the first time at the NAACP Image Awards. Now, with similar allegations swirling around his chemically treated hair and surgically altered face, he surrounds himself with members of the Nation of Islam and goes calling on Congress. The only thing missing was a dashiki and one of those Afro picks with the fist for a handle.

See a pattern here?

While Jackson has long had an altruistic streak, showing admirable concern for the world's impoverished children, his sudden interest in Africa -- "our sister continent," he called it -- is a new, cynical phenomenon.

Alas, many of us have seen too many celebrities who cloak themselves in blackness only when they find themselves in hot water.

It is to their credit that the Black Caucus as a whole, and most of its members individually, refused to let themselves be pawns in Jackson's gloved hands. It's sad that some did.

4/10/2004

JAIL? NOT EVEN CLOSE

Carter G. Woodson, the scholar credited with starting Negro History Week, once wrote, "When you control a man's thinking, you do not have to worry about his actions. He will find his 'proper place' and will stay in it. You do not need to send him to the back door. He will go without being told."

"In fact," Woodson added in "The Mis-Education of the Negro," "if there is no back door, he will cut one for his special benefit."

He could have said the same thing about prison, because his "back door" theory is acted out every time you see yet another hip-hop music video in which rappers voluntarily put themselves behind bars.

You know the ubiquitous fashion trend of sagging pants? That started in the joint before it spread to the videos.

Judging by what you see on TV, you'd think there were only two kinds of young black men: those who drive around in Bentleys surrounded by bootyful babes in bikinis, or those who spend their days behind bars.

Somebody, anybody, tell me when being a convict became cool? And how can we stop it?

The only thing worse than privileged young rappers literally placing themselves behind bars to enhance their street cred is hearing a privileged college basketball star figuratively placing himself behind bars.

By a show of hands, how many of you cringed when the UNC Tar Heels' star guard Rashad McCants compared being in college to prison? How many wanted to snatch him by the scruff of his neck, drag him over to Central Prison and show him what doing time is really like?

"I'm in jail right now," he said in a televised interview. "I'm just in my sentence, and I'm doing my time."

I was at UNC's Midnight Madness season kickoff last week, and believe me, Rashad, Carolina is no prison.

I like the kid and want to give him the benefit of the doubt when he says he didn't mean it, but it is distressing to hear a prison analogy flow so casually from him, especially when there are, by some estimates, more young black dudes in prison than in college.

Give most men older than 40 a camera and tell them to produce their own video and they'll make themselves king, president or, in my case, the Duke of Earl, with pretty women strolling through my dukedom.

You can bet we won't be "keeping it real" by putting ourselves in a cell.

Besides, what's real about a generation of young men who, like Otis Campbell -- the Mayberry town drunk -- save the cops the trouble by locking themselves behind bars?

Otis was fictional; thousands of black men in prison are an unfortunate reality, and those with creative control who put themselves in prison are making an unnecessary concession to that reality.

Some people want to excuse McCants by saying he spoke the truth, that the athletes are in confinement and are being used.

Bull-oney. If they are being used by the system, so is everyone who has a job. The key is being smart enough to use the system, too -- to get an education, enhance your NBA draft status or, better yet, give yourself a frame of reference that doesn't include prison.

——• 10/22/2004

JARRING ENCOUNTER WITH THE CONDOM DEBATE ├——

After what happened last week and this, Colin Powell can be forgiven if he longs for the relative safety of Vietnam during the war in which he served.

That's because Secretary of State Powell has been dodging a hand grenade hurled by his so-called allies.

All the dude said, at a forum sponsored by MTV, was that young people who have sex should use condoms. Period. He was not traveling around dispensing this quite commonsensical opinion just for the heck of it; he was responding to a question from a young lady.

Nowhere in Powell's response did he encourage young people -- or old ones either -- to go out and, in the jargon of today's youth, "get busy." But you would have thought he had done precisely that judging by the barrage of incoming missiles launched by Gary Bauer and other right-wing nuts. (And yes, before you write in to complain, there are left-wing nuts, but they did not weigh in on this issue.)

Bauer, president of American Values, sniffed that Powell should "stick to diplomacy. He's not the administration's top health official." Condoms, Bauer furhter declared, are "bad medicine."

Compared to what, Gar? AIDS? Syphillis?

When I think of Bauer and others of his unrealistic ilk, I am reminded of the quote by that great philosopher, Bugs Bunny: "What a maroon."

A couple of years ago a pastor entered my neighborhood barbershop a few seconds ahead of me. This is a guy of local renown, albeit one I've never known to speak out on any issue outside of his church's building fund -- and certainly not on the crime, unemployment or poor housing that adversely affect his community.

So, being me, I decided to have some fun. Motioning toward the huge jar of free condoms my barber keeps on his counter, I asked the reverend, who was seated beside me, "Hey Rev., what do you think of a barber providing condoms to his customers?"

I thought an appropriate answer would have been something like, "Oh, given the realities of unwanted pregnancy and AIDS, it's wonderful that he cares enough to encourage sexually acative young people to protect themselves in the clinches."

Fuhgeddaboutit. He launched into a rambling diatribe about how the barber was encouraging young kids to have sex, blah blah blah, and how he didn't feel comfortable patronizing such an establishment.

He then walked out, which meant just one thing: I moved up a seat.

If the righteous reverend had stuck around -- or if Gary Bauer and his unrealistic religious cohorts would come around -- I'd gladly, although not proudly, tell them that merely having access to condoms does not guarantee sex.

I know someone -- ME! -- who carried one around for five years and never came close to having sex. (When I finally did open it, it distintegrated.) So there.

Just as in the Vietnam War, Powell will survive this minor skirmish with the enemies of common sense.

That's because President Bush, unlike his predecessor, Bill Clinton -- who jettisoned former Surgeon General Joycelyn Elders in a flash for her comments on condoms and masturbation -- has shown no inclination to sacrifice Powell for his temperate remarks.

Good for him, and good for the country that someone is willing to use common sense when it comes to young people and sex.

2/23/2002

JESSE ... JESSE... AW, JESSE

It's getting harder and harder to defend this Jackson cat, even for me, a dude who has many of his records and used to wear my hair in a big 'fro the way he did.

But now, he has become a cartoon character more deserving of derision than envy.

Aha! Got ya. You thought I was talking about the Jackson with the pointy nose and fondness for sharing his bed with children, didn't you?

I'm not: I'm actually referring to the one with the unhealthy attraction to the spotlight: the Rev. Jesse Jackson.

As Michael Jackson's court date approached, I kept my fingers crossed and prayed, "Please, Jesse, please don't say anything."

You knew there was no chance of that, though, considering that Al Sharpton has eclipsed him as the top civil rights agitator and U.S. Sen. Barack Obama and his own son, U.S. Rep. Jesse Jackson Jr., both of Illinois, have surpassed him in terms of political influence.

Thus, it was not surprising that Jesse jumped onto the Michael bandwagon with the agility of a mountain goat, bemoaning the absence of blacks on the jury.

Michael isn't the only black man -- a term I use loosely here -- whose jury was not composed of his peers. He was, though, the only one whose trial was sure to garner international news coverage.

When the Rev. Jackson decries the absence of the singer's peers on the Santa Barbara County, Calif., jury, you naturally wonder, "What peers?"

Is he trying to say there are 12 other people in the United States, nay, on Earth, who've done to their bodies, faces and psyches what Michael has done to his?

If Jesse or anyone else shows me other black people who look like Michael, I'll demand their inclusion on the jury -- and then run, in case their condition is contagious.

For decades Michael has mutilated his face, straightened his hair and bleached his skin in an effort to appear as unblack as possible.

But when his albums stopped selling and his alleged fondness for little boys came out, he draped himself in the sequined cape of racial victimhood and accused Sony's president of racism for not promoting him enough.

Of course, Michael Jackson is not the first black celebrity to discover his ethnicity once he got in trouble.

Even O.J. tried to turn back black, albeit momentarily, after he found himself facing double murder charges in connection with the deaths of his wife and another person.

And darned if some blacks didn't fall for it, welcoming O.J. as though he were a prodigal son.

Now that Michael's possibly facing time in prison, where he could really get in touch with the brothers and they with him, don't be surprised if he shows up in court one day sporting a dashiki, eating a bowl of chitlins and reading Jet magazine.

Jesse called it "simply inconceivable" that blacks would be omitted from Michael's jury: He's probably right, but what was most inconceivable was the possibility of Jesse letting a case with this much publicity pass by without his butting in.

3/4/2005

JESSE JACKSON'S LATEST CAUSE ~ PAR FOR THE COURSE —

I don't know about you, but when I'm faced with a tough decision, I think of my two heroes, Fred G. Sanford and Dr. Martin Luther King Jr., and ask "What would those two dudes do?"

That's always a dangerous prospect, trying to predict what a fictional junkman and a slain civil rights giant might do, but I'm confident that neither would be marching outside a country club's golf course this weekend.

Yet that's what the Rev. Jesse Jackson is scheduled to do in Augusta, Ga. He -- and several other ministers, he claims -- plans to join Martha Burk of the National Council of Women's Organizations in her crusade to integrate the country club for women of means. Also slated to be on hand are those who want to keep the barriers up -- and possibly re-erect others that previously had been torn down.

Yep, those paragons of enlightenment, the Ku Klux Klan, will be in Augusta urging Hootie Johnson, president of Augusta National, to stand tall against women.

Me, I'm delighted that the Klan is wasting its time on something so insignificant.

As for Jesse and the other ministers, I'm disheartened for the same reason.

We've got way more important stuff to concentrate on than whether some rich Dixie chick gets to join the club.

During the early 1970s, when rumors of an affair between the Rev. Jackson and pop singer Roberta Flack abounded, Flack recorded a torrid love ballad called -- you guessed it -- "Jesse." I don't remember all of the words, but I know it was hot and contained the phrase "Jesse, come home."

That's what I'm singing now: Jesse, come home. There are too many important issues facing black Americans for Jackson to squander his diminishing gifts on getting some rich woman admitted to a hoity-toity country club.

Come home, Jesse. Black men are dying violently at an alarming rate -- most often at the hands of other black men -- depriving black women and kids of husbands and fathers.

Come home, Jesse, because many of those who aren't being killed are being criminally underserved by the school systems of this country. Illicit drugs, and the government's war on illicit drugs, are sending too many young dudes to the prison farm, to the graveyard or -- worse -- turning their brains to cream of wheat.

So come on home, Jesse. Sure, you've strayed and slipped and allowed yourself to become a joke, a caricature of what you could've been. I used to be a fan, but even I am amused and amazed that you, after 40 years in the spotlight, are still attracted to TV cameras like a reporter to a free buffet.

There's time to redeem yourself, J., but you can't do it by marching outside a golf club singing "We Shall Overcome." That way lies more scorn and ridicule

Some people will say "Dawg, you'd feel differently if Jackson, Burk, et al. were trying to gain acceptance -- no, make that 'membership': they are not the same thing -- for blacks instead of for women."

No, I wouldn't. It is of no consequence whether or not some rich black dude is allowed to join a country club and sip mint juleps on the veranda with rich white

guys. It was only in recent years that the Augusta club took in a black member, and that was under duress. I've yet to see any appreciable progress for the race as a result.

Several years ago, while a reporter in Gary, Ind., I covered the story of a prominent black businessman who allowed his name to be entered for membership in an exclusive all-white country club. He wanted to join, and was willing to endure the resulting tumult, he said, because it would help him make business contacts.

Another black dude, who thought the whole effort an exercise in silliness, summed it up: "What kind of business contacts are you going to make when they hate you?"

Right on. And to turn on its ear Groucho Marx's famous quote, I wouldn't belong to any club that wouldn't have someone like me as a member.

4/12/2003

JESSE SEES THE LIGHT AT LAST

I'm not a very religious man, but I'm fixing to try to get my soul right. You'd better, too.

Why? Because it's prophesied that just before the end of time we'll see some weird things. For instance, the prophet Woody (Allen, that is), wrote that in the last days, "the lion and the lamb shall lie down together -- but only the lion shall get up."

Far-fetched, yes, but not even the idea of a lion and lamb making nice is as weird as the idea that that old, pretty-much-toothless lion Jesse Helms would change his obstinately wrongheaded view on anything, much less AIDS.

Yet, such a transformation seems to be occurring inside Helms' head, as he and Franklin Graham, son of Billy, combined to address Christianity and AIDS at their Prescriptions for Hope convention in Washington earlier this week.

Helms made opening remarks at the invitation-only convention -- did anyone tell him some gays might be invited? -- and Graham acknowledged that the church has been slow to confront AIDS or to console those suffering from it.

I don't think we'll see either of them joining the Village People for an a cappella version of "YMCA." But they both seem to be recognizing that people with AIDS are worthy of God's grace.

Graham, unlike his revered daddy, Billy -- who went his whole career without saying anything controversial -- has at least shown a willingness to address issues his daddy pretended were of no concern to the church.

Papa Graham, remember, is the dude who, despite rubbing shoulders with every president since Eisenhower, never said a word at the time against the Vietnam War, about the civil rights movement or myriad other issues that threatened to rend the country.

But his son convened a conference at which Helms told attendees that he was "ashamed" by his inaction in responding to the AIDS epidemic. "I have been too lax too long in doing something really significant," he said.

That's a huge change for a dude who considered AIDS and Christianity to be incompatible for the first two decades of the deadly epidemic. AIDS was once considered a gay disease -- indeed, some church people viewed it as God's retribution for homosexuality.

Yet, in a perverse way, both AIDS and homosexuality have been potent political weapons for Helms, as he railed against funding for AIDS research and did everything but dress his political opponents in pink tutus.

Miracle of miracles, this is the second time in a week -- and possibly the second time in his long Senate career -- that Jesse Helms has done the right thing. Last week, he sought to remove some of the restrictions from scientists who use rats and birds in their research. Lab rats, he said, are living the life of Riley compared with some of their free-roaming counterparts.

That riled animal-rights activists, but on this one I'm with Helms: If it's between human suffering and a mouse getting jolted with an electrode, it's "So long, Mickey."

It's unlikely, but at this rate, Helms might -- in 20 or 30 years -- join me in an a cappella version of "We Shall Overcome." On the Martin Luther King Jr. holiday.

2/22/2002

JOBLESS BY THE NUMBERS

Mary Beth German, manager of Green Front Interior & Rugs in Raleigh, didn't go to work Saturday. She was sick.

Don't bother looking in the medical dictionary for German's ailment, though: It's not listed.

You see, she was laid low with a broken heart.

"I spent most of last week crying," German told me as we sat in her office on Yonkers Road and discussed the reasons for her sadness. Those reasons toiled right outside her door and throughout the huge furniture showroom as we talked. They are the six Mexican workers she is being forced to fire because their Social Security numbers didn't match up when the government checked them.

"I'm upset by it. The company's upset by it," she said, heartache thick in her voice. "Everybody's sad that they're going. We wish there was something we could do."

Ann Robertson, a Raleigh lawyer who specializes in immigration law, declined to speak specifically about the Green Front 6 but said the process of securing green cards for workers is lengthy.

"When workers are here illegally, they can't get legal status without leaving the country and applying," she said. If the workers have been in the country illegally for up to six months, they can't return for three years. If they've been here a year, they can't return for 10 years.

No wonder undocumented workers simply leave their jobs when they are discovered -- and reappear elsewhere, where the whole "hire 'em to fire 'em" process is repeated.

Sensing the depth of German's despair, I gingerly suggested that some cynics will conclude she's merely despondent over losing a cheap source of labor.

"Cheap? I pay them what I pay anyone else," she said. "I don't consider them a cheap labor pool; they're a high-quality labor pool. They're excellent, excellent workers."

Not all employers are as conscientious as German professes to be. Unscrupulous employers know that desperate Latino immigrants often accept below-minimum-wage pay.

A buddy of mine told me a story a couple of years ago that illustrated the point. After working several weeks as a carpenter on a construction site with Latinos, he said, he noticed that his paycheck was mysteriously and significantly lighter one payday.

"What's up, yo?" he asked the site foreman. Turns out the boss thought my pal, who is light-skinned and wears his hair in a pony tail, was Latino and thus working at a lower rate than other workers. My pal said that after he colorfully informed the dude that he was black and born and raised in Mebane, the paycheck discrepancy was rectified.

The problem of immigrant workers and their documentation -- or lack thereof -- is nothing new, but it intensified after Sept. 11, when anyone not legally in the country became suspect.

Several months ago Food Lion in Carrboro, among other businesses, had to dismiss dozens of workers whose numbers didn't match up. In response, the town's aldermen unanimously passed a resolution demanding the reform of U.S. immigration policy and laws. Given today's political climate, that resolution, I fear, has as much chance of making a difference as a snowball in Mexico. In July.

5/14/2002

JOE WILLIE AND SEXUAL HEALING

Who knew? Maybe Joe Willie was right.

After hearing about the doctor who accidentally invented a female orgasm machine -- he was merely trying to alleviate women's back pain -- I've concluded that my old mentor down in Rockingham knew what he was talking about all along.

If Dr. Stuart Meloy's surgically implanted device turns out to really work -- despite anecdotal evidence that it does, there has been no verifying clinical research -- then it appears Joe was onto something all those years ago.

I introduced you to Joe Willie in 1993, during a debate over whether North Carolina schools should teach sex education.

Like some of the more reactionary parents, I was dead set against it. But unlike them, I had no fear that kids armed with the basics of reproduction and contraception would suddenly become promiscuous and wanton.

No, my opposition was based on a simpler, more selfish premise: Why should today's kids be more enlightened than those of my generation? They should learn about sex the same way we did -- by hanging around the poolroom and listening to older guys lie.

Joe Willie, the most worldly guy our adolescent selves knew -- he'd been in the Army -- returned from overseas with myriad "tips" on women. He was also the first person to show us the condom he kept in his wallet. Talk about a big deal. And he only charged us a quarter to see it.

Alas, everything Joe told us about attracting women turned out to be wrong. For instance, I never met one who found me irresistible after catching a whiff of the pungent mixture of Hai Karate aftershave lotion and vanilla extract I splashed on per his instructions.

But what we thought was the biggest piece of misinformation from Joe Willie may turn out to be true. This is no lie: He once told us that if you pressed your forefinger into the middle of any woman's back -- whether she liked you or not was irrelevant -- she'd find you irresistible.

Girls at Rockingham Junior High found me irresistible, all right; they couldn't resist the urge to punch me in the eye, call me everything but a Reuben sandwich and tell their big brothers.

Now, though, Dr. Meloy, an anesthesiologist from up around Winston-Salem, may have stumbled upon validation of Joe Willie's theory. While implanting his device -- simply put, it blocks pain signals to the brain -- in a patient's spine, he put the electrode in the wrong spot: So long pain machine, hello sex machine and international celebrity for Meloy.

Lest anxious women and lazy husbands go rushing down to the local mega-drugstore seeking one of his pleasure machines, you need to know that there is only anecdotal evidence that it works, and it costs $15,000.

With the death last week of Dr. William Masters, revolutionary sex researcher, Meloy's invention could mark Joe Willie as the nation's foremost sex authority -- which might also make me try that Hai Karate and vanilla extract again.

2/20/2001

JORDAN SPEAKS ... AIR BALL!

There's an ancient proverb that says, "Be careful what you wish for; you might get it."

That has never been truer than now. For two decades, I wished that Michael Jordan would use the tremendous capital he had as the greatest, most beloved athlete in the world to speak out on something, anything, more significant than the state of his jump shot or the magical properties of his latest pair of $200 sneakers.

Alas, no matter what the issue, Jordan remained dutifully mum: slave labor, kids being killed for his overpriced shoes, politics -- nothing could get the dude to speak out. He'll forever be remembered for two things: for staying too long at the dance and for his pitifully pithy comment in 1990 when asked to support Harvey Gantt's Senate race against Jesse Helms. "Republicans buy gym shoes, too," he demurred.

Wouldn't you know it, though: When Jordan finally does speak out about something of relative importance -- the firing of his buddy Matt "I did it my way" Doherty as UNC's basketball coach -- he's as wrong as two overpriced, slave-labor-produced left shoes. "There's no way that 18- and 19-year-olds should be dictating the future of a coach," His Airballness said after his buddy and former teammate was shown the door.

My efforts to reach Jordan were unsuccessful, but I would have told him that 18- and 19-year-olds always dictate the future of coaches: If the kids don't knock down enough jumpers or snag enough rebounds, the coach will soon find himself on his brother-in-law's used car lot, greeting people with, "I can put you in this baby -- real cheap."

Depending upon how you want to view it, UNC Athletics Director Dick

Baddour knows he's in trouble -- or on the right track -- when heretofore Silent Mike and Lute Olsen deign to criticize the way he runs Carolina's program.

Olsen, the hoops coach at the University of Arizona, stuck his unexemplary nose into the Tar Heel situation last week by opining, "Thank goodness in my career I've worked for ADs that have had confidence in what I do."

The silver-maned Olsen also should "thank goodness" that he has worked for ADs who don't care that he seldom graduates a player, making him something akin to a pimp in tennis shoes. In The Chronicle of Higher Education, I read that, over the six-year period beginning in 1995-96, only 15 percent of Olsen's players graduated.

Baddour has critics with far more legitimacy than Olsen -- and so, unbelievably, do I -- after writing last week that Baddour made the right move in showing Grandmaster MD the door.

"You are a joke," wrote Michelle, a "UNC fan 4 Life." She added, "I'd like to see you read that article to Matt's face. You should be run out of town for the garbage you spew."

That was one of the kinder ones. As was this gem: "How dare you attack Matt. I feel sorry for you. You ought to be ashamed of yourself for attacking such a man. Have a good day, sir."

Speaking of proverbs, here's one Jordan should consider: "'Tis better to keep your mouth shut and have people think you're a fool -- than to open it and remove all doubt."

4/8/2003

JUDGING A JOB APPLICATION, 20 YEARS ON

Judge Samuel Alito is an ideological hit man who can't wait to take a shot at women's right to an abortion.

I only feel that way because that's about what he said.

Applying for a political appointment in the office of then-Attorney General Edwin Meese in 1985, Alito wrote an embarrassingly brown-nosing letter in which he expressed his admiration for Barry Goldwater and crowed "I am and always have been a conservative...It is obviously very difficult to summarize a set of political views in a sentence, but...I believe very strongly in limited government.

"I am particularly proud of my contributions in recent cases in which the government has argued in the Supreme Court that racial and ethnic quotas should not be allowed, and that the Constitution does not protect a right to an abortion."

Now, though, Alito declares that he wrote those things only because he was seeking a job. In other words, he said it -- but had his fingers crossed behind his back. So it doesn't count.

Oy. One is left with the impression that had Alito been applying for a position in Lyndon Johnson's administration, he'd have written a letter praising FDR and expressing support for the school lunch program, the War on Poverty and free dental care on demand for everybody.

Sen. Edward Kennedy, in television and newspaper interviews, has said he asked Alito, after interviewing him, 'Why shouldn't we consider that the answers you're giving today are an application for another job?'"

Why, indeed.

Kennedy also said, "He's obviously an intelligent and informed nominee, but the real criteria that all of us look for is whether the nominee is going to have a core commitment to the constitutional values and the rights and liberties and interest of the American people."

Sorry, Senator, but if Alito is to be believed -- disbelieved? -- his only core commitment is to advancing his career. That should make pro-lifers who feel they've found a kindred spirit just as skeptical as Kennedy and other pro-choice advocates.

Alito finds himself in a classic Catch-22 situation: either he was just telling the Reagan administration officials what they wanted to hear and he's really not that gung-ho on abolishing Roe v. Wade -- or he's a dissembler. Of course, he could have changed his mind over the years -- but he had his chance to say so, and he didn't.

Judging by the way Alito's statements from 20 years ago are coming back to bite him beneath his judicial robes, don't be surprised if future candidates for the Supreme Court are reluctant to express an opinion about anything. Ever.

Their Patron Saint of the Ambiguous Answer will be the recently confirmed chief justice, John Roberts, who practically tap-danced through his own confirmation hearings without expressing an opinion on anything.

From the moment young people express an interest in the legal profession, they're likely to adopt the stance of Roberts, or the motto of the mobster whose advice to a crony was "don't put nothin' in writin'." They're also likely to start at an early age couching their true feelings, so as not to give potential opponents ammunition with which to torpedo their candidacy decades hence.

Mom: Sandra, which doll would you like for your ninth birthday -- a redhead like we got you last year or the blonde?

Sandra: Mother, I have no real opinion. I am older and wiser now. I have great respect for precedent, but I also --

Mom: Aw shaddup. We're getting the E-Z-Bake Oven.

⊢ 11/26/2005

JUMPING THE GUN ON RACE ⊢────────────

Somebody'd better check the thermostat in hell, because they're probably feeling a chill down there.

You know how I always said I envisioned writing something kind about Bob Johnson when hell freezes over?

OK, here goes: The dude who mined black booties and thug imagery for billions deserves the pro basketball franchise he was awarded last week.

Yet some Charlotteans -- who accepted the former team's reptilian owner, George Shinn -- are disturbed that the owner of their new team is black and are complaining that he is the beneficiary of race preferences.

I know, I know. It seems laughable that a billionaire would have any acquisition tainted with charges that he got something only because of his race. Alas, nothing about race in America is laughable.

How unlaughable? So much so that a Web site eliciting comments about the new team was shut down because, it said, "the debate on the NBA 'talk forum' has declined to racial slurs, race-baiting and sexual comments about city officials."

A Charlotte Observer columnist, while not saying directly that Johnson got the team because of race preferences, wrote that "Trent Lott's mouth made it very clear affirmative action -- even in the NBA -- isn't outdated."

Say what? The columnist assured me that he didn't feel Johnson got the team because of his race, but the fact that affirmative action would be mentioned in a column on a billionaire -- even one with Johnson's obvious lack of civic responsibility -- is baffling.

I clicked onto Charlotte.com's discussion board just for fun, and the very first message I read bemoaned that "Charlotte has now become the absolute worst place in America for a white person to live ... Robert Johnson is a black racist, and BET is a black racist network."

How so, homeslice? Johnson might be a lot of things, but a racist? Why, I'd bet my entire Z.Z. Hill record collection that he has done way more damage to blacks than to whites.

For one thing, the bulk of BET's programming reinforces negative stereotypes about black men, women and youth.

Hmm, could the writer of that message be upset that there are too few white rappers and hoochie mamas?

Some people have a legitimate gripe: They are upset that the new arena for the team was shoved down their throats after they voted "no" on a referendum for financing it. That's cool: I'd be upset about that, too. But there is no mistaking whence most of the hostility springs.

For instance, one guy wrote, "Yanks and lib scum have ruined" Charlotte. "They are moving here by the millions and have ruined a great society that is now sinking into race-mixing and ... perversion."

Oy vey, homes.

Nobody -- and I mean nobody -- is more disappointed in what Bob Johnson has done with his network than I am. But anyone who hates the dude because of his color is an idiot: There are a whole lot of substantive issues on which to disdain him.

Like "Cita's World."

12/24/2002

JUSTICE FOR PETERSON ... AND HIS WIFE

You can't tell just from looking, but I have a lot in common with Mike Peterson, the political gadfly and murder suspect.

Oh sure, there are obvious differences: He's short and slight, while I'm a chiseled 6 feet 2, 230. OK, 240. Would you believe 250?

The similarities, though, are striking.

He writes a column; so do I.

He ran for political office and was rejected by voters; I received only 14 votes when I ran for office.

He was a decorated Marine Corps veteran; so was I. (OK, I really wasn't, but I've seen "Saving Private Ryan" twice.)

He's spent time in jail, and I, too, have been the involuntary guest of various states' hospitality.

But although I know I was innocent every time I went to the hoosegow, a jury has yet to decide Peterson's innocence or guilt in the death of his wife.

This column isn't about Peterson's innocence or guilt. It's about the people who presume to know his innocence or guilt -- mainly his innocence. They are the people who packed the courtroom Monday and who held a vigil outside the county jail last week, demanding that Peterson be freed on bail even though the district attorney was considering seeking the death penalty.

They seemed unaware -- hold it: Some of them were lawyers, so they had to know; perhaps they simply didn't care -- that there's a reason bail usually isn't set in capital cases. A dude facing the hot squat might be more inclined to forfeit his possessions and head to the South Pacific than a person who knows that the dirt nap isn't a possibility if he's convicted.

Listening to and watching Peterson's supporters and friends, you'd think District Attorney Jim Hardin was trying to lock up Mother Teresa when he asked that Peterson, as a condition of bail, hand over his passport and stay in North Carolina until the trial.

The guy seated next to me in the courtroom, a Peterson sympathizer, sighed in exasperation and muttered an unprintable when Hardin asked that bail be set at $1 million.

In an N&O story, a friend described Peterson as a dude who "seeks injustices to right, using his mind and heart to make things better for family, friends and even strangers." In court, some of his impressively credentialed friends considered it "almost laughable" that Peterson, "who wouldn't hurt a flea," might pose a danger to the community or flee the court's jurisdiction.

"Hey, wait a minute," I asked myself. "Is this a hearing for Mike Peterson or Mahatma Gandhi?"

Even the children -- the couple's from previous marriages -- are proclaiming his innocence. Others swear under oath that he is incapable of killing anyone.

Hmm. In "The Godfather II" movie, when Michael Corleone suggests rubbing out Hyman Roth, his attorney says that's an impossibility, to which Michael replies, "If history has taught us anything, it's that anyone can be killed."

Yeah, and if history has taught us anything else, it's that anyone can kill.

Michael Peterson hasn't been convicted of anything, only charged, and he deserves every assumption of innocence while awaiting his day in court.

His dead wife deserves something, too: justice.

1/15/2002

KING'S 'DREAM' FOR SALE

Nobody wants to see the Kings, the first family of Black America, on the welfare line.

If I'd known that Dexter, Marty, Coretta and the other members of Dr. Martin Luther King Jr.'s family were hurting for cash, I'd have gladly cut them some cheddar or taken up a donation.

Anything would be preferable to seeing Dr. King's image demeaned for dollars by his own family.

Brian Murphy, a spokesman for Alcatel USA, said response to that company's television and print ads featuring Dr. King's "I have a dream" speech has been mixed but "mostly positive. People have been saying, 'Right on, keep it up.' We're also hearing from people thanking us for making the speech available to generations that weren't aware of it."

C'mon, man. I find it hard to believe anyone is unaware of that speech. And if they are, they might also be unaware that a few people -- estimates range from 250,000 to 750,000 -- actually showed up to witness King's great flight of oratory. They won't see that in the first part of the Alcatel ad: Everybody has been airbrushed out, and King appears to be standing at the Lincoln Memorial talking to himself.

What's even more terrifying than that eerie image is the fear that, after Alcatel -- the deluge.

Murphy of Alcatel said, "We were very much trying to honor Dr. King," although I'm sure the company isn't wringing its hands in anguish over the millions in free publicity being generated by controversy over the ad.

The Alcatel ad, featuring a ghoulish, apparently digitized rear shot of King, is downright reverential compared with Cingular Wireless' television ad.

In that one, a snippet of King's most famous speech is played next to voices that were a little less historically significant -- Kermit the frog and Homer Simpson going "Doh!"

That's right. Kermit the #$ %% $#&* frog.

Ironic, isn't it, that the dude survived attempts by FBI Director J. Edgar Hoover to destroy his image, yet that image is being sold and sullied in death by his own family?

Think about it. If the family is willing to allow one of the civil rights movement's most sacred moments to be usurped to sell cell phones, who can say where they'll stop?

For instance, on the night before he was killed, King delivered his disturbing "I've been to the mountaintop" speech in which he foretold his death.

Must we now live in dread of hearing a computer-generated version of the speech in which Dr. King tells us, "You'll get to the mountaintop quicker in the new 4x4 Land Crusher by Toyota"?

A little-known but true historical tidbit is that King was actually running over his allotted time and Roy Wilkins, then head of the NAACP, was trying to get him to cut his "Dream" short. I'm glad he didn't.

Had King had more time, though, he might've finished with this rousing conclusion:

I have a dream that one day my four little children will live in a nation where they will be judged not by the color of their skin but by the content of their checking accounts -- which will be padded considerably by the residual income earned off cheesy, exploitative television commercials using my image.

4/3/2001

KRISPY KREME SELLS OUT

I'm through with Krispy Kreme doughnuts.

Nah, nothing to do with my Rubenesque waistline or dire warnings from my doctor.

It's OK to be a glutton for glazed doughnuts, but not for insults, and Krispy Kreme has insulted us North Carolinians for the last time.

The doughnut that broke the camel's back emerged from the deep fryer last week when the Winston-Salem-based company opened a shop in Harrod's, the hoity-toity store in that hoity-toity city London.

When Krispy Kreme went public and opened stores in New York, and then Seattle, while neglecting its home state, I bit my tongue. I figured, "They're Americans, and they have to live in New York and Seattle. The least we can do is share some of this legendary Southern sweetness with 'em."

When the company starts exporting that sweetness overseas, though -- at, apparently, our expense   then it's time to say, "Hold on there, old bean."

The merger of lowbrow Southern Americana with highbrow English pedigree has been, said Krispy Kreme spokeswoman Brooke Smith, "extremely gratifying .... Harrod's has many, many years of history bringing its customers unique experiences. It seems to be a great marriage."

Smith said the company will open 25 stores in the United Kingdom and Ireland within five years: She said nothing about opening another one in the Triangle to go with the single, forlorn, no-longer-24-hour-except- drive-through store in Raleigh.

At the risk of sounding xenophobic, it defies belief that fresh, hot Krispy Kremes are now available in London and not in, say, Fuquay-Varina.

Why would a beloved Southern institution neglect its base in favor of making a big splash across the Big Pond? Only last week I told you how NASCAR, the quintessential Southern pastime, was pulling races from the small Southern tracks that made it great in favor of larger venues in California, New York, Illinois and possibly overseas.

Now Krispy Kreme, maker of the quintessential Southern finger food, is also showering its confectionary affections on everyone but us.

Remember the classic "Beverly Hillbillies" TV episode where the Clampett clan inherit s a London castle? They flew over, and Jed introduced himself to his valet, Mr. Faversham.

Jed: "Howdy, I'm Jed Clampett."

Valet: "Faversham, sir."

Jed: "Well, Faversham to you, too."

I waited 30 years to go to London, just to try my "Faversham" greeting on some bloke, certain that he'd seen that episode and we could share a laugh, some crumpets and a spot of tea.

Alas, not one person got it, and they all looked at me as though I'd insulted the Queen Mum or said something bad about Prince Charles' ears.

Hmmph. I don't see why anyone who doesn't share such classic American humor gets to share our doughnuts.

I'm not going back to London -- not even for one of those doughnuts -- but if you go, do me a favor: Slap the first person you see eating a glazed with a knife and fork.

———————————————————————— 10/10/2003

KU KLUX SPIN

It's a lament we've all made: Where is a night-riding cross burner when you need one?

Efforts to find homegrown KKK members failed -- my old buddy and frequent caller "Joe C. from Johnston County" was nowhere to be found -- so I ended up chatting with Pastor Thomas Robb of Harrison, Ark.

Robb said he is pastor of the Church of Jesus Christ and bills himself as the national director of the Knights of the Ku Klux Klan. It was through the KKK that he added $100 to the $22,000 reward fund set up to help find whoever burned three crosses in Durham last month.

"We sincerely want them to catch those people who burned the crosses," Pastor Robb assured me. "They're making us look bad."

At the beginning of our conversation, Robb informed me that our telephone connection was tenuous. "So if by chance we get cut off, I didn't hang up on you."

The first time he "didn't hang up" on me was when I asked why the KKK would care whether black boys ran around killing each other. Wouldn't that work to the Klan's benefit?

Click.

Leaflets left at one of the cross-burnings attributed them to the KKK. The crosses were presented as warnings to Durham gangbangers, who were told to "cease and desist" with their fratricidal violence.

"Cease and desist"? Hmmph. That's like a cat warning a dog not to play in traffic or the Sioux warning Custer to stay away from Little Bighorn.

The Klan I know would be more inclined to bake cakes and send "thank you" notes to black predators than order them to stop doing what it used to do.

Bull, Robb said, objecting to my depiction of the Klan. He blamed

Hollywood for distorting its image.

"When the entertainment media says that burning crosses in a person's yard ... is what white people do when they are mad, then people may follow the script. Acts of intimidation are not what Christian white-rights organizations are about."

Ku Klux Klan is derived from a Greek word, kyklos, which means -- if you're me, anyway -- "RUN!" A burning cross was viewed as its symbol of domestic terrorism which meant, "RUN FAST! No, FASTER."

Not to Robb. "The lighted cross" -- he says lighted, I say burning -- "is an old Christian symbol still used in some churches. There are many instances where we've been blamed for things we didn't do.

"There was recently a situation at Trinity College in Deerfield, Ill., where minority students received threatening letters," he said.

Those letters, as Robb gleefully pointed out, were signed by the KKK, but an investigation determined that they were written by a homesick black female student.

Anyone who would employ such a trick suffers from more than just homesickness and should be allowed to withdraw from school -- after I withdraw my foot from her ... Oops.

The Klan's coffers are not as flush as they once were; court rulings have bankrupted it. Thus, its image-burnishing contribution of $100.

Still, Robb pointed out, "I'll bet that $100 represents a higher percentage of our income than the $5,000 the [federal] government has pledged" represents of its income.

—————————————————————————————————— 6/10/2005

L.A.-SMOG, STARS AND TEARGAS ———————————

LOS ANGELES -- Ever been read the "riot act"?

Naw, not the one where your dad yells at you for putting the empty milk carton back in the refrigerator or for not cleaning your room.

I'm talking about the riot act where a big ol' cop with a bullhorn and an attitude says, "You are hereby advised by the City of Los Angeles that you have 10 minutes to disperse or we're gonna start whaling away on your heads."

OK, that's not precisely what the dude said, but that's what it sounded like to me.

Because I'm allergic to tear gas, horse hooves and rubber bullets, I left the protest area with nine minutes and 40 seconds remaining on the clock and fled into the Staples Center to hear Bill and Hil.

The cops, as I later saw on television, thus began walking through the crowd and dropping tear-gas canisters as casually as men strolling through the park and dropping bread crumbs for pigeons.

While the images of barbed wire and helmeted cops astride huge horses are not the laid-back images most people have of California, it's a timeworn cliche that California is different from anywhere else.

Indeed, most of the protesters outside the Democratic National Convention were opposing or espousing issues you'd expect to see any place

- abortion, gun control and gay rights, among others. It's hard, however, to imagine protesters in Johnston County carrying signs saying, "Breast-feeding must be stopped."

The anti-breast-feeding leader was not amused when I asked whether he'd been breast-fed as a kid.

Things were a bit more tranquil back in my hotel room, where I have a breathtaking view of the parking lot where big-money Democrats disembark throughout the day from long, black limousines.

The only other difference between this hotel and a Motel 6 in Monroe is the book in the nightstand and the earthquake safety tips on the bathroom wall.

"In the event of an earthquake ... stay calm, stand in an open doorway with your back to the door or crouch under a heavy piece of furniture. Then, bend over and calmly proceed to kiss your butt goodbye."

OK, I made that last part up.

I'm not making up the book I found in my nightstand. It was not the Holy Bible. It was "The Teaching of Buddha," which I randomly opened to this passage: "In this Pure Land, there are boundless Light and everlasting life."

I don't know where that place is, but it isn't here. Los Angeles is an exciting city where, in some neighborhoods, you can tell the poor people because they're the ones driving their own Mercedes-Benzes.

But I haven't drawn an unlabored breath of air since I got here. That's why I have to stifle a laugh each time I hear radio ads and see billboards boasting how California fought the tobacco companies so its citizens wouldn't have to breathe second-hand smoke.

———————————————————————————————— 8/17/2000

LAST MEAL UNCERTAINTY A BITTER FATE ——————

I was hoping the dude would at least get one more last meal.

Under normal circumstances, you'd almost have to be Mother Teresa to work up a good head of sympathy for Willie Ervin Fisher. This is a man who beat and stabbed his girlfriend to death with a knife and broom handle and stabbed her 12-year-old daughter when she tried to stop the attack.

But as Fisher's soul is committed to heaven or hell -- I know which one I'm putting my money on -- after his execution for that murder last week, it's hard not to conclude that the state "done him wrong."

Think about it: How do you justify prepping a man for his death -- going so far as to feed him his last meal -- and then have a judge intervene three hours before he's supposed to take the dirt nap?

Then, 19 hours later, which was barely enough time for him to digest the fried chicken, mashed potatoes and cabbage he ate for his first last meal, prison officials rap on his cell door, strap him onto a gurney and send him to perdition anyway.

I wonder what's the protocol when an execution is temporarily aborted after a condemned man eats what is presumably his last meal. Do they let him eat another last meal the next night? If so, will the inmate alter his selection?

I'm guessing "yes." Who, after all, would order a meal of chitlins, cherry cheesecake, strawberry cheesecake and Cheerwine soda if they thought they'd have to be around to suffer the gastronomic consequences?

That's what happened a few years ago when an inmate here consumed just such a feast and then received an 11th-hour reprieve from his death sentence. I'll bet that about 3 a.m., when those chitlins and cheesecake started warring inside his belly, he was probably wishing the execution had been carried out.

Regardless of one's opinion on capital punishment, strapping an inmate onto such an emotional roller coaster before strapping him onto the gurney seems unfair.

To be sure, there are emotional sadists who figure that nothing -- not even telling the condemned man that the governor was setting him free and then shouting "NOT!" just before pulling the switch -- is too bad for someone guilty of a crime as heinous as Fisher's.

A far more typical opinion, though, was expressed by Dan Young, a Raleigh man who called me after Fisher was executed.

"I believe in the death penalty," Young said, "but this on-again, off-again thing -- man, that's what I call cruel and unusual."

That's what I thought, too, but Larry Moore, one of Fisher's attorneys, said Fisher was unperturbed by the legal flip-flops occurring with his life hanging in the balance. "He was serene," Fisher said. "He never showed the least bit of anxiety over his own death, but he wanted us to raise any issue that might help other inmates" on death row.

When Fisher's last ray of hope -- that Gov. Mike Easley had a conflict of interest because he was attorney general when Fisher was convicted and now was the man to whom Fisher was appealing for clemency -- was dashed by the state Supreme Court, Moore said, Fisher serenely accepted his fate.

But he didn't order another plate.

3/13/2001

THE LAST RIDE HOME FOR BROTHER

Sally Fisher-Ervin hadn't spent any time alone with her baby brother or even touched him for 10 years, so when the opportunity presented itself March 10, she put him in her daughter's SUV, climbed in beside him and headed home.

But first, she turned the air conditioner up really high.

Once en route, they stopped for sodas and then called family members and friends to tell them that she was bringing Ervin home so they could stop by and see him. After an impromptu, 10-minute family reunion in the front yard, Sally Fisher-Ervin took her baby brother to the funeral home.

For burial.

"Ervin" -- known to the state of North Carolina as Willie Ervin Fisher -- had been executed by lethal injection at Central Prison the night before for killing his girlfriend. Afterward, his body was taken to the medical examiner at WakeMed.

That's where Sally Fisher-Ervin picked him up the next day.

"I just got up that morning and said, 'We might as well take Ervin home, ' " she told me. "I just wanted to be close to him for a while."

Sally Fisher-Ervin, along with her sister, daughter, a family friend and an employee of the medical examiner's office, struggled mightily to fit her brother into the GMC Jimmy. "Honey, I was in the van trying to pull the body, and you know dead weight is heavy, and Ervin was a big, heavy guy anyway, " she said.

The back seat of the truck wouldn't go down all the way, so they had to lay him across the back seat. "We couldn't get him in straight, " she recalled. "When we finally got him in, I said, 'Ervin, we're about to take you home.' My sister and I sat in the back, one on each side of him, and we talked to him."

Getting Ervin into the truck was easy compared with getting him out of the morgue at WakeMed, his sister said.

"The medical examiner kept telling me, 'You can't do that, ' when we went to get him, but I said, 'Oh, yes, I can.' He made a couple of telephone calls and five minutes later came back and told us we could."

Fisher-Ervin knew she could, because as deputy registrar in the Vital Records office of the Forsyth County Health Department, she deals daily with the regulations of death. She knows the rules.

She also knows that some people will think she's crazy.

"I'm not a Looney Tune, " she said with a small laugh and disputed the contention of some people familiar with the case that she transported her brother's body in such an unorthodox manner to save on funeral expenses.

Indeed, Pam Walker, a spokeswoman for the Department of Correction, said the state will pay up to $300 for an indigent family if the funeral home writes a letter. Walker said, "We did not get such a letter for the Fisher family."

That's because, Fisher-Ervin insisted, money was not a factor.

"To me, it was like closure, " she said. "For 10 years, I was talking to him through glass and couldn't touch him. That was my brother; he was the baby. ... I still have days where I have my little crying spells where I can't deal with his death. But bringing him back home helped me out."

I'm guessing that, somehow, it helped her baby brother out, too.

5/18/2001

LATINO? SI, SI, HOMEY

I don't know how you missed it; it was front-page news across the country this week: Hispanics have passed African-Americans as the largest minority in the country.

Boo freakin' hoo. Such a designation could mean billions in federal dollars to certain areas for schools, housing and community development, but for individuals, being known as a member of the country's largest minority is akin to being the world's tallest midget or shortest giant: It means nothing.

That hasn't stopped some people from becoming angry over losing their most-favored-minority status, so I'll tell them exactly whom they should blame: Ricky Martin.

Naw, the Latin heartthrob isn't singlehandedly responsible for a Latino baby boom, but he is responsible -- and to a lesser extent, so is Jennifer Lopez -- for inspiring a growing number of black people to suddenly "discover" their Latin roots.

Don't look at me like that. Ever since Martin began shaking his bonbon all over the place, every light-skinned black person with even a hint of a curl in their hair has claimed to be half-Latino. With mouth agape, I recently watched part of a TV show called "J. Lo's Fabulous Life," which detailed, yep, her fabulous life. Who wouldn't want to be Latino if that's how they live?

Of course, Martin and J. Lo aren't the only reasons why it's now hip to be Latino and why they outnumber blacks -- depending upon how you classify who's black and who isn't: Once the U.S. Census put in a box allowing people to mark "other," I knew our numbers would diminish.

This is nothing new. Just between you and me, some black people have been passing for something else for a long time. Mr. Delaney, a Wesley Snipes-hued Jamaican merchant in our neighborhood in the 1960s, claimed on his passport that he was white. A grade-school classmate, no doubt influenced by the popularity of the old "Daniel Boone" TV series we all watched, once claimed he was part Indian. "Blackfoot, daddy-o," he said, until Mrs. Robinson, our sixth-grade teacher, put a stop to that by slapping him upside the head. (Teachers could do that back in those days.)

Remembering that, I shouldn't have been surprised a couple of years ago when my son's 12-year-old friend, Patrick, suddenly claimed that he was part Latino and started wearing pomade in his hair to make it wavy. He also proclaimed that we should henceforth call him "Rick."

The irony of all this is that I've heard the old-timers talk about a time, many moons ago, when it was actually cool to be black.

The president had declared "War on Poverty," the literati had discovered us -- Norman Mailer wrote a famous essay called "The White Negro" -- and it was nothing to read of fabulous parties where rich Manhattan liberals would hang out in their penthouses and sip Cold Duck with members of the Black Panthers.

Alas, that mythical period was short-lived, and Hispanics are now the chic minority.

Oh, well. I reckon I'll just learn to shake my bonbon, too.

As soon as I find out where it is.

1/24/2003

LEARNING WELL IS BEST REVENGE

In my accustomed role of peacemaker, I have devised a compromise in the battle between students at the University of North Carolina at Chapel Hill who want the names of slave-owning benefactors stricken from campus buildings and university hard-liners who shout, "Nevah!"

Since the first building in dispute is named after a slave-owning, purported grand pooh-bah of the Ku Klux Klan named William L. Saunders, a perfect compromise would be to name the building after - yep, you guessed it - me.

That way, the university wouldn't even have to pay to chisel his name off the building's facade.

Working against me is the fact that I never attended UNC and have no official connection to the school. Working for me, though, is the possibility that William Saunders was some kin to me. If he was, he came from the side of the family we don't talk much about, or if we do, it's in hushed tones. Li'l Willie, as we called him, was the white sheet, uh, sheep, of the family.

Sad to say, he wasn't the only one. You know how Confederate sympathizers are always claiming that some blacks actually fought on the side of the rebs during the Civil War? I know that's hard to believe, especially since Clarence Thomas hadn't even been born yet, but I have evidence that there is some truth to their contention.

Legend has it that another family member about whom we don't talk, Col. Beauregard Saunders - we just called him "B.S." for short - ran away from home at 11 and fought on the wrong side during the war. Of course, legend also has it that B.S. was half-crazy from licking turpentine off dead possums. He later claimed, unconvincingly, that he thought the crossed-rifle insignia on the Confederate soldiers' caps was actually an "X" that stood for Malcolm X.

Eboni Staton, a student at UNC and a member of the student organization leading the name-change charge, said in a story in the UNC campus newspaper that Saunders was "a murderer, a slave owner and the emperor of the KKK."

People who oppose changing the building's name probably say, "Yeah, but other than that, he wasn't so bad, right?"

I admire the students' fervor in attempting to make the university face up to its past and for just being committed to a worthy cause. It was beginning to appear that campus activism had died or was taking the form of student protests of the somnolent '70s - when our big issues were demands for longer visitation hours in the girls' dorm or for positive identification of the mystery meat served on Wednesdays.

As admirable as their activism is, though, the best way for the students at UNC to hurt the late, unlamented Col. Saunders is not to chisel his name off the building that bears it. No, the best way to have him spinning in his grave and going "What didn't I do wrong?" throughout eternity is to walk into Saunders Hall - even if the name isn't changed - and get a good education. Thus armed, they can work to create a world that won't tolerate another Col. William L. Saunders.

————————————————————————————————— 11/4/1999

LESSONS IN CLARITY AT THE END OF THE DAY ———

In the magnificent television mini-series "Lonesome Dove," two former Texas Rangers agonize as they prepare to hang one of their former colleagues who fell in with a bad bunch of outlaws. Sensing their displeasure with the task at hand, the lawman-turned-criminal, Jake Spoon, says "Well, adios, boys. I never meant no harm."

Then he spurs his horse from under him and is dead.

One of the ex-Rangers, Gus McCrae, after finally composing himself, says "He died fine, didn't he?"

Yep. And you could say the same thing about Eppie Lederer. She died fine.

You know Lederer by her professional name, Ann Landers. Landers, who in her advice column over several decades instructed millions on how to live, gave perhaps her most poignant advice in her final days on how to die. And she did it without saying or writing a word.

First, she kept her terminal illness secret from all but her closest friends and relatives. She did this, her daughter said, to prevent a barrage of letters and public expressions of sentiment from well-meaning fans. She also, no doubt, wanted to avert the dignity-stealing tabloid headlines and stories that usually mark the death of a celebrity.

In a television interview shortly after Landers' death, her daughter, Margo Howard, told of the final decisions her mother made.

"She said to me in the hospital in January when she was diagnosed, 'You know, we've always gotten things pretty much the way we wanted.' And one of the things she wanted was to edge off the stage rather quietly so her readers and many close friends did not know that she was ill....So she did get to do it on her own terms."

Even more impressive than the decision to keep her illness secret was the one to forgo life-prolonging -- which is not the same as "life-enhancing" -- treatment. Howard, discussing her mother's decision not to subject herself to painful treatment just to buy a little more time, said, "Well, my dear, she was 83 when she got the news and she decided she didn't want to go through all of the carrying on and the treatment... Mother thought in her mid-80s she wasn't really up for that. She wasn't willing to louse up, say, four or five months to get another year out of it."

Good for her.

Treatment exists for multiple myeloma, the type of cancer Landers had, but she eschewed it. As Howard noted during the television interview, former vice presidential candidate Geraldine Ferraro is being treated for the same type of cancer. She, however, is in her sixties.

The concept of "dying well" has been in my mind ever since I heard the details of Landers' death last month, but the story became even more compelling when I read accounts of the recent death of American missionary Martin Burnham, who was held hostage for more than a year by terrorists in the Philippines, and of two Buddhist monks slain in their monastery. One of the monks had written "To accept death lovingly, trusting in God -- this is our final obedience."

Gracie Burnham, Martin's wife, said of her husband, "He died well." He was killed, and she was wounded, during a rescue operation.

One of my favorite poems, by Dylan Thomas, advises,

Do not go gentle into that good night,

Old age should burn and rave at close of day;

Rage, rage against the dying of the light.

Some might think that notion contradicts Landers' decision, but I don't. I'm guessing that even Thomas would appreciate the dignity inherent in knowing when to exit life's stage -- and doing it on one's own terms.

7/13/2002

LET'S HOPE MCVEIGH TOOK HIS CAUSE
WITH HIM TO THE GRAVE

Li'l Timmy McVeigh is dead, and if there is any justice he's licking the dirt from between Satan's toes right now. But dead though he is, he won.

The terrorist who called himself a patriot paid the ultimate price for the Oklahoma City bombing that killed 168 people, but he went out - as most sociopaths long to do - in a blaze of glory.

Not the blaze of glory with guns a'blazin' like Randolph Scott, John Wayne and other celluloid cowboys. McVeigh went out in a blaze of popping flashbulbs, media attention and, I fear, adulation from an unofficial brotherhood of anti-government psychos.

Executing McVeigh, especially after the FBI admitted it had neglected to turn over information from its investigation to the defense team, only enhances his status as a martyr among like-minded lunatics. Far better it would have been to let him just rot away in anonymity in some prison cell, far away from the media coverage that, intentionally or not, made him appear heroic.

I spent the weekend leading up to McVeigh's execution in Washington, D.C., where media overkill is an art. It seemed as if every news station in the nation's capital had adopted an All Timmy, All The Time format, lest they be out-McVeighed by the competition.

The highlight - or was it the lowlight? - occurred when one station lured viewers with a "new development" teaser before cutting to a commercial. I, like a chump, waited anxiously for the new development, wondering if one of the lawyers had succeeded in getting their man another stay of execution.

Nah, nothing like that. From what I could discern, the only "new" development was that McVeigh was five minutes closer to being executed than he had been during the previous report.

Everyone who had any contact with McVeigh - friends, lawyers, casual acquaintances - was on television, offering "expert" insight into what drove him to commit the heinous act. Even when they had nothing edifying to add. For instance, Steven Jones, McVeigh's original attorney, was asked what drove his former client to blow up the Murrah Federal Building.

"Bullies," Jones answered with the self-assurance of the ignorant. And "horrific marital conflicts" between McVeigh's parents.

In other words, we're supposed to believe that someone committed the worst act of terrorism in U.S. history because he was teased by classmates in school and used to lie awake nights hearing his parents fight?

Bull. If that were the case, federal buildings would be going "KABOOM!" all over America, since I'd guess that adolescence was a painful experience for more teens than not. It trivializes McVeigh's evil acts to attribute them to something - schoolyard taunts - as traditional as apple pie.

Few people with knowledge of the crime think McVeigh acted entirely alone. "He ain't that smart," his former attorney said in one of his few cogent pronouncements. Even fewer think he is the only misanthrope who views the government as an enemy to be attacked by any means necessary. Anyone who thinks that way should've been listening to talk radio stations around the country during the days surrounding the execution.

Sure, what McVeigh did was bad, many callers said (without much evident conviction), "but what about Waco?"

In other words, what our government did at Waco - or, more accurately, what David Koresh did to his followers at Waco - was just as bad as what McVeigh did and, to their twisted reasoning, seemingly justified McVeigh's declaration of war on America and its citizens.

At least it did to McVeigh.

6/16/2001

LOVE ~ OR WHATEVER ~ FOR SALE

As far as disappointments go, this was a big one. I went to a massage parlor two nights ago, and all I got was a ... a ... massage.

The tired lady didn't even call it a massage. "We can't give massages," she explained with a straight face. "That's against the law. You have to be a licensed masseur or masseuse for that. What we do is give you a rub."

Whatever you call it, it wasn't worth $70 for 30 minutes and was about as titillating as watching a "Sanford & Son" rerun of Fred and Grady playing checkers. But as a journalist, I felt it was my duty to investigate -- for you, dear readers -- at least one of the numerous businesses you see in our state touting "all girl staffs" and hinting at something delightfully unsavory.

My interest was piqued after Raleigh police raided what they said was a bordello earlier this week and arrested or cited people on charges of operating a house of prostitution, engaging in prostitution or entering a dwelling for the purpose of engaging in prostitution.

Cops are alleging that men from all social strata visited the house of ill repute for a little afternoon delight during the weeks they had the house at 5838 Six Forks Road under surveillance.

But the men alleged to have run the joint and those cited for visiting it were all from Latin America. As were the women. Either they just picked a bad time to visit, or the place was providing a valuable service for young men new to this country who speak little English but are conversant in the international language -- moolah.

The informant who turned the cops on to the place said men were "paying $30 for 15 minutes of anything they desired."

To my jaundiced eye, if men were getting anything they wanted in an innocuous-looking house in a quiet North Raleigh neighborhood, one could only guess what was happening in a neon-lit building with a sign advertising "Girls Girls Girls." That's why I decided to visit one such place in Durham -- for you, remember -- and find out if anything more illicit takes place for money.

Not the night I went, it didn't. Oh, one woman offered to talk dirty to me for an extra tip, but I politely declined. "Shucks," I thought, "all I have to do is write a column about Billy Graham, and half the people in the Triangle will talk dirty to me for free."

Capt. David Laeng of the Durham Police Department said what happens in such businesses "falls way down on our priority list. We generally don't look into them until we get a complaint."

Of course, the only complaint they're likely to get -- "Hey officer, all I got was a rub" -- means that no crime took place.

Although moralists will disagree, many people see prostitution as a victimless crime. Think about it. Is the fact that consenting adults are having fun -- and money is changing hands -- really a crime we want police spending countless man-hours on?

I could be wrong, which as you know is quite unlikely, but I think most taxpayers would prefer to know their dollars are paying for protection from something more sinister than men who have more money than communication or social skills.

Want to tell Barry what you think?

7/13/2001

LUTHER'S DEATH IS LESSON

Is it wrong to be mad at a dead man?

Probably, but it's hard for me not to be angry with departed soul singer Luther Vandross.

Go ahead, accuse me of dissing the dead. But I'm not. I loved the dude, at least his first three albums. After that, he just seemed to remake those same three albums for the next 23 years.

Still, he was so popular throughout his career that there used to be national contests in which people vied to have Luther sing at their weddings. He was the original "Wedding Singer," although I always thought it would be cool to get him to sing one of his songs -- remember "It's Over Now"? -- at my next divorce.

The reason I'm angry at him is because, while Luther sang like nobody else, it appears he took care of his health like too many others -- especially too many brothers.

When he died last week of complications of diabetes, he joined a list of black men who've succumbed to similar complications in recent years: actor Paul Winfield, gospel singer Ronald Winans, fellow lovemeister Barry White.

The thing they all had in common is that they all checked out before reaching Social-Security-check-receiving age.

Luther, who died at 54, and the others probably needed a doctor like mine.

Each time my weight inches past an eighth of a ton, or I do something really stupid -- like eating 5 pounds of pork barbecue and washing it down with a gallon of Gatorade, sending my blood pressure into the stratosphere -- ol' Dr. Sawbones'll tell me just what he thinks of such a boneheaded move.

It's unlikely that there's a dude who hasn't benefited from Luther's dulcet tones saying things we wish we could say.

Back in the old days, before CDs replaced albums, you'd just drop the needle, dim the lights and let Luther do the rest.

Because of diabetes, he won't be around any longer to help smooth our romantic paths.

Dr. Allen Mask of Raleigh said the main problem with Luther was not lifestyle, but genetics. Noting that two of his siblings and his father had all died of diabetes-related ailments, Mask said ,"He was predisposed to it ... I'd taken care of him a couple of times when he came here, and he was really, really taking good care of himself.

"Sometimes, you can do everything you're supposed to do" and still be vulnerable, he said.

Mask said it is important to get a checkup and take your medicine, but equally important to monitor your health.

OK, by a show of hands, how many of you know men who neglect their health, yet schedule an appointment with Jake down at the garage as soon as they hear a strange noise under the hood of their car?

It may be understandable, in a historical context, why many black men are leery of going to the doctor: We all "know" somebody who knows somebody whose second cousin went to the doctor for a hangnail and came out minus a kidney.

Sorry, homes. That may be an acceptable reason for neglect to apologists who want to blame everything on past injustices, but not to me. It's merely irresponsible. Period.

Go see a doctor and get checked out. Even if you do, you won't be able to sing as well as Luther and Barry.

You might, however, be able to sing longer.

7/5/2005

MAKE CITY SAFE FOR LAP DANCING

I know I have but few claims to divine Providence, but if I could send a prayer to the Almighty it would go, "Dear God, Please save us from do-gooders." Amen.

The do-gooder I want relief from most immediately is the Rev. Carl Kenney, pastor of Orange Grove Baptist Church. He is on a misguided mission to close down a certain nightclub in Durham.

In the column he writes for another local newspaper, Kenney zeroed in this week on Brothers III on Angier Avenue, labeling it a scourge on the surrounding community.

The good pastor discovered this scourge, he claimed, en route to his church late one Friday night to get a book -- some Kierkegaard, he wrote -- to help him sleep.

Wow, what a coincidence. I discovered it the same way. I was searching for something -- let's call it "Kierkegaard" -- to help me sleep, too, when I saw scores of cars and decided to investigate. Unlike Kenney, who claimed that he stayed in his car, watched the procession of men streaming into the club and learned what happens inside from secondhand sources, I got out to see for myself. As a journalist, I had to. For you.

Besides, if there was some sin in there that needed to be rassled to the ground, I wanted to lend my support and jump on it, too. What I found, unfortunately, was not the evil, lowdown sin den that Kenney described, but a relatively benign place where men, rowdy but peaceful, stood or sat around enjoying the floor show. As far as I could tell, everybody was grown.

131

Kenney not only misrepresented the club, which doesn't open until 'round midnight, but he misrepresented its clientele. "There aren't many black men in Durham who haven't been to the strip club," he wrote, a statement that is so wrong it defies comprehension. It also makes you wonder how he reached that conclusion by sitting outside one night. On the few occasions I've been there, every race and ethnic group has been represented.

Kenney cited residents' complaints in asking why the club hasn't been closed. None of the neighbors with whom I've spoken recalled complaining, and a couple of cops even said the place serves a useful function: Far from being the breeding ground for crime that Kenney contends, they and I think the crime rate in the city may actually go down during visiting hours at Brothers III.

The reverend cited statistics showing police have been called to disturbances of varying severity at the club over five years. I checked those same stats and was unimpressed. I haven't kept count, but I suspect the cops would've responded to at least that many disturbances at my house -- if Sweet Thang hadn't gone back to her mama a couple of years ago.

Enterprising young ladies have traditionally worked their way through school by dancing, and I, a big fan of both education and self-help, have felt compelled to contribute to their educations. If Kenney succeeds in convincing city officials to shut down the establishment, I wonder how much money he will contribute to their educations.

I'll tell you what, though. If the Rev. Do-right can show me a single instance where the owner of Brothers III snatched some dude off the street, hauled him into the club and forced a lap dance on him, I'll be the first to help shut it down.

1/18/2002

MAKE ME A PERFECT MATCH

So, it's finally hit you that Bubblicious, your favorite dancer down at Thee Nasty Kitty, was only after your money.

Or let's say you spent the days leading up to the holidays weeping into your eggnog and singing "Please Come Home for Christmas." And he didn't.

It's now time to face the fact: They're not coming back.

What to do, what to do?

If you're like a lot of single people in the Triangle, you'll call Lisa and Bill Horst or some of the other companies offering services like theirs. The Horsts, a married couple, own the William Ashley matchmaking company, which, they say, helps people who've succeeded at everything in life but finding the right mate.

"We're not a dating service," Lisa Horst said. "We cater to upscale single professionals ... internationally acclaimed scientists, best-selling authors. We attract people who are interested in a lifelong mate, not just someone to date."

It's hard to find a mate, she said, because "there are a lot of transplants here and this is a very family-oriented area."

On a hunch, I decided Monday to call the Horsts and operators of other dating companies to see if the need for their services increased during the holidays when feelings of loneliness can be exacerbated.

As usual, I was right.

"Absolutely," said Lisa Horst, a former journalist. "It's hard to be alone for the holidays. You go to family dinners, and everyone's asking: 'Where's your date?' That makes this a very challenging time to be alone."

My own theory is that, just as people begin each new year by embarking on self-improvement projects such as joining a gym, they also make resolutions to get rid of -- or find -- somebody, too.

Divorce lawyers to whom I talked said they often see an increase in divorce filings after the holidays.

The Horsts met the old-fashioned way: They were walking their dogs in a Raleigh park and struck up a conversation. But they don't recommend you at home try that. "We were just lucky," Bill said.

Lisa said, "We'd tried all the avenues available here, but because we work at home it was hard to meet anyone."

The Horsts cite copious statistics to show that there exists a market for what they're selling: There are about 350,000 single people in the Triangle, nearly half of all households nationally are headed by people who aren't married, and more people work at home and thus are not likely to meet someone in the workplace.

That was the case with Bill Horst, he said. "I was single, but I was pretty much off the market. I had just moved here from San Francisco, where there was an active social scene.

"Between traveling for work, playing hockey a few nights a week and taking care of my dogs, I didn't get out much," he said.

It's easy to believe the Triangle would be fertile ground for a dating -- oops, matchmaking -- service, because every day when I cruise any of the Internet dating sites (strictly for professional purposes, I swear) I am astounded by the number of eligible singles from the Triangle.

Of course, if singles become disillusioned by Internet dating or matchmaking services -- and don't want to be standing under the mistletoe alone -- they could always take a page from the Horsts' playbook: Buy a dog.

————————————————————————————————→ 12/30/2003

MARION, HERE'S A QUICK FIX ├─────────────────────────────

Everyone knows the proverb about hell having no fury like a woman scorned.

But what about us? We dudes can become furious when scorned, too.

Just ask Marion Jones, who pulled out of a track meet this week. Anyone seeking an explanation saw only the part of her that fellow runners usually see: her backside.

Whether the speedy sisterwoman's pullout from the meet in London or recent lackluster performances had anything to do with charges that she was illegally juicing up, you knew she was in trouble when her former husband was summoned to talk to federal agents.

Imagine knowing that the man you'd shared a life with before pushing him from your gravy train was privy to potentially damaging info. Yikes.

Not only had C.J. Hunter been exed out of her lucrative, fabulous lifestyle -- I saw Jones and her new beau, Tim Montgomery, exiting a shiny Porsche at a local restaurant recently -- but he also works at N.C. State University.

What better motivation could Hunter need for tripping a former UNC-Chapel Hill star coming out of the starting block?

Hunter, in the tradition of scorned lovers everywhere, reportedly testified that not only did Jones juice up before big meets but that he himself was the Juiceman.

Since Hunter'd already admitted using banned substances before landing at NCSU -- where he, ahem, helps football players become stronger -- his reputation was already sullied.

Jones, too, was in a no-win situation even before Hunter's testimony. Do well, and people attribute your performance to drugs. Do poorly, then it's because your drug use was curtailed by the scrutiny.

Back when they were trying women as witches in Salem, Mass., the courts would throw a suspect into a lake. If she floated, she was a witch and would be burned. If she didn't float, she drowned. But at least her name was cleared.

With Jones, apparently, if she wins it's because she's using performance enhancers. If she loses, her career sinks faster than a falsely accused witch.

And her rep is still sunk. Considering what she's going through, she'd have to be on drugs to win with such accusations nipping at her Nikes.

It's heartbreaking to me that -- 36 years after John Carlos and Tommie Smith were banned from the Olympics for making a political statement -- scores of today's athletes, motivated by greed, are being banned for using illegal substances. They ought to be ashamed.

Jones needn't be ashamed, yet, but she needs her image rehabilitated before Athens. I have the perfect solution to begin her makeover: me.

Laugh if you want, but it seems obvious that successful, ambitious, athletic men -- sprinter Montgomery has also been accused of juicing up -- have caused her grief.

That's why I'm offering her me, a man who judges success by the number of times he catches "Sanford & Son" on TV and whose idea of a tough workout is running downstairs for another bowl of Cap'n Crunch.

Unlike her two most recent men, I've never been accused of using performance-enhancing anything, unless you count putting cheese in my grits.

Boy, I'd look good in a Porsche. Call me, Marion.

7/30/2004

MEAGER NIGHTLIFE COST US

Jerry Lee Lewis, also known as The Killer, once sang, "What's made Milwaukee famous has made a loser out of me."

Those of us in Raleigh, nay, the entire Triangle, can say the same thing: What's made this a great place to live, work and raise a family has made a loser out of us -- at least where the CIAA tournament is concerned.

This will hurt our civic pride, but the fact is that if you're not living, working or raising a family in the area, there's little reason to come -- especially after the morality cops closed down most of our beloved sin dens.

Oh sure, Leon Kerry, commissioner of the Central Intercollegiate Athletic Association, said the conference's desire to expand southward was a factor in selecting Charlotte over the Triangle after five profitable and fun years, and everyone with a laptop computer has offered their reasons for the change.

The real reason Charlotte was allowed to steal the tournament, though, is this: There is nothing to do in Raleigh after the games without getting in your car -- and driving to Charlotte.

As Kerry said of Charlotte in a Charlotte Observer story after the theft was formalized, "This town's a happening town."

It's doubtful anyone has ever said that about Raleigh. Sleepy? Yup. Happening? Get real.

Many of the thousands who fight predawn February frigidity during the tournament to attend the Tom Joyner Morning Show at the RBC Center do so because they know there will be little else going on other than basketball. That point was slam-dunked in February when a party sponsored by Magic Johnson drew close to 4,000 entertainment-starved people to the convention center.

Ascribing blame for allowing Charlotte's grand larceny is pointless. But I'll do it anyway.

Years ago I pointed out, quite accurately, that one reason we're often left sucking Charlotte's exhaust fumes is that Charlotte has dynamic leadership -- Bruton Smith, Humpy Wheeler and others, plus a sharp, young city council -- that can get things done.

In Raleigh, everything is seemingly done by committee.

Our bargaining position would have been enhanced if, for instance, Mayor Charles Meeker had possessed the juice to pull Kerry into a smoky room and say "Look, homes, tell a bro what you need, and I'm on it."

Alas, Meeker was left scratching his head in befuddlement and saying that the city and he had done everything they could.

Buffalo chips. To make us more attractive to future conferences -- I hear the World Tractor Pull Extravaganza hasn't booked a site yet -- we're going to need progressive leaders. That means leaders who realize that Raleigh visitors are no longer satisfied, as Barney Fife was, to get a corner room at the Y and send postcards of the Capitol back home to Thelma Lou.

They want exciting nightlife, which starts with nightclubs that stay open beyond 1 a.m. Thousands come here from places where the festivities don't crank up until midnight. By the time the last game ends and they run to their hotel room to splash on some Brut, it's already "last call."

To paraphrase country music icon Willie Nelson, the nightlife ain't no good life -- at least not around here.

12/17/2004

MEN MAKE A MENTAL ADJUSTMENT ├──────────────

I loved the movie "The Brothers," and not just because it had plenty of sweet young thangs running around with hardly any clothes on in one scene.

The thing I liked most was an opening scene that featured something I'd never seen before. There was a beautiful woman in a chair, and across from her was a good-looking, articulate dude seated on a sofa.

I know, I know: That's the opening scene in just about every movie you go to. The difference about this one, though, is that the woman was a psychiatrist and the man -- who was black -- was her patient.

"My, things have changed," I remember thinking. In the old days of black cinema -- say, the 1970s -- when a brother like Shaft had a problem, he'd just go out and kill something, love something or blow something up. Everyone knows that we don't go to a head shrink, right?

Wrong. Dr. Denise Barnes, a psychiatrist in private practice in Durham, said a sizable percentage of her practice is composed of men -- of all races.

"They are white-collar and blue-collar, black and white. I'm surprised and very pleased, because they are coming in on their own or encouraged by their significant other," she said.

One reason men might have been reluctant to seek head help in the past was because therapy was mainly associated with wimpy, whiny men like Woody Allen. Now, though, you can see a tough mobster, portrayed by Robert DeNiro, scheduling an appointment with his shrink in "Analyze This" while en route to kill a rival gangster.

In other words, movies have helped "masculinize" psychiatric therapy, a phenomenon I first noticed in high school. Teachers at Richmond Senior High School in Rockingham had despaired of ever getting boys to take a "Home Economics" course -- we thought it was too sissyish -- but they simply changed the name of the course to "Bachelor Living," and we rushed to sign up for it.

Barnes doubts that a single scene in a movie is responsible for the number of men seeking what she called "psychiatric assistance," but I'm guessing that movies such as "The Brothers" and "Analyze This" and the hit HBO series "The Sopranos" have all contributed to making such treatment more palatable to men.

As one mob wiseguy in "The Sopranos" stated -- or, more precisely, misstated -- upon learning that his boss was seeing a shrink, "There's no stigmata attached to seeing a shrink now."

Barnes said the same thing, albeit more articulately. "Some of the stigma may be reduced," she said, "and we have a more sophisticated population, especially in this area, who know you need to take care of your psychological as well as your physical health."

I'm about the most well-adjusted man I know -- OK, except for the time I thought my neighbor's dog was telling me to build a rocket ship out of Z.Z. Hill album covers -- but I don't think I'd be afraid to see a shrink if I needed one. Besides, there are times when every man could use someone to talk to besides the guy who asks, "Hey, bub. You want that straight or on the rocks?"

──┤ 6/1/2001

MIND THAT TATER LADLE

As a lover of haute cuisine - high-class food - I love nothing more than dressing up, splashing on some Brut, strapping on the ol' feedbag and heading down to my local Golden Corral.

The death of manners, though, is about to make me give up this uniquely American pleasure. In what other country can you pay $6.99 for dinner and eat until they have to back the truck up and wheel you out?

But I'm not giving up without a fight, because one shouldn't have to go to Delmonico's, Spago's, Roscoe's Chicken & Waffles or any of those famous Los Angeles restaurants I visited last week - for work, Boss, honest - to witness proper etiquette.

This is stuff you should have learned in kindergarten, or even before your ma and pa let you out of the house for the first time.

But since many of the people who dine at the precise same time I do didn't learn it then, I'm taking it as my civic duty to teach them. To wit, Mr. Manners' tips for dining out at buffets, tips which, if followed, will result in a more pleasurable dining experience for everyone, or at least for me:

- Wash your hands. Look, it's OK for you to come in after plowing the north 40 and plop down at the table without washing up at home, but your fellow diners at GC don't want to pick up the ladle for the mashed taters after you've left part of the north 40 on it.

- Don't lick your fingers. The surgeon general has warned - or would, if he ate at Golden Corral - that licking your fingers and then grabbing ahold of the gravy spoon in a restaurant transmits about 71 million cooties.

You know how when you enter the restaurant and the line goes directly to the cashier? They ought to make it go to the rest room, where people can wash their hands. Saying "But I washed 'em yesterday" is no excuse.

- Accompany small children to the buffet line. No matter how proud you might be that li'l Katie or Shaniqua is finally displaying independence, no one wants to eat banana pudding containing her grubby little fingerprints.

Over the years, I've sent scores of sticky-fingered crumb-snatchers fleeing to inattentive parents with just my baleful, mean-dude stare. No, really, you don't have to thank me.

- Go sit down. Despite the presence of tables and chairs throughout most restaurants, an alarmingly high number of people prefer to stand at the buffet table and sample every dish there.

- Scrap the tank top, fellas. Sure you're proud of your biceps, and Sweet Thang loves running her fingers through that forest on your back, but the rest of us could keep our food down if we didn't see your hirsute torso leaning over the green bean casserole.

I realize that with all of the problems in the world - violence in the Mideast, N'Sync rumored to be making a new album - bad manners at the Golden Corral might not seem of paramount importance. But that, and thousands of other little things we barely notice, detract from our quality of life.

Think about it: How much quality of life can you have when there are strange fingerprints in your mashed taters?

8/22/2000

MISGUIDED SNIPING AT AN HONOR ⊢──────────

As members of an unofficial brotherhood, columnists usually refrain from criticizing colleagues at competing newspapers.

But sometimes one must dispense with protocol and ask "Colleague, hast thou been drinking printer's ink again?"

Just such a time arose when I read a recent column by Michael Peterson in The Herald-Sun. Peterson, as he is wont to do, was unleashing a bilious assault on the Durham City Council. Most of his bile was aimed at council member Howard Clement, whom he took to the woodshed for proposing that cities sue gun manufacturers for gun violence - a tactic many big-city mayors are using to discourage companies from manufacturing cheap handguns solely to kill human beings cheaply.

Even though Clement is the coolest Republican I know, this proposal is as full of holes as a punk on Saturday night after a botched drug deal. Guns don't kill people, Howie: Bullets fired by misanthropic, maladjusted sociopaths do.

But the reason Peterson was peeved so personally at Clement - he called him the "big Kahuna" of stupidity - had little to do with the futility of suing gunmakers.

No, sirree. Peterson seemed angriest because Clement in 1996 awarded the key to the city to Johnnie Cochran, the attorney whose legal wile - along with Marcia Clark's and Christopher Darden's incompetence - kept O.J. Simpson out of prison.

In a mind-boggling bit of pseudo-logic, Peterson accused Clement of "mind-boggling hypocrisy" for opposing gun violence even though he honored Cochran for "successfully" defending Simpson. Huh?

"Howard wants to sue gun manufacturers, yet award a key to the city to a lawyer who defended an accused butcher," Peterson said, as if the link should be obvious to everyone. (Is he saying that lawyers who represent defendants accused of dastardly crimes are unworthy of such honors? Hmm?)

I realize, because some of you tell me every day, that mentally, I'm not the sharpest knife in the drawer. So could somebody, ANYBODY, please tell me what opposing gun violence and recognizing Cochran's jurisprudential excellence has to do with each other?

If pressed, I'd bet my lunch money that Simpson had a bloody hand in the deaths of his ex-wife and her friend. But a jury found him not guilty. If Peterson is so discontented with that verdict - which marked the first time anyone ever got away with murder in America (wink, wink) - that he wants to overthrow this country's legal system, fine. I might even be willing to help, since I've witnessed a legal verdict or two that displeased me.

But as long as the current system is in effect, someone needs to tell him, "Get over it, dudeboy."

Perhaps Peterson was unfamiliar with Cochran before the lawyer led Simpson's "dream team" defense. But Cochran's legal skills were venerated on the West Coast long before that. He reached the height of superstardom to me more than 20 years ago, when he was represented by a character on the greatest television show in history, "Sanford & Son": only then, his name was "Sonny Cochran" and he lost.

In real life, though - and to Peterson's everlasting chagrin - Johnnie Cochran seldom loses.

MOM'S LOVE FOR HER SON ISN'T UNCONDITIONAL

The man police captured last night in the death of 95-year-old Bob Carson should have every presumption of innocence until proven guilty. That's the law.

But, man, it takes considerable restraint not to jump to conclusions after talking to his mother.

When I asked Joyce Johnson on Thursday whether she thought her 19-year-old son, Jason Troy Johnson, could really be the dangerous criminal Durham police were seeking for Carson's death two weeks ago, I expected her to jump indignant - to say something like, "Not my baby," or, "They're looking for the wrong dude."

I expected her to hem and haw, as mothers do when they don't want to acknowledge - even to themselves - the worst in their children. At the very least, I thought she would qualify her answer with "Yes, but ..."

I mean, you know it's all over when your own mama refuses to defend you. Thus I was taken aback briefly when I asked Jason Johnson's mother if she thought he could have committed such a heinous crime, and she replied unhesitatingly, "I sure do. I hate to say it, but I sure do. He was always robbing people, taking their radios. ... He has always been full of anger, for what reasons I don't know."

Despite her matter-of-fact tone, the searing pain in her voice tugged at my heart strings as she told how her son started getting into serious trouble about two years ago and how she eventually had to kick him out.

"He started wanting to fight me," Johnson said.

"Would it have been different if he'd had a father around, someone to talk to while growing up?" I asked later in the conversation, assuming that his father was stereotypically AWOL.

"He had his father until four or five years ago," Joyce Johnson said, adding that one day she and her husband had a vicious fight.

That violent confrontation led to the dissolution of their relationship, but she fears it also led to the acceleration of her son's malevolence.

"I think he wants to be like his father," she said.

The last time Johnson saw Jason at her Suitland, Md., home was around Mother's Day, she said, just after "that incident occurred here."

"That incident" was a robbery and stabbing in Maryland for which an arrest warrant has been issued, police said. Johnson said she told her son, "Jason, I love you, but turn yourself in."

He didn't, but he called her that same night, and she figured he was headed south to Durham to stay with his girlfriend.

Despite the resignation in Joyce Johnson's voice, it's clear that she hasn't given up on her son. I asked her, "If I talk to Jason, do you want me to tell him anything?"

Just as quickly as she did when affirming that she thought he was capable of killing a helpless 95-year-old man, she replied, "Tell him I love him and to turn himself in."

I doubt that Johnson is hunkered down in his cell in the Durham County jail reading my column. But if someone close to him reads it, just tell him his mama is worried about him. And she loves him.

—— 6/16/2000

MORAL OUTRAGE LACKING ———

Is it me, or have some black people lost their #*$%& minds? Or at least their moral compass?

Check this out: We all know that, for some performers, death is a great career move, right?

Just look at the way the bank accounts of Elvis, Jimi, Tupac and others have swelled since they ascended to rock 'n' roll heaven.

But judging by the career trajectory of R&B singer R. Kelly, accusations of child pornography are also a great career move.

R., who faces 14 counts of child sexual abuse related to a videotape of him with a 13-year-old girl, has not missed a beat. He is more popular now than before concerns started surfacing about his preference for underage girls. He denies that's him in the video -- it sure looks like him -- but he did marry 15-year-old Aaliyah and reportedly paid off the parents of other young girls.

His CDs still sell in the millions, and he gets heavy airplay on black radio and television stations. Most infuriatingly, he performed last month at the Congressional Black Caucus' annual fund-raiser, and last week at N.C. A&T State University's homecoming.

My question is: "Just what does a bloke have to do to get censured by us? What heinous crime must one be accused of, or found guilty of, before we turn our backs on him -- excommunicate him from the race?"

Sure, the basic precept of our justice system is "innocent until proven guilty," and it is possible that the man urinating on a 13-year-young girl in that video could turn out not to be R.

But why not wait and see before you start bestowing upon him the legitimacy of our educational and political institutions? This would have been a great opportunity for the CBC to show some moral outrage and say "Not in our house, R. Not with all of these problems confronting our kids."

When you buy his CDs or concert tickets while these lurid charges are unresolved, you are saying it's OK to devalue the humanity of young black girls. Indeed, you're doing the same thing yourself. Stop buying his music. Stop listening to it. Now.

A&T's media relations director, Nettie Rowland, told me that "the Student Government Association invited him ... . I checked around and there were no protests."

What a pity. Of course, the sisters at A&T had nothing to worry about from the X-rated R.; he obviously prefers his conquests to be younger than college-age.

I've heard more black vituperation aimed at Bryant Gumbel -- he's deemed not black enough because he uses proper grammar and prefers white women -- than at R. Kelly, who faces prison for allegedly robbing girls of their innocence.

Yet, Jacquelin Dennis, director of the CBC event, said in a prepared statement, "We are confident that [Kelly's] performance will help us to achieve our goal to educate the next generation of leaders."

Well, heck, darlin', if making money by any means at all is the objective, I'm guessing you could make even more at next years' Black Caucus gala by hiring Mercedes, Bubblicious and other pole-climbers from the late, lamented Brothers III strip club to perform their famous hot-wax dance.

That wouldn't be any more shameful than inviting R. Kelly.

10/12/2004

MORE CHATTER, LESS JOY

Up to now, Feb. 3, 1959, was universally considered "the day the music died."

There's even a song -- "American Pie" -- that immortalizes the day a plane crashed, killing pop legends-in-the-making Buddy Holly, Ritchie Valens and the Big Bopper.

There was no such plane crash Monday, but I'm predicting that Nov. 25 will also be remembered by millions -- OK, probably just me -- as the day the music died.

That's the day WCHL changed from a charmingly eclectic mix of any kind of music you can think of -- can you imagine hearing Dean Martin, Sam Cooke, the Beatles and Steve & Eydie back to back? -- to what has become the flavor of the moment in broadcast circles. Yep, my favorite music radio station has gone "all news and talk, all the time."

And not just all news and talk, but "all Chapel Hill news and talk."

Jim Heavner, the man to credit or, in my case, to blame for this revolting development, said -- jokingly, I hope -- "if there's a shooting in Durham at high noon, WCHL will interrupt its broadcast only if a Chapel Hillian is shot."

Heavner, president of Vilcom, the company that owns WCHL, said, "I believe broadcasters have a responsibility to not only entertain, but to provide a service. ... A community radio station should be more than just a jukebox."

To which I replied -- to myself, of course -- "What's wrong with being just a jukebox?"

A jukebox sounds infinitely more appealing than befouling the airwaves even more with another station full of angry dudes calling for war.

Tuning to WCHL during the day was like opening a box of chocolates: You never knew what you were going to get.

With most music stations seemingly programmed by the same unimaginative demographics- and research-driven computer, each song sounds like the one before it.

On WCHL, though, I once heard the Temptations, Patsy Cline, Frank Sinatra, the Rascals and Connie Francis in one set. WITHOUT CHANGING THE DIAL! I know, because I was so impressed that I pulled over and wrote down the names of the artists.

Alas, those days are no more, and to hear Heavner tell it, I'm one of the few who will miss them. "You," he told me, "are a member of two minorities" -- by which I think he meant I'm a left-handed columnist and I liked WCHL the way it was. "We have had not one complaint over the change."

That was surprising, especially since I arrived at the station's new offices Monday expecting to be joined by hundreds of other angry music lovers in mourning. I even had a momentary vision of us storming the Bastille and locking ourselves inside the station, where we'd play "Louie, Louie" or Elvis' "If I Can Dream" until the cops broke down the door and hauled us out.

I lost my nerve upon realizing I was the only protester. But I didn't lose my sadness. To paraphrase Don McLean in "American Pie":

"I can't remember if I cried/

"When I read about his widowed bride.

"But something touched me deep inside/

"The day WCHL went all-talk, all the time."

⊢ 11/26/2002

MY HEART BELONGS TO ... DADDY? ⊢─────────

You'd have to have a heart of stone not to be moved by the recent story of the Raleigh man who stopped drinking when he gained custody of his two young daughters.

Ahhh, how nice that women would make a man put down the bottle, I thought -- especially since they've usually had the opposite effect on me.

The story on Lawrence Murray, who admitted to a serious drinking problem, and other men, focused on census figures showing a huge increase in the number of men who raise their children alone. The number of single dads raising kids rose 62 percent nationally and 95 percent in the Triangle since 1990.

As with anything else, some people saw that as bad news -- portending a breakdown of the traditional family structure -- while some saw it as a positive sign that men are more involved in parenting, blah, blah, blah.

Me? I see the increase in single fathers as a hopeful sign that we'll now get better "daddy" songs on the radio.

Think of all the great musical tributes to moms that just tug at your heartstrings. Every Mother's Day you can hear, ad nauseam, songs like "I'll Always Love My Mama," "Mama Tried" and "I'm the Only Hell My Mama Ever Raised."

Dads? Let's put it like this: If someone remade that old-timey paean to mothers -- "I Want a Gal Just Like the Gal Who Married Dear Old Dad" -- it would probably be called "I Want A Gal Just Like the Gal (Dear Old Dad Kept on the Side)."

That's because most songs, when they mention us at all, feature sentiments Hallmark doesn't put on its Father's Day cards.

Father's Day is Sunday, and I can't think of a song that would be a fitting daddy tribute.

Let's see, now. There's "Daddy Could Swear, I Declare," a backhanded compliment if there ever was one, praising a father for his ability to curse a blue streak. Then there's "Papa Was a Rolling Stone," about a misanthrope who "had three outside children and another wife." Who can forget the less-than-praiseworthy chorus?

Papa was a rolling stone.

Wherever he laid his hat was his home.

(And when he died) All he left us was alone.

A loan? Knowing papa, it was a high-interest loan.

The all-time bad-daddy song, the one that has sent more men crawling to the Jim Beam decanter than any other, is Harry Chapin's "Cat's in the Cradle," in which a work-consumed, neglectful father wakes up one day to realize that his son is now grown and doesn't have time for him -- in other words, is a chip off the old paternal block.

I've long since retired and my son's moved away.

I called him up just the other day.

I said, "I'd like to see you if you don't mind."

He said, "I'd love to, dad, if I could find the time.

"You see, the new job's a hassle and the kids have the flu

"But it's sure nice talking to you, dad.

"It's been sure nice talking to you."

Ouch. Say, hoss. Hand me one of those hankies, will ya?

Gosh, with "tributes" like that, it's no wonder that fathers are regarded as the baldheaded stepchildren of parents.

6/12/2001

NAACP NOT MAKING THE GRADE

The silence is deafening.

The Durham NAACP's normally shrill leadership has made no public denunciations, held no angry protests nor, to quote that old Negro spiritual, said a mumbling word about allegations of grade-fixing at Durham's Hillside High School.

Almost makes you wonder whether this is the same group that so loudly protested when hundreds of students, many of them black, were flunked last year and forced to attend summer school - which many of them proceeded to flunk also.

In an astounding example of illogic, the mass flunkings were attributed by some to racist school administrators and policies, and the Durham Committee on the Affairs of Black People called in the federal government to investigate the way the school system was treating black students.

Call me slow if you want to, but I can't for the life of me figure out why teachers who were racist and desirous of impeding an individual's or race's progress would actually fail students and force them to repeat a grade. Their devious purposes would be better served, it seems, if they passed kids, sent them forth into a world for which they were woefully unprepared, and then sat back and admired that destructive handiwork.

In the case under investigation at Hillside, the person accused of changing a student's grade - and of facilitating his entry into the world with inflated, undeserved grades - is a black principal, Richard Hicks.

I don't know about you, but I would consider that more hurtful - more, in a word, racist - than holding students back a year and re-exposing them to knowledge they didn't get the first time. Even a Durham Committee official has expressed alarm over the grade-changing allegation.

A kid I knew in high school actually thought school administrators who sent him to special education classes - where he learned to make a mean clay ashtray, ogle Playboy bunnies and sing "Kumbaya" - were his friends.

It wasn't until I - oops, I mean he - was out of school that he realized they cared not one whit about his ultimate welfare.

Durham NAACP President Curtis Gatewood has made holding Durham schools accountable and ensuring that they educate all of their students his raison d"tre. Somebody needs to, especially when you consider that many parents are criminally slack in involving themselves in their young'uns' schooling.

No one has been more critical than I of Gatewood for some of his frivolous crusades - who can forget when he attacked Santa Claus and Duke University's blue devil as injurious symbols?

There is no denying, though, that he and his organization keep this immeasurably important issue, one many people would prefer to ignore, in the public's consciousness.

How, then, can he ignore this obvious example of what Republican presidential candidate George W. Bush called "the soft bigotry of low expectations" - a mind-set that "Those po' li'l cullud kids can't learn, so let's just get 'em on outta here" - when it's right in front of him?

10/3/2000

NASCAR HEADED FOR CRASH

I'll tell you what. If y'all fight another civil war, this time I'm fighting for the South.

Naw, I haven't turned into Clarence Thomas, who used to fly the Confederate flag from his college dorm window.

The cherished Southern institution I'm willing to take up arms to preserve is stock-car racing.

Northern cities, with the help of carpetbagging NASCAR and television officials, are yanking races from small markets throughout the South in an effort to "grow" the sport.

Say, homes, "grow this."

Seemingly suffering the effects of sucking on Jeff Gordon's tailpipes for too long, NASCAR officials have forgotten that it was small venues such as Rockingham, Wilkesboro and Bristol, Tenn., that made them rich. Now blinded by greed, they're neglecting their roots.

Eugene McLaurin, mayor of Rockingham and a former schoolmate of mine, said that after 38 years of two races annually in his city -- races that draw about 60,000 fans each -- NASCAR has cut that to one.

"It's in February," McLaurin told me. "Last February, we had ice on the streets the day before the race. People won't buy tickets far in advance if there's a chance of bad weather."

He also noted that Rockingham's Subway 400 is the second race of the season, coming after the Daytona 500. "That's like following the Super Bowl," he said.

McLaurin is still negotiating with NASCAR, so he had to be diplomatic -- "We're not blaming anyone, but we feel we've helped grow the sport and we deserve a better date" -- and perhaps couldn't speak frankly.

But I can: This stinks.

NASCAR officials won't be satisfied until they've taken the sport international and removed every mullet from its fan base. They'll rejoice when that familiar cry -- "Say, hoss, slap some mo' mustard on that thang" -- is replaced in the stands with "I say, old bean, have you no balsamic vinegar? Jolly good."

NASCAR means a lot to the South, especially to small cities such as Rockingham. They derive their sense of identity -- and a big hunk of money -- from race fans. Bennett Deane, president of the Chamber of Commerce, said each race at The Rock means millions of dollars.

I felt a huge, and admittedly irrational, sense of pride when, in South Africa last year, I heard a newscaster refer to my little hometown and the race that had just been run there. Since the Chicken Box closed and no longer makes the world's best hushpuppies, what other distinction do we have?

We knew that once the North took Krispy Kreme doughnuts, which are easier to obtain fresh in Times Square than here, they wouldn't quit until they took the thing we love second-best.

Speaking of doughnuts, NASCAR officials probably saw how popular that Southern export became on the Big Board and with consumers and said, "Dadgummit, we could do that with Jeff Gordon and Little E."

Speaking of doughnuts again, I'll bet Big E is cutting some in his grave over this travesty.

Don't worry, though. This big expansion is going to crash, and racing will return cities such as Rockingham to the big time.

How do I know racing'll never be as big in California and New York as it is here?

For one thing, who's going to translate what the winner says for the TV audience?

9/26/2003

NEGLECT PLAYED ITS PART, TOO

Had I become a preacher -- and you'd better be glad I didn't -- it's unlikely I'd have had the courage to do what Bishop James Daniel did this week.

Days before two masked men entered Hilltop Food Mart on Hardee Street in Durham -- and, as we've seen countless times on our TV sets, cold-bloodedly, wordlessly killed a store owner -- two of the men arrested in the slaying stood in Daniel's Greater Joy Missionary Baptist Church and asked for prayer and guidance. In front of the whole congregation.

Daniel declined to say for print just what they asked, except that it involved "changing the direction their lives were headed."

He not only admitted that the men came to him but also admitted something that many people, in any profession, are loath to admit.

"I failed them," Daniel said, sitting in his wood-paneled church office. "That boy had cried out, and somehow we missed him. ...

"This city, this pastor, this community has failed them one more time. There is no recreation around here for kids except a drug-infested park. There isn't a swimming pool within five miles.

"When kids have nothing to do, they're going to do something."

Whoa there, Bish, I said. Don't be so hard on yourself. While some might say that Daniel's prayer failed, others could more generously say that, without his brief, prayerful intervention, even more destruction could have been wrought.

Even with prayer, the gunmen wrought enough, leaving poor Ahmed Raja's wife to raise two fatherless children.

Because of what Daniel called his church's "strong drug and alcohol ministry," he said, his heart was gladdened to see young men seek him out for prayer on Mother's Day.

"They stayed and ate dinner with us. We didn't have a second's worth of trouble out of them," he said.

A week later, when he saw the tape of the shooting, he said, "The bottom dropped out of my stomach." He said he thought he recognized the gunmen.

When an innocent man is gunned down right on camera, few of us want to discuss the need for basketball hoops and swimming pools. We want, no, demand, our pound of flesh.

Sure, vengeance is mine, saith the Lord. But in cases such as this, vengeance is too good to be left to him, right?

That's understandable, but even if you get the revenge you crave, the conditions that bred such a crime -- including lack of recreation and parental, or at least adult, guidance -- will still be there. And you'll have to seek even more vengeance.

"What they did," Daniel said, "was hideous, but I don't want to bury them. I can't get past that. I failed those boys. You" -- he said, pointing at me -- "failed those boys."

So did you.

The blame for Raja's murder lies ultimately with the masked gunman who pulled the trigger, no doubt about that.

It is not absolving him of responsibility, though, to say that neglect -- by parents, the city and others -- put the gun in his hand.

5/27/2005

NEPHEW'S DEAL SMELLS FISHY

Call it human nature, but each Valentine's Day romantics such as I commemorate history's legendary love affairs: Bogie & Bacall, Tracy & Hepburn, Puff Daddy & Jennifer Lopez.

One of history's greatest -- or at least most profitable -- love affairs, though, is occurring right here in North Carolina. Yes, I'm referring to the love between a man and his uncle.

The relationship between state Senate President Pro Tem Marc Basnight and his nephew, Hannon "Fish" Fry, is the stuff of legends -- and possibly of grand jury investigations. A News & Observer story Monday detailed how a state agency approved Fry for two loans totaling more than $63,000 at a time when other, similar businesses were going belly up. Not only that -- no one's sweating Fry for making just one payment on the loan in 10 years.

Oh sure, the N.C. Rural Rehabilitation Corp. initially wrote nasty letters threatening legal action if he didn't make good on the loans for his smoked fish business, but the tone of the letters suddenly changed from confrontational -- "Dear Deadbeat, send us our money or those #$%&* fish won't be the only thing getting smoked"   to "Say, hoss. You think you might want to pay on that loan sometime this decade? Pretty pleeeease?"

Everybody involved is denying that Fry got special treatment just because his mama is Basnight's sister, and I'd like to believe them. But gee willikers, it's hard to imagine some bloke off the street being approved for a loan two days before he filled out the application -- as was Fry. Was the loan officer a member of the Psychic Loan Network whose crystal ball told him Fry would pay back the loan?

If so, that ball was broken.

Fry, who blames his inability to repay the loans on dishonest business partners, said he hasn't "had 15 cents to pay on the loan." Yet, he is paying $1,600 monthly mortgage payments and $500 notes on his wife's BMW, which, he lamented, they've traded in for a Ford Expedition.

Basnight denies pulling any strings to secure loans for his nephew, and it's conceivable that Fry got the loan without invoking Uncle B's name. But if Fry is anything like me, he'd have made sure the loan officer knew he was connected by blood to the second most powerful man in the state.

Don't look at me like that. If my Uncle Sweet Willie was a powerful state senator, I guarantee I'd find a way to invoke his name to the loan officer.

Me: My, what a lovely day. Y' know, I was just telling my Uncle Sweet -- the powerful state senator who controls how much money your region of the state receives -- that it's a lovely day. By the way, Homey, I need $75,000 to open up a museum honoring the music of Z.Z Hill.

I'm guessing that Hannon Fry found a similarly subtle way to invoke Uncle Bas' name in the application process.

Loan Officer: Mr. Fry, you want $63,000, but I see that you list few assets or collateral.

Fry: Right. But "marc" my words, the fish business is going to be big because people eat bass nightly. Why, I myself ate so much that I finally had to cry "uncle."

Loan officer: Here's your money.

2/13/2001

NO GOAL FOR HER THIS YEAR

Sure, it's only the first week of December, but Christmas has already arrived for at least one Triangle resident.

That would be Ann Denlinger, superintendent of Durham Public Schools.

First, Denlinger, whose tenure has been marked by tumult, anger and -- most important -- improved student test scores, won over a group of black ministers who belatedly realized that, "It's all about the kids, stupid."

This group, Clergy Closing the Achievement Gap, is composed of some of the same preachers who once vociferously demanded Denlinger's resignation. Even though Denlinger in public emits about the same level of warmth as a new Frigidaire, those ministers have warmed up to her. They seem willing to look past her personality and work toward finding out why minority students perform worse on standardized tests than white students do.

Perhaps the ministers, upon realizing that efforts to oust Denlinger were futile as long as she had a 4-3 advantage on the racially divided school board, heeded the words of that old Negro spiritual "Get On Board, Li'l Children."

Or perhaps they simply realized that, regardless of who's in charge, black kids are going to need to know how to read, write and conjugate a verb.

They have thus gotten on board with Denlinger's program, as have -- and this is another part of her Christmas present -- Hispanic community leaders.

The biggest gift the at-times-taciturn superintendent will unwrap this holiday season, though, was the news that Curtis Gatewood was stepping down as president of the Durham branch of the NAACP.

Gatewood has been the biggest -- or at least the loudest and most persistent -- pebble in Denlinger's shoe since she took over six years ago.

Make no mistake. No matter how you feel right now, you're going to miss him. The dude could be a royal pain, and nobody criticized his grandstanding, confrontational -- even when diplomacy was called for -- style more than I did.

But even I concede that his heart, if not his head, was always in the right place.

As I wrote several months ago, despite whatever else you say about Gatewood, the dude was committed (OK, OK. Some of you say he should be committed) to bettering the conditions and performance of black kids in Durham schools.

Too bad more black parents aren't as committed to their own children's educational welfare as Gatewood was. If they were, then we might have been spared a few of those distasteful spectacles of, for instance, Gatewood being forcibly removed from school board meetings while shouting his trademark slogan, "No justice, no peace."

Denlinger and her former enemies are having one of those Hallmark moments in which they join hands, make smoochy-face and sing "Joy to the World." That's good; we could all use more joy.

That shouldn't obscure the fact that some measure of conflict is good for all concerned: It'll keep Denlinger on her toes, and it'll keep important issues -- such as the disproportionately high number of black kids who are suspended and expelled -- before the public.

————————————————————————————————————— 12/3/2002

NO HELP IN A TIME OF NEED ——————————————————————

Having a tough time getting around in the recent snow and ice storms that have many of us wondering whether we've moved to Green Bay by accident? Then hush up complaining for a sec and check out the saga of Carrboro's Jerome Jones.

Jones' disabled fiancee, Elva Garza, sensed one of her seizures and debilitating headaches coming on when the storm hit in December, so Jones dutifully trudged out for aspirin and batteries for their portable radio.

"We had no power, but I had friends who lived 15 minutes away, and there was a store near them, so I figured it would be all right," he told me Monday while recounting the nightmare that turned what is usually a short walk into a near-fatal two-hour ordeal.

Jones is blind, but at 44, he said, "very independent." On this night, though, his friends weren't at home when he got there about 9 p.m., the store was closed, and the ice and debris cluttering his normal path, along with the sub-freezing temperatures, caused him to become discombobulated.

"I got lost," he said.

After about an hour of Jones' stumbling, falling, crashing and crawling, a good Samaritan in a big truck -- "At least I'm assuming it was a big truck from the way it sounded," Jones said -- pulled up and offered to help.

"He told me not to move because I was about to walk into a ditch, and he offered me a ride. ... I have to be cautious because I'm blind," Jones said, "so I didn't get in. But I asked if he would call the police on his cell phone."

The driver called and drove away when Carrboro police arrived.

Bad move.

Jones said the officers asked for his ID and then told him, " 'We can't assist you. We're on emergency alert.' One said, 'I can point you in the right direction.' He told me to walk '50 feet that way and turn right at the stop sign.' I asked him how would I know when I was at the stop sign."

For a reply, Jones said, he heard the sound of the police cruisers pulling away.

At least another hour of stumbling, crawling, crashing and falling ensued, he said, before two more do-gooders drove up and offered to help. They walked him home.

Jones, incensed, called the police department to complain after telephone service was restored to the couple's home.

"I talked to the chief ... and she said the report stated that I had refused a ride," Jones said. "There I was, freezing cold, done fell down two or three times, lost -- and I'm going to refuse a ride from the police?" he asked incredulously.

Chief Carolyn Hutchison disputed Jones' account, telling me there's no such thing as "emergency alert." She said the report states that officers "asked if he needed assistance and he said, 'I'm lost. Just point me in the right direction.'

"Officers have a lot of discretion" in determining whether to offer a ride, she said. "Based upon what I know, they made appropriate decisions. It's clear that he was asked if he needed assistance and he said no."

I wasn't there that night, and neither was the chief, so the only thing that's clear is that one blind man had a horrifying night and that police should have used their discretion to make sure he got home.

────────────────────────────────────── 2/18/2003

NO NEED TO PROTEST THOMAS ├───────────────────────

Always in search of adventure, I recently donned my pith helmet, loaded my trusty side arm, grabbed 10 Moon Pies -- you never know how long these dangerous missions will take -- and set forth into deepest, darkest Chapel Hill.

My quarry? The legendarily elusive creature known as UncaThomas Reptilious.

The seldom-seen-but-much-lamented creature, which answers to the name of "Clarence," was on the UNC-Chapel Hill campus to speak to law school students and officials earlier this week, so I went to see him for myself.

Although Clarence Thomas sits on the U.S. Supreme Court, you will never see him except in the most tightly controlled circumstances -- usually in question-free photo ops or on C-SPAN addressing awed students or adoring philosophical soul mates.

His visit to the Triangle was similarly scripted.

I never got within rock-chunkin' distance of Thomas -- he accepted law school dean Gene Nichol's invitation only on condition that ink-stained wretches such as I be kept away.

One person who did get that close was Kaci Bishop, a first-year law student. She judged Thomas "brilliant" after he spoke to her class on civil procedure. "I was certainly impressed with his legal knowledge," Bishop said Thursday, "but I disagree with his politics and was disappointed that he dodged some of the questions" regarding his legal decisions.

Professor Charles Daye, who led a group of five law professors who protested Thomas, was disappointed with his refusal to countenance dissent. "The question was never whether or not he should be allowed to come and express his views," Daye said, "but whether we should suffer those views in silence."

They didn't: They held a teach-in to discuss some of Thomas' more egregious decisions the day before his arrival.

Not only does Thomas vote by rote with the most conservative Supremes, but he rejects any opportunity to demonstrate nominal compassion, such as when he ruled a few years ago against a prison inmate who sued after suffering a savage and debilitating beating by a guard. Thomas callously ruled -- get this -- that there was no way to prove the guard meant to debilitate the inmate.

Oy vey.

As much as I respect Daye and the others who oppose everything Thomas stands for, I think their protest was counterproductive. If anything, it served only to imbue that lame excuse for a brutha or a justice with more gravitas than he deserves.

Make no mistake about this. Thomas, despite the virulent emotions he stirs, is a mere historical blip -- a Negrophobic, self-loathing blip, but a blip nonetheless.

His significance begins and ends with the fact that he is the second black dude to sit on the court. Unlike his predecessor, Thurgood Marshall, Thomas did nothing of significance before being appointed, and he has done nothing to distinguish himself since being appointed, except go out of his way to antagonize people who hoped he would become an ally.

So my advice is to just chill, and pray that one day the dreaded UncaThomas Reptilious will be extinct.

———————————————————————————————— 3/28/2000

THOMAS' ADAMANT ADMIRERS

Now, I know that conservatives have their mental giants, such as Rush Limbaugh, but if the scores of responses I received after a recent column on Clarence Thomas are indicative, few of them will be trying to secure lodging at the next Mensa conference.

Good- naturedly likening Supreme Court Justice Thomas to a species of dinosaur -- I called him UncaThomas Reptilious -- I did indeed express a desire to see such objectionable creatures become extinct.

Imagine my surprise, then, when I received a couple of dozen angry responses from all over the country accusing me of wishing death -- or worse -- upon Thomas.

I did not.

Though I find Thomas' brand of conservatism particularly objectionable, I don't want to see him disappear from the face of the earth. He is far too valuable as a cautionary tale to our children, an example of what can happen when you stand downwind of one too many dyspeptic mules while plowing fields in Toenail, Ga.

That, incidentally, is where Thomas was and probably would be still had he not been the beneficiary of the same affirmative action programs he now denigrates at every opportunity and wants to eliminate for others. Either that or standing on somebody's veranda going, "Y'all want some mo' mint in this heah julep, suh?"

Not everyone appreciated my playful, gently chiding remarks about the unjust justice. For instance, Nathan W. of Raleigh wrote, "Your continued attacks on Thomas are old, worn out and wrong. ... What else would we expect from a pathetic, liberal columnist? By the way, were you an affirmative action hire for the N&O? Sure seems like it."

Nathan, I'm as much of an affirmative action hire as Clarence. Oops, I take that back. They hired me because I'm so sexy.

James R. wrote that he "blushed all the way through" the piece on Thomas. "Even a pretense of fairness? No. ... Does the newspaper pay you for this work? I hope not."

Yes, James, it does. But not enough.

Annie P. wrote, "Your article reveals just what a fool you are." Thanks, Annie. I'm glad to know it served some purpose.

Michael W. weighed in with, "Barry, you're a sniveling little p---ant who's never had an original thought drill its way into yo' nappy little head. ... I'll bet you think Al Sharpton is the smartest man you ever met."

Sorry, Mike. Never met the dude. And for what it's worth, I'm happy to be nappy.

Goshdarnit. It is so frustrating being misunderstood. The only reader who caught what I really meant to say was a dude named Norm. He wrote, "UncaThomas Reptilious? You were too kind to the #!%$*&. Plus, you insulted all reptiles, living, dead and extinct."

Despite the vitriol heaped upon me, I want Thomas to have a long, happy life. Just not on the court. Think about this: If EMI could pay Mariah Carey $28 million not to sing any more on its label, surely we can raise enough moolah to persuade Thomas to exit stage right.

If you agree, make checks payable to SCRAM -- Supreme Court Removal and Maintenance.

———————————————————————————— 3/15/2002

NO POINT IN YELLING ABOUT SILENT SAM ——————

When I first heard that professor Gerald Horne at UNC wanted the statue of the armed Confederate soldier removed from the Chapel Hill campus, I thought it was a joke.

"Hmmph," I remember thinking, "I'm more concerned about real guys with real guns than with some 87-year-old statue specked with pigeon poop."

Horne, the director of the Institute of African-American Research and the Sonja Haynes Stone Black Cultural Center, wants the statue of the rebel Silent Sam removed because, he wrote in The Chapel Hill News this year, "There is no better ... example of 'racial separatism' than the Confederacy and the statues that honor it."

Now, if someone had stopped and bowed reverently before the statue, promising Sam to avenge his 135-year-old defeat - "We gon' win the next one, Hoss" - I'd have been worried.

Worried, hell: I'd have packed up and headed nawth.

But no one did. Truth be told, more people slowed to look at the foolish man trying to copy the statue's inscription while being pelted by rain - ME! -

than actually looked at Sam.

Of the several passing students I asked about Silent Sam, none knew his history nor seemed particularly keen to hear it.

One student, obviously thinking Silent Sam was a former UNC basketball star, said he "played before I got here."

Two dudes I talked to, Aryano Bush of Raleigh and Charles Johnson of Durham, said they never gave the statue a second thought despite passing it almost daily. Upon learning that it was donated to honor "sons of the university who entered the war of 1861-65," Johnson said he still wasn't offended, but "it makes me wonder why they had to put it right in the middle of campus."

If removing the statue from its perch overlooking Franklin Street would obliterate not only the memory but the reality of the Civil War - if it would dry the tears and blood that were shed - I'd be the first to hook up a rope and pull it down.

But that won't happen. Those of us raised here in the South passed such monuments every day on our town squares or in front of the courthouses. They were as much a part of the scenery as kudzu and Moon Pie wrappers lying on the ground.

Sure, if the soldiers represented by Sam had won the war, I'd probably be on a plantation shoeing horses or going, "Y'all want some mo' mint in this heah julep, suh?"

But they didn't win, thank goodness. Still, I'm sure the soldiers who died on the wrong side of the slavery issue were loved by their families just as much as those who died on the right side. Honoring dead soldiers, professor Horne, is not the same thing as honoring their cause.

I received in the mail last week a booklet in which it is claimed the Holocaust never occurred.

Not only the survivors, but the gas chambers at Auschwitz and Dachau give vivid, irrefutable testimony to the preposterousness of such a claim.

Razing the South's monuments to the Confederacy would only make it easier, years hence, for other revisionists to argue that slavery never existed and that the Civil War was a little skirmish.

10/12/2001

NOT SORRY FOR CALLING THIS FOUL

During my week at Bible college -- before I discovered women and liquor and concluded that the voice I heard calling me to preach might not have been God after all but merely something I ate -- I learned that "a soft answer turneth away wrath."

That's why I am taking the high road and being downright Gandhi-like in my response to angry N.C. State Wolfpack fans. Many feel impugned because I reported that some of their number yelled out, "I killed your grandfather," to Wake Forest's star guard, Chris Paul, during Sunday's game at the RBC Center.

Paul's grandfather was beaten to death during a robbery in 2002, and I wrote that some fans reminded him of it.

Pack Athletics Director Lee Fowler, who called his Wake counterpart to apologize, has concluded that one to three people made the callous comment -- and they were quickly shushed by better-bred fans.

Wake's sports information director, Dean Buchan, who initially told me about the taunts, said again Thursday that Paul heard them throughout the game. (Buchan said he did not hear the taunts himself.)

Fowler's acknowledgment is a concession that many Wolfpack fans were unwilling to make. Scores of them called to say they heard nothing harsher than "Gee whiz, that was rather uncalled for, old bean" after Paul low-blowed Julius Hodge.

If you've ever attended a college basketball game, you know the crowd is more raucous than that, especially after the home team's star player has been forced to sing soprano.

Never did I say or imply that all of the N.C. State fans were engaged in the tasteless chant. Indeed, I wrote, "Not all of the Pack's fans engaged in the tasteless chant." Look it up.

Regardless of how many said it, it was vile and doesn't redound to State's glory.

Yet, Sweet Thang and the kids -- also known as Mrs. Kool & The Gang -- awakened to hear callers to local and national radio stations referring to me in a most uncharitable manner. The host of one local talk show said, "I don't know this Barry, but I don't like him."

I was crushed.

There was no intent to insult all State fans, some of whom I consider friends -- or at least used to. I merely intended to show that some fans take far too seriously the ability of hyperglandular teenagers to put a round ball through a hoop. Want evidence? One State fan told me, "You have got to be the stupidest [N-word] the white man has ever given a chance" to write. That was one of the kinder calls.

Foul-mouthed fans, however many there were, are not unique to State or even to the ACC. After University of Arizona guard Steve Kerr's father was kidnapped and killed in Lebanon, fans at some schools are alleged to have shouted "PLO" at him -- a reference to his dad's suspected killers.

Some State fans have asked when I plan to apologize for slandering their fine alma mater. My answer: NCSU is a fine school, and I'll apologize when pigs fly or Herb Sendek wins a championship. Whichever comes first.

I did not slander NCSU; I just called a foul on those punks -- however many there were -- who said what they said about that boy's granddaddy.

 3/11/2005

OFFERING A JORDAN~SIZED APOLOGY

'Dear Sir, please pardon my ..." Nah, that won't hack it. Hmm, how about, "It is with deepest regrets that I apologize for ..."

Nah, that doesn't make quite enough noise, either.

OK, try this one on for size: "Hey, Homes, sorry 'bout that."

Dadgummit, it doesn't matter how you try, there is just no dignified way to admit you screwed up. For the past week, I've been trying to think of a suitable way to apologize to Michael Jordan for a column I wrote about him and his humanitarian efforts.

I chided Jordan recently after his new restaurant pledged 23 percent of its opening-week take to victims of Hurricane Floyd. Me with my cynical self viewed that as a paltry public-relations ploy because his uniform number and the restaurant's name are both "23."

The column was ironic and funny, but it was also wrong. Unbeknownst to me, Jordan had already toured a flood-damaged area of the state and had written a check for $250,000. I don't care how much moolah you make, that isn't chump change, hoss.

Of course, within hours of the paper hitting the street, I was confronting a jangling phone and readers gleefully informing me of his largess - I couldn't tell whether they were more gleeful over his generosity or over my screwing up - and calling me everything but a Reuben sandwich.

Because I have written critically of Jordan once or twice in the past - he deserved it those times, though - I knew I'd be deluged by people calling me mean and jealous. (Imagine that: me jealous of him just because he is taller, richer and more handsome. Hmmph! Ridiculous, right?)

The N&O, as is its policy, ran a correction the next day, but I figured a goof-up of this magnitude deserved a personal apology.

At least I planned for it to be personal, but a Jordan spokeswoman in Washington, Ms. Portnoy - the possessor of a voice on whose bad side I didn't want to get even on the telephone, 300 miles away - insisted that I apologize instead to his fans.

Yeah, when pigs dunk, I thought. It was him I insulted and to him I wished to apologize. "It's a 'man' thing," I explained.

I sent the personal apology, but I decided a public one would hurt even more and would ensure that, next time, I make the extra phone call that could have averted this error. I'm also writing a check to the hurricane relief fund. It won't be for 250 large, but it'll help.

Even in my darkest hour, though, I did some good. A father who said he was having trouble getting his daughter to focus on college applications sent me an e-mail thanking me for providing the necessary impetus.

After his daughter read the Jordan column, he said, she told him she suddenly recognized the importance of a college education.

How's that, sweetheart?

"Because I don't want to grow up to be like ... Barry Saunders."

Hey pal, whatever I can do for the cause of higher education.

A reader, offering me solace, called to say she doubted that Jordan lost any sleep over my mistake.

Probably not.

But I did.

11/8/1999

OFFICER'S INSIGHT AVERTS TRAGEDY

The way Michelle Williams sees it, the police, prosecutors and a judge in Durham saved her from being murdered after their counterparts in Raleigh left her in peril.

Williams, 22, who police said was kidnapped at gunpoint by her former boyfriend last month in Raleigh, doubts she'd be alive had Durham police not rescued her from a van driven by her armed former boyfriend, Louis Stanley Leysath III -- and then moved to ensure he is locked up until trial.

She contrasted that with Raleigh authorities' "nonchalant attitude -- like, 'This is just another domestic dispute where she won't even show up' " in court.

"Thank God," she said, "for Officer Cornatzer."

R.S. Cornatzer is the Durham cop who went to Williams' apartment complex and waited after being alerted that the two might be headed there. He was greeted that Friday morning by the bizarre spectacle of a man and a woman jumping from a van and running toward him with their hands in the air, both screaming that they'd been kidnapped by the other.

Cornatzer knew the real deal and ordered Leysath, 23, of Wake Forest to the ground. A gun that he had allegedly tossed out of the window was turned over to police by a construction worker; Leysath was taken into custody and turned over to Raleigh police. He was charged with second-degree kidnapping -- which means that no gun was used and the victim was not beaten or sexually assaulted and was released in a safe place.

That wasn't enough for Williams. "I'm so frustrated with Raleigh police that I don't know what to do," she said.

She told of an eight-year relationship that began when both were 14, was marked by violence, and culminated in a nightmarish, high-speed trip down U.S. 70 during which the van ran cars off the road, she fought to hit the brakes and jump out, and Leysath threatened to kill her, her new boyfriend and himself.

Attempts to reach Leysath for this article were unsuccessful.

Court records show that he has been arrested three times and convicted once in Franklin County -- on charges of assault on a female. Other convictions include larceny and obtaining property under false pretenses.

"I don't understand how they got second-degree kidnapping out of that," Williams said. "... He had this perception that we were going to be together, but I told him I'd moved on." She said the relationship ended -- for her, at least -- in February 2003.

Moving on from a violent relationship, however, is a dangerous thing to try to do, said Kit Gruelle, a domestic violence expert based in Chatham County. "That is when the violence gets jacked way up and hard-core abusers can become homicidal," she said.

Gruelle uses the term "separation homicides" to describe killings that occur under these conditions.

Williams said she thought she was about to become a victim of one. "I don't know what happened that morning," she said. "He just snapped. In eight years, through all of the fights, I'd never seen Louis this angry. I knew I was dead, so I just prayed that no matter what happened, my kids would be taken care of."

The second-degree kidnapping charge brought a $30,000 bail. Leysath's parents posted it, and on March 9, he was free.

Williams was not.

"I knew he was going to come back," she said.

A need to act quickly

When asked why Wake authorities did not seek a first-degree kidnapping charge which, given Leysath's history, would have brought a higher bond, Assistant District Attorney Jennifer Knox said: "I'm not sure it fit the statute as to first-degree. He didn't sexually assault or injure her.

"We don't have any proof that he had a gun in Raleigh," she said. "We can presume that he had one, but we don't have any proof that he presented the gun to her in Wake County," she said.

Wake District Attorney Colon Willoughby said Friday that Leysath's extensive criminal history may have an impact on sentencing if he's found guilty, but could play no part in the severity of the charges resulting from the March 5 incident.

It was that history -- which included violence against Williams, among other things -- that made Detective John Stokes of Durham's domestic violence unit think he needed to act quickly.

Dismayed that only one charge was levied against Leysath, Stokes said he told Raleigh police, " 'Maybe that's how y'all roll in Wake County, but that's not acceptable here.' We told them we've already had nine homicides in Durham and we don't need 10 and 11."

Stokes concluded that Durham police had legal grounds for charging Leysath with offenses committed in their jurisdiction. Tipped off by a Raleigh cop that Leysath was free, Stokes moved to return him to custody.

After being unable to find him for several days, Stokes and a probation officer -- Leysath was already on probation -- and seven officers from various departments went to Leysath's parents' home in Wake Forest on March 12, subdued him after a struggle and brought him to Durham.

There, he was charged with first-degree kidnapping, possession of a firearm by a felon, assaulting a female, assault by pointing a gun, resisting a public officer, fleeing arrest with a motor vehicle and communicating threats.

'One messed-up fellow'

Bail was set at $150,000, but after listening to Williams' tearful, fearful testimony, District Court Judge Elaine O'Neal increased it to $250,000 and ordered Leysath to have no contact with -- to not even look at -- Williams.

Stokes recounted what happened next. As a bailiff led Leysath out of courtroom and he was out of the judge's line of vision, several spectators "jumped up and began shouting that he was making motions and mouthing something at" Williams. The spectators described to the judge what they had seen.

"When you're so crazy with rage that you'd make a gun with your hand and say, 'Bang, I got you,' in front of the chief district judge," Stokes said, "that is one messed-up fellow."

O'Neal apparently agreed and increased the bail to $505,000. A different judge cut it back to $250,000.

O'Neal, who has been subpoenaed as a witness in the case, declined to comment.

A court hearing for Leysath is set in Raleigh for April 12. A hearing in Durham is set for April 20. He remains in jail.

————————————————————————————————————— 4/3/2004

OH, MY; PAPA STRIKES BACK ————————————

Yo, Homeslice, chill out.

I admit I was wrong and vow to punish myself either by letting some beautiful woman spank me or by listening to the entire Kenny G. boxed set.

The crime I committed that warrants such a hideous punishment -- have you ever heard Kenny G.'s over-praised faux jazz? -- was to write earlier this week that there were no good "daddy" songs. I know all kinds of songs paying homage to "mama" but -- as Groucho Marx said -- great daddy songs begin and end with "Pop Goes the Weasel."

Or so Groucho and I thought. Some readers called or wrote to tell me that I am a #$%&*$@ idiot for overlooking such musical masterpieces as "Oh! My Papa," "My Son Calls Another Man Daddy," Conway Twitty's "That's My Job" and a score of other daddy songs guaranteed to make you cry - either because they are so sentimental or, in the case of Wayne Newton's "Daddy Don't You Walk So Fast," because they are so bad.

The man who wrote what I think is the greatest daddy song in the history of music, though, is now a high school teacher in Wadesboro.

Richard Spencer was the lead singer for a bar band called The Winstons when he penned a song called "Color Him Father," a saccharine ode to a mythical stepfather who marries a woman with seven kids and raises them as his own.

The lyrics are not Dylanesque or even Smokeyesque, and Spencer himself admits, "It's not a great piece of music." But the song struck a chord in 1970 America. It was a staple of AM radio stations and won Spencer a Grammy award for R&B songwriter, and versions of it hit No. 1 on the country, R&B and easy listening charts.

The idea and most of the words for the song came to Spencer after a painfully embarrassing incident when he was a child.

"When I was 13, we had something at school, and I had to wear a tie," he told me earlier this week. "My mother tried to tie it, but she didn't know how. It looked really bad. I went to school, and the other kids laughed at me. That's when I created an imaginary guy who would do all the things a real father was supposed to do, like teach me to tie a tie."

He had to create an imaginary dad, he said, because his own father was often missing in action. "He wasn't much of a father, but I loved him very much. I don't know why."

Spencer never repeated the success he had with that one song -- the band broke up a year later, and he drove a bus in Washington, D.C., while going to college, but he has no regrets about being a one-hit wonder. "That song was one of the important things in my life, and I'm glad I did it. It's like dating Halle Berry: Who cares if she eventually drops you; at least you had that experience."

Few of us are creative enough to write a hit song about our dad or about the man we wish Dad was, but all of us can show him how much we appreciate him. Father's Day is Sunday, and you ought to be able to think of something better than a necktie to give to the dude who taught you to tie one.

To hear a sample of "Color Him Father," point your Web browser to newsobserver.com/saunders

6/15/2001

ONE *%! DON'T STOP NO SHOW

Darn. I should've drunk more liquor. Maybe then I'd have enjoyed the show more.

But since I had only one beer -- at $9 a pop, that's all I could afford -- the stand-up comedians at the Big Black Comedy Show on Saturday night elicited only a few amused titters.

The show at the Entertainment and Sports Arena was so forgettable, in fact, that I've got a suggestion for a name for the next in the series of touring shows featuring well-known black comedians: the Big Black Not Much Comedy Show.

My main objection, and one expressed by others at the show, is not that the comedians plumbed new depths of gratuitous vulgarity: They did. That would've been forgivable if they'd displayed a hint of wit or originality. Instead, nearly everything the comedians said was a stale ripoff of stuff Richard Pryor said, funnier, 30 years ago. Pryor was the Van Gogh of vulgarity, but he used it to make poignant social commentary.

Pryor, Lenny Bruce and George Carlin constituted a holy trinity of profanity that could blister your ears with their cuss words. Those words, though, were the engine that drove their story, not the story itself, as it was Saturday night.

Jay Anthony Brown, who is often hilarious on the profanity-free nationally syndicated "Tom Joyner Morning Show" radio program each weekday morning, made sure everyone knew he was going to curse.

"I love to #$!$%&* cuss. ... Is anybody here offended by cussing?" he asked upon stepping onto the stage. "Then get your #$%#$%&*% out."

Bill Cosby, criticizing a young Eddie Murphy during the early 1980s, said it best: "There's a big difference between the seven-letter words Richard Pryor uses and the 14-letter words Eddie Murphy uses."

Indeed, Pryor was a Picasso of profane profundity, using words that could peel paint off a wall yet paint an insightful picture. The comedians Saturday night used such words in lieu of a story, to mask the fact that they offered insight into nothing.

It insults people who have paid money to be entertained when you're unable to spin a tale without relying on words a naughty 9-year-old can spout.

Anyone who grew up sneaking a listen to their parents' party albums can probably still remember classic comedic bits by Carlin, Redd Foxx and Pryor decades later. Yet I can't remember one bit from six performers I heard two days ago.

Most of the alleged comedy was so lame that I attempted to amuse myself by counting the number of times they said "#!$" -- the Big Kahuna of cuss words. I stopped at 75. Before intermission.

You're probably saying, "Dude boy, why'd you go if you're offended by cussin'?"

Hold the phone, you #$%#$%^&*. I'm no prude. You know those 14-letter curse words the comedians spewed? I hear worse every time I pick up my telephone. But then, so do the people who call me.

I don't mind vulgarity in a show; I just mind when the vulgarity is the show.

Thinking back, I recall one memorably funny line during the night. It was when the bartender said, "$18" for two beers.

"#$%^&* it. Gimme one."

6/25/2002

ONE BAD NIGHT FOR MANKIND

So I'm sitting there trying to keep the next teardrop from falling while thinking of the four young men who were killed Saturday night -- and trying to figure out yet again how to defend Durham against the attacks we know are coming -- when a commercial for a new video game comes on TV.

It wasn't for Pac Man or Kong or any innocuous game fit for children. This video game, featuring hip-hop mogul 50 Cent, was fit for no one.

All you need to know about his game is that his last CD was called "Massacre," the game is called "Bulletproof" and that he raps constantly about killing other young black men.

Fitty -- as he is called even by network news show interviewers who should know better -- was up to his old tricks. He was bulletproof, but the people he aerated on the video screen with a huge hand cannon weren't.

In real life, neither is he. And neither are the thousands of young black men who die each year at the hands of other young black men.

That's right. Unless you're one, you have little to fear from the homeys charged with committing a disproportionate percentage of crimes in society. Most of their deadly venom is spewed on anyone unfortunate enough to remind them of themselves.

Durham cops aren't giving up many details on the four deaths -- it would have been six if the shooters had been more thorough -- except to say they are drug-related.

Drugs are bad; drugs are illegal. Yeah, sure. We know. I've got a bet with a colleague on the number of calloused-hearted moralists who'll surely call me and say, perhaps while sipping their evening martini, that these men got what they deserved for dabbling in drugs.

Never mind that some of the victims may simply have been in the wrong place at the wrong time. Never mind that the drinks the callers themselves sip used to be bad, used to be illegal, used to get you killed.

Those young men didn't deserve what they got, and their grieving, inconsolable survivors certainly didn't deserve the lifetime of sorrow they got.

Police Chief Steve Chalmers promised that the killers would be captured. Too bad neither he nor anyone else can promise that it won't happen again.

One way to possibly lessen the chances of it occurring again, though, is to get guns off the street.

Don't laugh. I'm serious, even though it's such a quaint notion. The National Rifle Association has spent so much money convincing us that "guns don't kill people; people do," that talking about controlling access to guns for anyone makes one sound hopelessly naive or foolish.

If proposing getting rid of guns is foolish, try this one on: We also ought to get rid of malevolent music, video games like "Bulletproof" and violence-glorifying movies like Fitty's "Get Rich -- or Die Trying."

Why? Because too many young men are doing just that.

City Manager Patrick Baker, answering a question at the police news conference about the impact the quadruple slayings will have on his city, summed up solemnly by saying, "Saturday night was not a good night for Durham."

Homes, Saturday night wasn't a good night for mankind.

⊢ 11/22/2005

OPINIONS BY THE YARD ⊢

The colorful signs with the constantly changing numbers in Robert Stromberg's front yard aren't a tally of the number of times Roy Williams changed his mind before leaving Kansas for UNC or the number of times J. Lo has changed her hair style this week.

The numbers -- 3,500, 3,235 and 1,608 as of Monday -- deal with real real life. They are, respectively, of the number of civilians killed in Afghanistan, in the United States on Sept. 11, 2001, and in Iraq during the current war.

Accompanying signs -- "No Blood for Oil" and "No More Kill" -- leave no doubt for anyone driving on one of Durham's busiest streets how the residents at 1111 N. Duke St. feel about U.S. policy in Iraq.

"We all support the signs," Bill Weaver said, "but Robert is the one most responsible for them being there." He said the numbers of reported deaths cited on the signs come from a Web site called iraqbodycount.net, which compiles and estimates the number of civilian deaths.

Weaver, who works at a Durham bookstore, is one of four residents in the five-bedroom home with the activist front yard. I drive past the house daily and can attest that, even before the current military hostilities began, Stromberg, Weaver and their roomies viewed their yard as more than just a place to plant grass or to hold barbecues.

Among other causes, they've displayed their anti-television views by filling their yard with several sets, until the landlord made them move all but one. After President Bush sought additional military spending following 9/11 and Congress went along, a sign went up stating, "I Feel Safer."

If drawing attention is the goal, the yard definitely succeeds. When I stood knocking on the front door Monday afternoon, only a few of the dozens of passing cars failed to slow down and acknowledge the signs.

"Most people honk in support or flash the peace sign," Weaver said. "People stop and say they are real happy with the sign. ... It's been a mixture of positive and negative. The house has been paintballed three times. I assume those were negative responses."

Another notably negative response, he said, comes from the guy who apparently derives great pleasure from circling the block and yelling "Commies" at anyone standing on the porch or in the yard.

Stromberg, a technician for the Durham Arts Council, said the motivation for his talking yard came after he attended a museum and was moved by art that made a statement.

"It was in November, and people were putting up Christmas decorations. I decided to jump on the 'decorate-your-house' bandwagon and put a different spin on it," he said.

None of Weaver's neighbors were at home -- or perhaps they simply refused to answer the door when they sneaked a peek at who was knocking -- when I sought their views on the political signs in their neighbors' yard.

If they have anything to fear, though, it should be people who feel compelled to attack a house with paintballs or shout "Commies!" at anyone who dares to express an unpopular -- with them, anyway -- view.

4/15/2003

OUTRAGE IS ABSENT IN KILLING

Too bad the dudes who beat James Robert Dudley to death weren't white.

I mean that in a good way.

Maybe if the people arrested for stomping, kicking and beating Dudley to death in front of spectators outside a Raleigh convenience store Sept. 30 had been white, then you'd have heard of him and his death.

Alas, there were no renowned media hounds such as the Revs. Jesse Jackson and Al Sharpton rolling through for the TV cameras with their trademark brand of drive-by shouting, no activists in the streets.

As it was, fewer than a dozen people attended the antiviolence vigil held for Dudley a week after his death.

That's because the people charged with beating the intoxicated man to death with fists and a chunk of asphalt were all black. Like him. That, we know, tends to mute the outrage factor.

Of the 250 black North Carolinians who were homicide victims in 2002,

73 percent were killed by other blacks, 5 percent by whites and the rest by unknown assailants.

The absence of outrage outrages Dudley's older sister, Dorothy Clark. "It's just another black drug thing, a poverty thing, that doesn't mean a hill of beans to most people," Clark told me days after the vigil.

When I used to sin bad on Saturday night, I'd spend all day Sunday in church, or several churches, depending upon how many commandments I'd broken. That's the good thing about being a Baptist.

In the weeks before and after a front page News & Observer story chronicling Dudley's tragic life and violent death, I visited churches again. But I wasn't trying to outrun that old familiar hellhound that nips constantly at my heels.

I went hoping to hear someone rail against the brutality that caused people to beat a drunk man to death, allegedly over a $10 drug deal gone bad, while several people watched.

I'm still waiting.

One pastor, of a supposedly progressive church, told me unashamedly that he doesn't read newspapers and thus knew nothing of the crime.

Oy vey.

It's easy to castigate even the preachers who do read for not bemoaning from the pulpit Dudley's violent end, the same violent end that awaits far too many young men and women. It's also easy to understand why they didn't: Start preaching about the violent death of some homeless guy -- Dudley's address is listed on the police report as "Anywhere" -- and you'd have little time to preach about real sin.

There are few certainties in life, but one is that no one grows up expecting to be a junkie with his address listed as "Anywhere." Nor do they expect to have their life -- and death -- ignored.

Neither did James Dudley.

"Just because a man doesn't have anything doesn't mean he should be demolished or that he's worthless," Clark said. "James had people who loved him. He's not the first person to lose his way or get strung out."

A prophet of nonviolence spoke famously of his dream of living in a world of peace. Sorry, Doc, but that's too much to hope for.

I simply dream of a world where the murder of a homeless black man -- beaten to death by black thugs -- sparks the same anger that it would have had the perpetrators been white racists.

11/18/2003

PAPER CAN'T BEAT BULLETS

I don't reckon it would have made much difference no how.

Jerry Webster, who described himself as Erin Farb's closest friend, said Farb told him recently that she was about to seek a restraining order to keep her estranged husband, Roderick Morris Farb, away from her. "She'd been having problems with Rod ... and found out about some emotional problems," Webster said.

"She was going to try to get one Friday ... . What's a restraining order going to do if you know you're going to kill yourself?" he asked.

It was a rhetorical question. As this week's series in The News & Observer on domestic abuse shows, no piece of paper is going to stop an unhinged person intent upon killing someone he used to love and possibly, in his own demented way, still does.

At least one woman profiled in this week's series, Camille Blackwell of Salisbury, died clutching the restraining order intended to keep her husband, Michael Horne, away from her. He is charged with her death.

Webster, squinting in the sunlight peeking intermittently through the late Monday afternoon clouds, stood outside the house where Farb, a male friend and one of her children died that morning, along with Rod Farb, the suspected gunman.

If a piece of paper won't protect a woman, neither, apparently, will having a male friend stay with you for protection. Webster, who said he knew Erin Farb both as a customer at his Hillsborough dry cleaners and as a workout partner at the Sports Plex, said the man killed along with Farb was not a boyfriend.

"She told me she felt safer with a man in the house," he said.

As this case and others show, nothing will make women truly safer until men disabuse themselves of the notion that they have a right to abuse them.

Anthony Smith, a licensed psychologist and executive director of the Alase Center for Enrichment in Durham, said that without meaningful counseling, nothing can be done to prevent violence.

"There's always hope if he goes to counseling and seeks a way to deal with his issues," Smith said, "but batterers are typically insecure people. ... They are not likely to open up and be vulnerable, which is what's needed in counseling to get to the core of the problem.

"They can be very charming," he said. "Even when they're referred by the courts, they will say what they think the counselor wants to hear."

That same charm, Smith said, persuades many women to stay with abusers. "They either make the victim feel that she is less than they are and can't find anyone else, or they go through extreme measures to make up for their behavior. They do all these wonderful things like send flowers and candy and promise that it'll never happen again. But it will happen again."

Smith has advice for any dude who thinks he might be about to join the ranks of woman-beaters.

"Take a step back," he said, "take a deep breath, and ask yourself what will this action bring about in the long term. You need to find some other way to release that energy and find someone to talk to about the stressful situation."

Asking a potential batterer to get hold of himself sounds simplistic, but it's got to work better than asking a potential victim to get hold of a restraining order.

5/20/2003

PARENTAL CONCERN NEEDED

To many, Matthew Grant, the man sentenced earlier this month to life in prison for killing a Wake County deputy, is a wholly unsympathetic human being.

Whatever sympathy he is due, though, stems from the fact that his birth parents were emotionally and physically abusive or gone and that his grandparents, loving though they seemed, were overwhelmed. Indeed, that is part of the reason cited by jurors for sparing his life.

But what if Ma and Pa Grant had been more involved, if they'd monitored from an early age his choice of running buddies, his phone conversations?

Chances are, they -- his parents -- would be on the wrong side of the law.

The Washington state Supreme Court recently ruled that children have the same right to privacy as adults. It overturned a robbery conviction because some of the evidence in the case was obtained from a mother who eavesdropped on her 14-year-old daughter's telephone conversation: The robber called the girl and implicated himself in the crime.

Mom, who was worried about her daughter, put the call on the speakerphone, took notes and dropped a dime -- that's '60s lingo for "squealed to the pigs."

Instead of being lauded, as she should have been, Carmen Dixon was castigated by the courts for violating her daughter's rights.

Oy vey. What kind of world is this when concerned parents can't listen in on their child's phone conversations in their own house?

Look around: That's what kind.

Wake County District Attorney Colon Willoughby said he has never prosecuted a case in which key evidence was obtained by a listening-in parent, but that wouldn't deter him from proceeding.

"Parents can help be accountable for some of the activities of their children," he said, "so we ought to give them the authority to be nosy. It's an obligation. I'd think we need more parents looking into what their children are doing."

Nobody is saying crumb-snatchers shouldn't have rights, but there must be a common-sense balance between parental dictatorship and laissez-faire -- a hands-off approach.

This not an abstract issue. Rather, it could be one of life or death.

For instance, what if the parents of Briana Rawls, the 15-year-old high school girl killed in a stolen car last week, had listened in on the other line? It's just possible they may have heard the 14-year-old car thief tell her: "Hey, I'm fixing to boost a car tomorrow; wanna go for a spin"?

Viewed from a distance of decades, there were times that I wish my aunt had listened in on some of my calls and thus kept me out of some of the trouble I got into.

I wouldn't have liked it then, but I'd appreciate it now -- as I do the many times she grabbed something, anything, and hit me when I transgressed. (If you think listening in on them is bad, you'd better not even think of hitting the little drape-hangers.)

From a legal standpoint, Willoughby said, children become adults at 18, "when they are able to enter into contracts by themselves."

Yeah, like with the telephone company. And a landlord. That'll ensure them privacy.

12/14/2004

PAYING ATTENTION TO LIFE

Losing a loved one to violence has got to be bad enough in its own right, but losing a loved one that way and seeing his or her death relegated to the back end of a newscast must seem like another indignity.

All life is precious in God's sight, we're told, but to network executives, some lives are more precious than others.

It appears that the bulk of the TV time allocated for murder in the Triangle is going to the Mike Peterson murder trial that is being beamed nationally on CourtTV.

People love to see the mighty fall, and novelist and former newspaper columnist Mike Peterson is, in a way, our O.J. People are anxious to know whether -- and if so, why -- he killed his wife.

Make that "some" people are anxious to know.

The trial, with its combination of violence, wealth, sex and a loudmouthed former newspaper columnist, may be a ratings draw for CourtTV and newspapers. Over here on Cheek Road in Durham, though, Kathleen Peterson's death hardly registers a blip on the radar screen.

But then, hardly did the death of 15-year-old Karsheem Greene, either -- and he lived right here.

Karsheem was gunned down Tuesday night as he stepped from inside the U Save Foodmart on Cheek Road, across the street from the apartment complex in which he lived.

A door shattered by a bullet had been replaced when I got there the next day, but a pomegranate-size hole remained in a plate glass window, inches above a hand-lettered sign that read "No Standing In Store or In Front of Store."

Michelle Jones, a high school student I stopped as she walked in the rain, said she heard the shots that killed Karsheem and injured a young woman. Residents have said that is not an uncommon sound in the 100-unit complex.

This is, remember, the same complex on which police last year conducted a "rescue" -- Chief Steve Chalmers' characterization -- to free residents from what they described as the tyranny of drug dealers and gunrunners.

Unfortunately for the cops, a judge ruled that the raid and subsequent arrests were unconstitutional.

Still, it isn't hard to figure that the Peterson trial wouldn't be a riveting ratings winner in a neighborhood where people are more interested in avoiding violence than in watching a court case about it.

Jones said of the Peterson trial, "It's all over the news. You can't help but hear about it. I'll watch bits and pieces of it, but I don't pay much attention."

Any attention Jones pays to the case is more than Candi Walker has paid. Walker, who lives across the street from Cheek Road Apartments, said she wasn't even aware of Mike Peterson or his trial.

That would certainly disappoint Peterson, who loved controversy and publicity the way a hog loves slop. He shouldn't feel bad, though: Walker didn't know anything of Karsheem's death at the U Save a few hundred yards away, either.

She did have one immediate concern when I asked her about it, though. "Oh, no. The store is closed?" she asked.

She sighed with relief when I assured her that at the store -- as everywhere else in the neighborhood -- it's business as usual.

7/4/2003

PAYING PSNC NO BREEZE

The wait in the gas bill line was tough for everyone, but it must've been uniquely bad for David Perry of Durham.

"Man, this is worse than castration," Perry said as he was sent from the bulletproof window of the tiny check-cashing establishment to the pay phone outside one more time -- this time to call PSNC's central office to get his account number.

His "castration" comment drew a gasp from a very old lady teetering on a cane and groans from the men in line.

Perry, like everybody in the joint -- including me -- was trying to pay his gas bill and was frustrated by the inconvenience associated with that necessary task.

One guy -- I won't identify me because it'll make me look really stupid -- was especially frustrated, having initially gone to the building where PSNC's office used to be to pay his bill.

Perry said, "As much money as they make off of us, you'd think they could have an office." Then, sighing resignedly, he said, "But you've got to pay it. It's the wrong time of the year to get your gas cut off."

The angry responses and frustration I witnessed and felt in that check-cashing place were unusual, according to Jodi Roberts-Smith, a PSNC spokeswoman out of Charlotte. "There has been very little, if any, negative response" to closing down the PSNC offices in Durham, she said. "Once customers knew there was still a place to pay, they were fine.

"There are lots of ways customers can pay their bills," she said helpfully, besides standing in line at usurious check-cashing places. "They can pay on-line, and there's the traditional way of mailing your payment. Or you can ... pay over the telephone."

"There is," she added with prompting from me, "a convenience fee for that service."

Those are all good options -- but everyone who cooks and heats with gas doesn't have a computer or extra money to pay for "convenience."

This is, obviously, yet another in a list of PSNC decisions meant to improve the bottom line for its shareholders at the expense of its captive customers. Because PSNC is a monopoly, it can -- and obviously has -- adopted a policy toward its customers of "love it or lump it. Or freeze."

It was in that spirit that, several years ago, the company stopped what was a tremendous good-neighbor policy of relighting customers' pilot lights. After the new policy took hold, if your flame flickered out in the middle of the night -- the time they invariably do -- you were on your own. You could do it yourself, in which case you might blow yourself up, or you could call a contractor -- whose fee caused you to blow your top.

Company officials, without snickering once, recite the mantra that everyone who works for the company apparently must learn by heart. They told me then, as Smith-Roberts told me last week, "This wasn't a financial decision. This will help us serve customers better."

Hmm. Has your service improved since the company stopped lighting pilot lights and shut down its offices?

Mine neither.

Boy, I wish I had me a monopoly.

————————————————————————————————————— 10/7/2003

PEDALING INTEGRITY FOR FAVORS ————————————

The answer is so obvious, I'm amazed no one has thought of it before now.

You know how people are always complaining about crime, chewed-up sidewalks and poor municipal service in their neighborhoods?

The solution to these problems is simple: Everyone should just move next door to Durham City Council member Floyd McKissick Jr.

McKissick hasn't shown much leadership in most instances, but when it comes to getting things done for himself and his neighborhood, the dude is downright tenacious.

And as hypocritical as a preacher in a bootlegger's house. On Saturday night.

At last week's City Council meeting, McKissick praised overdeveloper John Silverman as "a person of integrity" and voted to approve plans for Silverman, with his controversial Renaissance Center project, to overdevelop yet another part of Durham.

Two years ago, though, McKissick lambasted Silverman's "lack of integrity." Silverman, McKissick contended then, reneged on a promise to build McKissick a sidewalk directly in front of his house. So incensed was McKissick that he cast the council's only "no" vote on the site plan for Southpoint mall.

What, one wonders, did Silverman do in the intervening 24 months to become McKissick's poster boy for integrity?

Why, he contributed money to McKissick's mayoral campaign, for one thing, that's what. He coordinated campaign contributions from acquaintances, for another. And he agreed to build a bicycle trail in front of McKissick's crib.

McKissick told me Monday that criticisms of the trail in front of his house are "total bull" and "frivolous."

"Bike trails are a nice amenity that we should encourage all developers to put in," he said.

Far from benefiting him personally, McKissick said, the bike trail will benefit pedestrians and cyclists from the Lakehurst subdivision, where, he said, his council colleague Thomas Stith lives.

"I've seen a lot of near-misses on Herndon Road" where motorists have almost hit cyclists and pedestrians.

It would be easy for us to dismiss McKissick as myopic and self-serving, but as Fred Sanford said, "Let he who is without sin -- pick up some." That means that, deep down, we'd all have tried to extract some promise from a deep-pocketed developer who needed our vote.

I asked several people what they'd ask for in their neighborhood if they were in McKissick's position, and the answers included a police station, a grocery store, a bar (my favorite) and a Starbucks.

I don't really blame Silverman for spreading a little cash -- in this instance, very little -- to get his multimillion-dollar project approved. But I do blame so-called public servants who'll not only sell us out, but sell us out so cheaply.

I reckon it's true what they say: Money talks and McKissick rides -- on a new bicycle trail right smack dab in front of his house.

— 6/26/2001

PETERSON FORTUNE GOES POOF ⊢

Remember all that money and the other assets convicted murderer Michael Peterson's attorney claimed his client had, back when he was fighting to stay out of the pokey? Fuhgeddaboutit.

At least, that's what Peterson and his attorney, David Rudolf, want you to do now.

After claiming throughout his trial to be a man of substantial means -- heck, I was fixing to ask him for a loan if he'd gotten off -- Peterson is now po' mouthing to beat the band. He asked Durham Superior Court Judge Orlando Hudson to declare him indigent so he could receive an attorney on the taxpayers' dime to handle his appeal.

Hudson, who acquitted himself well during the high-profile trial, is fixing to go on vacation, probably someplace where he can bask in the sun and in the fact that he won't go down in history as "the Judge Ito of Durham." He, in essence, politely told Peterson to "sell that crib, homes."

Not in those words, but it was obvious he found it unfathomable that the state would pay for the appeal of a convict with a million-dollar house.

Peterson's Durham mansion is now on the market, listed for more than $1 million.

Both in a previous interview and Monday when I talked with him, Hudson stated that this case represented the first time he's had a defendant claiming to be broke while listing assets of more than $1 million.

Of course, Rudolf was extolling his client's wealth during the trial in an effort to dispute prosecutors' contentions that Michael killed Kathleen because he was strapped and wanted to cash in on her insurance.

Want to know the definition of chutzpah? It's arguing, without cracking up at your own temerity, that your client is rich, then turning around and beseeching the state to pay for his defense because he is broke.

That's the kind of lawyer we all can only pray to have the next time we're staring down the barrel of a judge.

Rudolf, reached at his Charlotte office Monday, said he has filed a renewed motion "that goes into greater detail" about Peterson's finances.

Hudson told me he received the motion last week and will give District Attorney Jim Hardin a chance to look at it before making his decision this week.

It is, of course, possible that Peterson was rolling in the dough when the trial started. Brand-name legal representation and a stream of expert witnesses can eat up a couple of million bucks pretty quickly.

Rudolf, in his new motion to Hudson, wrote that "the trial was extraordinarily expensive" and that Peterson had to borrow money from friends and family members. Peterson, he wrote, "is clearly indigent" despite the value of two houses. "The assets are exceeded by the debts."

Peterson's bottom-line condition, of course, was hurt by a nasty old state law that says anyone convicted of first-degree murder forfeits any interest in property owned by the person he killed.

The well-heeled Forest Hills crowd that attended the parties for which Peterson and his wife were known -- and that supported him throughout the trial -- seemed incapable of entertaining the possibility of Peterson's guilt.

They'll probably have a harder time accepting that he could be broke.

⊣ 11/4/2003

PULL OUT VISA, BUY DEGREES ⊢

That's DR. Chump to you, pal.

The way I had it figured, anyone calling me dirty names in the future would have to start attaching a handle to their insults.

With the stroke of a pen, I was about to accomplish in five minutes what my guidance counselor at Richmond Senior High School said couldn't be done in 100 years: I was fixing to get my master's degree. Or doctorate. Over the phone.

Take that, Mr. Weathersley.

Alas, my dreams of revenge and a graduation ceremony -- it was to be held over at The Jiggly Room and catered by Akbar Johnson's House of Ribs and Hair Products -- ended abruptly after I told the representative from Somerset University what I do for a living.

"Oh, you're looking for a story?" he asked skeptically.

"Nawsuh" -- a Southern drawl is a great tool to make people underestimate your intelligence -- "I jes' wants a degree. I've always felt an emptiness cos I had to quit school rat befo' finishing.

"Besides, Sweet Thang says a man what ain't been colleged has no future," I said.

"What do you want your degree in?" he asked after deciphering what I'd said.

"English."

"How far did you go in school?" he asked.

"About two miles. Oh, I mean 'eighth grade.' "

"Do you want a bachelor's, master's or Ph.D?"

Not wanting to come off as a slacker, I went for the big 'un: a Ph.D. In this instance, that stood for "Piled high and Deep."

Neither my broken English nor being a middle-school dropout deterred him. I was still making admirable progress toward a diploma. "Sure," I said when he asked if I wanted to graduate summa cum laude.

The dean touted my "life experience" as diploma-worthy and was moving in for the kill ("Will you be paying with Visa or MasterCard?"). When I said $1,565 was too much, he discovered some scholarship money that I qualified for. Now, my degree would only cost $1,165.

Upon learning that I am a writer, he discovered something else he had to do. "I'll call you back," he said. Click.

I was crestfallen for about two minutes. That's how long it took to log onto my computer and find an e-mail message from yet another diploma mill promising "a prosperous future, increased earning power and the respect of all."

Who wouldn't want that, especially when you didn't have to work for it? That school, though, didn't even have a name -- at least not one it would divulge on its voice mail. "Thank you for calling the university," a woman with a very proper English accent said.

Chances are you've seen electronic advertisements promising a diploma or degree for a moderate fee. "No required tests, classes or books."

Judging by my experiences, the only book you'll ever have to crack to receive one of these degrees is a checkbook.

We've all heard reports of people, including high-ranking government officials, boasting degrees from "universities" that probably exist only in some slickster's basement.

Instead of paying $1,500 for a phony degree from a nonexistent school, it'd be cheaper and just as legitimate to do as I did: bestow upon myself a degree from my own school: B.S.U.

Want to guess what that stands for?.

6/15/2004

QUEEN BEE'S STINGING REJECTION OF
NEW HORNETS' NEST

Like most people I know in the Triangle I am loathe to compliment Charlotte on anything. Our feeling is, "what compliment can you pay Charlotte that its residents haven't already paid to their city?"

As a person who grew up in the shadows of the Queen City - it cast a huge shadow, one which reached all the way to Rockingham, 60 miles away - I know that people in that part of the state view Charlotte as Mecca, Jerusalem and Mayberry all wrapped in one.

Psst, just between you and me, it's not. Charlotte has the same civic and social problems as any other city, and in many instances those problems are writ larger because Charlotte - to its credit and detriment - tends to do things on a larger scale.

But whatever its shortcomings, we all owe kudos to the citizens of Charlotte for a bold action which I hope will be emulated by citizens around the country. Last month they resoundingly voted against paying for an arena to keep the Charlotte Hornets basketball team in the city. Team owners Jerry Shinn and Jerry Wooldridge claim that without a new arena to replace the archaic - actually, it's only 12 years old - Coliseum, they'll be forced to move the team to Memphis, where they have been promised an arena with cash-producing luxury skyboxes.

They applied for a move to Memphis last year, but withdrew it before the NBA ruled on its petition.

That request was merely a shot fired across the bow, though, a form of civic arm-twisting by Shinn and Wooldridge designed to let Charlotte residents know that if they didn't fork over the moolah for a new arena, they might take their basketball and dribble in someone else's city next year.

The response of Charlotte residents was heartening, especially in an era when people seem to derive inordinate pride in the accomplishments of high-paid mercenary athletes whose only true association with them is their city's name stitched across the front of their uniforms.

In a nonbinding referendum, Charlotteans overwhelmingly told Shinn, Wooldridge and the team to - in the words of Ray Charles - "hit the road, Jack. I hear they've got some great barbecue in Memphis. And give our regards to Elvis."

By a vote of 57,000 to 43,000, Charlotteans responded to the Hornets' blackmail threat to leave by saying, in essence, "Frankly, my bees, we don't give a damn."

Because the referendum is nonbinding, don't be surprised if elected officials seek a way to provide funding for a new downtown arena despite voters' wishes. Already they're trying to see if the outdated coliseum - did I mention that it's only 12 years old? - can be retrofitted with the luxury skyboxes all pro sports team owners crave.

A few years ago when Charlotte was on the verge of becoming a veritable New York City with sweet tea, the Hornets' threatened defection wouldn't have posed such a threat to the city's psyche. But with the possible loss of corporate citizen First Union Corp. to an Atlanta bank and US Airways struggling for its life after a failed merger attempt, city officials may be willing to move heaven and earth to ensure that they don't lose the city's first professional sports franchise - even if it means circumventing the will of the citizens.

I'd love for the team to stay. It's a fun team to watch as presently constructed, although it's not about to win an NBA championship.

The real winners, though, are the residents of Charlotte, who've shown they won't be held captive by wealthy team owners.

7/28/2001

'R' RATINGS REALLY MEAN 'RID~OF~KIDS'

Rainy weekends are made for two things, only one of which I can write about in a daily paper. That thing is going to the movies, where you can sit in the dark and stuff yourself with popcorn, pop and chocolate-covered raisins.

But some inconsiderate knuckleheads are ruining that low-brow pleasure by committing an act of unimaginable vileness and stupidity: bringing young kids to movies clearly meant for adults.

Here's a tip, Ma and Pa Kettle: If you can't find or afford a baby sitter, stay at your #!*&% home and wait until the flick comes out on video. Trust me. We don't want to hear your crumbsnatcher fidgeting and whining inside the theater after paying $7 to see a movie -- $50 if we've bought popcorn, Raisinets and a large soda.

If I ruled the world, the first thing I'd do is propose a constitutional amendment forbidding parents to bring kids into "R" rated movies. Anyone who did would be pelted with Raisinets and forced to watch every movie Adam Sandler ever made.

I'm angry not only because I recently had to pay twice to see "Baby Boy" -- the second time so I could actually hear the dialogue without some kid telling his momma every five minutes that he had to go tinkle. I'm also angry and disturbed that young kids are being robbed of their childhood by being exposed to cinematic sex and violence at an age when they should be thinking babies come from a stork.

If some beetle-browed, lascivious stranger waylaid your 9-year-old, took him home and watched an "R" rated movie with him, he could and should be arrested for child abuse. Yet, if some ignorant parent does it, it's called bonding.

It's possible, but not likely, that the parents I saw at "Baby Boy" with tots in tow thought it was a Disney movie about a baby boy.

It wasn't. It was an adult movie with violence, profanity and sex, although not enough of the latter for my buddy Ed. But he's 43 and can handle what he sees on-screen. That preschooler sitting with his parents in front of me in the theater -- at the 9:30 p.m. show -- can't.

My friend Michelle, a middle school librarian in Durham, said that when she warned a girlfriend not to bring her two young daughters to see "Waiting to Exhale" because of explicit sex scenes, the mother proudly replied, "My babies have seen sex before."

No doubt they have, and therein lies much of our problem: Our children are becoming benumbed to violence and sex and growing up way too soon. I recall a scandal in Rockingham decades ago when a fifth-grade classmate's mother allowed her to wear stockings to school instead of socks.

The girl was sent straight home to change because the teacher, Miss Fulton, thought she looked "too grown."

I wonder what she'd say if she saw parents dragging their children to see movies like "Baby Boy"?

We can't shield our young 'uns from everything, but that's no reason we should aid in stealing their innocence. So the next time you go to an "R" rated movie, leave your kids at home. Or be prepared to duck the Raisinets.

9/25/2001

R&B TELLS OF LOTTERY INTRIGUE

From the minute Kevin Geddings vowed never to step down as a state lottery commissioner, you should have been looking for a window at which to place a bet on just how long it would be before he quit.

Men know from experience that when someone is that insistent about staying -- "Oh, big sugar, I will nevah leave you" -- it's a sure thing she has called and told mama to clean out the spare bedroom.

Oh, so I'm the only one that has happened to, huh?

Geddings blusteringly attempted to convince anyone who questioned his relationship with an outfit called Scientific Games that he had nothing to hide -- even though he did. As a public relations professional used to advising politicians, he knew how damaging even the appearance of impropriety would be to the lottery.

In this instance, there seemed to be not only impropriety, but incest: House Speaker Jim Black appointed Geddings to the lottery commission, even though Geddings insists he told Black he was a former business associate of Alan Middleton, who became a Scientific Games vice president. Middleton, whose company would love to get the contract to run the North Carolina lottery, helped write the lottery bill.

Meredith Norris, Black's former political director, has said she monitored legislation (but did not lobby) for Scientific Games. What she did was arrange hook-ups -- dinners and cruises -- for and between powerful people. I have a buddy who does that, but we sure don't call him a monitor.

With that much incestuousness, if the lottery were a baby, it'd come out with two heads and three eyes. Or stillborn, which it now may be.

Geddings could have quit with some honor weeks ago for the good of the lottery. Resigning just hours before his ties to Scientific Games came out leaves him honorless. And brainless.

Black's spokeswoman, Julie Robinson, told me Thursday that "the speaker is focused mainly on looking ahead. ... Mr. Geddings misled the speaker."

Money, a poet once wrote, is like manure: It's no good unless you spread it around. Scientific Games spreads cash; those who deny the company's influence spread the other.

Attempts to reach Black himself were unsuccessful, so with apologies to Martha and the Vandellas and their hit "Jimmy Mack," here's an ode to a man of few words. Maestro, hit it:

Jimmy, oh Jimmy Black,

Why don't you call me back?

I call you on the phone

At least three times a day.

Since this lott'ry stuff came out

You've got nothing to say.

Well, you promised us that you'd keep it cool

But Jimmy, you played us all for a fool.

They took you out to Mo's Diner

And fed you off of their finest chiner.

Then that lott'ry bill -- you snuck it in

And made sure that your friends would win.

The whole thing was done pretty weaselly

And we've barely heard from Easley.

He acts like he has nothing to do

But Jimmy, he talked just as sweet as you

'Specially when y'all were ramming that lott'ry through.

Jim, you can't hold out very much longer

You or the lott'ry could soon be a goner.

Oh, Jimmy ...

11/4/2005

RACE-BASED JUSTICE? THOMAS DOESN'T SEE IT

Strong evidence exists that Thomas Miller-El deserves to take the hot squat or whatever method of execution they're using down in Texas these days.

But what, pray tell, should we think about Clarence Thomas?

Miller-El was convicted and received the death penalty for robbing and murdering a motel clerk in 1985. He appealed his conviction on the grounds that the Bowie County, Texas, prosecutor unfairly rejected most blacks from serving on the jury -- thus denying him a fair trial.

A series of appeals courts denied his request for a new trial, but, surprise of surprises, the U.S. Supreme Court -- no one's idea of a bastion of liberalism -- concurred with Miller-El. This week the justices ruled 8-1 that the jury selection process deserved closer scrutiny both by the trial judge and the appeals courts.

The Supremes didn't say let him go. They didn't even say he deserves a new trial. They just said the lower courts and judge should take a closer look at the way jurors were selected and dismissed.

Guess who cast the lone vote against such a seemingly reasonable measure?

Yup, Justice Uncle Thomas.

Writing for the majority, Justice Anthony Kennedy wrote, "The statistical evidence alone raises some debate as to whether the prosecution acted with a race-based reason when striking prospective jurors...The prosecutors used their peremptory strikes to exclude 91 percent of the eligible African-American (prospective jurors), and only one served on petitioner's jury."

Uncle Tom....er...Associate Justice Clarence Thomas, disagreed. In his gratuitously antagonistic dissent, Thomas said that under his reading of the law and rules authorizing appeals in cases like Miller-El's, defendants face a high hurdle of having to prove the allegations in an appeal by "clear and convincing evidence." He said proof of discrimination was weak and that the case for historical bias on the part of Dallas-area prosecutors was circumstantial.

This is not the first time Thomas has gone out of his way to try to circumscribe the rights of defendants and to stick it to blacks and anyone else who opposed his ascension to the nation's highest court.

Several years ago, he dissented in a case in which an inmate sued after he was debilitated by a beating administered by a guard. There was no doubt that the inmate was beaten, but Thomas dissented because, he said, there was no evidence the guard intended to debilitate him.

Forgiveness is my middle name, so I've tried for years to glean something positive from Thomas' tenure on the court.

Perhaps, I told anyone who would listen, Homey will chill out and come to like himself -- and by extension blacks -- more once he's been on the bench for awhile. Maybe, I kept telling myself, the dude isn't as bad as civil rights groups and I initially thought.

Bull. He's worse. Seemingly at every turn, Thomas goes out of his way to antagonize blacks and liberals -- either because knowledgeable blacks and liberals opposed his appointment to the high court or perhaps out of some pathological self-hatred.

Just as troubling as Thomas' vote against the rights of defendants to face a jury of their peers is the erroneous notion fostered by prosecutors that black jurors are unwilling to convict black defendants.

Whatever empathy black jurors are suspected of feeling for black defendants is more than offset by the realization that blacks are far more likely than whites to be victimized by crimes committed by black defendants.

It is racist and unfair to disqualify citizens from performing their civic duty simply because of some prosecutor's preconceived and unsubstantiated feelings.

3/1/2003

RACISM TUNE HITS SOUR NOTE

I swear, at first I thought it was a beauty pageant to see who had the prettiest hair.

There was Fat Al -- OK, he has dropped 100 pounds, so we have to call him Formerly Fat Al -- Sharpton standing with aging and fading pop star Michael Jackson.

Michael: Oooooh, how'd you get your hair to look like that, Albert? I ... I'd give anything to get that kind of lift in my 'do.

But no, they weren't talking about how to get your hair to lie down like that. They were talking about, get this, racism.

No surprise about Al. Talking about racism has pretty much been his raison d'etre since he burst onto the national scene. The surprise was hearing Jackson, a man who has fled his blackness the way a snail flees a salt shaker, complaining that he has been done wrong because of the color of his skin.

Speaking of which, what the heck is the color of his skin? It's certainly nothing you can find in your kid's crayon box.

It has, instead, the toxic hue of a Negrophobic entertainer whose self-loathing was chemically carried to a crazy extreme.

What did Tommy Mottola, whom Michael called "the devil," and the suits at Sony do to Jackson to elicit squeals of racism and lead him to partner up with Sharpton and Johnnie Cochran? Did they refuse to let him use the executive john or deny him some other perks?

Nah. What they did, Jackson said, was fail to aggressively promote his latest album, "Invincible" -- resulting in legacy-tarnishing sales.

With all due respect to both Sharpton, who has indeed done some good things for the cause, and to Jacko, who has never done anything for any cause other than his own, I'd like to say, "Blow it out yer ear, pal."

I wasn't even going to mention that surreal news conference with Al, Johnnie and the beloathed Gloved One, so sure was I that I had merely slipped into a coma after drinking one bottle too many of MD 20/20 fortified spirits. But then, a couple of livid readers assured me that I really had seen what I thought I'd seen.

A dude named Norm from Raleigh wrote to say he thought cries of racism were "downright funny, and more than ironic, coming from a turkey whose own denial of his race was extreme enough to be a sickness, a man who in his obsession to escape his blackness became a sick caricature of someone white."

Jackson blames the disappointing sales -- 40 million worldwide for "Thriller," a couple of million for "Invincible" -- on Sony's alleged refusal to promote it. The company said it spent $30 million making the album and $30 million marketing it, and I've certainly heard its songs on radio stations.

Alas, to Michael's obvious chagrin, they've all been "urban contemporary" stations -- the new phrase for "black" -- instead of the pop stations where he enjoyed such popularity in the 1980s.

I don't care where or if they play his records, how many he sells or anything else. I do care, though, that it demeans the struggle of the millions of black people who battle against racism daily for some rich chump with the race consciousness of an armadillo to self-servingly drape himself in the flag of race victim. Especially when he has done everything he could to deny his race.

7/9/2002

RALLY ROUND A DRIVE~IN

Put the past year of Bob Groves' life story on the screen at his drive-in movie theater, and you'd have a tear-jerker that would make "Love Story" look like a Disney musical.

The screen of his theater burned down Aug. 22, destroying irreplaceable mementos.

Groves' beloved father died four months ago, and his girlfriend of 28 years, Kathy Bednarz, died months prior to that.

"We got along perfect," he said. "I guess you could say she was my soul mate."

So on a rainy, muggy Monday -- with the door of his mobile home wide open to catch a breeze -- why is Groves smiling?

He is smiling, he said, because of the way people have rallied to aid him during this period of travail. "It makes it real nice to see how much the community wants to help," he said. "Everybody is pitching in."

Progress Energy will donate the huge poles for the screen if Groves gets a logging truck to transport them up from Wilmington. Other companies have offered employees, hammers and nails, ice. A nonprofit foundation, "Save Our Starlite," has been set up in the Triangle at RBC Centura Bank to accept donations for the drive-in.

Contributions had started even as the ruins smoldered, said Robin Evans, who was answering the phone in the unpowered concessions building Monday. "People will drive up ... and drop off money," she told me as the steady rain made the gloomy day gloomier. "Everybody who's ever been here has a fond memory of a first date or something and wants to see it reopened."

My fond memories include taking my then-small son and his buddies to the drive-in, where they could watch movies from the truck's roof. Each time Groves, who sold tickets, would peer into the truck as we pulled up and ask, "How many you got hiding in the trunk?"

Those could've been fighting words, accusing me of trying to avoid a $3-per-head kids' admission price. Groves, though, said it with such a disarming smile that it was easy to laugh off.

No one has fonder memories of Starlite or drive-ins in general than Groves, 52. He has worked at them since he was 12, as a projectionist since 13.

Few things are as evocative of Americana as drive-in theaters, and few things are as sad to see as an empty one with the poles for speakers standing a forlorn, lonely sentry before charred poles that once held a screen.

The uninsured screen will cost about $35,000 to replace. "I'd had insurance for 15 years when Fran ripped us apart, but the insurance company wouldn't pay. They said it wasn't part of my business," he recalled. "Now, I'm a drive-in theater, but they said the screen wasn't part of my business."

Groves spends his days plotting the Starlite's return -- he hopes in about 60 days -- with just his huge German shepherd, Sir Robert Blackhawk, Blackie for short.

"I really have no family anymore. The people who work here are my only family. ... The theater can be rebuilt, but the memories can't be replaced," he said. "I guess now we can make new memories."

If you want to help him make new memories or want to help a place where you can make some of your own, send contributions to any Centura Bank.

8/31/2004

READER NEEDS TO 'CHILL'

It's hard to tell whether the man who wrote the vicious letter was angrier because I, in his opinion, made light of a serious issue or because I wrote about driving down the street eating skins and listening to Bobby "Blue" Bland.

Whichever it was, he'd better be glad I'm such a nice guy. Otherwise, I'd be inclined to slap him baldheaded up and down Capital Boulevard.

This is what happened: In a recent column about Col. Richard Holden becoming the first black commander of the state Highway Patrol, I noted that the sky didn't fall, there was no mass exodus of whites from the state nor were the highways suddenly overrun with black motorists taunting troopers while burning rubber and sticking out their tongues at them because their new boss is black.

In short, I noted, everything proceeded normally. As it should have.

But this guy, who must've read my column while in the midst of an alcohol-induced stupor - or, more likely, had someone read it to him - accused me of predicting an exodus of whites and a proliferation of law-flouting black motorists.

Oy vey. I don't mind someone disagreeing with me, even when they misinterpret what I've said. But then he got personal, and anyone who knows me knows I'm a sensitive, easily bruised spirit. Indeed, that's why some people - OK, just me - call me Mr. Sensitive.

"Barry 'Chicken George' Saunders is the house nigger now," he wrote. "He took an extremely serious issue and reduced it to his trademark gibberish. The issue is not about people like you, who 'eat pork skins.' ... Is there any other major newspaper that allows such shallow, repulsive writing?"

The writer, who calls himself Mad Dog, then made the most scurrilous accusation ever leveled at me: He blamed me for the Triangle's population boom. "The population in Wake County is increasing daily. Maybe it's The N&O they like. Where else can a white person pick up the daily paper and read an editorial with black folk 'eating pork skins'? And to top it off, the article is written by a fried chicken-eating, watermelon seed-spitting black man with a big stupid grin on his face."

Ha! Shows how much he knows: I'm not grinning. I confess, though, that I do love a good watermelon and I spit out the seeds - unless I'm lunching with the Queen of England, in which case I discreetly place them in a hanky when no one is looking.

And yes, I have been known to wail along loudly with Bobby "Blue" Bland when he sings "I believe my woman is putting something in my food."

Since there was nothing in my column that made light of the problem black motorists face when statistics show we are stopped and searched in disproportionately high numbers - I've written often and seriously on the humiliating, at times tragic, consequences of such stops - I can only conclude that Mad Dude is angry because of what I eat.

I didn't know it at the time, but apparently letting white readers know we don't all eat duck a l'orange and listen to Tchaikovsky makes me a race traitor. Sheesh.

I'll tell you what, Dog. I'll try some of that symphony crap if you eat some pork skins with hot sauce and listen to some blues. Because you need to chill, Homes.

——— 6/14/1999

RESILIENCE OFFERS ITS OWN REWARD POST-REAGAN ⊢——

This is a great country. Ronald Reagan's presidency proved it.

No, this isn't another of those embarrassingly effusive hosannas being strewn before Reagan's casket by a press corps that has seemingly lost its objectivity and memory.

America's greatness was demonstrated by Reagan's presidency because, darn it, we survived it.

The newsroom of the Atlanta Constitution was a sad place on the night in 1980 when Ronald Reagan defeated -- "defeated" my eye; massacred is more like it -- President Jimmy Carter.

Carter was a native Georgian whom many in the newsroom knew personally from his days as governor. They felt a kinship to him and he to them: a stack of Constitutions was delivered daily to the White House, allowing me to delude myself into thinking that maybe, just maybe, President Carter in one of his down moments read some of the obituaries I wrote.

The sadness among the staff was caused by something deeper than Carter's humiliating defeat, though. It was also caused by fear.

It's hard to remember now, with Reagan being beatified upon his death, that the late president inspired fear in many people. That was especially true of the newsroom receptionist who called him "Ray-gun."

Drunk on Heinekens and sorrow, I caught the subway home in the wee hours of the post-election morning -- downcast that the president-elect would never read my obituaries and fearful that his policies would give me more to write.

The coup de grace occurred when I stumbled up to my no-bedroom apartment and flicked on the TV. The movie playing was "Bedtime for Bonzo."

You could look it up.

Like millions of people, I went to bed that night and many others fearing the sky would fall, that we'd wake up in a war. Nothing less than Armageddon would have surprised me coming from this dude.

It didn't happen.

America and democracy survived eight years of Reagan's presidency, and we'll survive four -- or eight -- of George W. Bush's.

That sentiment was first expressed after Reagan's election by comedian/ activist Dick Gregory, who has never succumbed to reason when a conspiracy theory would do. The essence of his comment was that we were here before Reagan was elected, and we'll be here after he's gone.

He knew, as we should, that democracy as practiced in America has a self-correcting mechanism that prevents it from getting too far off-track regardless of who is driving the train.

That mechanism is the Constitution.

It is, ironically, precisely when the country experiences its greatest tumult that its greatness becomes apparent.

Political assassinations in most countries are followed by tanks rolling and blood flowing through the streets.

All of our political assassinations or attempted assassinations were followed by a seamless, peaceful transition. OK, Secretary of State Al Haig did go bonkers and screech "I'm in charge here" after Reagan was shot, but he was given a hot toddy and promptly calmed down.

Again, the Constitution dictated who would succeed in case the President was incapacitated.

We have heard incessantly over the past week inane blatherings about how Reagan "made us feel good about ourselves."

I wonder if any of the thousands who were kicked out of mental institutions and onto the streets feel better about themselves, or the air traffic controllers who were fired for exercising their constitutionally protected right to strike for better wages? What about the homeless people, whose numbers increased greatly during his reign? Of course, Reagan said they were homeless by choice. You could look that up, too.

Or how about the "welfare queens" whom he ridiculed and blamed for every social ill, or the thousands of kids who couldn't attend college because of Reagan's gutting of grants programs?

You reckon they feel better about themselves? Hmmm?

Near the end of Jerzy Kozinski's novel and movie "Being There" -- no, I'm not going to compare Reagan to Chance the gardner, although many have -- the eulogy was read for super-rich political kingmaker Benjamin Rand. In it, Rand's philosophy was expressed thus:

"I have no use for those on welfare, no patience whatsoever... But, if I am to be honest with myself, I must admit that they have no use for me, either."

That wasn't read at Reagan's funeral Friday, but it could have been.

6/12/2004

RESTORING A GOOD NAME

Next to "I swear, your honor, I thought she was 18," the most common lie uttered in court is "That's not me. You've got the wrong man."

Or, in this case, woman.

Weird thing is, when Phyllis Marie Roberson of Raleigh tells cops they have the wrong woman, she is telling the truth.

Oh, there's another Phyllis Marie Roberson out there keeping police busy, but that one is 21 years younger and lives in Edgecombe County. She did 30 days in jail for beating up someone.

An assault charge is what's known as a red flag when you're applying for a job as a nurse, as the Phyllis Roberson in Raleigh did recently.

She thought she had a good chance to get the job at Triangle Family Services until they called. "They said there was a charge against me for assault," Roberson told me earlier this week. "I said, 'That's not me.' "

Unlike her 25-year-old namesake in Rocky Mount, the Raleigh woman, 46, has had limited connection with the legal system. There are infractions for not wearing a seat belt and not having her driver's license on her.

She explained, "You know how it is when women change their pocketbooks and forget to take their license out, don't you?"

Not really, but I do know how it is when someone with a similar name is intimately connected to the criminal justice system and the law thinks it's you. That's why I travel under a fake name in the whole state of Georgia.

Fortunately for the good Phyllis, she finally convinced her prospective employers that she hadn't beaten up anybody. "I told them, 'I've never assaulted anyone. I've been in jail one time, and that was as part of my nursing training.' "

Despite getting her name cleared in that instance and getting the job, which she starts next week, Raleigh's Phyllis fears that she might not be able to convince the next cop who pulls her over and runs a background check.

"I'm just so upset and nervous about this," she said.

Although this'll be small consolation if her credit is ruined or if she finds herself involuntarily snuggling with a cellmate named Big Bertha, Roberson's problem is not unique.

Bill Nicholls, trial court administrator for the judicial district that includes Edgecombe County, told me about a magistrate whose career was imperiled because the criminal misbehavior of his same-named pa kept rearing up and biting him in the backside. His solution: "He changed his name," Nicholls said.

"Or you could go into every job interview and warn them up front that there's someone out there" messing up your good name, he said, "but that's not the way you want to start a job interview."

"This is a genuine problem," Nicholls said. "The courts have been trying to get identifiers beyond the traditional ones of names and birth dates. Unfortunately, there are a lot of people dedicated to keeping us in the courts employed, and they don't always give the right birth dates or Social Security numbers."

Tell me about it. Because of the misdeeds associated with my name in Atlanta, I changed my name while there last summer. For some reason, though, I don't think the hotel clerk believed I was Denzel Washington.

10/7/2005

RIGHTEOUS INDIGNATION POURS FORTH

I'm no theologian, and my knowledge of the Bible is admittedly skimpy. But I doubt that there's anywhere in the Good Book where God instructs somebody to be fruitful and multiply -- alone. With a typewriter.

Who among us has heard a preacher say, "Let us turn now to the Book of Tyrone, where it says, 'If thy typewriter offendeth thee, take it and shove it up #$@%&^*, you #$!%&%*.' "

Hmm, that must've been in one of the lesser books of the Old Testament.

Yet, I received that and several other colorful suggestions from Christian readers who didn't like me questioning why the Rev. Billy Graham was named one of the most influential Southerners in the 20th century.

Silly me. Because Graham was as quiet as a church mouse on two of the biggest events of the 1960s -- the anti-war protests and the Civil Rights movement -- and has still uttered nary a word about the death penalty, I ranked him way behind the inventors of the Moon Pie, cheesy grits and Krispy Kreme doughnuts in terms of influence.

To many readers, that was blasphemy, or as one so graphically put it, like making "hamburger out of our sacred cow."

"Billy Graham has done more for America than you or any of the people you mentioned in your damned movement," said one dude, "especially Martin Luther King. He was an adulterer and was out whoring around the night he got killed."

Hey, pal, let he who is without sin -- pick up some. Besides, no one ever said King was a saint.

Another self-professed Christian wrote praising Graham and said, "The hat makes you look like a pimp who just lost his Lincoln in a card game to a crack dealer."

Sorry, homeslice. I lost my car -- a Caddy, not a Lincoln -- shooting craps, not playing cards. Nyah, nyah, nyah, nyah, nyah.

One woman wrote, "Cheesy grits are good, but they won't get you into heaven."

Naw, but if done up right -- with the correct seasoning and some red-eye gravy -- those bad boys will taste heavenly.

Besides, anyone who says grits can't lead you to God apparently has never heard of Al Green: Soon after a spurned lover threw hot grits on the soul singer, he became "the Rev. Al Green."

A woman wrote, "Don't you see all those people with tears streaming down their faces when Billy Graham has his altar calls? He has brought more people to Christ than anyone in the past 50 years."

Yeah, but how many of them stayed once the tears dried?

Some people, alas, agreed with the reader who wrote, "God has served Billy well."

"You are right on about Billy," one lady wrote. "The cheese thing, though, makes me PUKE."

My, such a delicate constitution. The antidote to her condition can be found at the Pan Pan Diner in Durham, where they make the world's best cheese grits.

Another reader agreed that Graham's influence was minimal, but asked, "What is a Moon Pie?"

Oh, it's nothing but a couple of round -- uh--oh -- Graham crackers wrapped around marshmallow and dipped in chocolate. Talk about heaven.

⊢ 7/17/2001

SARDINES A BIG STINK IN ABERDEEN ⊢

Anybody with any home-training at all knows there are certain things you never do in front of others: pick your nose, listen to Kenny G records or eat sardines.

Engaging in the first two acts is self-evidently tacky; the latter marks you as a low-born, unsophisticated weed bender who thinks dressing up means putting a crease in your bib overalls.

It also makes you my friend.

"Love" is a strong word for something that's dead and crammed in a can, but that's how I feel about sardines.

Despite the stigma and the stink attached to them, sardines are the quintessential poor man's delicacy of country boys who don't give a rat's toenail about what others think of them or their gastronomical cravings.

In a world in which public approval is coveted, you probably think such people don't exist. They do, and hundreds of them will gather down in Aberdeen from 11 a.m. to 1:30 p.m. today for the eighth annual International Sardine Festival.

The festival was started by Randall Moss - "as a joke," Moss said - when his daughter forbade him and other employees of her manufacturing and distribution company to eat the stinky (I prefer "malodorous") little fish in her office.

"Then we went right outside, and she told us we couldn't eat them there, either," Moss recalled when I talked with him Thursday. So he and several friends and co-workers, cast out and disconsolate, wandered down to nearby Aberdeen Lake on U.S. 1. There they found a sardine sanctuary where, free of persecution, they could eat sardines and soda crackers.

And verily, they were good.

Sensing he was on to something, Moss cultivated the gathering to include vendors - he invites more to come - music, larger crowds every year. He expects today's crowd to exceed the nearly 400 people who showed up last year. The sardine golf tournament won't be held this year because of a scheduling conflict with the course, he said.

Just as "love" is not the precise word to describe one's feeling for dead, pickled fish, "organize" doesn't precisely describe what Moss does. For instance what, I asked, is the main qualification you're looking for in the Sardine Queen y'all crown each year?

"Somebody we can get to run," he replied with a laugh.

Wouldn't the event draw larger crowds, and thus more money for the local charity to which donations go, if it were held on Saturdays?

"Probably, but 'When it works, don't fix it' is my philosophy," he said. "You don't really want to organize it; that'll mess it up."

The Port Clyde Sardine Co. donated 30 cases of sardines for this year's festival, he said, and he expects to have to buy more. Along with sardines, the menu for the festival consists of Moon Pies - truly the food of the gods - Coca-Cola, Sprite and, of course, soda crackers.

There is, alas, no wrong way to eat a sardine. I prefer mine mashed up with onions: I call it sardine pata. Regardless of how you eat them, though, few things in life are more forlorn and pitiful-looking as a sardine without a soda cracker.

─────────────────────────────────────── 10/13/2000

SAY IT AIN'T SO, JESSE ────────────────────────

No, Jesse, no.

Don't go out like this, pal. Please.

After a lifetime as a race-baiting commentator and politician, Jesse Helms now is trying to present himself to posterity as a moderate.

Helms, a former U.S. senator, has written a book that is due out in September. It's supposed be an autobiography, but much of what I've heard from my colleague Rob Christensen's critique of the "uncorrected" version sounds like science fiction.

For instance, when Jesse writes that he never opposed integration -- just "forced integration" -- anyone with even a brain stem must ask: On what far-off galaxy was that, Jesse? Because down here on Earth, son, you seemed to view integration with the same affection that a snail has for an overturned salt shaker -- none at all. Integration was, in your political and social life -- remember, you voted against admitting blacks to your church -- something to be avoided at all costs.

In the unholy trinity of modern-day political bigots, Jesse is Mr. Big: Even ol' Strom and George Wallace came around a little bit near the end, but Jesse has remained unrepentant.

To some, Jesse's one redeeming quality over the decades was his willingness to stand up for what he believed in, to risk being unpopular. It'd be a shame to see him ruin that now by lying.

Some people swear that Helms in one-on-one situations is the quintessential courtly Southern gentleman. On the two occasions I've talked to him, that was true -- even though he did tell me the whole civil rights movement was a waste of time. Maybe to you, Senator, but not to me.

His wife, to whom I spoke, seemed like a dear woman.

But that is not enough. Miss Dot, I'm sorry to tell you this, but your husband is an evil man. He stood -- and voted -- against everything that would have made this state, this country, great sooner. The great progress we've made in both? That was made in spite of him.

You'd have a hard time convincing anyone who listened to his comments in 1965 on the death of Viola Liuzzo otherwise. She was the Detroit woman who, moved by televised images of racial brutality, went to Alabama to help register blacks to vote in 1965. She was murdered for her efforts.

In commentary on WRAL, Jesse blamed not the Ku Kluxers who shot her twice in the head, but President Johnson and Dr. Martin Luther King Jr. for provoking the killers: "[W]hy and how did the rage of these men become so great as to prompt them to commit such an outrage? Can it be honestly said there was no deliberate provocation of violence?"

Oooh, Jesse, God is going to get you for that.

Indeed, don't be surprised if, at 83, Helms wants to pull the wool over the Big Guy's eyes. With a past like his, who wouldn't?

The dude showed that he could admit he was wrong by reversing his opposition to AIDS funding. It is on the race question, though, that Jesse never admitted he was wrong. He was, we are now supposed to believe, just misunderstood.

He was also a master at couching his baser feelings in coded, high-sounding but shallow protestations of principle.

Others require less evidence. We figure: If it talks, acts and votes like a racist -- it's Jesse.

6/14/2005

SCHOOLED IN THE WAYS OF DISCIPLINE

We've all seen those hapless, pitiable parents on TV shows such as "Maury" and "Queen Latifah" pleading, "Maury, help! I can't control my 12-year-old," or, "Queen, help! My 6-year-old beats me."

Mike Phillips has seen them, too, and he is determined not to become one of them. That is why, when the principal at his 6-year-old son's school called to say the boy was misbehaving yet again, Phillips left work, roared over to Middle Creek Elementary School and commenced to introduce his belt to his son's behind.

Right there in the hallway. Then, he said, he sat the boy down and explained why.

All right, stop that cheering.

Phillips' action may draw cheers from some quarters, but from the school system it elicited a stern letter and permanent banishment from school property.

In a letter from Corey Duber, Wake County Public Schools director of security, Phillips was told, "Your actions were said to be totally inappropriate for the school environment and were further described as bordering on child abuse. ... [E]xcept in the case of medical emergency, you are no longer permitted on the property of Middle Creek Elementary School. Failure to adhere to this directive will result in immediate legal action."

Ouch. I don't know about you, but where I grew up, schoolhouse whippings - administered either by parents or Principal J.C. Watkins with his notorious leather strop - were as much a part of school as abacuses and chalk. We all left home with this parental admonition ringing in his ears: "Don't make me have to leave my job to come up to that school."

If they did, you knew you would get it both for acting up and for making them miss a payday.

Phillips said he was shocked by the school's draconian response. "That was such a harsh letter, especially for the first time," he said when I talked to him in his office at Men at Work Car Wash in Raleigh recently. His voice, even when he is being reflective, is like a thunderclap. "I whipped my son. I didn't whip anybody else's kid," he said. "Now they try to take me out of his life. I guess there isn't any due process in the school system."

Duber said he took the action he did because Phillips "scared everyone at the school. We can't tolerate that."

Phillips was incensed by Duber's dictum that school business must be handled by Phillips' wife. "My wife doesn't handle discipline in my family," he said resolutely. "That's my job."

Duber told me he notified Child Protective Services, but a spokeswoman at CPS refused to say whether the case had been referred to that department. She did say, however, that beating your young'un, even at school, was "not necessarily child abuse. ... North Carolina law does not prohibit corporal punishment. We would investigate it, and if it doesn't meet our standard for abuse, we don't contact the parent."

Phillips said he has heard nothing from CPS but has since moved his son to a private Christian academy.

"Whaddya do, whaddya do?" he asked haplessly. "You're an uncaring, absentee parent if you're not involved, but you're an abuser if you discipline him."

4/6/2001

SEE WHAT YOU HAVE DONE

If you're old enough to remember Captain Kangaroo, Puff the Magic Dragon or nickel candy, you probably also know someone who served -- and possibly died -- in Vietnam. And you may not even be aware of it.

I wasn't, not until I went home to Rockingham earlier this month and thumbed through an ancient copy of Leak Street School's yearbook. Stopping at a picture of a tall, slim kid who looked familiar, I asked, "Whatever happened to Jimmie Ellerbe?"

"He died in Vietnam."

Whoa, talk about putting a damper on a visit home.

You know how philosophers are always debating whether a tree falling in the woods makes a sound if there's no one there to hear it? They ought to be pondering whether a young life taken in war diminishes us, even if you don't hear about it.

I was angry that such a friendly guy died in a war that most people now acknowledge was a mistake. I also was angry that someone who'd made the ultimate sacrifice for his country could die and the world not sit up and take note -- or at least not let me know.

Lucille Lea wanted to make sure that a similar fate would not befall Justin Onwordi, who died in Baghdad on Aug. 2 in a war that history also will likely classify under "mistake."

Lea, executive director of Lea Funeral Home in Raleigh, called me Tuesday. "I thought you should know about this young man who has made the ultimate sacrifice for his adopted country," she said. "I don't want his life to pass unheralded."

Onwordi's life should be heralded, as should every other soldier who gave his or her life on a battlefield. I sat in the funeral home's chapel during the wake Wednesday, listening to the Onwordi family's anguished wailing -- an anguish that was unallayed by the posthumous awarding of the Army's Purple Heart, the Bronze Star and the Good Conduct Medal. The awfulness of war became personal, and I wanted to snatch President Bush and Secretary of Defense Donald Rumsfeld by the collar, drag them before Onwordi's coffin and his grieving family and say, "See what you've done!"

Onwordi, a Nigerian immigrant, gave his life for a country of whose citizenship benefits he hadn't yet been able to fully partake. He joined the Army -- he became a medic to help heal and comfort rather than kill -- in 2001, a year after he got to this country.

It's impractical, sure, but wouldn't it be great if there were a law requiring the president, the vice president and all of the old men who make wars but don't fight in them to attend the wake -- we used to call it the 'settin' up' -- or funeral of every soldier killed in a war?

I would have loved to have seen Vice President Dick Cheney, who received five deferments to keep himself out of military service, try to explain to Ebony Onwordi and month-old Jonathan Onwordi how the death of their husband and father was necessary in a country that poses no threat to us.

Cheney, questioned about his absence from the military, has been widely quoted as saying, "I had other priorities in the '60s."

His priority now should be apologizing to the families of Justin Onwordi and every other soldier who did what he himself was too cowardly to do.

8/20/2004

SETTING THE POST-SEPT. 11 SENSITIVITY METER WAY TOO LOW

Maybe it's the fact that I've been me for 44 years - which means I've been called everything but a Reuben sandwich - but not much offends me.

Certainly not hearing James Taylor singing "Fire & Rain" on the radio in the days immediately following the World Trade Center and Pentagon attacks.

The disc jockey who played it must not have gotten the memo - or maybe worked for a station that didn't implement a list of records that supposedly were to be shelved lest they remind listeners of the attacks or, worse, offend them.

(As reporters later tried to track down the story, Clear Channel Communications denied ordering stations to censor songs, noting that the suggested list was e-mailed to others by one station programmer.)

The "banned" songs ranged from the ludicrous - the aforementioned "Fire & Rain," John Lennon's "Imagine" - to the absurd, like "Big Old Jet Airliner" by the Steve Miller Band. (The absurdity of the latter is not that a song about a jet airliner might have seemed in poor taste following the attack, in which planes were used as weapons, but that it actually sounds like the dude is singing "Big ol' Jed had a light on.")

The list, I concluded, was either a cynical attempt to garner publicity or to flout the patriotism of a huge, impersonal corporation, or, more charitably, a desperate attempt to do something - anything - to display sensitivity to survivors of victims of the cataclysmic event.

Who, I wondered while perusing the list, could be offended by Van Halen's "Jump," Carole King's "I Feel the Earth Move (Under My Feet)" or the Gap Band's "You Dropped a Bomb on Me"?

Nobody, right?

That's what I thought, too - until I received a call from a woman complaining about something even more trivial.

Seems she had turned to the Cartoon Network to lose herself in animation as a way to escape the barrage of news about the terrorist attacks. Me, I did the same thing, but I chose "The Brady Bunch" marathon, a series about a fictional family upon which reality seldom intruded.

Alas, such was not the case for the woman who sought solace in cartoons. Turns out there was a scene in one of the shorts in which some characters were constructing a huge building and, as often happens in cartoons, it came crashing down just as the last brick was laid. (Of course, if the short was like most cartoons, it only took them three seconds to reconstruct the darned building.)

That was too much for the caller. She said "I don't know how long in advance they pick the cartoons, but it seems that someone could have looked at that one before it came on."

And done what, exactly? Censor it so that it wouldn't remind people of the World Trade Center?

I kept listening, trying to detect in her voice a hint of something that would let me know that this was a gag call from someone playing a joke. I heard nothing to indicate that she was yanking my chain.

I wish I had, because even before the Sept. 11 attacks we were a nation filled with people quick at the slightest provocation.

A Chicago columnist who noted the same thing - people offended by songs, flags on clothing and cars, ads in magazines - wrote of spending an evening with some New York City firefighters who were taking a break from searching for their dead comrades and others.

"These guys have buried friends and they're still digging for bodies," he wrote. "They don't have time to be offended by trivial crap. Why don't we follow their lead?"

I'll drink to that. And play "Fire & Rain" on the jukebox.

10/6/2001

SHALL WE OVERCOME THE URGE TO EXAGGERATE, REV.?

Jesse, of all people, ought to know better. And he ought to be ashamed.

The Rev. Jesse Jackson further diminished his rapidly shrinking stature when he compared a peaceful march in Connecticut for better wages and job security to one of the bloodiest episodes of the Civil Rights Movement.

That's exactly what he did prior to being arrested earlier this week while participating in a march with striking Yale University clerical and maintenance workers. That's a noble cause, no doubt.

Event organizers and Jackson know that his fame attracts a certain level of media attention, and there's nothing inherently objectionable about trading on one's fame as a type of currency. After all, the Rev. Martin Luther King Jr. was in Memphis on behalf of striking sanitation workers when he was assassinated. So, in New Haven, Jackson apparently had his heart in the right place.

But to trade on his association with one of the seminal events in American history to add historical heft to his latest cause du jour is objectionable and in poor taste.

"This is the site of national Labor Day outrage," Jackson told about 1,000 people before being whisked off to jail. "This is going to be for economic justice what Selma was for the right to vote."

I've always said I wanted someone to walk up and slap me if I was ever heard to utter that banal catch-phrase "Don't go there," but that's precisely my response to comparing a demand for better wages and job security -- again, a genuinely noble cause -- to the right to vote and not be beaten by cops.

Let's see, now. As far as I can tell, none of the striking workers at Yale have had their homes firebombed, been beaten or assaulted with water hoses for demanding better wages. There were no cattle prods, no billy clubs swung with relish by state troopers, no tear gas.

Two days after television and newspapers portrayed the state-sponsored violence on Selma's Edmund Pettis Bridge on March 7, 1965, demonstrations of outrage and support occurred across the country. As Atlanta congressman John Lewis, who was beaten severely during the march, has said, "Something about that day in Selma touched a nerve deeper than anything that had come before. People just couldn't believe this was happening, not in America...I thought I saw death that day."

Five months later, President Lyndon B. Johnson pushed through the Voting Rights Act -- an act propelled legislatively, no doubt, by the image of men, women and children being whomped by cops in Alabama.

Is that what Jesse is comparing his latest peaceful arrest to? He ought to be ashamed.

One of the failings of the post-Civil Rights era generation is that they -- we -- haven't done a proper job educating our children about what our parents and grandparents went through to secure these rights for us. Jackson doesn't help things by seeming to trivialize Selma, a signature event, to get his 15-second soundbite on the evening news.

This appropriation -- make that "misappropriation" -- of civil rights tactics and imagery is not unique to media-hounds such as Jesse.

One of the more egregious examples occurred during the 1980s. I was living in Atlanta and watched as residents of a wealthy enclave protested a proposed highway near their neighborhood by bodily blocking bulldozers and singing "We Shall Overcome."

It was with a mixture of anger and bemusement that I watched them belittle one of the transforming eras in American history.

It is with much sadness that I watch Jesse Jackson do the same thing.

9/6/2003

SHARING TIME ON A HOOK

There are three things you'll never get most men to admit: that they once liked disco music, that as kids they found Bugs Bunny strangely erotic when he put on high heels and red lipstick -- oh, so I'm the only one, eh? -- or that they bought a time-share vacation that they didn't really want.

That's what makes my buddy Dr. Jeffrey Scales unique.

"I just finally bought it out of exhaustion," said Scales, showing more courage than most men would if they had done the same. "They wear you down."

Remember Joe Walsh's song, "Life's Been Good"?

"I have a mansion, forget the price/ ain't never been there, they tell me it's nice."

That's how Scales feels about his time-share villa in Austria. "My dad says it's great," he told me, "and the pictures I've seen of it make me want to go. If I ever get a chance."

His situation was one I found myself in just last month, when Sweet Thang, the kids and I -- also known as Kool & the Gang -- went to Orlando to take advantage of a package I purchased from a seductive telemarketer: three days, four nights in a sunny vacation resort for only $99. And dig this: All I had to do was take a tour of the joint, listen to a brief, "no-pressure" sales pitch and split.

To make sure that I yielded not unto temptation, I left credit cards and checkbook at home.

Foolishly believing honesty to be the best policy, I tried the tack taken by another buddy who'd been hoodooed by the same outfit: He told his tour guide from the get-go that he wasn't interested in buying anything and was merely taking advantage of a cheap vacation. The guide, he said, graciously accepted his honesty and saved his spiel for the next sucker.

That, I'm guessing, was me.

Just like an overanxious teenager in the back seat who keeps trying to get to second base while his girlfriend cries "Foul!" my sales guy kept telling me "I respect you" while blatantly ignoring my pleas.

When he saw that I didn't agree that mortgaging my life for the privilege of two weeks a year for the rest of my life at the resort was the best thing I could do to show the gang I loved them, he tried to get a sympathy purchase out of me. Again, like that overanxious teenager.

Why else would he confide to me, a bloke he'd known all of 35 minutes, that he had a newborn and that his wife had been laid off from her job?

What happened near the end of my tour was the closest I've come to being kidnapped since the time a guy in a long black car with tinted windows lured me over by saying he knew a place where pancakes grew on trees and "Sanford & Son" was on TV all day. I was home from college for spring break so I said, "Why not?"

This time, though, I declined the offer, but the dude wasn't accepting. So I removed his hand from my arm and stood up.

"He's leaving, he's leaving," he shouted, and four people intercepted me at the door.

"You didn't read your contract," an exasperated supervisor said after every other attempt to keep me failed. "You must stay for 90 minutes and you've only been here 60."

I returned dutifully to my seat for 30 minutes more of a more intense sales pitch, during which I kept thinking, "Whew, I'm glad I didn't bring my checkbook."

3/11/2003

SHE PAID THE PRICE OF LOVE

It was only in the past month, after six years of triple-checking the locks of her apartment, constantly peering from behind the shower curtain, expecting to be assaulted again by her imprisoned former husband, that Tanisha Bagley got her first good night's sleep.

Before that, she said, "I'd wake up thinking he'd broken out of prison and into my apartment. Every time I'd brush my teeth or take a shower, I'd think he was standing there."

With her ex scheduled to be released from prison next month after a six-year term for kidnapping and raping her, it seems natural that her fear would increase. It hasn't. Not even after being told he's still bent on revenge.

"I've been told, 'You're crazy for staying here,' or, 'You should leave,' " she said. "The human side of me says, 'He's going to come for you,' but I've always had a relationship with God, so another side says 'God has brought you this far, so don't question him now. ... Get it together, girl.' "

The girl has gotten it together, big time. In the year since I introduced her to you in a column about her ordeal, she has become sought-after as a speaker on domestic violence and has written a book, due out today.

"The Price of Love" is about Bagley's relationship -- beginning when she was 14 and her ex was 15 -- that led to marriage, three children and a decade of abuse culminating with her kidnap and rape. Part of the proceeds of the book, available at priceoflove.com, will fund her proposed shelter, ENSHRINE. That's an acronym for Everyone Needs Support Help Respect Inspiration Nourishment and Empowerment.

That formula helped Bagley overcome daunting obstacles. "When I was rebuilding my life, things got tough," she said.

"The women's shelter was full, but they offered to let us sleep on a church's pews," she recalled. "I didn't want to do that, so I stayed in an abusive relationship for an extra year simply because there was no place to go. I would never advise anybody else to do that."

She worked two jobs, one of which was cleaning toilets at 4 a.m. in a Raleigh office building.

"I'd cry my eyes out, because I knew I was supposed to be doing something, and it wasn't cleaning toilets.

"I went on public assistance, which hurt me to my heart, because I never wanted to do that. I never wanted to get divorced or be a statistic. ... Everything I tried so hard to avoid I ended up doing."

She also ended up becoming a survivor helping others. "I've always wanted to open a facility, a Club Med, for other Tanisha Bagleys who feel their situation is hopeless," she said.

Bagley got a good break -- as opposed to the ones she usually got from her violent former husband -- when Rhonda Powell, a victim's advocate with the Raleigh Police Department, invited her to speak at the department's annual Domestic Violence Awareness Month in October 2003. "From that day on, I knew that's what I was supposed to be doing," she said.

The book tells women and girls the warning signs to look for and when they should leave: "After the first slap. If he hits you once, he'll hit you again. When he shows that first sign of control, of what you wear, where you can go, who your friends should be -- run. That's what I should've done."

———————————————————————— 11/5/2004

SHOE BOX STILL HOLDS A STENCH ————————

When James Lampley was arrested at the State Fairgrounds in September 1998 and accused of pointing his video shoe box under the dresses of unsuspecting women, you figured he'd at least be suspended from his state job -- and sentenced to jail, a shrink or film school.

No one, at least none of his co-workers I talked to, imagined that he'd emerge from the scandal unscathed and end up being promoted to section chief for the general accounting/financial management section of the state controller's office. Yet that is precisely what happened last week, when Lampley was given a $6,900 raise to $82,000 a year.

The aspiring Cecil B. DeMille of state government was charged six years ago with two counts of assault on a female after two women told fairgrounds cops that some dude was traipsing around pointing a strategically placed shoe box at women.

Smooth, Jim, smooth.

The cops observed, then grabbed Lampley, nipping his film career in the bud. One charge against Lampley was dismissed, and he was allowed to plead guilty to disorderly conduct on the other.

Laketha Miller, controller, and Jack Chappell, chief of program benefits for the Department of Health and Human Services, were out of the office Monday, and Lampley didn't return calls. Chappell, at the time of Lampley's arrest, dismissed it as "not related to state government."

Lampley's offense was, however, related to being a decent human being. Any man who lurks around taping under women's dresses is either socially maladjusted or a creep. Lavonda Van Benthuysen of the Office of State Personnel said "the state could take action against an employee if the agency feels their off-the-job behavior could have an impact on their ability to do their job."

No one, apparently, thought Lampley's arrest would harm his ability to work with women, but I'll bet that as his rank in state government goes up, the hemlines in his office go down.

Matt Cleary, the fairgrounds' top cop, said when Lampley was arrested that he was "not very cooperative," so there was no way to know what he was going to do with his footage.

Maybe not, but I've got an idea. Filming women without their knowledge and then posting it on the Internet is big business. I located 759 Internet sites with the phrase "hidden upskirt camera" in their names.

There were not yet any called "Women of the State Fairgrounds."

Here is my musical tribute to Lampley and his ability to stay employed and out of jail or the Hoo Hoo Hotel, sung to the tune of the Okaysions' "I'm a Girl Watcher." Maestro, hit it:

I'm a girl watcher

I'm a girl watcher

Watchin' girls go by

My my my ...

I wonder if you know

that you're putting on a show.

Come here and stand by this here shoe box.

Whenever I detect members of the other sex

I look to see if they're wearing a dress, Lord.

Then I'm a girl watcher ...

In an e-mail message announcing Lampley's promotion, Controller Miller praised his "wealth of knowledge" and called him a "true team player."

Yep, and he and his magic shoe box will always be available to film company picnics.

———————————————————————————————— 8/3/2004

SOME TIPS FOR DEALING WITH FLASHERS ————————

Honest, it was merely a coincidence that the Triangle was hit with a rash of flashers at the exact time I left for vacation and can't account for my whereabouts.

In case you missed the news, Cary has had more incidents of indecent exposure so far this year than all of last year - 21 at last count. Recent flashers have been described by witnesses as white, black, Asian and Hispanic.

I don't know about you, but I find it oddly reassuring that perversion knows no boundaries and that these freaks who like to turn the other cheek while showing off their physiques constitute their own perverted Rainbow Coalition.

Of the reported incidents so far this year, the weirdest must've been the one in which a lady said a man sprang from an alley in North Cary about 8 a.m. and began chasing her car with his shorts around his ankles.

Two things strike me: First, I didn't know Cary had alleys, and second, I can't picture the chase without laughing.

Lest such incidents cast all men in a bad light and make women think we're all pigs, I feel a civic duty to offer them advice on how they should respond the next time they are confronted by a nekkid man they don't know.

Several of the alleged flashing incidents began when a man called an unsuspecting woman over to his car. First of all, the next time you approach the car of some strange man seeking directions - don't! Better yet, snarl, "Do I look like Rand McNally to you, chump?"

If you are one of those Good Samaritans who just can't stand to see someone lost and feel the need to help anyway, try to maintain your composure when you discover he's cruisin' nude.

Your first inclination would be to run away shrieking in horror. Anyone's would. That, however, is precisely what the inadequate pervert wants since knowing that he could strike fear into someone would simply boost his fragile ego.

Dr. Lee Walker, a Cary police psychologist, said flashers are men who feel inadequate and have "serious problems."

Gee, and here I was thinking that anyone who'd drop trou in front of strangers and chase cars was well-adjusted.

Dr. Lee suggests that women show no behavior when confronted by a flasher. Hey, what fun is that? Here are far more appropriate responses which, if done right, will send the puny perp running home to cower in his stuffy attic next to his vintage, alphabetized collection of Playboy magazines dating back to 1966:

- Point and fall down laughing hysterically, or say,

- "Evenin', ma'am."

- "That's nice, but does it come in adult sizes?"

- "Gee, I didn't realize it was that cold out here."

- "Hey, didn't I see you on the 'Tonight Show' 30 years ago marrying Miss Vicki?"

Smirk if you want, but my tips are superior to what I heard from a local TV reporter who said police suggest women "keep an eye out."

Funny, but it seems that's just what the flashers want.

8/11/2000

'SOMEBODY DOESN'T LIKE YOU'

Mack O'Neal doesn't know how he ended up in prison.

Wait. That's not quite right. He doesn't know how he ended up back in prison.

O'Neal escaped from the state prison in Hillsborough in 1972 and lived a relatively crime-free life in Los Angeles the whole while. After that much time on the lam, the 58-year-old Durham native could be excused for figuring he wouldn't have to pay for his crime - burning private property in 1969 during a demonstration against the Durham Housing Authority - at least not until St. Peter made a head count in that big correctional facility in the sky.

But in December, O'Neal found himself handcuffed on an airplane, escorted by an extradition officer and once again trading in his name for a number after being stopped by L.A. police.

"The cop told me, 'Somebody in North Carolina doesn't like you,'" O'Neal explained when I interviewed him last week at the New Hanover Correctional Center in Wilmington. "He said they got an anonymous tip" that O'Neal was wanted in his home state.

A spokesman for the state Department of Correction said of O'Neal, "That fellow just had some bad luck. We've got thousands of outstanding warrants," implying that a 27-year-old one could easily slip through the bureaucratic cracks.

Mack O'Neal wishes it had. "Everything I did in L.A., I did under the name Mack C. O'Neal Jr.," he said. "I drove a taxi for 10 years, and every ticket I got was under my own name. I even drew disability insurance under it."

His first thought after being arrested, he said, was: "Carmen. I thought she'd turned me in."

He turned toward Carmen O'Neal, his 35-year-old daughter who sat in on the interview in a tiny office at the prison. She denies ratting him out, even though both admit she had ample reason to. She'd even threatened him three days before his capture. "I wish I knew something on you, you #&%$," she'd said on a venomous message left on his answering machine. "I'd send you to jail. I hate you."

The decades-old hatred smoldered because she thought he'd abandoned her mother and her for a woman in Los Angeles.

"Carmen didn't know I was on the run," O'Neal said. "She hated me for all the wrong reasons."

"I hated you for leaving," she snapped.

O'Neal is philosophical about his fate. "I don't mind being locked up, but I hate it when they say I'm going to be released on a certain day and that day passes. I want 'em to let me go or charge me with something," he said.

The bad news for O'Neal is that no release date has been set. The good news is that he apparently isn't facing escape charges. Richard Davis, assistant superintendent for programs at New Hanover, said O'Neal's maximum release date - if he has to complete the original three-year sentence - would be Jan. 30, 2001.

Or, the parole commission could decide that a tired old man who got caught up in the social tumult of the 1960s and has lived nearly three decades being decent deserves a break.

2/22/2000

SOUTHERN CULTURES ON THE SKIDS

Billy Graham? There must be some mistake.

A list of the most influential Southerners of the 20th century was published in the spring issue of the journal Southern Cultures, and evangelist Billy Graham came in near the top.

Fiddlesticks.

No one can argue seriously with the list's top four picks - Martin Luther King Jr., William Faulkner, Elvis and LBJ. They all had a profound effect on the South, and thus on the world, in their chosen milieu.

But the Rev. Billy's impact? Negligible, at best. Now, if you were to compose a list of most popular Southerners or those who accomplished the least with the most, Graham would be at the top. Yet, during the most turbulent, exciting period in this century -- the 1960s -- when Americans were embroiled in a war for civil rights and others were trying to get us out of a war in Southeast Asia, Graham was MIA -- content to barnstorm the country mouthing pious irrelevancies and sanctimonious trivialities while George Beverly Shea sang "How Great Thou Art." But, boy, could he sing it.

It's significant that three of the top six on the list -- King, LBJ and George Wallace -- probably had as many detractors as admirers. But Graham? Everybody liked him. And therein lies the problem.

In most things Southern, I'd gladly defer to the judgment of sociologist John Shelton Reed, cartoonist Doug Marlette and writer Roy Blount Jr. who, among others, were on the panel ranking the most influential Southerners.

But I think they confused Graham's renown and popularity with influence. I have infinitely more respect for Wallace than for Graham. Wallace had a profound, albeit a profoundly negative, effect on the South, but at least you knew where he stood on everything. Can you say the same for Graham?

Nope. That's why he doesn't deserve to be on the list.

Neither, or so I initially thought, does Michael Jordan. I've often criticized Jordan's refusal to speak out on anything that didn't personally profit him, but how can one lightly dismiss the influence of a man who persuaded people to spend $150 for a pair of gym shoes that some exploited Indonesian made for $2.79?

Now, that's influence. Too bad he didn't use it for something other than selling sneakers.

George Washington Carver, the scientist from Tuskegee, Ala., did more with a peanut and an ear of corn than Graham when he had the ear of every president and Jordan when he had the ear of everyone. Yet Carver's influence was rated behind both of theirs. (To be fair, though, George's jump shot was a bit suspect.)

Any list of influential Southerners that includes neither Vernon Rudolph, the founder of Krispy Kreme, nor the dude who invented the Moon Pie -- truly the food of the gods -- is automatically suspect.

Not only would those two culinary pioneers be on my list, but I'd also reserve a spot near the top for the man or woman who first thought of adding cheese to grits and stirring it up.

I'd like to shake that person's hand. As soon as my arteries unclog.

→ 7/10/2001

SOUTHERN FRIED GREED ├────────────

Lawd ha' mercy, but those must've been some good hush puppies.

That was my conclusion after reading this week's story about lobbyist extraordinaire Joe "Drink up: It's not coming out of my pockets anyway" McClees.

There was nothing surprising in the revelations that Big Money McClees, a lobbyist for the N.C. Technological Development Authority, lavished upon myriad beneficiaries gifts, pheasant-hunting trips and luxury hotel rooms -- paid for in part with taxpayers' money.

Hmmph, any lobbyist worth his tasseled alligator loafers does that.

What was surprising was the revelation that McClees, known to the

beneficiaries of his state-sponsored largess as "Brother Joe," spent a lot of money on cornmeal. Hmm, could it be that Brother Joe was a member of a secret cult that worshipped hoe cakes? Or perhaps, with Jell-O being passe, he would head over to Thee Dollhouse, pick out a couple of dancers and pay them to rassle in cornmeal? Hmmm, note to self: Remember that one.

The TDA paid McClees more than $600,000 over the past three years, but I was looking for an angle beyond your everyday, run-of-the-corn-mill greed. Thus, I hoped that McClees was a modern day reincarnation of Robin Hood, the mythical dude in tights who stole from the rich and gave to the poor.

Only McClees, I was thinking, instead of giving money to poor people, would sneak into their homes during the night and leave -- get this -- hush puppies. How else to explain his billing the TDA more than $1,300 for cornmeal?

Sure, he took clients, friends and the people who approved his inflated expense accounts to fancy Italian restaurants, but that was just business. The people he really cared for, the little people of North Carolina? He fed 'em hush puppies. Or so I hoped the facts would prove.

Speaking of facts, it's a scientific one that a fried hush puppy is nature's perfect food, containing the recommended daily allowance of carbohydrates, nutrients, protein and flavor. Not only do hush puppies stick to your ribs, but -- as anyone who looks at me with my shirt off can attest -- they stick to your belly.

New York Times writer Rick Bragg recently wrote of his mother feeding him sweet tea in his milk bottle as a baby; I remember those days, too. I also knew mothers who used day-old hush puppies as pacifiers. It was nothing to see little babies crawling around on their hands and knees, gnawing on a crisp but succulent hush puppy and sipping tea from a bottle. Show up on my doorstep at the right time and you're likely to find me doing it now.

It is impossible to overstate the importance of hush puppies to the Southern diet. Thus, instead of reviling McClees as a spendthrift who over the years spent thousands of dollars of our money on food, fun and frivolity -- and wasted the rest -- I was ready to extol his efforts to improve the diet of poor Tar Heels by feeding them hush puppies.

Alas, I discovered later in the story that McClees was not, as I had hoped, engaged in gastronomic altruism: The cornmeal he spread -- to powerful legislators -- was merely to help him make more dough.

4/30/2002

SOUTHPOINT CAN'T BUILD CHARACTER

One of the best juke joints I've ever been into - this was back before I became the paragon of virtue that I am now - was a place in Rockingham called the Crooked Window.

It got its name - no fooling - when the owner, a guy named Fun, heard how much it would cost to replace the cracked and crooked picture window at the front of the establishment.

"Fellas," Fun announced when told of the prohibitively hefty price, "we are open for business."

To us regulars, the window and the general scruffiness of the joint contributed to its character and were essential to its appeal - OK, that and the fact that Fun would sometimes give us a beer on credit.

But character is something that can't be faked, as the developers of the Southpoint shopping complex will discover. They are, it appears, trying to build character into the project, to make the Streets of Southpoint an "experience" rather than just a place to go pick up a pair of black pumps or some BVDs.

Randall Stone, vice president of the superambitious mall's architectural company, said in a News & Observer story this week, "We're trying to take the mall out of the mall."

The more I read of plans for the mall - plans that include faux manhole covers, street signs and metal shutters similar to the ones on Durham's vacant cigarette factories - the more I am convinced that they are really trying to take downtown Durham out of downtown. What else can you think when the food court is supposed to resemble a refurbished tobacco warehouse and the kiddie play area's furniture looks like construction-site barriers?

As far as I can tell, the only thing the mall will be missing from the real downtown experience is one of Durham's legendarily cantankerous panhandlers going, "Can you loan me $2 for something to eat, Hoss?" and the courtesy patrol writing parking tickets. They can probably appropriate some of that ambience by piping in on giant loudspeakers Petula Clark's 1960s urban anthem, "Downtown."

Don't confuse me with the anti-growth zealots who condemn the project because of its largeness. No sirree. I, as an espouser of the theory that nothing succeeds like excess, welcome Southpoint.

Sure, it's almost big enough to have its own congressman, but one mammoth mall is preferable to 20 more extraneous, landscape-defiling drugstores or the cookie-cutter, characterless strip malls that already threaten to rob Raleigh of its remaining charm.

Downtown Durham is woefully inadequate to house a project of Southpoint's size, but the fact that that mall is seeking to replicate downtown should hip others to the underdeveloped gem with its massive potential for growth.

The Southpoint project reminds me of another song - it won a Grammy as song of the year in 1979 - by the Doobie Brothers, "What a Fool Believes." It was about a lovesick dude and had a line describing him thusly: "He's trying hard to re-create what had yet to be created."

Southpoint's developers, on the other hand, are trying hard - and spending millions - to re-create what has already been created. And it's right downtown.

1/13/2000

SPARKS FLY OVER PAYMENT

It was only after the customer-service representative taking payments for gas and electric bills stopped cursing, throwing chairs and telephones and kicking tables that he realized he was in serious pain.

"I think I broke my #$@%&^* leg," the clerk said as he grimaced and took my money through the bulletproof payment window this week.

What caused the man to go electric -- had his explosion occurred in a post office, you'd say "postal" -- was a request by Edward Gilchrist: "Give me my money back so I can go pay my electric bill."

Gilchrist, as so many Durham residents do when they lack checking accounts or Internet access, had gone several days earlier to a check-cashing establishment -- one that also sells genuine imitation leather handbags and gaudy fake diamond watches -- to pay his Duke Power bill. But the electric company hadn't received his payment and was about to cut off his service.

Durham residents have long lamented the hassle of having to deal with such places to pay utility fees -- and being charged an additional dollar or so for the, ah, convenience.

Their lamentations have fallen on deaf ears, though. As much money as Duke Power and PSNC make, you'd think they could provide a central location for residents to pay bills.

Can't our political representatives do something about the fact that if you pay your gas bill where you pay your electric bill, there's a fee? Or, if you pay your electric bill where you pay your gas bill there's -- you guessed it -- a fee and the bill won't be credited for three days?

That's why Gilchrist was trying to get his money back.

"They told me to come here, get my money and then go pay" at Duke's Avondale Drive center, Gilchrist explained calmly but firmly through the thick glass as his wife, Gwendolyn Green, stood beside him.

The clerk, who wouldn't give me his name, refused to give Gilchrist his money. He did, however, call Duke Power so Gilchrist and Green could straighten out the mess.

After much difficulty, he succeeded in sliding the telephone receiver through the small opening for payments, but when Green put it to her ear, she heard only a dial tone.

Either the dial tone or Green's insistence on a refund set homey off. He tossed the phone, threw chairs and kicked the table, all the while unleashing what must've been an impressive stream of curse words. I say "must've" because he lost his temper in a language I didn't know. I understand every fourth or fifth word, none of which are suitable for retransmission.

"He's probably calling me all kinds of names," Gilchrist said, "but I don't care, as long as he gives me my money."

When the man kicked at the chair with his foot, he missed but connected with his shin.

"Ooh, that's gotta hurt," I winced. He profanely confirmed it when he took my money.

I told a representative at Duke Power's customer service center in

Charlotte, who said her name was Lynn, about the incident at the check-cashing establishment. She said, "We don't recommend or condone paying your bills there. We tell our customers 'Do not pay at those places.' "

They won't have to tell Edward Gilchrist again.

⊢ 2/25/2005

ST. AUG'S GETS WRONG ADVISE ⊢

I was a student at St. Augustine's College for only about long enough to eat lunch 25 years ago because of a slight misunderstanding between the basketball coach and me: I thought I should be on the team; he thought I was more valuable sitting in the stands cheering.

Yet, despite my brief semester on the bucolic college campus, I am as saddened by the turmoil that keeps coming out of there as any alumnus could be.

First, President Dianne B. Suber announces potentially devastating, if not fatal, staff cuts that could slice the number of teachers by a quarter.

Second, the school's chief academic officer quits in disgust after, he said, Suber ordered him to have the flunking calculus grades of 11 students changed to passing. Suber said she ordered the grades changed out of fairness to students who should have been told they were not ready for the advanced course.

Fairness? C'mon, Prez, you know better than that. By all means, ensure that students get proper guidance, but you are doing no one a favor when you give them grades to which they are not entitled. I believe students should pass courses the old-fashioned way: by copying off the paper of the kid sitting next to them or having an affair with their teacher.

Most recently, the new president ordered student newspapers confiscated ostensibly because a dude who'd been stabbed on campus was showing his butt - literally - in the latest issue of the campus newspaper. More likely, though, she wanted to quash the accompanying front-page criticism of campus security.

In defense of campus security, students who peddle reefer from their dormitory rooms - as police contend the stabbing victim was doing - should be required to pay for their own private security, because unsatisfied drug customers are less likely to report questionable business practices to the Better Business Bureau and more likely to use violence.

Not only was confiscating the student paper a disastrous display of Realpolitik - might makes right - but it also was a boneheaded public relations move that accomplished precisely what President Fidel, I mean Suber, wanted to prevent: focusing attention on campus activity.

As a former college newspaper editor, I could've told her that students rarely sit around breathlessly awaiting the arrival of the campus newspaper - unless they know the president doesn't want them to read it. Oh sure, there was the occasional hot story - never proved - that administrators were slipping something into our food to dampen students' sex drive, but usually a hard-hitting, controversial story was one that presumed to identify the mystery meat served in the cafeteria on Wednesdays.

With their heavy-handed tactics in this matter, St. Augustine's administrators ensured that the student newspaper - and the issues they so wanted to keep quiet - would receive prominent play in newspapers and on local TV news.

For an ailing school struggling to reach enrollment goals, a grade-changing scandal, to-the-bone staff cuts and dictatorial administration tactics are not what the doctor ordered.

5/16/2000

ST. AUG'S REACTION WOEFUL

I don't know what's more offensive: that a top official at a local college goes to court this month on charges of assaulting and threatening his wife -- or the college's response to the charges.

When I called St. Augustine's College to inquire about the assault and threat charges being faced by Director of Admissions Timothy D. Chapman, I expected at least a hint of shock or outrage. None was forthcoming. Instead, I got this from spokeswoman Mildred Robertson: "The institution has no comment as it relates to that issue. It is a personal issue, not an institutional issue."

Say what?

Let me get this straight: The director of admissions, the person most responsible for determining what type of student gets into your school, is being hauled into court to face charges that he, with knife in hand, according to police reports, told his wife in April, "This is it. This is the last night. It is going to be either me or you," yet that is not considered an institutional issue?

Are they saying that the 48 hours Chapman spent cooling off in the pokey after police said he threatened his wife with a knife and punched his 13-year-old stepdaughter don't reflect on the school?

I'd like to hear President Dianne B. Suber say that to the parent of some 18-year-old young lady whose welfare is being entrusted to the college. Suber, speaking reluctantly to a reporter after Robertson's woefully inadequate comment to me, praised Chapman as "extraordinarily competent" and noted that "there are two sides."

True, and everyone is entitled to the presumption of innocence. That's why no one is calling for Chapman to be tarred, feathered and fired. Yet. That presumption of innocence, though, does not mean St. Augustine's should stick its head in the sand. The school should -- no, must -- distance itself from this "exemplary" dude and him from it pending the resolution of these disturbing charges.

If Chapman doesn't have enough respect for the institution to take a leave of absence so as not to further sully the school, then Suber should insist that he take a leave and handle his personal family business. Now. If he's exonerated, welcome the dude back. If he's found guilty , hand him his walking papers and change the locks.

Several calls to Chapman's office were unreturned.

St. Aug's, after years of declining enrollment and the threatened loss of its accreditation, has seemingly gotten on the good foot thanks to Suber and, according to her, Chapman. Enrollment has increased, and the school's continued accreditation seems assured.

Do administrators want to risk stalling that momentum because of a misguided sense of loyalty or paranoia?

As a former student -- I attended about long enough to eat lunch, leaving after being cut from the basketball team -- I have fond memories of St. Aug's and would gladly church up to help pay for that new $23 million expansion project.

Few others would be inclined to cough up some dough, though, if they suspected that the second-most-powerful administrator on campus had assaulted his wife. Or that school officials didn't think it was important whether he had.

———————————————————————————— 8/12/2003

STADIUM SORCERY WRECKED TECH ————————————

Poor Georgia Tech. When its heavily favored football players left Kenan Stadium dragging tail after being thrashed 34-13 by the UNC Tar Heels last month, they must have felt they'd been cursed.

Perhaps they had been.

Days before the Sept. 18 game, Dawn Bunting, the wife of UNC head coach John Bunting, was seen escorting a veiled, stooped figure around the empty stadium. The woman was burning sage and making incantations.

Georgia Tech's chances for a victory might have gone up in smoke long before the kickoff.

UNC Athletics Director Dick Baddour confirmed that the unusual pregame ritual had taken place, calling it "just a big joke."

"You've got to know Dawn," he said. "She's fun-loving, passionate and spirited. ... If you thought that was serious -- Lord, no. "

He said the woman accompanying Bunting was a good friend and longtime Tar Heel fan. She was not, he said, from New Orleans, where the Buntings previously lived and where Voodoo is a religion.

The sage ritual was also practiced in St. Louis when Bunting was an assistant coach with the Rams from 1997 to 1999.

"The year we went to the Super Bowl, they said the city was cursed and that the only way to get rid of the curse was to burn sage," he said Thursday at UNC's practice.

"So on Saturday nights before games ... a lot of people started burning sage. It was a little bit of fun. Of course, we started winning and everybody had more fun."

Asking if burning sage were going to become a new Carolina tradition, particularly with Saturday's big game against N.C. State looming, Bunting responded, "We need to win first. What are we, 2 and 1 at home? I'm sure we'll be burning some sage tomorrow."

Georgia Tech Athletics Director Dave Braine couldn't be reached for comment. A secretary was laughing too hard to say if the school might want a voodooless rematch.

———————————————————————————— 10/8/2004

WHY NOT A LITTLE VOODOO?

Laugh if you want about UNC coach John Bunting's admission that he invoked a little voodoo to help his team, but you can bet he's not the only coach who has resorted to extreme measures upon being unable to recruit a 6-foot-2, 240-pound tailback who runs the 40 in 4-flat.

As much pressure as there is on Division I coaches, if they thought putting a whammy on the opposition would work, they would all be channeling Miss Rudolph -- the voodoo lady with the three-legged monkey that comedian Richard Pryor made famous.

I was skeptical, but being a true-blue Tar Heel fan, I still had a little chant prepared for today's game against the N.C. State Wolfpack.

Bubble, bubble, toil and trouble;

Help our tailback score a couple;

And when their kicker starts to kick;

Let the ball to his big toe stick;

Hee hee hee, cackle cackle;

Make the Wolfpack miss the tackle.

When I first heard about the voodoo lady burning sage at Kenan Stadium before a game, I called up Coach Bunting just to get the voodoo queen's telephone number: I wanted to see whether she'd put a mojo on a woman I love but can't stand.

One reader, calling himself Charles Brown, insisted that voodoo has long been in use at UNC. "For years, I have been begging Saunders to investigate the link between voodoo and UNC," he wrote after Friday's story. He noted that each time the Heels won a basketball championship, it was in New Orleans, where voodoo is a religion.

As evidence, he cited the strange way both of those championship games ended: with Georgetown's Fred Brown throwing the ball directly to UNC's James Worthy in 1982, and then Michigan's Chris Webber calling a timeout his team didn't have in 1993.

OK, dawg, you've got a point, but it didn't hurt that both of those teams had All-America players and the greatest coach ever, right?

Besides, employing a witch doctor to burn away evil spirits is not the most extreme or worst thing a coach has done to win games. It's certainly not as bad as castrating a bull to motivate your team, as Mississippi State University coach Jackie Sherrill did several years ago.

How, you ask, can castrating a bull motivate a team of young men?

Hey, how could it not? I don't know about you, but a coach who snaps, "Drop another pass, Stonehands, and this is what we're gonna do to you," would motivate me to play well more than any "win one for the Gipper" speech.

As a Tar Heel fan, I wanted Coach Bunting to summon whatever forces were at his disposal to win the game against the Wolfpack -- as long as he didn't resort to wearing silly shades and prancing around on the sidelines in ruby red slippers as his counterpart does.

10/9/2004

STATE GETS THE COLD SHOULDER

If this keeps up, we Tar Heels may develop an inferiority complex.

This year alone, we have watched as two North Carolina cultural icons -- NASCAR and Krispy Kreme -- courted other areas at our expense. NASCAR pulled races from some tracks here, and Krispy Kreme opened a shop in merry olde England while the entire Triangle still has only one.

Now, to further lick the salt off of our fatback, a Civil War movie set in North Carolina has been filmed in Romania.

Marla Tambellini of the Asheville Convention and Visitors Bureau expressed disappointment that the soon-to-be-released "Cold Mountain" wasn't filmed on and near the the real Cold Mountain in Haywood County. But she said she hoped the area could "piggyback" off the movie's popularity.

"Those of us with a deep and abiding love of the mountains had our hearts set on it being filmed here," she told me Thursday. "On the other hand, we hope it shines a spotlight on the mountains of North Carolina and creates awareness."

There are, as Tambellini said, "areas of pristine wilderness" still there, so many that producers of the movie "The Last of the Mohicans" had no trouble capturing an era that preceded the Civil War.

Kind of makes you wonder whether the folks at Miramax studio had another, baser reason -- such as cheaper workers -- for choosing a poor Eastern European country to tell a uniquely Southern story.

I couldn't reach director Anthony Minghella -- he's probably hiding from anyone with a Southern drawl -- but he said in a published interview that he chose Romania because "the landscapes look like the 19th century in a way that nowhere in America" does.

OK, let's concede that North Carolina doesn't look like the North Carolina of two centuries ago. In some places it doesn't look like the North Carolina of two years ago. At least then there was a chance of seeing a corner lot that didn't have a "Future Home of ... " sign on it.

Still, there are remote regions of North Carolina that have pretty much gone untrodden and undeveloped -- and not just the Global TransPark.

Despite the overdevelopment, creative direction could have kept the movie in the state. For instance, computers could've digitally removed those intrusive cell phone towers and billboards for Thee Dollhouse.

The billboards could even have been incorporated into the script, as when the Confederate general promises his men a night of R&R at Thee Dollhouse -- "It's just three exits yonderways" -- if they fight with good courage.

A civic snub similar to this occurred several years ago when I was doing time in Indiana -- OK, it only felt like I was doing time -- and producers of a movie on the Jackson family, which famously hailed from Gary, sought a more picturesque locale for the biopic.

They chose Pittsburgh. Yes, Pittsburgh.

Gary officials were livid and wanted to ban the family from ever returning, even though Michael, Tito and the others hadn't been back to Gary since Michael was black.

As disappointed as Tambellini and others are over losing "Cold Mountain," they can take solace in knowing at least that Pittsburgh wasn't our stand-in.

⊢ 12/19/2003

STRIP CLUB MOURNED AT CLOSING ⊢

Under most circumstances, holding a wake at midnight would sound weird, ghoulish even.

But late nighttime was the right time to say goodbye to an old friend in Durham to whom death came Thursday afternoon with the stroke of a judge's pen.

When Superior Court Judge Ronald Stephens slammed down his gavel and issued an order preventing Brothers III nightclub from opening -- possibly forever, but at least until a hearing -- he killed what many considered the most notorious, sleaziest, off-the-chain strip club on the East Coast.

That's why so many men in the Triangle are in mourning.

It's also why about a dozen people -- club owner Ben Fletcher, beefy bouncers, beefier dancers, a couple of longtime patrons -- gathered Friday night for an impromptu farewell in the club's gravel-and-dirt parking lot the day after the judge's ruling. A trunk went up, a cooler came out, libations and memories flowed.

A stream of cars bearing would-be patrons or dancers who had not read the papers or seen on television the news of the judge's ruling emerged from the darkness at one end of Angier Avenue. The cars, ranging from coughing, belching hoopties to gleaming limos and pimped-out Escalades, streamed by, slowed, then headed dejectedly back into the darkness. They transformed into a funereal procession when informed by an employee, "We're closed, Dawg."

Brothers III was no "gentlemen's club," although gentlemen came. Professionals and college athletes, businessmen and college professors were among those who trekked to the the cinderblock building.

It's possible that you may have smelled, as police contend in their affidavit, burning marijuana mixing with the enticing aroma of exotic body oils and sweat. But you would have also heard Fletcher on those occasions silence the DJ and admonish whoever had lit up to "take that [expletive deleted] out of here."

His armed and big-armed bouncers weren't shy about bouncing rule-breaking or unruly patrons out the door. They seldom had to, though, because most of the dudes knew what a jewel the club was and had a proprietary respect for it.

Despite the occasional minister -- I recognized one despite his big, floppy hat and made sure I commended him on a recent sermon when he emerged from the club's V.I.P. room -- nobody came to B3 to bone up on Bible verses. Many of the dudes standing in front of the club's four stages on weekend nights had also stood in front of judges during the week, though not for Brothers III activities.

The club was what it was. Unapologetically. There are things some men like. They don't brag about those things, but neither should they have to apologize for them.

Civic leaders never mention places such as Brothers III in brochures touting what's good about their city. Such clubs aren't for everyone, nor did Brothers III try to be. Fletcher often asked, "Is anyone here offended by nudity? If you are, come see me, and I'll give you your money back."

Nobody ever took him up on his offer.

That's another reason why nighttime was the right time for mourning.

5/25/2004

'BINGO' WAS SLOW FOR B-3

By closing down the delightfully notorious Brothers III nightclub last month, the Durham Police Department has made Triangle streets safer. Or so they say.

Cops have a job to do, and we should all appreciate it. My only question is this: If the club was as much of a sin den as the police affidavit reads -- that 40-page document has "best seller" written all over it -- why did it take about two years of undercover work to gather enough evidence to shut it down?

The first undercover officer to visit the joint did so June 21, 2002, according to the affidavit compiled by the city attorney and presented to Superior Court Judge Ron Stephens as evidence that the club constituted a nuisance to the community.

The last officer -- no, officers; they went back as a pair -- to go deep undercover into that world of what police say was drugs, prostitution and violence did so March 11, 12 and 18 and May 14, 2004.

The first police investigator wrote in the affidavit, "On June 21, while working in a covert capacity at the request of the Durham Police Department, I went ... and heard or observed the following."

Since people younger than 80 may read this column, my editor forbade me to write what the officer observed and heard.

Apparently unsure or unbelieving of what he'd witnessed, he went back again. And again. And again.

He heard and observed on each subsequent visit -- Aug. 2, 3 and 17 of last year -- the same things he heard and observed the first time.

I'm guessing that when the officer returned to the squad room with his tall tales, his colleagues in the department's Special Operations Division didn't believe him and had to see for themselves. ("Aw, c'mon, man. Nobody can do that with a beer can.") Or else they did believe him and had to see for themselves. How else to explain subsequent undercover visits that described, in strikingly similar details, the same activities?

Some people -- OK, just the club's owner and me -- contend that crime, instead of increasing, actually went down whenever the club was open. Our theory is that you can't be out robbing people when you're getting a lap dance.

As a habitue of the Durham County courthouse and the club, I can attest that their clientele overlapped.

Police spokesman Norman Blake was skeptical that the club was actually a crime- fighting establishment.

"If you have some statistical data to support that hypothesis, I'd love to see it," he said, laughing.

Each officer who visited the club seemed to come away with the same conclusion: "We must shut that den of iniquity down -- but not right now."

With the city's budget stretched, I'm guessing that Police Chief Steve Chalmers handed out undercover assignments to B-3, as it was affectionately known to legions of crestfallen fans, in lieu of raises.

The court's ruling is that the building can never again be used for adult entertainment. Last I heard, it'll be converted into a church.

I don't know about you, but I plan to be there for the first service -- not just to hear The Word, but to see whether they left the poles up.

Let the church say "Amen."

—— 6/8/2004

STRIPPED OF HIS `DUDENESS' ———————————————————

Yo, it's been real, but after more than four decades, I'm being asked to give up one of my favorite activities.

No, not that one. My other favorite activity -- being a black dude.

Seems that some black readers, upset over recent columns, are demanding that I turn in my membership in the "brotha'hood."

What, you might wonder, was my offense that led these strangers, independent of one another, to conclude that I had somehow forfeited my right to be black?

Did I reveal the secret handshake necessary to get into "Brothers III" nightclub? Nope. Did I print out and publish the lyrics to Marvin Gaye's classic but pretty near indecipherable, "Got To Give It Up"?

Un-unh. My offense, as near as I can tell, was to criticize a couple of black celebrities or events -- an apparent violation of the 11th Commandment: Thou shalt not criticize other blacks, regardless of how exploitative, despotic or just full of hooey they might be.

For instance, when I wrote a couple of weeks ago about soul singer R. Kelly, a man noted for his alleged affinity for underage girls, it was -- to some readers -- an act of treason worse than anything Clarence Thomas (now that's a real Uncle Tom) ever committed.

One reader, "Conspiracy Sister," suggested that R. is the victim of a government plot involving the CIA, FBI and COINTELPRO, the same groups involved in "killing Malcolm X, Dr. King and perhaps JFK."

"People like you," she concluded, "are a menace to the media community."

Perhaps, but not to 14-year-old girls.

I really incurred the wrath of my (former?) brothers and sisters when I wrote about the unfunny and vulgar comedians at the recent Big Black Comedy Show, a show which was indeed big and black but was woefully short on comedy and in which every other word, seemingly, was #$%^&*&^%$#.

One dude, Jules, wrote, "So they cursed a little bit. Big deal. You are a playa hater. What the #$% have you ever done for the black community? Writing #$##$%^ columns like this definitely won't help. ... There is no hope for #$%#$# like you."

That's remarkably close to what another reader said when I wrote about R. Kelly. "You should've been the first person to point the finger at Whitey but instead you bring down a brother," she wrote. "Is this the price our ancestors paved the way for, for you to forget what happened?"

I politely told her that if she showed me the white man who made R. Kelly -- or whoever the grown man is in that infamous, depraved video -- do those despicable things to that little girl, I'd write mean things about him, too.

Another dude wrote last week accusing me of "portraying yourself as a strong, smart, streetwise black man. Many people believe this image to be true, but I know it is nothing more than a coverup for your actual self."

Alas, he never told me who my actual self is.

Another reader, leveling what he must have considered the most damning of insults, wrote, "I'll bet you're the kind of Negro who rushed out and bought a U.S. flag after 9-11."

Ouch. Now that hurt.

7/2/2002

SURVIVAL: HER BADGE OF HONOR

Cutting one of those hospital-issue pork chops with a plastic knife and fork would tax the most dexterous among us.

It was a feat worthy of "Believe It or Not" when Dorethea Hart did it Thursday. "Last week, she couldn't even move her hand," said her cousin, Ann Hunter-Paschall, as she sat by Hart's bed at UNC Hospitals. "She's come a long way. She's been through a lot."

Through hell, you might say.

Fortunately for Hart, she slept through two months of the trip.

Hart is the Durham woman I introduced you to in January after she'd been dragged through the city's streets by a car going 70 mph. She was in such bad shape that doctors kept her in a drug-induced coma for two months to give her body -- and, just as important, her mind -- time to heal.

Detective John Stokes, who has made the case a mission, said at the time that her injuries were "the worst I've ever seen, and the person is still alive."

Hart remains scarred from the back of her scalp to her feet, but she can, at last, smile. As she did proudly after cutting the pork chop without assistance.

When I entered her room to get her side of what happened Jan. 3, I prayed that she'd forgotten. She hadn't.

"I just know I went for a wild ride," she recalled.

Thea Edward Newman has already told police his version. He said he had stopped to give Hart a ride but panicked and zoomed off when his no-driver-license-having self saw cops. No, he said, he didn't know Hart's foot was caught in the seat belt or that he was dragging her. Nor, he insisted, did he hear her screams. That's odd, because I can still hear them now; can't you?

Hart said that Newman, who is in jail charged with assault with a deadly weapon, would sometimes give her money when she needed it. She would then give him the only thing she felt she had to offer.

"I just sensed something wasn't right that night," she said. "He didn't seem like himself. He took out his gun. ... I was hysterical and threw my shoe at the police car."

About the trip that left her skin along a two-mile stretch of Liberty Street, Hart recalled, "I was screaming. I thought I was dead. God said, 'You're gonna make it. You're gonna live.' "

Most people, after a nearly three-month stretch in a hospital, would want to stay far away from one. Hart, though, can't wait to return -- once she leaves. "I want to work in a hospital," she said. "Being here has made me want to work here. I owe these people everything. They saved my life.

"I want to dedicate my life to God, to live life, go back to school, make something out of myself," she said.

Whether she knows it, she has already made something of herself: a survivor. With help, she could become an inspiration to other women who think the only thing they have to offer can be bought by men in cars.

When I told her of the scores of calls and letters I'd received from people inquiring about her, tears welled up. "People want to do something to help me?" she asked, astonished.

Her medical bill is more than $50,000. For those who still want to help, an account has been set up in her name at the Cooperative Latino Credit Union, P.O. Box 25360, Durham, NC 27702.

3/26/2004

WHO WILL BE THERE FOR HER?

I'll bet you my whole Al Green eight-track tape collection that if Thea Edward Newman had been accused of dragging a dog down Liberty Street in a car going 70 mph, people would be screaming for his head. Or other body parts.

You know that group that gets ticked off every time somebody drops a possum -- People for the Ethical Treatment of Animals? Its members would be demanding justice and condemning the practice of dog-dragging.

Don't you think Dorethea Hart deserves as much consideration and sympathy as a possum?

Alas, there is no Society for the Prevention of Cruelty to Women, Especially Marginalized Ones. Hart was dragged down a Durham street Jan. 3, and Newman is in jail for it, charged with assault with a deadly weapon.

Hart's relatives refused to talk, apparently because they're ashamed of her alleged lifestyle, which police say included getting into cars with strange men.

A woman who answered the phone at Hart's uncle's home said the family didn't want to talk because Hart "was out there being wild. ... We tried to tell her to sit down, but she wouldn't listen."

In the police report I read, Newman told police that he saw a lady on the street who appeared to need a ride. Being the good Samaritan that he is, he offered one. When she wanted to get out -- so desperately that she broke out a window and threw her shoe at a police car to get an officer's attention -- he politely sought a less-crowded street, one without the dreaded Po-po because he had no license, had just gotten out of the pokey for nonsupport and didn't care to again take advantage of the county's hospitality.

He swears that as he fled the law at 70 mph for a mile or two he didn't know the woman's foot was caught in a seat belt, that he didn't hear her screaming as the pavement ripped the skin from her body.

That's odd, because I can hear her screaming now, and I wasn't even there.

Of course, this self-serving scenario is all Newman's, because Hart is still in a coma. Doctors at Duke Hospital put her in one because her injuries and the pain are so bad that they want to give her body -- and just as important, her mind -- time to heal.

Even if it is possible to heal from such an ordeal, it won't occur without a lot of help and support. Somebody needs to cry for Dorethea Hart, to visit her when she comes to. Can you imagine awakening from such a nightmare and finding no one there, no flowers, no cards?

If family members won't -- the woman I talked to wasn't overflowing with the milk of human compassion when she said, "She ought to be glad she's just hurt and not dead" -- then members of the family of the human race should.

Detective John Stokes insisted he'll investigate this case with the same tenacity he would if she were some blue-blood society matron. I believe him.

"I don't care what she is," Stokes said with rising emotion. "Nobody deserves that. Her injuries are the worst I've ever seen, and the person is still alive. The worst part is, she was conscious through the whole thing."

No, the worst part is that there may be no one there when she becomes conscious again.

1/9/2004

TAILGATE BOOZING PREVAILS

The way N.C. State University officials threw up their hands and despaired of banning alcohol from pre-kickoff tailgating parties, you'd think 100-proof Jack Daniel's wafts down from the atmosphere near Carter-Finley Stadium and Coronas spurt from the water fountains.

Strolling through certain sections of the State Fairgrounds hours before a Wolfpack game can indeed make you think the air is composed equally of oxygen and Jack -- so heavy is the smell -- but that is no reason to give up on trying to halt excessive pre-game boozing.

Yet, conceding defeat is just what NCSU officials have done.

"Some have suggested we ban alcohol, but that just isn't practical," Tom Stafford, vice chancellor for student affairs, told The News & Observer days after two men were killed in a parking lot full of tailgating fans. The shootings occurred just after the start of the Pack's first game Sept. 4.

No definitive link has been established between alcohol and the deaths of the two men, but certain parking areas had been frightful places to venture long before that fatal violence. Parking lot hassles were even cited by some fans who gave up their season tickets.

When interim Chancellor Charles Barnhardt acknowledges that he has been known to knock down a drink in the parking lot, you have to appreciate homey's honesty. You also have to question his judgment for essentially admitting that football and drinking are inseparable, thus giving students the excuse to say, "Hey, if the chancellor has to take a nip to enjoy the game, who am I to fight booze's irresistible pull?"

As usual, I have come up with a solution, one that will make a ban on alcohol not only practical but effective: Breathalyzers.

You read that right. Just as airlines sometimes prohibit people from boarding a plane when they are too high to fly, NCSU officials could prohibit spirited fans from entering Carter-Finley when they are already too full of spirits.

Of course, such a policy would not go down smoothly for those who think getting blitzed on game day is a constitutional prerogative.

SECURITY: Sorry, sir, but could you blow into this before entering the stadium?

FAN: Say, pal, why don't you blow the ... .

SECURITY: WHOMP!!!

Of course, NCSU officials don't just tolerate drinking, they encourage it by, for instance, providing "pass outs" -- which allow fans to leave at halftime, refortify their school spirit from the trunks of automobiles and then return to the game.

Yo, bartender, pour me a shot of hypocrisy with a lemon twist.

If by "impractical," school officials mean there is no way to prevent all drinking in the lots, they're correct. Even at UNC-Chapel Hill, which bans alcohol on campus, fans surreptitiously sip brandy and white wine from Dixie cups or from the head of their commemorative Jim Beam decanters that look like Elvis.

Etiquette maven Emily Post would disapprove: She'd suggest long-stemmed crystal flutes for the white wine.

Alas, if alcohol consumption should be allowed anywhere, it's at -- no, in -- Kenan Stadium, where Tar Heel fans need a cup of something strong to help them forget what's happening on the field.

—— 9/17/2004

TAKING THE LONG VIEW ——————————————————

Banks C. Kelly III remembers the reception he received upon returning to America from serving in Vietnam in 1971.

It wasn't pretty, he recalled when I spoke with him Monday. "That was a very unpopular war, and probably the low point for the military," the former Army Ranger recalled. "I came back when there were a lot of people upset" with anyone in uniform.

Although some might consider it unpatriotic to use anything French these days -- even French expressions -- Kelly could be excused if he feels he is experiencing deja vu, since the virulent antiwar protests of our present military action in Iraq rival in some places what was happening during the middle of the Vietnam War.

Kelly insists, though, that he didn't take antiwar opposition personally then, and he tells his son, Army Capt. Todd Kelly, not to do so now.

Banks Kelly, who still serves as a lieutenant colonel in the National Guard as the state contracting officer, said he lets his son know in letters -- he hasn't spoken to him since January -- that his country and its citizens appreciate his service. "We try to be reassuring to Todd that everyone is behind him," Kelly said.

Todd Kelly, like the three generations of Kellys preceding him, is serving his country during hostilities with a foreign country.

The 1990 graduate of Cary High School is commander of C Company, 2nd Battalion, 7th Infantry. Following in the jump boots of his dad, Todd is an Airborne Ranger.

Todd's great-grandfather Banks C. Kelly Sr. rode in the cavalry with "Black Jack" Pershing as that legendary general sought to quell the border raids of Pancho Villa from Mexico.

His grandfather Banks C. Kelly Jr. survived the attack on Pearl Harbor and the sinking of the cruiser Helena in 1943. "He was afloat for several days before he and other survivors landed on a small, Japanese-controlled island" where they hid out before being rescued, Banks C. Kelly III said.

I asked Kelly whether dinnertime conversation around home is dominated by military talk when the three surviving generations get together.

"We do have some conversations along those lines, yes, we do," he said in a wistful tone that let you know this was an understatement and that he longs for more such conversations.

Kelly III was drafted into the Army, but his father -- who is scheduled to be released from the VA hospital this week after suffering a heart attack earlier this month -- and his son Todd both enlisted.

"I imagine it's just something he wanted to do on his own, not something where he felt pressure from us," he said.

A frustrated Todd Kelly is quoted in the March 31 edition of Newsweek magazine by a reporter traveling with his battalion. Considering the military commitment the Kelly family has made to this country, if anyone had a right to tell antiwar protesters to kiss a Scud missile, you'd think it would be these guys.

You'd be wrong, though. Kelly III said, "We feel that everybody has a right to believe in what they believe as long as it's done peacefully."

Ah, at last: someone who remembers what makes America great.

4/1/2003

TEEN SEX GETS SILENT TREATMENT

I'd heard rumors, as a zit-faced, socially maladjusted teenager, of girls who were - let's see, what's a good way to put this? - not too discriminating about where and with whom they had sex.

But to me, they were like unicorns: oft-heard-of creatures who were never seen.

At the time, such girls were objects of desire, and the boys who were invited to partake of their favors, objects of envy. Now I consider them objects of pity.

Despite that, the kids involved in the Enloe High School sexcapades don't deserve to have their lives ruined.

None apparently has been, except perhaps for the girl and one boy.

All punishments were meted out not because of criminal behavior by the sexually adventurous adolescents - there was no crime - but because the kids violated, get this, a school policy specifically forbidding sexual activity on campus.

What happened in the locker room between the 15-year-old female sophomore and the male students did not constitute a crime - "There was no money or force involved," Principal Lloyd Gardner told me - but the disparity in punishment could constitute, at the very least, an outrage.

Suspensions for most of the boys, some of whom were football players, ranged from eight to 10 days, causing some jocks to miss one game. The girl and the kid with whom she was actually caught in flagrante delicto by an assistant principal were suspended for the rest of the school year.

Such a disparity would be justified if, say, the girl had used a gun.

She didn't, and thus there is no justifiable reason for her to be punished more severely than the boys. Indeed, there is evidence that she is less deservingof punishment and more in need of help. I asked Gardner and Wake schools spokeswoman Stella Shelton what good could come from suspending a student so obviously in need of psychological treatment and whether such help would be offered.

"The school system works real hard with kids who've been suspended from school," Shelton said, refusing to comment specifically on this case, "but there are some kids whose needs are beyond the scope of the system to help."

Gardner added he would recommend such help to the parents, "but it's up to them" to accept.

School system officials were reluctant to discuss the embarrassing case either on the record or off. For one thing, federal law requires them to protect the identity of the students involved. For another - and I'm guessing this is of paramount importance - they want to protect themselves from possible charges that they should have intervened sooner.

Moments after talking to Gardner, I drove past a billboard on U.S. 70 with a picture of a mother and daughter. What it lacked in proper syntax it made up for in poignancy. "Talk to your kids about sex. Everyone else is," it read.

When I called the girl's mother, she quickly slammed down the phone. I didn't feel too bad, because I have the impression that I'm not the only person with whom she doesn't discuss sex.

10/14/1999

TERROR LIST CASTS WIDE NET

Most of us would consider it a major inconvenience, a bummer, if we were prevented from boarding an airplane because our name ended up on a no-fly list designed to keep the friendly skies friendly.

To James Martin, though, being stopped at RDU, detained and informed that he was on such a list last month was the coolest, most exciting thing to happen in all of his years on Earth.

All nine of them.

That's right: James, a student at Partnership Elementary School in Raleigh, found himself listening as his mother tried to explain that he was no terrorist.

"He thought it was kind of neat that his name was on some national list," Greta Martin told me. "He was excited."

He was less excited, she said, when they arrived at their Orlando, Fla., destination without their luggage -- which had been held up and searched. "He had to borrow a friend's swimming trunks," she said.

We've all heard stories since Sept. 11, 2001, of little old ladies in wheelchairs and babes in arms being stopped by Transportation Security Administration officials and searched for weapons because their names matched a person of interest or because someone thought they looked suspicious.

I called the TSA on Monday and asked how a 9-year-old with no known terrorist ties ends up on a no-fly list.

They end up on there, I was told, "like anyone else. He obviously has a name that matches someone who can't fly," a customer support representative who identified himself only as Demetrius told me. "Everyone with that name will remain on the list and will be stopped until that person is captured."

In a tasty bit of irony, TSA policy forbids support representatives to give their last names, but TSA spokesman David Steigman confirmed everything Demetrius told me.

Of her son, Greta Martin said, "A stewardess recommended using his middle name and asked if I'd thought of changing his name. That is not an option because he's named after my husband's father."

Steigman said such an extreme measure shouldn't be necessary. People with names matching wanted persons -- say, Osama bin Laden Jones -- can clear their name by, he said, filling out a passenger identification verification form.

(By the time you say "passenger identification verification form" three times, though, your flight might be gone.)

Martin is black, and her husband is a British citizen of Asian descent. Their son, she said, "has an African-American-Asian look that looks like he might be from one of those countries" that exports terrorism.

But gee, he's only 9.

Now, I do know a grown dude, a frequent flier, who said he is often selected for random searches because his hair is wavy. (Just between you and me, the waviness of his hair depends upon how much Murray's hair pomade he puts in it to slick it down.)

Despite the inconvenience of being stopped, searched and arriving in Orlando several hours before their luggage, Greta Martin said, "I can't say it's a bad idea to double-check, but are they going to let someone who's a real threat slip through while they're minding the kids?"

10/18/2005

'THANK YOU' IS HEARTFELT

Helen Thomas has a ton of gratitude to go along with the ton of thank-you notes on her table.

Only thing is, she doesn't know where to send the notes.

That's why she asked me to thank the scores of people who hooked up her family with a houseful of furniture and other furnishings. After I wrote about Thomas, Kathy Pope, the woman who told me about her, and I both received more than 100 calls and e-mail messages in three days from people offering furniture and money.

"I only met two families, Courtney's and Loretta's," Thomas said. "But so many people helped us. People donated everything you see."

When I introduced you to Thomas in March, girlfriend was shooting bad. Really bad.

Through a combination of mental illness -- she has been diagnosed as bipolar and clinically depressed -- bad decisions and bad luck, she and her three children had been homeless. They had slept behind buildings and washed up in a fast-food restaurant's restroom.

The duplex they were crowded into when I met her was like the Taj Mahal compared with the back of a McDonald's.

I met Thomas through Hillsborough dentist Joseph Gatewood, who owns the three-bedroom house they now call home. Her rent is paid for by the Orange County Housing Authority.

The house, like the family's new mood, is neat, expansive and bright.

"My kids love this place. I love this place," Thomas said as she took me on a tour of the Hillsborough house. When we got to her son's room, she cautioned, "Don't look in there. It's dirty."

So, of course, I looked -- and saw, except for the unmade bed, what was perhaps the neatest 12-year-old boy's room in the world.

Thomas realizes that even though she is off the street, she isn't yet out of the woods. "I thought I was going to have to go back into the hospital. I had an episode, but the doctor increased my medication.

"I just have to stay on my meds, try to stay focused so I don't get in the rut I was in," she said.

That rut was caused primarily, she said, by her inability to take care of her family. Being able to provide a roof for her children has alleviated some of her panic attacks, but now she sometimes feels "overwhelmed" by the responsibility of running a home.

I explained that feeling overwhelmed is not unusual.

Thanks to many of you, Thomas doesn't have to battle her old demons while cowering behind a fast-food restaurant or walking the streets. She has a furnished home.

"This right here is my haven," she said. "I don't want to go anyplace. I always want to go home."

Her doctor, she said, has other ideas. "He thinks going to school would be a good thing," she said. She hopes to become a certified nursing assistant.

Almost as much as for the furniture, Thomas is grateful, she said, for the way "everybody gave to me and my children even when they didn't know us. They didn't pass judgment on someone like me. ... I thank God every day."

Just because you didn't receive a handwritten thank-you note, rest assured that Thomas thanks you, too.

And so do I.

5/20/2005

THAT CHILL IS IN YOUR WALLET

The envelope lying on the desk mocks me every day, taunting me for being such a pantywaist.

C'mon over here, punk, and open me up, it beckons. But I refuse for fear of what is inside.

The envelope that has lain unopened for two weeks contains no anthrax germs, the toxic micro-organisms that had Americans afraid to open letters or packages a few years ago.

It holds something more frightening than anthrax or even a letter from your ex's attorney: It holds -- eek! -- my PSNC Energy gas bill.

Frightened, no terrified, by the stories of friends who have already opened their gas bills only to be pimp-slapped to the floor by the figures, I've allowed mine to sit, hoping that if I ignore it long enough it'll go away.

It won't, of course. Ignoring it will only ensure that the kid and I will wake up one morning as a couple of frozen Fudgsicles.

A PSNC representative assured me Thursday that relief is on the way -- meaning future bills shouldn't be quite so terrifying.

PSNC spokeswoman Angie Townsend said the company filed a request with the N.C. Utilities Commission that would, if approved, translate into nearly a 12 percent decrease for the total year-round residential rate, beginning in January. That would equal about a $21 monthly decrease during the winter for a typical user, she said.

Hallelujah, but it does little to assuage one's fear of bills that have already been delivered. Hikes in August, October and November mean that any reduction now will have to be a doozy to offset what we're now paying.

Townsend actually sounded sincere when she said the company has been "very concerned that some people won't be able to pay their bills."

"Call us if you get a bill you feel you can't pay," she told me. "We have short-term options."

She even gave me a telephone number for people needing help, (877) 776-2427, and a list of conservation tips to help people stay warm without having to take out a second mortgage.

Among the company's tips are setting your thermostat to between 65 and 68 degrees while at home, caulking around leaky windows and lowering the setting on the hot water heater.

Those are good, but there are other ways to fight the high cost of not freezing this winter. Here are my tips for keeping warm:

- Feed Sweet Thang. A lot. In previous winters, I've discovered that the fluffier she becomes, the warmer I stay. There have been subfreezing nights when I've had to crack a window just to get a cool breeze.

- Build a fire. You could play it off as being romantic and rustic, but only you'll know that it's your way of keeping your heating bill manageable.

- Turn off your heat on the coldest night of the year -- and spend the night at a friend's house.

- Become a fan of three-dog night.

No, don't go around annoying everybody by singing "Jeremiah was a bullfrog" or wearing bell-bottoms. The term derives from an old folk custom in which, on cold nights, people would sleep with their dogs in bed with them for warmth.

Thus, a forecast for a brutally cold night might be, "Looks like it's gonna be a three-dog night."

With PSNC's new price reductions, perhaps it'll only be a two-dog night.

—————————————————————————————————————— 12/30/2005

THE CASE OF THE SHAKY PAST ————————————————————

The private investigator must have checked the mental calendar in his head to make sure it wasn't April Fools' Day when he saw the picture of the person I wanted him to investigate.

Naw, the picture wasn't of some woman who'd run off with my money or my heart, nor was it of the syphilitic snake who stole my entire Z.Z. Hill record collection.

The private dick from Durham was befuddled because the person I wanted him to get the lowdown on was me.

It started like this, see: When I was rejected for a gun permit - don't ask: it's a long story - last year, the reason given was that there is a warrant for my arrest in Georgia.

"Ha ha," I laughed, figuring it would be a simple matter of calling the law down there and setting them straight. Why, I hadn't been in trouble in Georgia since that unfortunate misunderstanding with the undercover Atlanta policewoman 22 years ago. But a couple of days as an involuntary guest of that lovely city's municipal facilities and a small fine had put that matter to rest way back then. I think.

Anyway, after a few frantic months in which I had to opt out of attending my college class reunion in Atlanta - couldn't risk being recognized by the law down there - it became obvious that no mere telephone calls were going to settle this.

"Sorry, Hoss. We can't tell you nothin' over the 'phone. You gon' hafta come down heah and straighten this 'mistake' out in person," I was told by each of about a dozen people I talked to.

Yeah, right. I had visions of myself strolling confidently into a Georgia courthouse, but being dragged out in handcuffs - or else sitting in a jail cell playing "That's the Night That the Lights Went Out in Georgia" on a harmonica while my son paraded in front of the jail with a sign reading "Free My Daddy" or, more likely, "Who's Going to Fix My Lunch For School Tomorrow?"

Since the authorities wouldn't talk to me about me, I called up some company on the Internet that'll investigate anyone's past.

That was a bust, so I visited the shamus to see if he could find out if I'm really public enemy No. 1 in Georgia.

I was disappointed immediately, because I expected some wise-cracking, sharp-dressing smoothie like Humphrey Bogart in "The Maltese Falcon." This dude, wearing a clip-on necktie, looked like an insurance adjuster or the night manager at KFC. No matter how he tried to reassure me that I wouldn't end up on an episode of "America's Most Wanted," all I could think was, "Humphrey Bogart wouldn't be caught dead in a short-sleeved dress shirt."

But at least he was better than the detective who, over the telephone, merely told me to slide an envelope with his fee - and, he added as an afterthought, some vital info - under the door to his office. I'm no detective, but that made me suspicious.

I'll keep you posted on the outcome, but if anybody's planning to be in Atlanta anytime soon, stop by the post office and see if you see my picture so you can tell me what I - I mean someone using my name - has done.

5/9/2000

THE DOOR IS OPEN FOR SENSE

Ignorance is no excuse. If you're anything like me, you've heard that line from cops more than once -- usually after being arrested for something to which you've pleaded ignorant, if not innocent.

It never worked for me, nor should it work for Dent Davis, general manager of the Durham Hilton hotel.

Homeslice is pleading ignorant of the historical context and harm of his edict forbidding N.C. Central University students to enter his hotel through the front door. He rescinded that requirement after students and administrators protested, but not before claiming it was meant only to keep the students from clogging the hotel lobby, not to keep black students out of view.

Melissa Thompson, a spokeswoman for the company that manages the Hilton, told me that Davis is guilty only of a "poor choice of words" and that the policy was meant to keep the students "safe."

Sure, pal. This is the same hotel that, a few years back, required the predominantly black clientele at its then-popular Blue Chips nightclub to use a back entrance. I stopped going when they made the front entry off-limits, although I occasionally drove by just to see if others would meekly go to the back and shiver in line for the chance to get into a nightclub. Alas, hundreds did every weekend.

I didn't blame the hotel. I figured that people who'd willingly subject themselves to such treatment probably deserved it.

But these college kids don't. They have no other choice until the dormitories are expunged of the toxic mold that made them uninhabitable.

Davis, who initially denied that there was a contract prohibiting students from using the lobby, apologized, and the university quickly absolved him of malicious intent. Still, a suitable punishment -- and history lesson, to boot -- would be to make him read "Roots" or watch that TV classic about slavery and its aftermath.

Given Davis' apparent lack of sensitivity, he might watch the movie backward -- from the end to the beginning -- so it would have a happy ending.

Davis is not the only one in need of a reality check. Some NCCU students need to get a grip, too, after whining about hotels in which they're staying not furnishing staples such as sheets or toilet paper.

Boo freakin' hoo. Those students need to crack open the autobiographies of either Booker T. Washington or Benjamin Mays to see what real college hardship is all about.

For instance, Booker T. wrote that, while waiting outside the college administrator's office for his admissions interview, the woman mistook him for a janitor. She handed him a bucket and a mop and left: Washington rolled up his sleeves and cleaned the office.

Had he gotten offended and called the woman a dirty name -- as my younger self might have done -- he would have felt better, but it's unlikely he would have become what he did -- founder of Tuskegee Institute.

Likewise, the NCCU students should not let the absence of, say, maid service or toilet paper -- or even Jim Crow treatment from Davis -- make them forget why they're in college.

If anything, they should be motivated to build their own hotels. Then they can hand people like Davis a mop and a bucket, instead of a position of authority.

8/29/2003

STAY OFF THE HORN

Repeat after me: "I'm never blowing the car horn again. I'm never blowing the car horn again. I'm never ... "

Wednesday night was the second time that simple act has almost led me to a deadly confrontation, so I'm vowing, with you as my witnesses, never to honk my horn again.

What if I see an old man crossing the street against the light? Perhaps I'll yell, "Watch out, Grandpa," but I'm not touching the horn.

There was nothing insistent or overbearing about the tap I gave my horn when the car in front of me refused to make a right turn not just on red, but on green. After several seconds, I tapped my horn -- thinking Homeslice might have fallen asleep at the wheel -- to get his attention.

I got it, all right: He flashed me a one-finger salute. Or was it his IQ? If I read him correctly, he was telling me -- in sign language -- to be fruitful and multiply. Alone.

Not content with that, the dude pulled up beside me at the next light, lowered his window and leaned over to unleash a torrent of profanity, which -- if cuss words were water -- would have alleviated our drought.

Any response by me might have escalated a minor skirmish into front-page news, so my own window remained up, and I looked straight ahead, wondering why it was taking the traffic light two hours to change.

The driver no doubt pulled off feeling good, as though he'd somehow punked me. Me? I was dismayed that someone could get so upset over a little horn beep. More than that, I was shocked that he was seemingly willing to fight -- and possibly die -- because of it.

You know, as well as I, that I'm Dr. King and Gandhi rolled into one: the most peaceful guy you'd ever want to meet. But the driver of the other car didn't know that. I could've been an armed idiot, for all he knew. There are things over which you should confront a stranger -- abusing a child, buying a Kenny G CD, for instance -- but not a beeping car horn.

I get flipped off verbally or manually daily, but something about this fleeting encounter with a stranger scared me. What, I wondered, made the man -- who didn't even have the excuse of being young -- so angry?

Did he take the horn beep -- did I mention that it was a very light beep? -- as a challenge to his manhood?

If so, he doesn't need access to a 2,000-pound automobile.

By no means do I think I was without blame in the incident. In retrospect, I realize I was tempting fate by blowing at a stranger driving a Ford Granada with whitewall tires. That alone should have told me he was a candidate for what folks in Rockingham used to euphemistically call "the nervous hospital."

I blew only because I knew what time they put a new tub of meatloaf out at the Golden Corral -- it's a thing of beauty before folks start tearing into it, lying there all golden brown and orange under the heat lamp -- and if I hurried I knew the kid and I could make it before the other patrons stabbed it with their own steely knives.

The meatloaf was delicious in that lowbrow, institutional way I love. But it wasn't worth fighting over. Thus, I'm never blowing the car horn again, even if it means missing the meatloaf.

10/18/2002

THE GIFTS OF GENUINE GENEROSITY

Few things make me cry. A letter from Sweet Thang's attorney, being stuck in an elevator playing Kenny G Muzak or having a lap dance interrupted when some drunk bumps into the jukebox are among the things guaranteed to get the tears flowing.

But sometimes random acts of kindness can move me, too.

For instance, the enthusiastic and consistent willingness of Triangle residents to rally to the aid of their neighbors in trouble always overwhelms me.

Remember that handicapped 9-year-old kid I told you about last week who died and whose grandmother couldn't afford to bury him? Triangle residents responded by sending in more than $20,000, enough to pay for a casket and funeral for Dontravius Antonio Jones, as well as enough to allow Passage Home and Vital Link Community Burial Fund to start a fund in his name so that other poor families will be able to bury their loved ones, too.

It would be easy to say that such generosity was merely a product of the season. We all know misanthropes who for 11 months don't speak to us and have no regard for their fellow men and women, but who suddenly discover their humanity during the holidays. I hate that and am often tempted to tell them to take their perfunctory "Merry Christmas" and stick it up their "Ho-Ho-Ho."

That's not the case this time, though. Triangle residents are always willing to share with those less fortunate, not just at Christmas. Each time I have introduced you to people in need, you've responded heroically:

- There was that brilliant but poor kid whose feet were size 24 and whose parents almost had to mortgage the house just to buy him a pair of shoes. Thanks to your generosity, he is at Morehouse College in Atlanta, well-shod and continuing to excel.

- There was a homeless woman who had to pay attention to the weather to see whether she would be able to sleep outside or whether she'd be forced to spend a portion of her teeny weeny Social Security check to bed down in a flophouse motel. She now shares a nice home with a reader who was moved by her plight.

- Then there was, more recently, the intrepid dentist whose office was torched by drug dealers angered by his anti-drug activism. People from across the country, but primarily throughout the Triangle, sent in thousands of dollars and other gifts, including a dental chair and an X-ray machine. One doctor even invited him to share office space until he could open his own office again.

"That," Dr. Curtis Bowens said of your generosity, "was the only thing that kept me going, because that was a low point."

In many instances, readers not only requested but demanded anonymity to dispel any notion that their generosity was inspired by a desire for publicity.

Stories about what a great place the Triangle is to live usually focus on the mild weather, the low jobless rate, the number of drugstores (do we really need one on every corner?) or the number of Ph.D.'s who live here.

To me, though, the real essence of the Triangle is found in the number of people with hearts who live -- and love -- here.

→ 12/15/2000

THE HERD PROVIDES LESSONS ├──────────────

Could the answer to what's ailing much of the black community be found in a dead rhinoceros?

Preposterous.

No, the answer was found in what has been killing the rhinoceroses: elephants.

Yep, that's right. Elephants.

Conservationists at South African national parks were bewildered in recent years by the frequent discovery of mutilated rhinoceroses. A rhinoceros is a bad dude in its own right, so they knew that whatever was responsible for the atrocities had to be equally bad -- or perhaps part of some strange religious cult.

Turns out the culprits were not fanatics who thought they could discern life's meaning by reading the intestines of a dead rhino but rampaging elephants.

Not just any elephants, either. The outlaw elephants were young males who'd been orphaned when their parents were killed as part of an effort to control the elephant population in some national parks.

Growing up without an adult male, the elephants became aggressive, violent, volatile and anti-social, often attacking without provocation.

Sound familiar? Don't look at me like that. And don't even think about calling to accuse me of comparing young black men to elephants.

I'm not. What I'm comparing is the behavior of young males, probably of any species, who are bereft of older males upon whom to model their behavior.

The violent behavior among the young bull elephants subsided, almost magically, when older males were reintroduced to the herd. To break it down, the presence of older males chilled the young ones out.

In America, the herd of black men has been culled by the judicial system, by self-destructive behavior that makes some men no good to themselves or anyone else, and by laziness.

As a result, a generation of young black men has learned about manhood from rap music and Black Entertainment Television (BET).

Oy. No wonder we're in trouble.

The older dudes we grew up watching in the pool room in Rockingham may not all have been of sterling character -- although some were -- but from them you could learn how to behave and, just as important, how not to behave.

For instance, by sitting back and watching grown men arguing over a game of six-ball, calling each other everything but a ham sandwich, you learned how far you could go -- or not go -- in an argument.

Young guys today never learn that lesson, resulting in every argument potentially turning into a life-or-death gun battle.

Fortunately for us, there are people and organizations trying to fill the void. A group to which I belong, the Triangle East chapter of 100 Black Men of America, mentors and works with young boys who have no older males around. A conference for black dudes and anyone who cares about them will run from 9 a.m. to 3 p.m. Saturday at the Hayti Heritage Center on Fayetteville Street in Durham.

They'll address, among other things, the impact of hip-hop on society, respecting women and leadership.

For more information, call chapter president Tony Jeffreys at 662-4925.

9/16/2005

THE IMAGE IN THE MIRROR

Being 16 years old is difficult under the best of circumstances, when the tiniest zit, the smallest physical imperfection, can -- no, will -- make you the target of humiliating, soul-scarring taunts from your peers.

So imagine how hard it is to be 16 and missing seven teeth. Right in front. Yikes.

Almetta Davis, a sophomore at Jordan High School in Durham, doesn't have to imagine it. She has lived the past seven years saddled with and saddened by that image staring back at her in the mirror. And she is so ashamed that she won't eat in restaurants because chewing is such a laborious, awkward chore. "When we go to family functions, she'll bring her plate home and wait until she gets in her room" to eat, her mother, Valerie Kenion, told me.

On an August day in 1994, Almetta was crossing Fayetteville Street when she was struck by a car driven by Lavonia Allison, the Durham activist who has dedicated her life to fighting for the poor, oppressed and disenfranchised. Allison was not charged in the incident.

After listening to Almetta's story -- Allison never returned my phone calls -- all I can say is, "Whew, I'm glad Allison likes poor people, because I'd hate to see how she treated them if she didn't."

It is hard to reconcile the image of Allison the tireless, ubiquitous battler for children's rights with the woman who, Kenion said, has never talked to or tried to help the young girl whose smile was destroyed in that 1994 accident. (Allison was re-elected chairwoman of the Durham Committee on the Affairs of Black People on Thursday night.) Yet Valerie Kenion, a nurses' assistant at Lincoln Community Health Center, said Allison has shown not one whit of concern for the little black girl with missing teeth and broken ribs.

"I've never talked to her, she has never called," Kenion told me. "She dropped some fruit and ice cream by when I wasn't home" a day after the accident. And, according to Kenion, Allison tried to persuade her pastor to get Kenion not to sue her. It didn't work: She sued, claiming Allison was driving recklessly, but the settlement is sealed.

Almetta has recovered from her physical injuries, her mother said, and in a very short while, she will be able to look in the mirror and smile at the image staring back at her. When I told my dentist, Dr. Joseph Gatewood of Hillsborough, about Almetta's plight, he quickly volunteered to make the young girl smile again. That's not surprising: Gatewood received an award earlier this year from GlaxoSmithKline for his work with children. If you want to help restore a young girl's smile, you can reach Gatewood at (919) 732-9306.

Kenion was adamant that she isn't trying to "exploit my daughter or anything." She said she would have never brought it up had a reporter for the Independent weekly newspaper not asked her about it.

Getting help from someone who has dedicated her public life to helping people in need shouldn't require a lawsuit. Nor should it be like pulling teeth.

Besides, if Allison wanted to help set things -- and teeth -- straight, she could have merely called her son. He's a dentist.

————————————————————————————————— 12/14/2001

THE LATEST PORTRAITS OF U.S. SOLDIERS' SACRIFICES ——

Wow, what a pair of great guys. If President Bush, and his father before him, were any more sensitive, I don't think America could survive them.

So concerned are they for the sensibilities of Americans that they want to protect us from seeing caskets bearing fathers and mothers, sons and daughters, after they've been killed in Iraq and are being returned to the United States.

It's for our own good and for the good of the slain soldiers' survivors, they tell us.

If you believe that, you'll also believe I've got the location of a station where you can buy $1 gas.

The reason the Pentagon instituted its policy of forbidding pictures of the flag-draped coffins of fallen soldiers during the Persian Gulf War in 1991 (in the first Bush's presidency), and is still enforcing it now, has nothing to do with protecting the sensibilities of survivors of Americans killed in Iraq. To buy the White House rationale, you'd have to believe that survivors would not be able to accept the sight of row upon row of flag-draped coffins being readied for homecoming ceremonies.

The real fallout feared by the White House, during the presidencies of both Bushes (and in the intervening Clinton years), is political.

It's instructive that Fox News Channel, which has become the journalistic equivalent of a Bush administration public relations firm, has neither shown the photos nor, as far as I know, reported on the flap surrounding them. To do so would make the war and its deadly effects even more tangible for millions of Americans. That would not redound to the political glory of Fox's favorite president.

Nothing makes a war more real, or amplifies the senselessness of this particular war, than the sight of scores of caskets being readied for shipment to local funeral homes. Those quiet, stark images, even more so than the bloody pictures we routinely see on television, speak eloquently of the war's savagery and loss.

During Vietnam, the first "television" war brought directly into our homes, bombings, death and mayhem were nightly staples of both television and print journalism.

The one image that remains, though, is a quiet one. and also the most powerful. A national weekly magazine published, with no text, individual pictures of scores of U.S. servicemen. They apparently had nothing in common except the uniforms they wore. Only elsewhere in the magazine did readers discover that these were the soldiers who'd been killed during a week in Vietnam.

That was as poignant as the solemn pictures that appeared in newspapers and on TV this week of rows of flag-covered cases used by the military to transport remains, after many such photos were made available through the Freedom of

Information Act.

Fox News does not think the sight of U.S. dead in coffins is newsworthy. Nor has the network given much attention to the woman who photographed flag-draped coffins in a separate instance -- she said she wanted Americans to appreciate the dignity and care with which the remains were treated -- and was subsequently fired by the contractor who employed her.

Wanna bet that Fox would find it mighty newsworthy if she'd been fired for, say, posting on the Internet a picture of Bill Clinton with an intern?

A picture, the old saying goes, is worth a thousand words, but when it comes to protecting this president and a war that Fox has boosted, a picture isn't worth a single word.

If President Bush was really concerned about the sensibilities of survivors, he would have made sure there were fewer families touched by death in Iraq, by not rushing into a war based on faulty intelligence.

⊢ 4/24/2004

THE NAME OF THE JOB GAME ⊢

Several months ago, Sweet Thang and I were in a hoity-toity part of Washington, D.C. -- by mistake: we'd gotten lost -- and were about to enter some expensive Georgetown boutique.

The lady in front of us stopped in the doorway, turned and snapped, "Keisha, you'd better come on, girl. They're getting ready to close."

Imagine my surprise when a tall girl with a flowing blond mane brushed past us and into the store: It was Keisha.

In a country where the top rapper is white and the top golfer is black, it is inevitable that you'll eventually encounter a white girl named Keisha.

Poor thing.

Judging by a study conducted by professors at the University of Chicago Graduate School of Business and MIT, Keisha could have a hard time getting even a job interview just because of her name. People with names like Keisha, LaQuisha and Tamika -- what I lovingly call "sista names" -- were less likely to get called in for an interview, regardless of how glowing their resumes, than applicants with names like Emily.

It's true, as Shakespeare wrote, that a rose by another name would smell just as sweet. It's also true that Rose is more likely to be called in for an interview than Shaniqua.

A black comedian on television recently said that, if elected president, he'd pass a constitutional amendment prohibiting black women younger than 21 from naming a child alone. I knew what he meant because I, too, have often wondered what -- or even if -- some mothers were thinking when they attached certain made-up appellations to their children.

What can we conclude from the study by two prestigious institutions of higher learning? Just this: that unless your kid has a wicked crossover dribble, a hyperactive pituitary gland or a 95 mph fastball, naming him Rasheed or Shaquille can negatively influence his job prospects.

Of course, we can also conclude that life won't be a crystal staircase even if you name her Crystal: A race-neutral name will only work until she enters the office for the job interview.

Nashica Thompson is black, but she said she never worried about her name sounding too ethnic when she graduated from N.C. State University with a degree in accounting.

"Fortunately for me, when I got out of college I went to work for my father's company," said the 27-year-old comptroller for Thompson Hospitality Inc. "I have friends who use their first name as an initial and use their middle name on resumes if their first name is Afrocentric and their middle name is Crystal or something like that.

"That way, they at least can get in the door and make a good impression."

Her father, Donnell Thompson, hasn't had to worry about getting in the door and making a good impression in a long time.

A former UNC and professional football star, Thompson used his off-seasons to acquire the business acumen needed to become successful in the restaurant and hotel industry, ensuring that he'd never have to submit a resume that could be rejected by a screener who thought his name was "too ethnic."

Names don't come much more ethnic than his. Indeed, you'll know we've achieved true equality in this country the day a president named Donnell -- or Colin -- takes office.

1/17/2003

THE OWL THEORY TOO LOONY

A good friend, the saying goes, will come down to the jailhouse and bail you out.

A great friend will be sitting in the cell on the bunk beside you when you come to, going "Man, that was fun."

The best friend, however, will come up with an alibi, no matter how ridiculous it makes him look, to get you out of the pokey.

That's why everyone needs friends like Larry Pollard and Nick Galifianakis.

No greater love hath any man than that he would risk his reputation -- and, possibly, a stint in the Hoo Hoo Hotel -- for his pal.

That's what Galifianakis and Pollard have done with their theory on Kathleen Peterson's death, a theory which they hope will spring their friend Michael Peterson from prison.

Naw, they're not saying it was the butler who killed Kathleen Peterson on Dec. 9, 2001. They're saying it was the bird.

Embarking upon a flight of fancy that famed oddball and movie director Alfred Hitchcock might've dreamed up after smoking a dime bag of wacky weed, Pollard and Galifianakis -- hereafter referred to as the duh-namic duo -- contend that an owl caused the gashes in Kathleen's scalp.

(Aha, I caught you looking at the date on this paper. Now that you know it's not April Fools' Day, read on.)

The marauding owl theory had been floating around the Internet even during the trial, which ended in October with Michael Peterson sentenced to life in prison. Pollard recently wrote a letter to District Attorney Jim Hardin urging him to re-open the case because new evidence made it "morally, legally and ethically the right thing to do."

Pollard was out of town and couldn't be reached, but when I talked to Galifianakis on Monday, he said he expected ridicule after The Herald-Sun wrote about their theory.

"When Larry first told me his theory," Galifianakis said, "I responded facetiously, 'Hoo, hoo done it?'

"The more I thought about it, I realized that it was plausible" and the district attorney should pursue every plausible theory, he said.

Galifianakis said neither he nor Pollard, whom he credits with hatching the theory, doubts Peterson's innocence. He declined to say what Peterson himself thinks of the theory.

Even more difficult to believe than the owl theory is that there are true believers who remain devoted to Peterson's cause.

Even during the trial I was struck by the loyalty -- if it wasn't blind, then it was nearsighted -- of rational-seeming people who'd suspended their powers of reason.

Indeed, to buy their theory, you'd also have to buy that the owl was not only murderous but conscientious, too.

How else could one explain, as Hardin noted in his response, the absence of feathers or copious amounts of blood leading outside from the death scene?

Could the hoity-toity Forest Hills neighborhood be plagued not only by murderous owls but owls who clean up after themselves? Hmm.

Hardin, ever the gentleman, responded to Pollard with a polite letter. "We appreciate your concern," he wrote, but he described the bird theory as "not credible."

Me, I would've summed it up in one word: cuckoo.

────────────────────────── 12/16/2003

THE PATH OF LEAST RESISTANCE

Time was, being an old man meant something. It meant you were accorded a measure of respect - even if by default because, as the late philosopher Mudbone once said, "You don't get to be old by being no fool."

Those days are long gone, and not only are old men no longer respected, but hell, it seems they're under attack in the Triangle by younger men who place little value on their own lives and none on anyone else's.

Take the three dudes who broke into Roosevelt Williams' home Monday. Please.

Williams, 72, known to friends and relatives as "Jackie Boy" or "Jack," was shot when the men kicked open the door of his home and burst in.

Except for the bloodstained splinters on the ground and the puddles of blood on the floors, the neat little duplex apartment looked like the humble abode of a man who had worked at low-paying jobs all his life and was content to spend his twilight years minding his own business and chilling out with friends.

Because Williams' Fargo Street neighborhood is not the first place you'd expect a robber to come looking for a prosperous retiree to knock off, I asked one of Williams' buddies why he was singled out for a bloody home invasion.

"Your guess is as good as mine," Roosevelt Roberts said with a shrug. OK. My guess is that predators who pick old, poor retirees are cowards seeking the path of least resistance, not the biggest payoff.

Despite some high-profile murders or assaults on old people in the Triangle this year - including the slaying of a 95-year-old man - seniors are 10 times less likely to be victims of violent crimes, according to a Justice Department study released this year.

That's small consolation to Williams' friends, several of whom milled about outside his apartment in the rain Monday, trying to comprehend what happened and why.

Williams was shot in the arm and taken to Duke Hospital. Police don't consider his wound life-threatening, but they're not considering his other infirmities. Roberts said his buddy is diabetic, is on dialysis for a kidney disorder and suffered a stroke last year.

"Anything goes in this neighborhood," he said, sighing heavily. "Young guys around here think they're Al Capone, Frank Nitti. ... Jack's a nice guy. He'd help you out. These jitterbugs don't care."

Roberts said he answered Williams' door Monday morning when a young man knocked and insisted upon entering. "When I saw him do this" - here, Roberts imitated a man pulling a gun from his waistband - "I slammed the door, but he kicked it in" and was followed inside by two masked men.

"If that door holds," Roberts said, shaking his head ruefully, "he don't get in."

In a perfect world, old people would only have to fret about getting to the Golden Corral restaurant in time to catch the early bird special. In Mary Lee Tucker's Liberty Street neighborhood, they fret about getting inside their homes before young thugs commandeer the streets.

"They used to give you respect," said Tucker, who is Roosevelt Williams' cousin. "My husband and I used to could sleep out on our porch. Now, we can't even sit on it."

9/19/2000

THE RIGHT TO BE A JERK INALIENABLE

You know how sometimes you go to a sandwich shop and they try to scrimp on the fixin's if you don't watch them carefully?

That's what happened to me about a year ago when I went to a sandwich shop operated by Arab-Americans in downtown Raleigh.

Feeling that I was being shortchanged on seafood in the $5 seafood-and-crab sub sandwich, I said, just as kindly as you please, "Hey, Homes, put some more seafood on that bad boy."

The sandwich maker looked up, glowered and snapped, "Shut up. I know what I am doing."

The packed shop fell silent, and everyone waited for my reaction. Now, I'm 6 feet 2, 240 -- OK, 255 -- and I might have reached behind the counter and snatched the thin guy over and proceeded to pound into him the fact that "the customer is always right."

Of course, I also might have snatched back a nub where my arm used to be.

Instead of escalating the tense situation, though, I merely laughed. I was genuinely surprised and delighted that the dude was not intimidated by me just because I'm a big ol' mean-looking dude. I was also delighted to see that being a jerk transcends one's heritage.

The sammitch-maker ended up putting more faux crab on my sandwich, and I, satisfied, paid him. Of course, I vowed never to set foot inside his shop again.

Even while making that vow, though, I realized that the sandwich-maker was a jerk who just happened to be Arab-American, and when you think about it, that's what makes this country great: We all have a constitutionally protected right to be jerks. (You can look it up: It's in the section that says "Congress shall make no laws abridging a person's right to freedom of religion, speech or jerkhood.")

For instance, when Mr. James King of King's Grocery Store in Rockingham would give me the evil eye -- well-deserved, too, because I'd go in there and order 75 cents' worth of three-for-a-penny cookies, which he had to count by hand -- I didn't ascribe his anger to all black men. Nor do I attribute the jerky behavior displayed toward me by my sandwich guy to all Arab-Americans.

I thought about that sandwich-maker last week when my son and I stopped, as is our custom, at a neighborhood Arab-American-owned store to load up on supplies for the drive-in movie. The men who work there are always very professional but not overly solicitous.

Last week, though, their attitudes had changed perceptibly -- had become, dare I say it, mellow. One actually smiled when he said, "Thank you. Come again."

It was disconcerting. Of course, after the events of Sept. 11, I can understand how people of Middle-Eastern descent might be sensitive about seeming brusque or offensive. But the reality is, they have as much right to be that way as anyone else. After all, not everyone is like me: soft-spoken and humble. Being a jerk -- as well as forgiving jerky behavior -- goes hand in hand with being a good American.

Think about it: Being tolerant of others is easy when they are model citizens, but it's when you encounter the jerks that every culture produces that true tolerance is achieved.

10/2/2001

ANOTHER BRICK IN THE WALL

Until a couple of weeks ago, the most dangerous thing Zeyad Hindi had ever held in his hands was a fishing pole.

That was before a loudmouthed but well-intentioned -- and extremely good-looking -- N&O columnist wrote about an incident that occurred in Hindi's sandwich shop.

You may recall that I recently wrote about my visit to the shop and how, when I asked a dude to put some more fixin's on my sandwich, he snapped, "Shut up. I know what I am doing."

Far from being condemnatory, the column was a reasoned defense of Arab-Americans' right to be -- as some members of every other ethnic group are -- jerks.

It's a constitutionally protected birthright of every American, hyphenated or not.

Alas, that is not how some retromingent moron took it. One day after the column ran, a dirty, lowdown skunk tossed a brick through the window of Hindi's shop.

A day after that, Hindi found himself in a pawnshop trying to decide what kind of gun to buy.

"I was afraid for my crew," he said when I talked with him Monday. "I asked the man in the pawn shop, 'What does this do?' and, 'What is this for?' There were so many guns. ... I didn't know what I was doing, and he figured that out. He asked me, 'Have you ever even held a gun before?' "

He hadn't, and his wife and myriad friends on the Raleigh Police Department dissuaded him from arming himself. Since some people, like the cowardly brick-thrower, are likely to use the attacks of Sept. 11 as an excuse to vent their latent anti-Arab-American sentiments, police have increased their patrols not only around Hindi's shop but also around other Arab-American-owned businesses.

Hindi, who arrived in this country 21 years ago from Kuwait and graduated from Shaw University, represents the kind of success story we should be proud of, not resentful toward.

The personable 37-year-old was not the person who told me to shut up during my earlier visit to his shop, and he seemed genuinely aghast and hurt that such an incident could have occurred there. "I wish you had called me when it happened," he said. "That person would have been fired."

Hindi has two American flags in his shop and a sign noting that 10 percent of his profits will be donated to a fund for survivors and victims of the Sept. 11 attacks.

Although Hindi's insurance paid the $600 cost of replacing his broken window, it'll take more than that to repair his broken heart and to let him know that the actions of one brick-chunking punk do not represent the feelings of most Americans.

There was a great -- but easy to overlook -- scene in the movie "Rocky" in which the slick promoter asked the title character, who was about to be given a shot at the heavyweight boxing title, "Rocky, do you believe America is the land of opportunity? Apollo Creed does."

So, too, does Hindi. I hope he still does after the brick went through his window.

That's one reason I went by Hindi's shop: to assure him that the brick-thrower represents the worst of America, not the best.

10/16/2001

THE TEACHER NO STUDENT LIKED

It was always easy to tell which students had gotten Mrs. Jennie W. Hager's class on the first day of classes at Leak Street School in Rockingham.

Just look for the kids walking around in a stupor, stunned expressions on their faces, as though headed to their executions. Mrs. Hager's legend had been passed down and embellished over the years, so everyone "knew" before they even entered her classroom that she was mean and that their social life was essentially kaput for the year: She was famous for assigning lots of homework and requiring you to actually work for your grade.

Oh man, being in Mrs. Hager's class was the absolute worst thing that could happen to a kid, and I saw the toughest guys in my neighborhood lose the color in their faces at the prospect. Believe me, that wasn't easy in my neighborhood.

Today is the first day of classes at some schools throughout the Triangle, and some parents have discovered a way to keep their kids out of the classes of teachers whose reputations for toughness precede them.

"Parents have gotten real savvy," a Durham administrator told me Monday. "They'll write letters describing their child's learning styles and what kind of teacher their child would most benefit from. ... Some kids need a highly structured teacher, some need a touchy-feely type."

I reckon it's a good thing that schools allow such flexibility and parents are able to pick teachers in some instances, but I shudder just thinking about how Principal J.C. Watkins would have responded if one of us had told him we didn't want to be in a certain teacher's class because our personalities didn't mesh.

For Mrs. Hager to have had such a formidable reputation, though, I marveled - even as a kid - at how there was a constant stream of former students visiting her house every Christmas when graduates returned from up North. (In those days, we got out of the South on the first thing smoking the day after receiving that sheepskin.)

You know that lame television series "Survivor"? Man, that's a day at Hilton Head compared with Mrs. Hager's class. But former students always returned to pay homage to her, and the respect, love and sense of pride in surviving her class could be heard in their voices decades later.

Mrs. Hager realized that being a good teacher is not a popularity contest, but just because a teacher is popular doesn't mean he or she can't be good. Some make a class so interesting that students clamor to get in, while others relate to students as buddies while retaining their respect.

Mrs. Hager, though, knew that she had a responsibility to gird our loins with knowledge we'd need to confront an often-hostile world. Yet, our ignorant selves thought she was just being mean, especially when she'd indelicately snatch your transistor radio from your ear when she caught you trying to sneak and listen to the World Series during her class.

So if your kid comes home from school today with an ashen, terrified look because he drew the one teacher no one at the whole school wanted, don't panic.

8/8/2000

THE VOICE OF REASON ON RADIO

I was recently driving down a tree-shaded street in Rockingham, a town that hasn't changed much since I left at 18, when I heard an old, familiar voice coming from my car radio. "Nah, couldn't be," I said.

But it was. Jimmy Smith was still there on WAYN-AM radio, and suddenly everything seemed right with the world. Since it was after 9 a.m., I didn't get to hear his trademark cowbell -- which he used to ring each morning to exhort listeners to "get up and fix some cheesy grits" -- but his voice brought back warm, safe memories of getting dressed for school and trying to think of a good excuse for not having my homework done.

You know how radio stations are always coming up with dumb or offensive stunts, such as the one in Denver where the disc jockey dropped a chicken off a third-floor balcony?

The closest thing to a radio stunt I can remember in Rockingham was when Smith would call the mayor at home early in the morning to find out what happened at last night's City Council meeting. You could get some interesting responses if the mayor was still groggy when he answered. You'd also hear -- get this -- local news, obituaries and birthdays.

The closest thing to such hometown-flavored radio in the Triangle these days is mornings on WPTF-AM, when Donna Mason and Maury O'Dell might ask people for their favorite pumpkin pie recipe or something.

Too quaint for the new millennium? Possibly, but when the only options are off-color "humor" or nationally syndicated schlock jocks who couldn't find their way from Raleigh to Cary with a map, recipes for pumpkin pie can be comforting.

You know how I've been picking on a local Clear Channel radio station for cutting off my favorite songs before they ended? No more.

Cutting off a record is an act of beneficence compared to what one of their DJs, Bubba the Love Sponge Clem, is on trial for doing in Tampa: He allegedly castrated a wild boar in the station's parking lot as a publicity stunt.

My contempt for such stunts -- and for much of what passes for local radio programming -- is boundless. And judging from the hundreds of responses you sent me after I wrote about it recently, so is yours.

The consensus is that people want more music -- and not the same #$%#@& songs over and over -- less talk and DJs who at least act as though they're interested in music.

With rare exceptions, the DJs in Rockingham and other little-bitty Southern towns were hardly the most scintillating personalities. But at least they had personalities. And a sense of decency. They would never pull a stunt like the one dreamed up by a couple of former Clear Channel jokemeisters at a Dallas station last summer. Just for the heck of it, they made up a story that pop icon Britney Spears had been killed in a car crash. Classy, guys.

Jimmy Smith has been at the family-owned WAYN his entire career, so he has no idea what it's like to work for a huge corporation driven more by ratings points than by scoring points with its listeners.

"I have friends in that situation, and they're very tense about it," he said.

I'd be tense, too -- and looking over my shoulder for Bubba Clem.

8/8/2000

THE VOTES GO AGAINST THE SINGER

Several months ago I was at a neighborhood multiplex theater in Raleigh, trying to decide whether I could afford to buy a large box of popcorn and still pay the rent that month.

A well-dressed, prosperous-looking dude approached and asked my name. I told him, but only after making sure he wasn't trying to serve me with a subpoena for that, ahem, unfortunate incident in D.C. earlier this year.

"That's who I thought you were," he said. "I read your column. Make sure you stay around until the end of the movie and hear my son sing."

"Who's your son?" I asked.

"Brian McKnight," he replied, not even trying to hide his well-deserved pride. That pride was even more apparent when he emerged from the theater 90 minutes later. Tears filled his eyes while he related to me how his son had been chosen to write the theme song for "Men of Honor," a movie starring Oscar winners Cuba Gooding Jr. and Robert DeNiro.

I've never been impressed with celebrities -- OK, one: Miss Delicious, who used to dance at the late, lamented 14 Karat Dinner Theater -- and certainly not with their parents. But I was moved and touched by my encounter with the man who claimed to be McKnight's dad. (I didn't ask him for I.D.) I only wish I could see Pops again so I could tell him -- to paraphrase an old blues song -- "Papa, you'd better talk to your son."

You see, it turns out that McKnight, a smooth, soulful balladeer, offended millions of black people recently with his revelation on a nationally syndicated radio program that he doesn't vote and is, to put it kindly, distressingly apolitical.

Three angry people called me the morning of McKnight's interview on the "Tom Joyner Morning Show" to vent their anger and vow never to buy or even to listen to another Brian McKnight song.

Three people do not a national movement make, but earlier this week, I received an e-mail message -- one that had been forwarded to about 50 people -- calling for a boycott of McKnight's music.

Joyner and his cast members are not promoting the boycott, but because registering blacks to vote has long been one of their pet projects, they were mightily displeased by McKnight's comments and had a whole lot of wicked fun at his expense.

Now, nary a soul I've talked to was offended that McKnight sang the national anthem at the Republican National Convention last year. They wrote that off as, "Hey, it takes all kinds" or "The dude's just getting paid." But his comment about not voting and his subsequent statement about his lofty income tax bracket making him immune to the vicissitudes of electoral fortune tore his designer drawers with many fans. Make that "former fans."

I hate to see McKnight's career fatally damaged like this -- he is, after all, one of the few performers out today who can actually write a literate song -- but I am delighted to see so many people take umbrage at his disdain for voting.

They know, as McKnight obviously does not, the high price our ancestors paid for us to get that right. They also know that one's tax bracket shouldn't make them impervious to that fact.

9/7/2001

THEIR EARS SHOULD BE BURNING

Basta!

What'd you call me?

No, no. I said "basta." It is not an insulting name, it's an Italian word meaning "enough."

And "enough" is precisely what we should be saying to all these men running around wearing earrings.

Basta, already. It's time to face facts, guys. Unless you're in a rock 'n' roll band or in the road show of "Pirates of Penzance," there is no reason to be running around with a diamond stud or a gold hoop hanging off your lobe.

Am I the only one who thinks earrings are inappropriate for a certain gender -- at least after a certain age? Nah. Your wife, girlfriend and co-workers feel the same way, but they won't tell you because they fear hurting your feelings.

Not me. Dude, lose the earring. I lost mine several years ago. I got it -- as we men do just about everything else -- because some woman told me she'd like me better with one.

So, I got my ear pierced and deluded myself that it was a bold fashion statement for awhile -- until my insurance adjuster, Orkin man and auto mechanic all showed up at my house within a month of one another making the same statement.

Even Michael Jordan, who pulled off wearing an earring better than any man alive -- five years ago, that is -- looks dated with it now.

Iconoclastic comedian George Carlin was right: Wearing an earring back in the days when you could get your butt kicked for wearing one was a cutting-edge statement of individuality and courage.

Now, though, when every CPA who ever attended a Jimmy Buffett concert or smoked a doobie 20 years ago wears one or two, it is merely a misguided fashion statement -- like wearing a ponytail or your baseball cap backward -- made by dudes trying to convince themselves that they are still hip.

It ain't working, pal.

The earring, I've concluded, has become the red Corvette of the new millennium, something donned by middle-aged men who feel they have become, in the words of a character on the late, unlamented television series "thirtysomething," "invisible to teenage girls."

Well, they see you now. Only problem is, when they notice you strolling through the mall now, they're saying, "Golly, look at the old geezer with the earring."

The only thing worse than seeing some geriatric dude with an earring is seeing some little kid wearing one because his mother or father thinks it makes him look like a cute little gangsta.

You can almost -- I said almost -- excuse grown men because they are, presumably, mature enough to make their own decisions and know, or will after reading this, that people think they look silly.

You can even forgive teenage boys, whose main goal traditionally has been to do things that infuriate their parents.

But it's the younger boys, some as young as 5, sporting earrings that should worry us. I figure no one should wear an earring or a ridiculous haircut unless he's old enough to pay for it. And even then he ought to think twice.

4/13/2001

THERE'S TOO MUCH OF RUBEN

I've got just two things to say to Ruben Studdard, the 25-year-old dude who won all of that money on television, beat our boy Clay and is now officially an "American Idol."

The first is, "Say, homes, lemme borrow $100."

The second is, "Lose some weight."

Don't look at me like that. Anyone who cares about the corpulent crooner -- or even about good music -- will tell him the same thing.

Recent months haven't been good for music fans. Edwin Starr and June Carter Cash went to that big juke joint in the sky, and Luther Vandross and Barry White are both suffering from serious weight-related illnesses that could've been prevented.

In recent years, Luther's weight fluctuated so greatly that he looked like a different person each time you saw him. Surely someone could have risked expulsion from his inner circle by telling him "Yo, dawg. That isn't cool."

Obesity is a national problem -- did someone slip Big Macs into the national water supply? -- and everyone needs friends who'll tell them they're getting too big.

Ruben, you're getting too big.

Simon Cowell, the obnoxious "American Idol" judge, freely commented on the weight of women contestants, telling even the most deliciously plump ones that they needed to lose a few pounds. Yet, did anyone ever hear him comment on Ruben's Rubenesque frame?

I don't know about you, but if I could come back as anything, it would be as a 1960s-era R&B singer. Man, I'd have more fun than the law allows.

The only drawback is that R&B singers seldom reach rockin' chair age. There aren't but three singers I'd stand in line in the rain to see: Sam Cooke, Otis Redding and Z.Z. Hill. As the Righteous Brothers sang in one of the under-appreciated songs of all-time:

If you believe in forever, then life is just a one-night stand.

If there's a rock 'n' roll heaven, then you know we've got a helluva band.

Neither Sam nor Otis nor Z.Z., tragically, lived long enough to get within sniffing distance of Social Security. All died young, but none ate his way to an early grave. That appears to be what awaits Ruben if loved ones don't intervene. Here's a tip: If you adore him so much -- heck, if you voted for him -- send him Jenny Craig's phone number.

Talent and excess go together like chitlins and hot sauce. Even Elvis battled carbs and drugs toward the end and would've benefited greatly had someone suggested he not, say, eat that fifth peanut-butter-and-banana sammitch deep-fried in butter.

A colleague said her father, noting Aretha Franklin's prayer vigil for Luther, commented, "She ought to be holding one for herself."

Amen. One "American Idol" fan wrote to tell me "This may get me booed around here, but this is not a North Carolina thing, it's not a black and white thing. ... Both of these guys can sing, but as a man of 'substance,' it's fascinating that the fat guy won."

It's actually too soon to tell whether Ruben really won. Let's wait to see whether they name a sandwich after him.

Oh, they've already done that. OK, then, let's wait and see whether he can, oh, see his feet while standing up when he's 26.

5/27/2003

RUBEN'S 'REDNECK' VILIFIER

Last week when I discovered that I was white, I decided to head straight for the bank to get a loan.

Come to find out, though, it -- my being white -- was all a mistake made by hundreds of angry readers.

After I wrote a compassionate yet witty column suggesting that Ruben Studdard -- the man who beat Raleigh's Clay Aiken for the title of "American Idol" -- should lose some weight so he'll be around to enjoy his newfound fame and wealth, I was assaulted by hundreds of verbal grenades accusing me of denigrating the corpulent crooner.

Because the story was forwarded across the country without my picture -- if you've never seen me, I look just like Denzel; if you have seen me, sorry -- many people assumed that I was some disgruntled "redneck" upset because Clay lost.

How do I know that? Because several wrote, "You are a disgruntled redneck upset because Clay lost."

When you're me, you get used to being called dirty names, but never, as this time, whitey (by a white woman), redneck or trailer park pimp. The worst insult came from a woman who called me a ... a ... KENNY G FAN!!! "He is thin and white, just like you like them," she wrote.

The only thing that prevented me from responding with a worse insult was my Christian upbringing -- and the fact that there is no worse insult.

For instance, I could laugh when a couple of Rubenites' letters began, "Were you born this stupid?" and "Get a grip, whitey ... . You need to get over the fact that a smooth, talented FAT black man won."

It broke my heart to tell her that, except for the "smooth, talented" part, they were describing me. So I didn't.

Some health-care professionals thanked me for addressing the problem of obesity and noted that people of Ruben's size are walking advertisements for heart disease and stroke. Most, though, agreed with Carmen from Georgia, who stated, "You are obviously a hater of blacks ... . What are you going to do when a BIG FAT BLACK WOMAN becomes president?"

I'll say, "Right on, sister." And, "Lose some weight."

Renee lovingly noted that "Ruben has fat on his hips, but you have fat between your ears," while Michelle from Texas said, "You are one of the most ignorant columnists I have ever read. ... It is obvious just how red your neck is."

Another began, "Just because you're a reporter doesn't give you the right to make people feel bad about how they look. I'm sure you're not God's gift to women. You are probably from one of those trailer parks in Belmont, Gastonia or Mooresville."

A law school student named Tiyesha, in one of about a score of e-mail messages I traded with her, wrote, "Say, homes, don't be upset because you are stuck in a low-paying job ... while another brotha is making money and doing what he loves."

A white reader, figuring he was writing to a kindred spirit -- someone equally upset over what Ruben's victory supposedly signified for America -- wrote, "Just goes to show that except for NASCAR, white guys don't get any breaks."

6/3/2003

THE WORST IT'S SAMMY BY A MILE

It was a misstatement of fact that couldn't go unchallenged, especially since it appeared right here in this newspaper.

My colleague, Mr. Check It Out, wrote recently that he had a remarkably dreadful CD containing "arguably the worst-ever cover versions" of some beloved songs. It was by Elva Ruby Connes Miller. She was known simply as Mrs. Miller to both of her fans.

I listened to it - or to as much of it as I could stand before I would've begun looking for a train in front of which to throw myself. I admit that it was impressively awful.

But the worst? No way. Because a few weeks ago, I bought the worst CD ever made. It's by Sammy Davis Jr.

Mrs. Miller can almost be forgiven her transgression. Who knows, maybe she recorded these songs as a lark or an attempt to win a bar bet. But Sammy's CD is far more insidious precisely because he should've known better than to remake an albumful of songs that should never have been made in the first place. He was, after all, a member of the Rat Pack, hanging out with Dean and Frank, and was probably its most talented member overall. (Did you ever see Frank dance?)

So why did he consent to sing the theme from "The Mary Tyler Moore Show" and "MacArthur Park"? Want to know how bad this turkey is? "The Candy Man" is the best song on it.

Listen, Hoss. You haven't heard bad until you've heard Sammy sing "Shaft." He wasn't content to merely defile Isaac Hayes' song about "the cat who won't cop out when there's danger all about" - hmm, sounds like me, doesn't it? - by changing it from a funky urban tale to an over-orchestrated Vegas lounge tune.

No sirree. Sam changed the lyrics to include such imaginative gems as this, which he tried to rap:

"Hey man, can you dig him? Looking so cool in all that leather. ... He's bad bad bad bad bad bad bad. ... Go ahead with your bad self, John Shaft."

The song is so devoid of soul that, by comparison, it makes the Mormon

Tabernacle Choir sound like Parliament Funkadelic.

I know celebrities such as William "Captain Kirk" Shatner, Bruce Willis and Eddie Murphy have made records so awful that they should've been prosecuted. Those efforts, though, were more tributes to their oversized egos than to a realistic assessment of their talents.

As I once heard someone ask, "If it's a crime to defile national monuments such as Mount Rushmore, why isn't it a crime for Bruce Willis to defile 'My Girl'?"

It's true that when Sammy died he was pretty much financially tapped out, so it is conceivable that the CD titled "Mr. Bojangles" was just a way to earn some moolah to satisfy the tax man and other creditors.

I'm guessing, though, that this tearfully bad musical monument to vapidity and bad taste satisfied no one but fans of kitsch.

If you want hear how bad this CD is - and who wouldn't? - dial 549-5100 and enter category 2229. If you're calling from Wake Forest, Clayton, Smithfield or Fuquay-Varina, call 836-2830.

But don't listen on an empty stomach. Better yet, do.

7/22/1999

THEY CUT TO CHASE OF CHANGE

Talking to Ann Atwater as she sits serenely, her hands folded gently in her lap, you figure it would take something pretty bad to make her want to commit murder.

Say hello to C.P. Ellis.

Ellis was worse than pretty bad when Atwater reached into her pocketbook at a Durham City Council meeting, pulled out her knife and approached the front of the council chamber. Her destination: Ellis' throat.

A member of the Ku Klux Klan at the time, Ellis was yet again dropping "N-word" bombs all over the joint. Atwater's temperature was in the red zone.

"I was not one of those 'turn-the-other-cheek' people. I am now," she said, "but back then, I was getting ready to cut him."

"Back then" was the early 1970s and Atwater and Ellis were frequent combatants squaring off before the City Council -- Ellis urging the adoption of apartheid-like rules that would, for instance, keep blacks off city streets, and Atwater fighting for what she felt were her rights as a black woman.

Neither she nor her knife reached Ellis' throat. "Councilman John Stewart came down and grabbed me by the arm and said, 'Daughter, don't do that. That's what they want you to do,' " she recalled while sitting in the lobby of the Meadows of Oak Grove assisted living center in Durham.

Ellis, who lives at the center, had moments earlier been awarded a plaque by Duke University's Office for Institutional Equity for 30 years of working to heal the racial divisions he'd once exacerbated.

Benjamin Reese, vice president of Duke's Office for Institutional Equity, said, "C.P. hasn't received the accolades he deserves. He and I went to dinner several years ago, and I was very taken by his commitment to racial equality."

Ellis, wheelchair-bound and senile, seemed unaware that he was the guest of honor, but a hint of recognition seemed to spread across his face when he saw Atwater. And why wouldn't it? The pair is just as connected, 30 years later, as they were when they were insulting each other and beseeching the city council on behalf of themselves and their respective constituents.

They have been the subject of a book, "The Best of Enemies," and a documentary film, "An Unlikely Friendship." Atwater and Diane Bloom, the filmmaker, will join a panel discussion following the movie's showing at the Richard White Auditorium on Duke's East Campus at 7 p.m. Friday.

The former enemies became allies, living, breathing examples, Ellis' son Tim said, "that people can change. I was just a young kid, but I was proud to see my dad doing something that seemed important when he stood in front of the City Council. I didn't understand the ramifications of what it would mean 30 years later."

Ellis has said that he changed his wicked ways when he realized the harm his racial intolerance was doing to his children. He and Atwater later helped lead the effort to desegregate Durham's schools.

Tim Ellis, a heavy equipment operator, said that the transformation he witnessed in his father helped a decade later when Tim became addicted to drugs. "I saw that my dad wasn't the same person he used to be, and I knew I could change. We're proof that you can change. It just takes openmindedness."

———————————————————————————————————— 1/13/2004

THEY GET THEIR SAY ON CLAY ————————————

Forget about it. Stop asking. Tain't gonna happen.

No matter how many calls and e-mail messages I receive from people who think the State Fair got taken for a loopy ride by paying Clay Aiken $200,000 for Monday's two performances, I'm not writing about that.

After I suggested that possibility in May when the deal was made for one show for $100,000, I was assailed and called everything but a Reuben sandwich -- and a Ruben fan -- by angry Aiken fans.

Regardless of what one thinks of his music, the State Fair can't possibly make back its investment. Couldn't Tiffany Budd, the fair's promotion specialist, have said, "Yo, Clay dearie, since you're already in the neighborhood, want to hang around and do another show for, say, $50,000 and all the turkey legs you can eat?"

Clay strikes me as a sincere, courtly chap -- who could use a few pounds of turkey legs. He might've gone for such a deal, too, but those of his fans from whom I heard took pride in his exorbitant fee. You usually have to go to a bowling alley -- or show up at your first ex-wife's house at 2 a.m. -- to get called the names I was hit with after thoughtfully suggesting that maybe, just maybe, we fairgoers had overpaid for Clay.

Won't say that again. I will say, though, that the fair will have to sell a whole lot of turkey legs to offset the hole it went into to book Clay at that price.

Some people got the impression that I was an anti-Aiken, just because I said the only thing he could do worth $100,000 would be to travel the state and paint all of our houses.

A typical response of the close to 500 I received after that initial column was this one from Dave: "If the hard working people of some hillbilly county want to [urinate] away their money watching Clay, what is it to you? What else should they spend their money on?? Prisons? Welfare? Crack mothers?

"Why not have a rap group in, loot the place and shoot each other up?"

A reader from Wausau, Wis., called Clay "a man with a heart of gold and a voice of pure heaven. ... We are sick of singers spewing foul language and lewd behavior. ... You are a #$%*@!^&." Honest.

Gail F. wrote, "You have lost me as a reader unless I see some apology. ... Clay is definitely the American 'eye-doll.' "

Another self-described Claymate wrote, "Wake up and smell the coffee. He is a great singer with a great personality and an all-round nice person -- which are three things more than you have going for you."

Me? Not a great singer? She obviously has never heard my soul-stirring a cappella rendition of Chuck Berry's classic "My Ding-a-Ling."

A Claymate named Bunny wrote a very un-Bunnylike response: "Get a grip, dude, or better yet, some journalistic talent. ... My advice? Crawl back under the rock from which you come."

Connie, a fan from Raleigh, wrote that Clay "is the hottest singer since Elvis and Sinatra. I am not a person of wealth, but I have gladly paid more than my mortgage for floor tickets to see Clay in concert every chance I get. ... I just thank God that he is coming home to Raleigh."

So, now you see why I won't be writing this time about Clay not being worth $200,000. To some people, maybe he is.

10/19/2004

THEY'VE GOT HIS NUMBER

There are only two possible explanations for what's happening: Either someone can't take a joke or I've got a secret bank account so secret that even I don't know about it.

As a joke last year, I responded to one of those e-mail messages seeking my checking account number -- so the family of some deposed African ruler could transfer millions of hidden dollars and graciously share some with me -- by giving them a made-up account number: I figured that since my rewards would no doubt be fictitious, so should the account number.

The number I sent them -- along with a nonexistent $20,000 of the requested "good faith" contribution -- was 634-5789.

Yes, that's the title of the classic Wilson Pickett song from 1966 , the one in which he advises Sweet Thang:

If you need a little lovin', call on me. ...

I'll be right here at home

All you got to do is pick up the telephone and dial now: 634-5789.

Alas, that must've been the magic number, because since sending out that smart-alecky response, I have received more than 100 similar entreaties asking to use my checking account number to spirit out even more hidden moolah.

The pleas usually come from the family of some slain military leader who died before he could flee with millions in fleeced loot. The untraceable cash, so the story usually goes, has been kept in a footlocker at the bus station, awaiting a sap -- er, make that kindly soul -- like me to provide an account number into which it can be wired.

For my help, the dead dude's grieving widow offers to share some of the money with me.

The pleas seeking to separate me from my money have, at least, become more creative. In the latest one, I was informed that I am the only living survivor of Mr. Mark Mark, an oil company executive in Nigeria who, along with his wife and three children, was killed in an automobile accident.

The bank representative, Mr. Al Hamza, wrote: "I decided to track his last name over the Internet, hence I've contacted you to assist in repatriating the money and property left behind. ... Since I have been unsuccessful in contacting the relatives, I now seek your consent to present you as the next of kin since you have the same last name."

Huh? Since when did my last name become "Mark"? Not being one to quibble over such things, especially when $20 million is at stake, I decided the dude could slap a dress on me and call me "Cleopatra."

With the theme song to "The Jeffersons" playing in my head -- "Fish don't fry in the kitchen/beans don't burn on the grill" -- I sent my consent, along with my checking account number (634-5789) to Al at the Diligent Bank in Lagos, Nigeria.

Math was never my favorite subject, but even I know that 40 percent of $20 million would mean no more waiting for the "blue light special" at Kmart just to buy a bag of Funyuns . It would be "Goodbye, Mickey D's, hello, Red Lobster."

Not only that, but if things go the way Al Hamza promised, this is the last Labor Day I'll have to work.

9/2/2003

THIN BLUE LINE NEEDS MORE GREEN

Hmmm, let's see. Maybe we aren't as outraged as we should be because Raleigh police Detective David Powell was off duty and working a second job as security for a nightclub when he got shot last week.

Would the public outcry, of which I've heard little, be greater if Powell had been shot while, say, responding to a bank holdup instead of moonlighting at some sports bar? Probably.

If we were smart, though, we'd be even angrier that he was shot while working off-duty. We'd be angrier still that he had to work while off duty.

It defies logic that we can continually find money to pay for new sports arenas -- often underwriting the cost for multimillionaires -- but can't come up with enough money to pay cops a wage that allows them to spend their leisure time in a leisurely fashion.

This may strike you as a blatant attempt to suck up to cops. It's not. The one time I tried that, it didn't work. (I put one of those stickers on my car that said I'd contributed to the Police Benevolence Association. I thought the cops would cut me some slack the next time I got stopped for speeding. Yeah, right: I got a ticket within a week.)

No, I'm speaking out for cops because they deserve more than they're getting. I don't know about you, but when I encounter a cop, I want him to be refreshed and in a good mood, not overworked, resentful and terse. The best way to ensure that is to let the dudes and dudettes in blue spend their off days enjoying their families while grilling in the back yard, not grilling some kid with a fake I.D. who's trying to get into a club or confronting some drunken punk who wants to impress his girl by mouthing off to a guard.

Instead of working overtime, Powell should've been chilling at the crib or out on a date with his wife, enjoying the rewards he deserves for providing the last line of defense between us and society's pathological predators. Believe me, they're out there, and the fact that you think they're not means the cops are doing their job.

Of course, even if Powell had been home that fateful night, his wife most likely wouldn't have been: She's a cop, too, and she was working off-duty security -- as do 75 to 95 percent of all Raleigh cops.

In the wake of Powell's shooting, acting top cop John Knox vowed to review the department's moonlighting policy.

Negatory, chief. You ought to review the city's overtime policy, which usually "pays" officers who work overtime with compensatory time, not money.

That would be cool if officers could take comp time to the Piggly Wiggly or to the bank.

Cop: "Excuse me, sir, but I'd like to buy a house. Got no money, but I've got about 2,000 hours of comp time stored up. What can you show me?"

Bank officer: "I can show you the door outta here."

Stop me if you've heard this one before, but something seems very wrong when the people who protect our butts and property have to work two jobs in order to earn enough for luxuries -- nay, necessities -- such as vacations and money for their kids' educations.

—— 8/3/2001

THIS GOAL JUST ISN'T WORTHY ————

Whew, that's a relief. Just when it appeared that black people couldn't get upset about anything, along comes an issue that has apparently reignited our fire for social justice.

The war in Iraq? Nope.

The way the cops beat that fat guy to death in Cincinnati? Get real.

What has seemingly ignited a spark is -- sit down for this one, Loretta -- the scheduled release today of Ruben Studdard's new CD.

On Monday morning, I heard two syndicated radio show hosts urge blacks to mark today as the day to rush out and purchase the American Idol's new CD, as though our lives, or anything else, depended on it.

Since the beginning of November, I have received dozens of frantically

forwarded electronic letters urging me to do the same. One of these came from the head of a national civil rights organization whom I won't name because he probably would, or should, be embarrassed.

This dude has never to my knowledge expressed outrage over the fratricide, a fancy word for brothers killing brothers, that has destructively rippled through our communities, or on how to persuade Bush to send our young'uns home from Iraq.

Yet, with what I presume was a straight face, he forwarded a letter urging me to "go out and buy one or two copies and make sure your friends buy a copy so we can surpass Clay's" sales.

Surpass this, chump.

With all of the pathologies blacks face -- fatherless kids, crime, high blood pressure -- I figured nobody but Studdard's record company could really care how many CDs he sold. I called J Records in New York and asked whether this alleged competition with Clay was designed to boost sales by making a phony appeal to race pride.

"That would be kind of trifling," Biff Warren, J's senior director of publicity, said with a laugh. "That's a fan thing. We had nothing to do with it. We've shipped 1.3 million units, and with this kind of groundswell, we think Ruben's going to do very, very, very well."

Years ago, I boarded a plane in Charlotte and passed rasslers "Nature Boy" Ric Flair and Ivan "the Russian Bear" Koloff sitting in first class. They were drinking and laughing together like old comrades.

I'd screamed myself hoarse the previous night, urging Nature Boy to rip Koloff's arm out of the socket and beat him with it. Imagine my disillusionment upon seeing them kicked back, sharing cocktails.

The people trying to foment a rivalry between Ruben and Clay are destined to be similarly disillusioned since, Warren assured me, "They have a great personal and professional relationship. They tour together."

Not only that, he said, but J Records, Ruben's label, and RMG, Clay's label, are part of the same company.

Darn. Of course, that'll make no difference to people determined to see a racist conspiracy lurking behind every CD. For instance, one e-mail message stated, "With our dollars we can surpass Clay ... and remind America who won their 'American Idol' competition."

I don't know about you, but I can think of more important things than reminding America who won a made-for-television "event." And I can think of a million more things we can do with those dollars besides buy Ruben's CD.

12/9/2003

THIS TIME THE COURT GOT IT

I'm the last person in the world to make light of somebody's mental illness. Willie Nelson could've been singing about me when he sang,

"I know I've done weird things, / told people I 'heared' things / when silence was all that abounds. / There've been days when it pleased me / to be on my knees, / following ants as they crawled across the ground."

Despite such empathy, I knew something was screwy when a jury ruled in 1998 that Dr. Myron Liptzin had to pay Wendell Williamson $500,000 plus interest and court costs for not curing Williamson and preventing him from going ballistic along a Chapel Hill street nearly six years ago.

Williamson, after thinking things over from the comfort of his room - not, you notice, cell - at Broughton State Hospital in Morganton, decided that Liptzin, not he, was responsible for his actions and sued him for his own personal injuries, career damage and hospital confinement.

Stop me if you think I'm wrong, but wouldn't someone strolling down a quiet street firing at innocent people likely suffer some personal injuries - say, from police who also are armed?

As for career damage, one could logically conclude that Williamson probably did suffer some of that. After all, few CEOs or law firms are clamoring for employees with "created deadly mayhem on a quiet street" as the most recent accomplishment on their r"sum"s.

Fortunately for Liptzin, other shrinks and all mental patients present and future, an appeals court unanimously overturned the verdict last week and decided that no one - except for maybe that lame psychic with the phony accent on those dreadful television infomercials - could have predicted that Williamson would saunter down Henderson Street firing an M-1 rifle at innocent people, killing two and injuring a police officer.

Can you imagine the repercussions if that verdict had been upheld and a man had actually been rewarded for unleashing such a devastating level of violence against society? Doctors either would decline to treat mentally ill patients for fear of being liable if the patients subsequently became violent, or would start confining or lobotomizing every patient who reclined on their couch.

I remember being wholly unsympathetic to Williamson or his alleged mental condition in the days and weeks after his rampage. Even though he killed two people and injured a police officer, he was found not guilty by reason of insanity and confined to a mental institution for an indeterminate length of time.

I was criticized by scores of readers as being callous and insensitive for suggesting that, instead of protesting to keep Williamson confined, I'd be protesting to get him released - so I could administer a justice the jury seemed unwilling to.

Those readers were right. It was insensitive, perhaps gratuitously so, to insinuate that Williamson's violent acts were wanton and willful. Even though they weren't, it's ludicrous to blame a doctor - with whom Williamson admittedly never even discussed violence - for the tragedy that destroyed several lives, including Williamson's.

12/26/2000

TIPPING THE TABLES ON TIPS

When I was about 9, we used to shop at the A&P grocery store in Rockingham. I always went with my aunt because I knew that if I begged enough, she'd buy me a honeybun.

Or hit me and say "shut up."

I still remember the taste of those honeybuns, but I also remember a befuddling sign on the store's door that read "No Tipping Allowed."

Being stupid, I had no idea what that meant, so each time I left the store I'd glance furtively around, looking left and right, and then tiptoe out of the store -- expecting to be nabbed by the no-tipping police.

I now know what tipping means, but apparently, if some waiters and waitresses from whom I've heard are to be believed, not many black people do.

A Cornell University School of Hotel Administration study confirms that waitresses and waiters -- black and white -- across the country feel the same as those who've been calling me for years: that "blacks don't tip" and they'd rather not serve us.

Well, kiss my grits, homeslice.

Shortly after the story broke nationally a few years ago about blacks complaining of poor treatment at Denny's restaurants, I heard from a local Denny's waitress who, with admirable honesty, stated "You're right. We don't treat blacks the same because black people don't tip."

She hung up before I could ask her whether , perhaps, there was a correlation between the fact that "we don't treat blacks the same" and blacks not tipping.

Johnny Silver of Raleigh has been a banquet manager or a waiter for 13 years. He works at the Holiday Inn at RTP.

Silver, who is black, thinks many blacks don't tip, but not always because they're cheap. "Some of them just may not know," he said. "If you never went out with your parents to eat, or go out with them and never see them tip, you don't know" to do it, either.

"When I get black customers, I try not to have any preconceived ideas because as a waiter, when I go out I can tell when a waiter doesn't want to serve me," he said. "If the service is bad, leave something -- even if it's a quarter. That way the waiter'll know, 'I must've done something wrong.' "

Any waiter who says his preconceptions about black diners don't affect his level of service is kidding himself. It's just as Maurice White of Earth, Wind & Fire wrote so eloquently in his song "On Your Face:"

"Ain't it funny that the way you feel shows on your face?

"And no matter how you try to hide, it'll state your case."

Likewise, anyone who thinks customers can't tell when they're being served under duress -- because their waiter drew the short straw and got stuck with the black couple -- is crazy. They're also crazy if they don't think their attitude is going to affect the service provided and the tip received.

For good service, I'm like Fred Sanford's friend Big Money Grip : glad to pay for it. When it is obvious the server would prefer not to have my table, and it shows in his or her face and service, the tip is 15 percent or less. If it is so bad that I don't want to leave anything, I ask for the manager and complain. So should you.

If the service is good, though, you should show your appreciation. Not knowing is no excuse.

7/22/2003

TOO LATE FOR BEING RELEVANT

OK, at least we know the dude reads the news.

The Rev. Billy Graham, who went through the 1950s and 1960s uttering scarcely a syllable about the social upheavals rending the country, is still not chatty, but on television earlier this week he sounded a note of skepticism of both the supposed spiritual transformation of Nation of Islam Minister Louis Farrakhan and of Farrakhan's stated desire to be a force for racial harmony.

"I doubt if he could. I know him," Graham said.

Farrakhan, like most people who find themselves knock, knock, knocking on heaven's - or wherever's - door, emerged from his near-death bout with prostate cancer seemingly eager to shed his racist raiments and intent upon cloaking himself in the robe of racial reconciliation.

I can see how such a transformation might be hard to swallow, and I don't knock Graham for knocking Farrakhan. I've done the same thing myself in this space and fail to see how anyone, at least with a straight face, could defend the Muslim minister against charges of antisemitism.

Regardless of how one feels about the sincerity - or lack thereof - of Farrakhan's transformation, it is disheartening that Graham has waited until the twilight of his career to roar. Maybe it's this new millennium thing: Since Graham said little of relevance during the civil rights movement or the Vietnam War - he did express schoolmarmish disappointment in President Nixon's "vulgar" language during Watergate - perhaps he wants to leave a legacy of relevancy.

Too late. He had a chance to be relevant during the 1950s when he was considered the conscience of the nation and 14-year-old Emmitt Till was being mutilated and murdered for allegedly whistling at a white woman in Mississippi, or when Rosa Parks was being arrested for refusing to give up her bus seat in Alabama.

But one needn't go back all the way to the '50s. He could've been relevant during the 1960s when he had the nation's ear and cities were burning and anti-war protesters were being gunned down on college campuses and women were fighting for equality and Dr. King was being killed.

He would've certainly been relevant if he'd told George Wallace, when that strutting, pouty-mouthed Alabama governor was defying the law and blocking the university door, "George, you'd better sit yourself down and let those young 'uns in that school."

But nooo. Graham, to quote an old Negro spiritual, "never said a mumblin' word." I know he didn't because I used to watch - this was before cable, and you could only get three channels - whenever he was on television. I loved those crusades and get chills just thinking of George Beverly Shea singing "How Great Thou Art."

Graham wrote that he adopted the racial attitudes of the rural South "without much reflection," although he eventually forbade segregated seating at his crusades.

Sorry, Homes, that won't cut it.

Farrakhan, as Graham said, may indeed be the wrong man to lead us into a racial Shangri-la. That's a shame.

A bigger shame, though, is that Graham might've been the right man - and didn't even try.

————————————————————————————— 1/6/2000

TRAGEDY BREEDS KINSHIP ————————————————

It was probably my first smile all day, considering that I'd been awakened by a telephone call telling me, "Man, they just blew up the World Trade Center."

But a couple of hours later, while walking on Hargett Street in Raleigh, I witnessed a heartwarming incident that made me laugh out loud. A FedEx truck and a UPS truck were stopped, side by side, waiting for the light to change. One driver was black, the other white, and their doors were open to take advantage of the beautiful fall day.

They nodded at each, and the FedEx driver shouted, "Damned shame about the World Trade Center, wasn't it?"

"Yup," his UPS-driving counterpart shouted back. They both shook their heads resignedly and, when the light changed moments later, drove on their way. I'll bet they had forgotten the minor encounter -- after all, they had spoken a combined total of 10 words -- by the next block. But that brief conversation will remain etched in my memory forever because to me, it epitomized what is great about our country.

Here you had two dudes, employees of competing companies -- and members of often-competing races -- expressing their mutual concern for what had happened to their country. Under ordinary circumstances, these men delivering time-sensitive packages might not have even acknowledged each other.

As it was, their conversation on an anything-but-normal Tuesday was brief and perfunctory. But it spoke loudly about what is great about the United States: We are family. Like it or not.

Think about it. The same as any family, we as a nation have our problems and don't always get along.

It's like that cousin you never could stand but whom you tolerated because he is your favorite uncle's son and is, therefore, blood. That's why, when that bully held his head under water at the swimming pool when you were kids, you rushed to his defense.

It is the same with the United States. We might not always like one another -- hell, can sometimes barely tolerate each other. But when attacked as we were earlier this week, we can drop the hyphens from our particular ethnic groups and become simply Americans rallying around our flag.

What I witnessed in that brief moment between the two delivery guys has been played out on our television sets every minute since the attacks on our country and our consciousness began. Who among us didn't swell with tears and pride upon seeing firefighters from across the country descending on New York -- without even being called -- to help look for their fallen brethren?

In the streets of New York, a city whose residents seem to take a perverse pride in their yawning indifference to their fellow man, people are risking their own lives and well-being to help people to whom they would not have muttered "Howdy-do" the previous day.

Of course, once they get the streets cleaned up, the buildings re-erected and life returns to a semblance of normalcy -- and it will -- then we can go back to being hyphenated Americans who barely tolerate each other.

Or maybe not.

9/14/2001

TRUE TO YOUR VOTE, FALSE TO POLLSTERS

Anyone who knows me knows I never lie - except on those rare occasions when I don't tell the truth.

Now, though, I'm encouraging everyone else to lie too. Naw, not to your wife about that strange lipstick stain on your collar, or to your boss about your expense account receipts. I'm asking you to lie to pollsters who pry into your voting habits and preferences.

It's gotten so you can hardly stick your neck out the door without bumping into a pollster asking you for whom you're going to vote, and why.

I know we live in an information age, but why oh why is it important for us to know, for instance, that George W. Bush is leading among voters who drive 1958 DeSotos, while Gore is tops with left-handed golfers who drive Volvos?

As journalists, we crave information the way a wino craves an unopened bottle of MD 20/20, so it may sound strange that a columnist would encourage people to mislead pollsters. I do so only because the preservation of the cornerstone of democracy - voting - is at stake.

If the prevalence of polls continues, citizens may not even feel a need to vote. They'll already know the outcome of the election.

Thus, we as good citizens should do anything we can to discourage the current emphasis on polls. One way to do that is to lie to pollsters. It is our patriotic duty.

And there's little doubt that polls not only predict political results, but influence them.

In 1980, television stations were reporting that Ronald Reagan had clobbered Jimmy Carter in the presidential race even as voters on the West Coast still stood in line to cast their ballots.

It's likely that some of those prospective voters in the lines or en route to them heard these reports, said "Aw, to heck with it" and returned home, thereby ensuring an even larger plurality for Reagan and dooming the political bids of Democratic candidates for other offices in California who'd hoped to be swept into office on Carter's coattails (such as they were).

Although that fiasco led to much subsequent hand-wringing over the media's role in reporting poll results, not much was learned, because in 1988,

Barry Saunders

ABC News - anxious to be first with a dubious scoop - reported that its polls showed Michael Dukakis would lose the presidential race to George H.W. Bush.

These "results," right as they turned out, weren't reported minutes or even hours after the polls had closed: they were announced before - yes, before - the final debate between Dukakis and Bush.

There is no disputing that most polls have a bias, but not in the way Republican voters and candidates claim: they swear that the polls discriminate against them when they report GOP candidates are leading - they're just trying to lull Republican supporters into a false sense of security -or when they report their candidates are behind - in which case the "left-leaning" pollsters are trying to discourage GOP voters.

The truth is that poll results can and do discriminate for or against anyone running for office: just let a candidate, for whatever reason, get a "bump" in his numbers. He is suddenly reported on, portrayed and viewed as a winner, while any candidate whose numbers slip even slightly is considered to be floundering and is portrayed that way.

"When I use a word," Humpty Dumpty said in "Through the Looking Glass," "it means just what I choose it to mean - neither more nor less." So, too, do polls mean exactly what pollsters chose them to mean.

So look 'em in the eye and lie.

10/14/2000

UNC ADS AMOUNT TO SELLOUT

The horse is already out of the barn. Or, more accurately, the ads are already as good as on the wall.

So kwitcherbitchin, because nothing will prevent UNC-Chapel Hill from defiling the Dean Dome and Kenan Stadium with advertisements.

The best you can hope to do is to contain the damage and hold the board of trustees to its word that any ads will be "limited and tasteful."

I reckon that means we won't see "VIAGRA" flashing on the backboard every time an opposing player shoots a crucial free throw, right? Right?

Not in the first year, at least.

Let's hope it also means we will never see a "tasteful" sign on the wall in the Dean Dome -- perhaps beside one of those classic team photos -- peddling adult diapers "for when you dribble long after the game is over."

There are, to be sure, advertisements that will be tailor-made for sports venues, especially with the arrival of Miami and Virginia Tech to the ACC. Because those schools seem to perennially put more players in the pros and on probation than in Ph.D. programs, their arrival will be giddily anticipated by -- who else? -- bail bondsmen.

If done with restraint, such ads can be tasteful. And who's more tasteful and restrained than bail bondsmen?

For instance, what bail bondsman wouldn't want his "soft signage" -- the board of trustees' phrase, not mine -- displayed where Miami's Willie Williams can see it? Or Virginia Tech's recently arrested quarterback Marcus Vick?

250

"Say, homes. Are you better at eluding tacklers than cops after a night of underage drinking and driving? Uh-oh. Better call Booker T. Dostoevsky's Bail Bonding Service. 10-percent discount for All-Americas."

Those of us who remember the days when ACC hoops were sponsored relatively unobtrusively by The Pilot insurance company still haven't made peace with those Nike swooshes on the sacred uniforms once worn by Charlie Scott, Lee Dedmon and Larry Miller. It'll take even longer to get over ads inside the Dean Dome.

As with most things regarding UNC-CH, I consulted my buddy Duff Morse, a '79 UNC-CH grad and the greatest Tar Heel fan in the world.

"I don't like it," Morse said of the imminent onset of the ads, which he feared will make his alma mater's arena look as though it's some hicksville county civic center.

Indeed. Weren't increased revenues the purpose of holding our noses and welcoming Virginia Tech and Miami into the conference? Oh? You thought it had something to do with competition? Silly you.

The trustees should just admit that the need for more moolah is prompted by their desire to raise the teams' armament level to keep up with Miami and Virginia Tech.

That motivation will ultimately result in UNC-CH recruiting more players whom, like Miami's heralded but hell-raisin' linebacker, Williams, it wouldn't have previously considered.

How much longer will it be before the trustees are "forced" yet again to make an unsavory concession, such as renaming the Dean Dome the Jones Sausage-Dean Smith Center?

The day that happens is the day I'll become one of those ABC (Anybody But Carolina) fans.

7/23/2004

UNC COACH SHOULD KICK HIMSELF

It's conceivable that John Bunting, during his just-begun tenure as head football coach at the University of North Carolina, could win a boatload of national championships. Or at least beat N.C. State.

But the dude has gotten off on the wrong foot with me and, I suspect, other Tar Heel fans because of the way he went after a 19-year-old punter who decided to move closer to home.

It was a tasteless, bullying response to an understandable human emotion: homesickness.

UNC fans are anxious for a winner, but if Bunting's response to Blake Ferguson's departure is indicative of what's to come, they might ask themselves what price they're willing to pay for one.

I guarantee you that some Heel fans are now going, "What in the heck have we got here, Margo?" In a few short years the football program has gone from the supersmooth (some would say too smooth) Mack Brown to the courtly (too courtly?) Carl Torbush to Bunting, a "Great Santini" of a coach willing to apply a scorched-earth policy against a teenager who, like all of us, just wants

251

to go home.

Tar Heel fans couldn't imagine Dean Smith ripping into some kid who decided he'd rather shoot jump shots closer to Ma and Pa. Dean would've said something like, "We regret to see Blake leave. He's an outstanding young man, and we wish him well in his future endeavors." And then he would have helped the kid find another school.

He certainly wouldn't have acidly questioned the kid's manhood. "It seems to me as if he's afraid to compete," Bunting said. "That's not the kind of player I want to have around here ..."

"I think he's afraid. I think he's afraid to go out and kick against his brother at Oklahoma. He'd rather travel home and watch the game."

He said some other uncomplimentary, pretty near incomprehensible things about the kid not having "what it takes" to kick in front of God and national TV. Take my word for it: A red flag should go up any time a coach invokes God and country in the same sentence as football.

Bunting is either a master motivator -- his remaining players might be willing to do anything to avoid being the subject of his public put-downs -- or an insensitive lout. Who among us, at 19 or 20, didn't consider leaving school and returning home, ready to replace dreams of conquering the world with thoughts of "Hmm, I wonder if I can get my old job back sweeping floors at the Piggly Wiggly?"

I myself was so homesick that for my first week away at college I couldn't get to sleep until I'd called home and listened to my aunt fuss at me -- just like old times.

Fortunately for most of us, we didn't have the Great Buntini lambasting us in the media as some kind of pantywaist mama's boy.

I know Bunting is supposed to be this macho, take-no-prisoners guy, but he needs to realize that, even though he's a full-time coach, the young men in his charge are not full-time players. They are students, players -- and, as Bunting just found out -- sons.

I don't know about you, but I think it's cool to see a kid who places his love for family ahead of punting for God, TV and Bunting.

8/17/2001

UNUSUAL, BUT NOT CRUEL

Some inmates at the new Cumberland County jail in Fayetteville must be asking, "Jail, where is thy sting?"

They're the ones with the big smiles on their faces.

Others, the ones holed up in their cells pouting, are asking, "Where the heck are my wings?"

Two female jailers were suspended last week after being accused of providing drugs, sex and Buffalo chicken wings -- among other favors -- for some inmates.

The SBI is investigating the charges, which, if true, would render meaningless the millions of dollars spent on the recently opened high-tech jail aimed at preventing inmates from getting their hands on contraband.

I've known dudes -- heck, I've shared cells with some -- who viewed the standard "three hots and a cot" you get in most jails as luxuries. To find out now that some inmates in Fayetteville supposedly received drugs, sex and chicken wings almost makes me wistful for the days when I was not the paragon of virtue you see before you today.

As if these allegations weren't harmful enough to Fayetteville, a city struggling with an image problem as bad as Durham's, we recently learned that two former cops have admitted to hiring prostitutes.

What must be most galling is that the jail boasts state-of-the-art "telejustice" innovations designed to prevent contraband from reaching inmates. The architecturally impressive facility, dubbed the "Taj Moose-hall" by some -- OK, just by me -- in honor of Sheriff Earl "Moose" Butler, uses video visitation and arraignment centers designed, its Web site says, to "eliminate drugs, contraband and confrontations and ... improve morale."

I could be wrong, but I'm guessing morale improved every time inmates saw their angels of mercy approaching with the chicken wings.

In some societies, sex, drugs and chicken wings are three of the five essential ingredients for a happy life -- the others are "air" and a Barry White CD -- and the people who provide them are known as angels.

The extras supposedly available in the Cumberland County jail must have had people -- criminal and law-abiding alike -- looking forward to being popped by police and tossed in the pokey.

Now perplexed Fayetteville cops understand why, for the first time, they had suspects chasing them down, or why they encountered suspects who not only didn't proclaim their innocence, but who gleefully proclaimed their guilt.

SUSPECT: Yessir, Mister Officer, that's me. I'm the one what did it. I broke in that house and stole that TV. Now, take me to jail.

COP: Sorry, sir. The person we're looking for has outstanding parking tickets.

SUSPECT: That's me, too. I haven't paid a ticket since 1969. I know my rights. Now, take me to jail. And bring that bottle of hot sauce.

The moral of this tale is, sadly, that no high-tech gadgetry will work when you have enterprising, free-market -- okay, reasonably- priced-market -- jailers looking to capitalize off a captive audience.

The other moral is: If you're going to smuggle in Buffalo chicken wings, make sure they're boneless. That way, you can eat all of the evidence.

7/11/2003

Barry Saunders

WAR? NOT WITH THIS MUSIC

After listening to our president semi-convincingly proclaim in his State of the Union address this week that Saddam Hussein is the biggest threat we face -- even bigger than the North Koreans or Michael Bolton being spotted near a recording studio -- I was almost ready to join the warmongrels clamoring to attack Iraq.

Alas, there is one compelling reason we can't: The soldiers would have nothing to listen to.

Think about it. How can we in good conscience send

our guys off to fight when the pop music charts are dominated by P. Diddy, Christina Aguilera and Justin Timberlake?

The music soldiers listen to during wartime has traditionally related to their experiences and kept them apprised of what's going down back home. As it did during the Vietnam War.

The music of that period is as deeply imbedded in the memory of those of us who were around then as phrases such as "demilitarized zone" and "Tet Offensive." When our boys went to Vietnam, they were able to keep at least a tenuous connection to "the world" -- as they called the United States -- via the music piping out of transistor radios and eight-track tape players.

Marvin Gaye plaintively asking "What's Goin' On?", Freda Payne demanding "Bring the Boys Home" or even Country Joe & the Fish wondering "What are we fightin' for?" let them know that the folks back home hadn't forgotten them.

Music with a sense of urgency provided the soundtrack not only to what was happening in Nam but also to the upheaval occurring in city streets.

No one expects a bunch of apolitical, self-absorbed poseurs to suddenly become Dylanesque, but couldn't they, with war imminent, try making music with some relevance?

For instance, to the uninitiated it sounds as though Levi Stubbs was singing a simple love song when he thundered on "Reach Out (I'll Be There)": "When you feel that you can't go on/because all of your hope is gone/and your life is filled with much confusion/because happiness is just an illusion."

Yet those words provided musical motivation for people fighting for equality in the sweltering heat of Alabama and for soldiers fighting for -- what the heck were we fighting for? -- in the sweltering heat of Vietnam.

A buddy of mine, Mike Hoke from Raleigh, served in Nam as a lieutenant colonel in the Marines. Speaking like a Marine earlier this week about the importance of music during his tour of duty, he told me, "I'm as serious as a case of lung cancer about this ... . My guys and I would listen to 'Trouble Man' by Marvin Gaye about sunset, and our testosterone level would get so high we'd pity any fools who took a shot at us during the night. ... Imagine trying to [get geeked up to fight] by listening to Ricky Martin."

I used to hear slightly older guys in Rockingham who'd been to Nam talk about the importance of receiving care packages from home that included eight-tracks or cassettes of their favorite music. Can you imagine sending someone a care package with a Celine Dion CD?

...and the horse you rode in on, Saunders!

Come to think of it, that might lead to the war being over more quickly, because the recipient would no doubt want to return home so he could smack whoever sent that crap.

1/31/2003

WASHED~UP JOCKS WALK, NOT RUN, PROUD

Gordon Miller knows exactly the type of guy who will be interested in joining his new organization, "Washed Up Jocks of America."

Guys like him. And me. "If you've ever had dreams of athletic glory" -- long after any realistic chance of attaining those dreams has passed -- "or sat in class when you were a kid practicing signing your autograph, you'd be interested," Miller said earlier this week over lunch.

Miller's day job, the one that pays the bills, is as president of DNJ Mortgage. The job he's wanted since he was 10 years old, though, was to be a starting pitcher -- or at least a middle reliever -- for his beloved Detroit Tigers baseball team.

He was a star baseball player as a kid and saw Michigan State as a step to his inevitable destination, The Show. Like most washed-up jocks, though, Miller said he ran into an undiscerning coach who didn't appreciate his ability. "He only focused on speed, but I had excellent movement on my pitches."

The coach was unimpressed. Miller left and played for a local semipro team where, wouldn't you know it, yet another dumb coach was underwhelmed by his artistry.

Reality set in -- as it must for all of us -- for Miller at 23, and he figured he'd better get an education. The chance to play was gone, but the embers still smoldered.

Therein, for many former athletes who practiced signing their autographs in anticipation of hordes of awed children, lies the most tormenting part of our lives. It is often when we are at the peak of our ability, as good as we're going to get, that the steel-toed boot of reality comes along and kicks you in the ... er, uh ... teeth and tells you it's time to hang up your jockstrap.

That moment came for me when the trainer on our college basketball team wiped up the court with me, and I faced the undeniable -- believe me, I tried to deny it -- fact that the NBA wasn't pining for lead-footed, 6-foot-2 set shooters.

Oh sure, we all still make the occasional weekend foray into the gym or onto the diamond, where we might wow our friends by knocking down four or five jump shots in a row or by smacking a couple of pitches over the fence during the company softball game.

Alas, such accomplishments feel good for a while -- until Sweet Thang has to break out the extra-strength liniment -- but they won't get you 10 seconds on "SportsCenter."

Those who want to come out of the closet and admit their own washed-upness can join what Miller hopes will be scores of other washed-up jocks in this weekend's Washed Up Jocks 1K Walk and Super Bowl Party outside Woody's City Market sports bar in downtown Raleigh at 3 p.m. You can register there or on his Web site, washedupjocks.com.

Don't fret if your most strenuous physical activity of late has been ripping the top off a bag of Funyons: 1K is less than a mile, and your $10 registration fee will get you all the beer you can chug, as well as cheerleaders exhorting you by name (if, that is, you bring your own cheerleaders).

The idea for the organization came not from Miller's own life, although he admits that he is the prototypical washed-up jock, but from the younger brother of his best friend.

"He was the first all-state football player in his school's history," Miller said. "He averaged about 28 yards per carry in school, and he got a college scholarship. When he injured his shoulder on his first play in college, he was done.

"I told him, 'You're as washed up as the rest of us now,'" Miller recalled with disconcerting glee.

"It's like being an alcoholic," Miller said of washed-uptitude. "The first step is acknowledging you have a problem. You have to come out of the closet. 'Hi, I'm Gordon. I'm a washed-up jock.'"

Of course, not all washed-up jocks become Al Bundy, the TV character whose post-high school life as a shoe salesman was so dreary that he constantly told anyone who'd listen -- and many who wouldn't -- how he'd "once scored four touchdowns in a single game for Polk High."

But many of us do.

—————————————————————————————— 1/30/2004

WE NEED ANOTHER CLASSIC ————————————

It's enough to make you want to run over man's best friend with a brick-laden sleigh.

Like most of you who appreciate good music and important cultural innovations, I wondered for the longest time how they got those dogs to bark "Jingle Bells" on that record.

I discovered decades later that you can make dogs, and many human beings, do anything with copious amounts of 90-proof eggnog, a liver-flavored dog biscuit or an electric cattle prod -- set on low.

The amusement of that uniquely American "barking dog" song -- and most Christmas music -- wears off and can send you looking for a ledge to leap from after you hear it for the 10,000th time.

Can't anybody out there write a Christmas classic?

The obvious problem is that nobody writes a classic; worthy songs just become classics.

Sometimes unworthy songs do, too, songs that can never be played too few times. Like the cringe-inducing "Grandma Got Run Over by a Reindeer."

There are also some songs that you never tire of hearing during the holiday season, despite their inane lyrics.

Your soul would have to be in your foot to ever tire of Burl Ives or the Temptations singing "Rudolph the Red-Nosed Reindeer," Mel Torme or Nat

King Cole singing "The Christmas Song," Elvis snarling "I'll have a blue Christmas without you" or Charles Brown crooning "Please Come Home for Christmas."

It must be noted that the Surgeon General of Love has determined that the latter song should not be played by anyone who has been drinking liquor in despair because Sweet Thang flew the coop.

Then there are the liquor-house Christmas classics, songs that go down great with a $2 shot and a fish sammitch from the local bootlegger's crib.

Said music is for adults only, though, because children could be irreparably damaged by hearing Albert King singing "Santa Claus Wants Some Lovin'" or Clarence Carter growling his yuletide classic "Backdoor Santa":

They call me Backdoor Santa

I make my runs at the break of day

I make all the young girls happy

While the boys are out to play

Well I ain't like old Saint Nick

He don't come but once a year

I come runnin' with my presents

Every time you call me dear

I keep the back door open

In case anyone smells a mouse

'Cause wouldn't ol' Santa be in trouble

If there wasn't no chimney in the house?

Have mercy. It is impossible to improve upon such holiday sentiments, but each year we are assaulted by new and extraneous versions of old holiday standards.

I mean, do we really need to hear Beyonce or any other singer with one name singing "Oh Holy Night" with a hip-hop beat?

Is the world really yearning for the latest country music flavor of the week -- all duded up in his designer jeans and big hat -- to belch his rendition of "Sahhhhhhhh-lent notttttttt, hoooooooly nottttttt" as though nobody has ever done it before?

Heck no.

12/23/2003

WHEN THERE'S DANGER ALL ABOUT...

Y'all will have to forgive me if I'm not my usual jovial, Mr. Sunshiny self.

Relax. I've gotten over the disappointment of "People" magazine once again snubbing me for its "Sexiest Man Alive" cover. (They've obviously never seen me in my red, black and green Speedos.)

My distress today is caused by the fact that the movie "Shaft" opened yesterday and I wasn't in it.

If you want to get technical about it, no, I have no previous acting experience -

unless you count the time in Mrs. Watkins' first-grade class when I played one of "The Three Little Pigs."

Actually, it was just my left hand with a painted sock on it playing one of "The Three Little Pigs" as a hand-puppet, a role I repeatedly screwed up by - I swear - sticking up the wrong hand.

Despite that inauspicious acting debut, I figure I am singularly qualified to play John Shaft, the super cool New York private eye: I have seen the original "Shaft" 137 times and know every line of dialogue and every nuance he makes.

Thus, the only explanation for Director John Singleton passing me over is spite. Pure and simple.

You see, Singleton called me a couple of years ago after he'd read my column on his movie "Rosewood." It was an excellent movie with a serious theme that had the misfortune of coming out at the same time as the lightweight, buffoonish "Booty Call." He graciously thanked me for the column, in which I lamented the fact that moviegoers streamed into theaters to see "Booty" while "Rosewood" withered on the box office vine.

This, word-for-word, is how my conversation with Singleton ended:

Me: "So, what're you working on next?"

Singleton: "I'm doing a remake of 'Shaft'."

Me: (Laughing my head off): No, really, man. What're you working on?

In retrospect, I doubt that was the response he wanted to hear, and it probably explains why he didn't put me in his #!$%& movie.

Singleton seems like a cool guy - as evidenced by his gracious telephone call - whose great misfortune was that his first movie, "Boyz In the Hood," turned out to be a masterpiece of the urban 'hood genre. When your first movie as a 22-year-old is hailed as a classic, anything you do as an encore is going to suffer by comparison.

(Witness Orson Welles and the curse of "Citizen Kane": the man who starred and directed, at 25 years old, in what many consider the greatest movie ever made ended up obese and doing Paul Masson wine commercials in his final act.)

And when it comes to "Shaft," nothing is going to compare favorably to the original. The 1971 movie was by no means a masterpiece - it's downright tedious in spots (Forgive me, Richard Roundtree) - but it was an important movie nonetheless.

For one thing, just about any black dude you saw in a movie B.S. - Before Shaft - was either dead before the opening credits rolled, a bug-eyed Sambo afraid of his own shadow or the chaste Sidney Poitier, who hardly ever got the girl, even when he married her - as he did in "Guess Who's Coming To Dinner?"

Shaft, unlike Sidney and us blokes in the audience, always got the girl. Always.

Yet there were two things about the original "Shaft" that defy explanation and which I hope Singleton fixed:

First is how Shaft, lying near death on his girlfriend Ellie's couch after being shot, went flying through a high-rise's window an hour later - with gun a-'blazin' - to rescue the kidnapped damsel.

The second is how someone as cool as Shaft had a girlfriend named "Ellie."

6/17/2000

WHO GOT DOHERTY? DOHERTY

I'm a lot like that dude Caine from the 1970s-era TV show "Kung Fu."

Like him, I'm sloooow to anger, but once you get me riled up, you'd better watch out, Jack.

Riled up is what I'm getting, too, after hearing people characterize the resignation of UNC basketball coach Matt Doherty as an instance of "the inmates taking over the asylum."

(Just between you and me, I'm guessing that Doherty resigned from UNC the same way Custer resigned from life at Little Big Horn -- quite involuntarily.)

Saying the inmates have taken over the asylum is meant to imply that a new breed of spoiled jocks staged a mutiny and forced out a coach who only wanted what was best for them.

Hogwash. First of all, I see no inmates, just a group of kids who, predictably, chafed under the dictatorial temperament of an insecure coach.

What's disturbing is how easily the word "inmates" -- as well as the opprobrious term "coach-killer" -- falls off the tongue of so-called experts on television and those jock- sniffers who burn up the lines on radio call-in shows.

If anybody killed Doherty's coaching career, the culprit is he.

I went on campus Thursday looking for players to ask how they felt about being blamed for running off a coach.

Alas, they were all probably in class or in their dorm rooms studying hard for exams, and I could find none to ask.

I was, however, at a Carolina practice early last season for about two minutes. That's how long it was before Doherty cleared the gym. I heard the coach use language on a player that made me blush. It was the same language that, used in a different gym, got me tossed in jail.

That happened in 1973 or '74, when cops slapped the metal bracelets on me and hauled me off to jail in Rockingham for assaulting some joker who'd gotten on my bad side on a basketball court.

I never laid a glove on the chump, but I strung together a paint-singeing string of epithets that landed me in the hoosegow charged with -- get this -- verbal assault.

I didn't even know that calling someone everything but a Reuben sandwich because they didn't perform on the court was a crime. Nor, apparently, did Doherty.

A player on the Green Bay Packers football team once praised (?) coach Vince Lombardi's egalitarian treatment of the team's players. "He treats us all the same," the guy said. "Like dogs."

Perhaps Doherty's methods would have won a championship 30 years ago, but they are as outmoded now as the short-shorts players of that era wore.

In 1982, when UNC won the collegiate championship, Freddie Brown of Georgetown bailed out Doherty -- who had just choked and shot the ugliest missed free throw in history -- by throwing the ball to a Tar Heel player and preserving the win.

This time, though, there was no one there to bail him out when he shot the air ball of his life.

4/4/2003

Y'ALL COME, GUV

Now is the time for all good citizens to come to the aid of their governor.

With Gov. Easley and the first family being forced out of the Executive Mansion due to dangerous mold, we must rally 'round the flag and ensure that they have a place to stay.

That's where we come in. You know how politicians are always spouting about their desire to stay in touch with the common man?

As the most common man I know, I'm inviting the governor and his clan to stay at my crib. No, don't thank me. It's the least I can do.

Since Sweet Thang gets ornery around people she doesn't know -- as well as those she does know -- the Easleys would have to leave after a few days and possibly stay with other families across the state.

Jill Lucas, the governor's deputy press secretary, said in an e-mail message that "The Governor and First Lady will be temporarily housed in state-owned property during the renovation. ... The specific location has not yet been determined."

You can bet it won't be some Motel 6 or the Rock 'em, Sock 'em Motor Lodge. Too bad. The governor could enhance his populist appeal by eschewing some fancy-pants town house with scented soap and staying in a cheap motel or with a regular Tar Heel family. Like mine.

Having the governor as a guest would prove your patriotism while ensuring that long-sought improvements were made on your street. No mayor wants to take a chance on the governor twisting an ankle on a raggedy sidewalk in his city.

As for me, I'd surely gain the upper hand in my battle with a neighbor who complains that my parked car encroaches on his property line. With the governor as an overnight guest, I could go, "Say, pal, I've got your property line. Right here."

Think about it. In any neighborhood dispute, having the governor stay at your place automatically makes you BNOB -- big neighbor on the block.

This is not just about politics or us, though. It would also bail out the governor. If first lady Mary Easley's mom is anything like my last almost-ex-mother-in-law, she's probably telling her daughter, "See, I told you he wouldn't be able to keep a roof over your head."

There is, admittedly, a huge problem with the governor staying with regular folks: His popularity will soar so high that all elected officials in the state will be searching for a family with which to bunk so they can prove their Everyman credentials.

Why, we couldn't run down to the Piggly Wiggly without encountering some legislator hanging out on the corner going, "Psssst. Yo, pal. Can I make a pallet on your floor tonight?"

We'll have kids fleeing the playgrounds in terror, shouting that a hobo with a tote sack is following them home.

"Honey, that's no hobo. That's House Speaker Jim Black."

Black: Pardon me, kind sir. But have you room in your home for a selfless public servant to crash for the night -- and simultaneously shore up his poll

...and the horse you rode in on, Saunders!

numbers before the next election?

Dad: Sorry, hoss, but Marc Basnight just left. After what he did to Sweet Thang's good towels, she said we ain't having no more politicians over. Here's a biscuit, though.

8/9/2005

YOU KNOW YOU'RE OLD WHEN

I guess you could call me lucky. Naw, I didn't hit the $197 million powerball or even find a parking spot in downtown Raleigh at noon.

I'm lucky because I know the exact moment I got old.

It happened last week after I finished reading - yes, reading a girlie magazine and actually heard myself lamenting that there were too many pictures of nekkid women and not enough stories on politics.

I used to think that watching "Soul Train" with the sound turned down or buying that first Barry Manilow compact disc signaled the onset of "oldness."

But that was nothing but middle age, Hoss.

The best definition of turning old was expressed by a self-absorbed, aging yuppie character - weren't they all? - on the late, unlamented television show "thirtysomething."

He knew he was old, he said, when he realized that he was invisible to teenage girls.

If you're under 30, you probably think you'll recognize when it's time to hang up your disco shoes and start drinking more buttermilk and less Jack Daniels.

No, you won't. Why do you think so many great athletes hang around too long and embarrass themselves? Money? Of course. But another reason is their unwillingness to admit when it's time to spit on the fire and call in the dogs.

Freud claimed that sex is the driving force of all life. Darwin said it is self-preservation. Both were wrong.

The real driving force in life is being able to fit into last year's jeans.

The best way to fight old age is not to deny its existence or to join a health club. (OK, that'll help with the jeans.)

First, you have to recognize it so you can gird your loins for battle.

Here then, as a public service, are some signs to let you know that you're getting old:

When your fingers don't automatically punch the car radio dial the instant you hear a Neil Diamond song, or when you think, even fleetingly, that Michael Bolton sounds almost as good as Percy Sledge.

The first time you say "Not tonight, dear; I have a headache" - and you don't. Or you do.

When you stop talking trash during pickup basketball games at the Y because you can no longer back it up.

When you lie down to take a nap to rest up for a big night on the town with your buddies but you don't wake up until the next morning.

When you no longer cluck your tongue disapprovingly upon seeing a balding, potbellied old man driving a 'Vette with a sweet young thang beside him because

261

now you think it's possible that she really loves him for who he is.

By no means should we accept decrepitude as an inevitable byproduct of aging. The poet Dylan Thomas was right when he wrote about growing old "Do not go gentle into that good night ... Rage, rage against the dying of the light."

I plan to rage against it, yes indeedy. But first, I have to take a nap.

YOUTHFUL WOES NO EXCUSE

Naw, Homes. Y'all have got to do better than that.

A jury, in deciding to spare Matthew Grant's life for killing Wake County Sheriff's Deputy Mark Tucker, cited Grant's oft-mentioned troubled childhood.

I could be wrong, which, as you know, is unlikely, but there ought to be a better reason than a dysfunctional family for sparing a cop-killer's life.

Think about it: If being abandoned by your parents, among other things, is now sufficient reason to keep a bloke off death row, then we might as well tell the dude who administers the sleepy needle to go home.

I'll bet you a nickel to a nail that not one of the 183 inmates awaiting a date with the state's executioner boasted a Beaver Cleaver-Theo Huxtable childhood, one in which Ward or Cliff waited at the crib to help with homework.

Judge W.R. Duke wrote to me in October: "This may come as a shock to you, but it has been my experience as a Superior Court Judge that almost 7 to 8 out of every 10 people who appear before me, well-dressed or otherwise, black or white, male or female, have one characteristic in common: They have had no significant relationship with their biological 'daddy.' Check it out."

That's not a shock at all, judge. After Grant's arrest, remember, it was his own biological daddy who said the boy was a hoodlum. Ouch.

Still, it's not as if Grant croaked some fellow ne'er-do-well in a fit of anger. He killed a cop who had dedicated his life to serving and protecting us.

Since when did a troubled childhood trump that?

Barry Winston and Thomas Maher, two of Grant's attorneys, said the jurors indicated to them that it did.

"You can't possibly encapsulate all of the things that went into their decision, but the foreperson said they agreed that the death penalty is intended for the worst of the worst," Winston said. "They felt this case didn't fit that. ... His bad childhood was an important part, too."

Maher said the combination of Grant's age and childhood helped save his life. "If you're 30, then childhood becomes less of a part," he said. "When you add the type of childhood he had and the inherent immaturity of an 18-year-old, then it becomes very important."

It would be easy -- and wrong -- to think that being a blond white boy helped spare Grant. The last person to kill a cop in Wake County, the dreadlocked Kawame Mays, also got life when the jury deadlocked on his sentence.

Cops would probably feel better about dispatching their dangerous duties if they knew that anyone who caused them to make the ultimate sacrifice was in turn going to have to pay the ultimate price.

From the time Grant was arrested, it was sometimes hard to tell who was the victim. I mean, the day after Grant's arrest, Sheriff Donnie Harrison was quoted as saying, "It's sad for both families. It's sad for Mark's family. ... A young man's life is wasted."

Boy, when did Big D get so sensitive?

A casualty of the excessive gnashing of teeth over Grant's childhood has been a proper acknowledgment of Tucker's sacrifice. Let me be, if not the first, then perhaps the last to say, "Thanks, deputy."

12/3/2004